NOVELL'S

ZENworks™ for Desktops 3
Administrator's Handbook

RON TANNER AND BRAD DAYLEY

Novell.
PRESS

Novell Press Provo, UT

Novell's ZENworks™ for Desktops 3 Administrator's Handbook
Published by
Novell Press
1800 S. Novell Place
Provo, UT 84606

ISBN: 0-7645-0792-3
Printed in the United States of America
10 9 8 7 6 5 4 3 2 1
1O/QR/RR/QQ/FC
Distributed in the United States by IDG Books Worldwide, Inc.
Distributed by CDG Books Canada Inc. for Canada; by Transworld Publishers Limited in the United Kingdom; by IDG Norge Books for Norway; by IDG Sweden Books for Sweden; by IDG Books Australia Publishing Corporation Pty. Ltd. for Australia and New Zealand; by TransQuest Publishers Pte Ltd. for Singapore, Malaysia, Thailand, Indonesia, and Hong Kong; by Gotop Information Inc. for Taiwan; by ICG Muse, Inc. for Japan; by Intersoft for South Africa; by Eyrolles for France; by International Thomson Publishing for Germany, Austria, and Switzerland; by Distribuidora Cuspide for Argentina; by LR International for Brazil; by Galileo Libros for Chile; by Ediciones ZETA S.C.R. Ltda. for Peru; by WS Computer Publishing Corporation, Inc., for the Philippines; by Contemporanea de Ediciones for Venezuela; by Express Computer Distributors for the Caribbean and West Indies; by Micronesia Media Distributor, Inc. for Micronesia; by Chips Computadoras S.A. de C.V. for Mexico; by Editorial Norma de Panama S.A. for Panama; by American Bookshops for Finland.

For general information on IDG Books Worldwide's books in the U.S., please call our Consumer Customer Service department at 800-762-2974. For reseller information, including discounts and premium sales, please call our Reseller Customer Service department at 800-434-3422.

For information on where to purchase IDG Books Worldwide's books outside the U.S., please contact our International Sales department at 317-572-3993 or fax 317-572-4002.

For consumer information on foreign language translations, please contact our Customer Service department at 800-434-3422, fax 317-572-4002, or e-mail rights@idgbooks.com.

For information on licensing foreign or domestic rights, please phone +1-650-653-7098.

For sales inquiries and special prices for bulk quantities, please contact our Order Services department at 800-434-3422 or write to IDG Books Worldwide, 919 E. Hillsdale Blvd., Suite 400, Foster City, CA 94404.

For information on using IDG Books Worldwide's books in the classroom or for ordering examination copies, please contact our Educational Sales department at 800-434-2086 or fax 317-572-4005.

For press review copies, author interviews, or other publicity information, please contact our Public Relations department at 650-653-7000 or fax 650-653-7500.

For authorization to photocopy items for corporate, personal, or educational use, please contact Novell, Inc., Copyright Permission, 1800 S. Novell Place Mail Stop PRV-A231, Provo, UT 84606 or fax 801-228-7077.

For general information on Novell Press books in the U.S., including information on discounts and premiums, contact IDG Books Worldwide at 800-434-3422 or 650-655-3200. For information on where to purchase Novell Press books outside the U.S. contact IDG Books International at 317-572-3993 or fax 317-572-4002.

Library of Congress Cataloging-in-Publication Data
Tanner, Ron.
    Novell's ZENworks for Desktops 3 administrator's handbook / Ron Tanner and Brad Dayley.
        p.   cm.
    Includes index.
    ISBN 0-7645-0792-3 (alk. paper)1
        1. Graphical user interfaces (Computer systems)
    2. Z.E.N.works. I. Dayley, Brad. II. Title.
    QA76.9.U83   T37   2000
    005.4'38--dc21   00-048720

Welcome to Novell Press

Novell Press, the world's leading provider of networking books, is the premier source for the most timely and useful information in the networking industry. Novell Press books cover fundamental networking issues as they emerge — from today's Novell and third-party products to the concepts and strategies that will guide the industry's future. The result is a broad spectrum of titles for the benefit of those involved in networking at any level: end user, department administrator, developer, systems manager, or network architect.

Novell Press books are written by experts with the full participation of Novell's technical, managerial, and marketing staff. The books are exhaustively reviewed by Novell's own technicians and are published only on the basis of final released software, never on prereleased versions.

Novell Press at IDG Books Worldwide is an exciting partnership between two companies at the forefront of the knowledge and communications revolution. The Press is implementing an ambitious publishing program to develop new networking titles centered on the current versions of NetWare, GroupWise, BorderManager, ManageWise, and networking integration products.

Novell Press books are translated into several languages and sold throughout the world.

Phil Richardson
Publisher
Novell Press, Novell, Inc.

Novell Press

Publisher
Phil Richardson

IDG Books Worldwide

Acquisitions Editor
Ed Adams

Project Editor
Julie M. Smith

Technical Editor
Jay Raines

Copy Editor
Julie Campbell Moss

Copy Editor
Patsy Owens

Project Coordinators
Danette Nurse
Louigene A. Santos
Marcos Vergara

Graphics and Production Specialists
Robert Bihlmayer
Jude Levinson
Michael Lewis
Victor Pérez-Varela
Ramses Ramirez

Quality Control Technician
Dina F Quan

Illustrators
Rashell Smith
Gabriele McCann

Proofreading and Indexing
York Production Services

About the Authors

Ron Tanner is a networking professional who has been with Novell since 1993; he currently has a Director position and is working in the CTO office designing the next generation products at Novell. Prior to being with Novell, Ron worked at AT&T Bell Laboratories developing advanced networking systems. Ron has been involved with the ZENworks project since its inception.

Brad Dayley is a software engineer on Novell's Critical Problem Resolution team. He has nine years of experience installing, troubleshooting, and coding Novell's products. He co-developed an advanced debugging course used to train Novell's support engineers and customers and is the co-author of *Novell's Guide to Resolving Critical Server Issues*.

I dedicate this book to TT, MRT, KT, JNT, and my Peach Queen. LYA.

— Ron Tanner

For D, A, & F!

— Brad Dayley

Foreword

In today's world of the Internet, each business must remain highly focused on their business and products. They must work each day to keep abreast of technology and one step ahead of their competitors. The systems that each employee uses must be readily available, functioning perfectly in order to keep up with the needs of the corporation. Any significant downtime or delays can be extremely costly in loss of productivity, resulting in a loss of business vitality.

One of the most used and potentially abused portions of any corporate environment is the desktop. The desktop is the interface for the user into the corporate network system and is, for most, their primary tool to perform their work. The workstation must meet the personal demands of the user, and must have access to the necessary tools and business processes, at a moment's notice. If there is a severe hardware or software failure, the IT departments must be able to respond quickly and efficiently in order to get the desktop back into working order, keeping the productivity and processes of the company moving effectively.

IT departments, in order to fulfill this critical job function, must have an effective desktop management solution. This solution must be flexible enough to provide the ease of traditional centralized management and yet must also give each individual user the custom environment that they need to accomplish their work with peak performance. ZENworks for Desktops leverages the power of Novell's eDirectory to provide a customized, distributed desktop management solution to each user of the network. It also gives the IT department the centralized power and tools they need to keep the demand for a smooth functioning business a reality.

In this latest release of ZENworks for Desktops, Novell has increased the value and power of desktop management by providing additional capabilities that will improve any IT department's efficiency. *Novell's ZENworks for Desktop 3 Administrator's Handbook* is concentrated exclusively on the deployment and use of ZENworks for Desktops in any computing environment. This book covers many aspects and features of ZENworks for Desktops, including the more advanced subjects, and can make the installation, deployment, troubleshooting, and use of the product a smooth and rewarding process. This book should be in every administrator's arsenal of references.

Craig Miller
Vice President and General Manager
Net Management Service
Novell, Inc.

Preface

The computer industry has made incredible progress with information sharing since the introduction of local area networks (LANs) in the 1980s. These advancements have produced services and tools that increase user productivity while decreasing their workload. Companies have come to rely on networks for virtually all aspects of business, such as accounting, payroll, mail, communications, advertising, banking—the list goes on and on. All this comes at a price, however. In return for having a high speed network to increase employee and company productivity, each business must also incur an often enormous support cost. Novell recognizes this and provides a solution—Zero Effort Networks, or ZENworks, for Desktops.

ZENworks is the first directory services-based desktop management tool that reduces the cost of owning networked PCs and makes using networks easier. ZENworks for Desktops builds on this initial release and leverages the functionality of NDS to make Windows-based desktops easier to use and manage without sacrificing power or flexibility. It allows the network administrators to leverage NDS to ensure that users can focus on their business, not their PC. With automated application delivery and repair, desktops-customized for user's needs, and with easy problem resolution, ZENworks for Desktops gives users all the power of the PC without as high an administrative cost for making it work.

This book is your guide to leveraging ZENworks for Desktops to distribute applications, manage users, and maintain desktop PCs. This book provides steps to setup and use the advanced features of ZENworks for Desktops to cut your administrative efforts and costs, while making the network environment much more friendly to users.

▶ · ◀

Who Should Read This Book?

This book is for anyone responsible for setting up or maintaining a Novell network. If you are a network administrator, technical support staff, CNE, or consultant this book will give you the edge you need to streamline application distribution and manage users and desktops much more efficiently. You will save valuable time by using the advanced features of ZENworks for Desktops to automate time consuming tasks such as application distribution and workstation management.

How This Book is Organized

This book is organized into the following chapters to guide you through installing ZENworks, setting up ZENworks in NDS, and then leveraging the advanced features of ZENworks to reduce your network management costs:

Chapter 1: Introduction to ZENworks for Desktops
Chapter 1 provides a high-level overview of the ZENworks for Desktops system and its components. Additionally, it discusses the different packaging of ZENworks for Desktops that are available and what is new in this latest release.

Chapter 2: Installing ZENworks for Desktops
Chapter 2 discusses the prerequisites and design considerations of installing ZENworks for Desktops. It also takes you through the installation of the server and client pieces of ZENworks for Desktops helping you avoid any pitfalls that could result in later problems.

Chapter 3: Setting up ZENworks for Desktops in Your Tree
Chapter 3 identifies the steps that must be taken following the install to get your ZENworks for Desktops system up and functioning. In order to get the full effects of ZENworks for Desktops you must deliver the proper agents to the workstations in your system and import workstations into your tree, allowing you to manage all of your desktops centrally from your NDS tree.

Chapter 4: Creating Application packages Using snAppShot
Chapter 4 discusses the snAappShot utility and how to use it to create an application object template for later distribution. It discusses why and when you should use snAppShot and describes how snAppShot creates the application object template. It also discusses how to use snAppShots advanced features including: preferences, special macros, and partial installation detection.

Chapter 5: Creating and Using Application Objects
Once you have an understanding of application object templates from Chapter 4, Chapter 5 will cover using the template to create application objects and setting them up for distribution. This chapter will also familiarize you with how to set up properties to customize your application objects and how the new application system incorporates Microsoft MSI.

Chapter 6: Setting up Application Distribution

Once you have set up the application object into your eDirectory, as described in chapter 5, you need to set up the application distribution environment. This chapter covers using ConsoleOne to set up application users to receive applications, application foldering, and automating application object distribution.

Chapter 7: Setting up User Policies

ZENworks for Desktops provides several policies that describe how the system should deal with users. Chapter 7 discusses the various policies that are associated with users of the tree, how to set them up, and the value that they can provide to your system.

Chapter 8: Setting up a Workstation Policy Package

Chapter 8 identifies the various workstation policies that are available in the ZENworks for Desktops system. These policies effect the behavior, security, and desktop of all the workstations in your network. This chapter tells you how to setup these policies and make them effective in your network.

Chapter 9: Creating a Container Policy Package

There are additional policies that are available for ZENworks for Desktops that help in describing how the ZENworks for Desktops system can be most effective in your tree and network. Chapter 9 discusses these policies and how they affect the behavior of the agents that are doing the work of getting your settings to your desktops.

Chapter 10: Creating a Service Location Policy Package

ZENworks for Desktops agents must locate several resources in the network in order to perform their jobs. These resources could be SMTP servers or databases. Chapter 10 discusses how the Service Location Policy package can be used to identify where these resources can be found by the agents.

Chapter 11: Creating a Server Policy Package

ZENworks for Desktops has now introduced agents that are located on your NetWare or NT servers and are used to facilitate such activities as imaging and inventory. This chapter discusses how the policies in the Server Policy Package can affect the behavior of these server agents.

Chapter 12: Using ZENworks Workstation Inventory

The inventory system in ZENworks for Desktops allows you to capture the hardware and software components on every workstation in the tree. This chapter discusses the inventory system of ZENworks for Desktops and how to best deploy the inventory system throughout the network and tree to get all of your information about your workstations in the right place.

Chapter 13: Imaging a Workstation

ZENworks for Desktops allows you to take images of your workstations and apply them to any and all other workstations in the network. Imagine being able to fix a workstation by simply requesting that it re-image itself from your administration workstation. Can you believe that you can even include application objects into these images? This chapter defines how the imaging system works and how you can get those images to contain exactly what you want and the most efficient way to get them onto those workstations.

Chapter 14: Maintaining a Workstation

Chapter 14 identifies the other programs and systems that accompany the ZENworks for Desktops product that will help in identifying problems with desktops in the network and getting those problems fixed. These tools include Remote Control and Remote Diagnostics.

Chapter 15: Using Software Metering with ZENworks for Desktops

Chapter 15 discusses how to use the ZENworks for Desktops software metering features to give your organization the ability to manage software licenses and track software usage by using ZENworks for Desktops application management and Novell's Licensing Services (NLS). This chapter discusses how to use the NLS manager and/or NWAdmin32 to create a licensed or metered certificate and then how to assign users to licenses.

Chapter 16: Integrating ZENworks for Desktops with ZENworks for Servers

Novell, Inc. has introduced additional ZENworks type products. One of these is ZENworks for Servers that allows you to perform tasks on the server much like you do for the workstation. ZENworks for Servers includes a function called Tiered-Electronic Distribution which will move files efficiently through the network and place them on servers. ZENworks for Desktops has the capabilities to interact with ZENworks for Servers making it easy for you to move your application objects and files throughout the network to your various application servers, keeping all of them up-to-date with the latest software. This chapter discusses this interaction between these two ZENworks products.

Chapter 17: Troubleshooting ZENworks for Desktops

ZENworks for Desktops is an extremely powerful tool which will save network administrators much needed time. However, because of the complexity of network environments, problems can occur that prevent ZENworks for Desktops from doing its job. Chapter 17 covers how to troubleshoot and diagnose those problems in the following areas: desktop management, distributed applications, policy packages, NDS, and NetWare errors.

Appendix A: Understanding eDirectory Changes for ZENworks for Desktops

Appendix A identifies all of the objects and attribute changes that ZENworks for Desktops performs on your Novell eDirectory tree.

Appendix B: Using snAppShot to Create Application Object Package

Appendix B first discusses a detailed example of using the snAppShot utility to create an application object package for distribution to other workstations. Second, Appendix B gives a detailed review of the application object template created. The purpose of Appendix B is to give you practical experience and knowledge of application object templates.

Appendix C: Other ZENworks for Desktops Resources

This appendix lists other places one can go to find out and get more help with their ZENworks for Desktops implementation.

Appendix D: ZENworks Inventory Database Schema

This appendix discusses the inventory schema that is used in the database to record the inventory of the workstation. This appendix describes each of the tables in the database and gives SQL examples to extract your own information from the database.

Acknowledgments

Our sincere gratitude goes out to the following persons, without whom this book could not have come in to being:

To Ed Adams, thanks for helping to keep this book alive through all of the struggles getting it kicked off the ground. I'm sure we drove you crazy — at least until you shipped us over to Julie.

To Julie Smith, thanks for your patience through the process and for being cordial even though we pushed everything out and went down to the wire.

To Julie Moss, who gave our words their final polish.

To the ZENworks team that, although leaner, has put a great number of significant features in this update. Thanks for making a great product that can benefit all those who have a network and users to support. We're looking forward to many new versions to make the product even better.

To everyone in Novell who allowed us to pick their brains, including but not limited to (with apologies to any whose names we have forgotten) Matthew Lewis, Krishnan R., Kelly Norman, Alan Jex, Frank Morse, David Rivers, Drake Backman, Kevin Wilkins, and Nile Thayne.

To our technical editor Jay Raines, our profound thanks for rooting out our errors and putting ZENworks into production at Novell, Inc. We know this book is significantly better thanks to your careful review.

Contents at a Glance

Contents

Chapter 8   Setting up a Workstation Policy Package   221

Chapter 9   Creating a Container Policy Package   263

Chapter 10   Creating a Service Location
Policy Package   275

Chapter 11   Creating a Server Policy Package   **287**

Chapter 12   Using ZENworks Workstation Inventory   **317**

## CHAPTER I

Introduction to ZENworks for Desktops

This chapter provides you with a brief introduction to ZENworks for Desktops, including its availability, packaging, high-level features, and relationship with other ZENworks family products from Novell, Inc.

The ZENworks Family

Although this book is about ZENworks for Desktops, several other ZENworks products are now available from Novell, Inc. Currently Novell offers the following products in the ZENworks family:

► **ZENworks for Desktops** — A desktop management system that manages many workstation aspects.

► **ZENworks for Servers** — A system that enables you to manage servers and to distribute files across the network.

► **ZENworks for Networks** — A policy-based system that enables you to set up QoS (Quality of Service) for your network and routers.

All ZENworks products rely significantly on the directory, specifically Novell Directory Services, to provide a greater manageability level, and greater ease, for each component in the network.

What is ZENworks for Desktops?

ZENworks for Desktops is a desktop management system that has been developed by Novell, Inc. The ZENworks in ZENworks for Desktops stands for Zero Effort Networks and is named to reflect the zero effort required for end-users and the minimum effort necessary for the administrator to manage the desktops in their systems.

The end result goal of ZENworks for Desktops is to reduce the total cost of ownership (TCO) of dealing with all the workstations in the network. This is achieved by special attempts to reduce the effort necessary to manage the desktops.

ZENworks for Desktops is segmented into three desktop management and maintenance areas, which are discussed in the following sections. These include Application, Desktop, and Remote Management.

NOTE

ZENworks for Desktop 3 has dropped the support for Windows 3.*x* systems. Your ZENworks for Desktop 2 (that is, ZENworks 2) continues to function and co-exist with ZENworks for Desktop 3. However, all the features associated with manual workstation import and Windows 3.*x* systems can only be managed in NWAdmin32 and have not been moved to the new ConsoleOne management tool. So if you have a mixed environment (ZfD 2 and ZfD 3) you may be switching between NWAdmin32 and ConsoleOne until you have completely eliminated ZENworks for Desktop 2 from your system.

Application Management

The ZENworks Application Management area for Desktops is designed to easily deploy applications from the network to individual desktops. These applications can be automatically installed on the workstation or just have an icon applied to a desktop that references a software executable or installation bundle on a server in the network. All the applications that are deployed to the desktop enable the administrator to control when they are deployed, how they are applied, and who or which desktops get certain applications.

ZENworks for Desktops then also enables you to customize the settings for each individual user by referencing values in Novell Directory Services (NDS) and embedding them in the registry keys and files for the particular applications. Then, when that application is deployed to the desktop, these values are customized for the particular user. In addition to customization, the ZENworks for Desktops Application Management portion includes the ability to help you equalize the usage on the network through its load balancing features, and attempts to make the application always available with its fault-tolerance features.

With the integration of NDS, ZENworks for Desktops Application Management makes sure that the applications follow the user to whichever desktop they use in the network, keeping their connection to the network always functioning in a familiar way.

ZENworks for Desktops Application Management has features that enable you to distribute and assign applications to users, thus making the management of application for desktops and your users on the desktop, simple and consistent.

ZENworks for Desktops Application Management features are currently provided for the following platforms: Windows 95, Windows 98, Windows NT, and Windows 2000.

Desktop Management

Desktop Management refers to the ability for the administrator to effect direct changes on the desktop and manage the registry, Novell clients, desktop images, printers, and even ZAW and ZAK policies of the Windows operating systems. With the Novell Directory Services advantages, you can make changes to a Configuration object that affects the client, for example, and then have it applied to all or a portion of the workstations in your entire organization. Due to the inheritance rules of NDS, and the introduction of Workstation objects into the tree, these Configuration objects can be applied to many users and workstations in the tree by associations with objects, groups or containers.

Microsoft introduced to their Windows environments the products ZAW (Zero-Administration Workstation) and ZAK (Zero-Administration Kit) as a first step in enabling administrators to manage the workstation. These products resulted in registry settings that could be stored in a .pol file and then accessed by each workstation as it attaches to the server. These registry settings would then be applied to the workstation, resulting in the interface the administrator wanted for the users. ZENworks for Desktops has taken the ZAW and ZAK features of Windows to the next level by providing these registry manipulations (resulting in desktop changes) and placing them into the NDS tree. Rather then having to create a .pol file and then have that deployed across the network servers, an administrator can administer the exact same features in NDS. Once the ZAW and ZAK features have been administered into the NDS system, that "policy" can then be applied to any workstation in the system or follow any users as they move from desktop to desktop, regardless of which server they are working on in the tree. Novell, through ZENworks for Desktops, has truly introduced fault-tolerance and manageability to these policies introduced by Microsoft.

ZENworks for Desktops also enables the administrator to create a Configuration object for the Novell client. Then all workstations that are associated with this Configuration object use the configurations specified to manage the client. There was one customer that was told by Novell that in order to fix the problem they needed to change only one line in the net.cfg file of the client. The customer was not too happy because they had over 10,000 clients of that type and determined that it would take them years with their current staff to make that change. Now, with ZENworks for Desktops, one administrator can make the change in one Client configuration policy object and the change would be forwarded and made to clients of all associated workstations, and then become effective the next time the users log into the system. Now this one change can be done in minutes instead of years.

In addition the ZENworks for Desktops Desktop Management feature includes a desktop hardware inventory. An inventory *sweet spot* is stored in the Workstation object that is associated with the physical workstation device. This inventory can be useful to the administrator in understanding the workstation capabilities as they manage and maintain the desktop. Additionally, ZENworks for Desktops provides a complete hardware and software scanning capability that is stored in a separate database. A link exists between the Workstation objects and the database, allowing you easy access to the scanned information. Reports are also included with ZENworks for Desktops that provide you useful, tabular information of what is stored in the scanned database.

Included with the ZENworks for Desktops Desktop Management features are enhanced versions of the original Workstation Manager 1.0 (WSM) features that include dynamic NT account management. Enhanced versions of the account management give even greater control to the administrator on having automatic accounts created on NT for users logging into the system. When these users log into NDS they have a local account automatically created and customized for the particular user. When they log out this account can remain or may be removed from the local NT system.

Through the ZENworks for Desktops Desktop Management features, Novell provides the ability to manage all desktop aspects including access to basic Windows features and to the automatic printer deployment. Like many ZENworks for Desktops features, these capabilities follow a user as they move across the organization from one workstation to another, and that includes your printer drivers and printers.

ZENworks for Desktops Desktop Management features are currently provided for the following platforms: Windows 95, Windows 98, Windows NT, and Windows 2000.

Remote Management

The ZENworks for Desktops Remote Management feature includes the ability to discover information about the workstation and to do some remote diagnostics and repairs on that workstation. As mentioned earlier, ZENworks for Desktops introduces into the tree a new object representing the workstation. This Workstation object is associated with the physical desktop and is a repository for information about the specific desktop. The administrator can then use this information in determining how to most effectively maintain and repair that desktop.

In addition to the introduction of the Workstation object, the Remote Management feature of ZENworks for Desktops provides the administrator with the capability of NDS Authenticated Remote Control and a minimal Help Request System. The NDS Authenticated Remote Control feature keeps anyone that does not have rights to remote control a *particular* workstation from being able to remote control the system. This way administrators and end-users are assured that only authorized personnel can remote control their desktops. The Help Request System enables end-users to send mail to help desk personnel that have been identified and administered in NDS for problems on the workstation. The e-mail that is sent includes information about the error, the user that is currently on the system, and the Workstation object NDS directory name enabling the administrator to quickly go to the Workstation object. By quickly getting to the object, the administrator can then discover the type of desktop involved, the system hardware inventory, and from the object they can automatically remote control the desktop (if they have appropriate rights) and make any repairs necessary on the desktop. This should considerably reduce the travel time to a desktop and therefore the cost involved in maintaining these systems.

To help in workstation diagnostics and repair, Remote Management of ZENworks includes remote diagnostics, chat, and file transfer capabilities. These also require proper rights in the NDS tree in order to perform the tasks.

ZENworks for Desktops Remote Management features are currently provided for the following platforms: Windows 95, Windows 98, Windows NT, and Windows 2000.

What Packages of ZENworks for Desktops Are Available?

The following sections discuss what features are included in each ZENworks for Desktops package. ZENworks for Desktops is currently available in three packages:

- ► ZENworks for Desktops
- ► ZENworks for Desktops Starter Pack
- ► ZENworks for Desktops and other ZENworks Family Bundles

Because ZENworks for Desktops only requires access to a file system and the existence of Novell Directory Services, ZENworks for Desktops works in an NT server only environment with the use of Novell's NDS for NT product. This enables the ZENworks for Desktops benefits to not only be available to the NetWare customers, but to the NT customers as well.

ZENworks for Desktops

This ZENworks for Desktops package includes all of the product features *and* the latest Novell clients. It is sold as a separate package and is available through standard Novell, Inc. channels. This package is not intended to be included with any other offering (except with the price break bundles discussed following). This ZENworks for Desktops product includes all the features of Application Management, Desktop Management, and Remote Management. As additional features are added to the product line they will always be included in this package.

ZENworks for Desktops Starter Pack

This packaging of the ZENworks for Desktops system is free to all Novell, Inc. customers and is available with most Novell products including NetWare. The ZENworks for Desktops Starter Pack is also available from the Novell Web site (www.novell.com) and is free for downloading.

The ZENworks for Desktops Starter Pack includes most Application Management and Desktop Management features of ZENworks for Desktops and the latest clients. It does not include any Remote Management features including the following: NDS Authenticated Remote Control, Help Request System, Remote Management tools (chat, file transfer, and diagnostics) and Desktop hardware and software inventory. These features are included only in the full ZENworks for Desktops product offering.

ZENworks for Desktops and ZENworks Family Bundles

The full-featured ZENworks for Desktops product is expected to be made available as a bundled option with other ZENworks-family products. This can give you a price break and enable you to have other ZENworks products in your site.

Previously, ZENworks was bundled with ManageWise. The ManageWise functionality is expected in a ZENworks for Servers release, and you should be able to get a price break for getting both ZENworks for Desktops and ZENworks for Servers in a bundle.

► • ◄

What's New for ZENworks for Desktops 3?

This text's first edition was based on ZENworks 2 and now Novell has provided the product's next release. The name has been changed to ZENworks for Desktops 3 to distinguish it from other ZENworks-family products. Suffice it to say that ZENworks for Desktops 3 has all the features from the previous ZENworks releases plus the additions discussed in the following sections.

Hardware and Operating System Platforms

ZENworks for Desktops 3 has been updated to handle the new Windows 2000 systems and support it fully. The Windows 3.1 system support has been dropped, but because ZENworks 2 and ZENworks for Desktops 3 can coexist you can continue to support your Windows 3.*x* environments through ZENworks 2 and NWAdmin32.

ZENworks for Desktops 3 works in either a NetWare only, NT only, or NetWare and NT mixed server environment. If you need ZENworks for Desktops 3 to work in a pure NT environment then you need to run NDS for NT or eDirectory for NT in order for the NDS directory to be available.

New Administration Environment

ZENworks for Desktops 3 has moved supported functionality to the new ConsoleOne administration utility that Novell now supports. Administration features that were supported in the previous ZENworks product and continue support in ZENworks for Desktop 3 have been migrated to the new ConsoleOne interface.

With the administration tool change, ZENworks for Desktops 3 has updated the interface and administration in many parts of ZENworks for Desktops. The most apparent change is the consolidation of the workstation policy packages. Previously, one had a different policy package for each workstation platform, often administering the same items repeatedly in each package. Now ZENworks for Desktops 3 has consolidated these packages into a single workstation policy package. You still have the ability to provide different policies for each environment by going to a tab in the dialog and administering differences for the specific platform. If you have no differences, then the platforms get their policies from the common page in the policy package.

ZENworks for Desktops 3 also includes, as additions, policy packages for servers. These packages were originally introduced with the ZENworks for

Servers 1.0 product. Because ZENworks for Desktops 3 has several policies that affect services that are now on the server (for example, auto-workstation import, imaging), then it has brought these same server packages into their product providing the relevant server policies. This coordination is important because it enables ZENworks for Desktops 3 and ZENworks for Servers to coexist on the same system, and seamlessly have the same server policy packages.

Application Management

The following major features have been added to the ZENworks for Desktops 3 product.

MSI Integration

ZENworks for Desktops 3 now fully supports MSI (Microsoft System Installer) packages. You can create an Application object in the directory from an MSI package and then have that MSI package distributed by simply associating the Application object with the user, as you did in ZENworks 2.

When a user clicks the application, the application uses the MSI system to install on to the workstation from the identified servers. Because the Application Management of ZENworks for Desktops 3 enables multiple source paths, the system retrieves the MSI package from whatever source path is currently available.

MSI-based Application objects support the entire new ZENworks for Desktops functionality including uninstall, imaging, and disconnected modes. The MSI support also includes the ability to associate transform files with your distributions.

Application Uninstall

All applications that are installed via ZENworks for Desktops to the workstation can now be uninstalled from the workstation. This new feature even uninstalls applications that had been previously installed with ZENworks 2.

The uninstall deletes all files, INI entries, and registry entries associated with the application, and observes any shared DLL reference counts. This works for both MSI and non-MSI applications.

Disconnected Application Launcher

The Novell Application Launcher, which is the software that handles the work on the workstation, has been updated to run when the user is disconnected from the network; and, even though the workstation is disconnected from the network, the user can still use the familiar interface to launch, install, and perform verifications on their local applications. Applications that are network only applications will, obviously, not be available.

An administrator can mark an Application object as downloadable, enabling the system to download and cache the application on the local file system. From this cached location the application launcher performs its install and verifications. The local cache can also be on a CD, or other removable storage, that the user puts into their system.

Application Reporting Enhancements

Additional schema elements have been added to the reporting system to enable you to get better reporting. Additionally, the system can now write directly into the database rather than relying on SNMP events that can be lost.

The database tables have been updated to have a table for successes and a table for failures, allowing for a greater flexibility in reports.

Imaging Application Launcher Support

In ZENworks for Desktops 3 a new imaging support system exists. This system enables you to take an image from the workstation and store that image on a server and then have an Image object in the tree pointing to that image. You can also have Application objects (and all associated software) injected into the image in the tree.

When the image is placed onto a workstation, all these associated applications are also copied and installed to the workstation during the restore process. This enables you to have a base image, and then an application set (that has been injected into the image), represent your workstation system.

When the user first attempts to launch an application that has been preinstalled with the imaging system, the HKEY_CURRENT_USER information in the Windows registry is updated and the application is launched. The copying of files and the HKEY_LOCAL_MACHINE entries, both lengthy processes, were included in the imaging process.

Tiered Electronic Distribution Integration

Tiered Electronic Distribution (TED) is a distribution system that is provided in the ZENworks for Servers product. The TED system enables an administrator to distribute files to any or all servers within their network.

ZENworks for Desktops 3 includes plug-in modules that extend the TED system to include distributing application files and objects throughout the network. With these extensions you can have TED automatically distribute your applications across your application servers. Additionally, you can have TED create companion Application objects throughout the tree and have them automatically associated with users and the applications, giving the end-user the best performance by referencing a server closer to them.

Workstation Management

The following sections describe the major changes in the Workstation Management area that have been enhanced in the ZENworks for Desktops 3 version.

Microsoft Group Policies

Microsoft has introduced with Active Directory a Group Policy concept that enables setting various security and application settings on users that are members of a specific group. Novell, with ZENworks for Desktops, has incorporated this Group Policy into NDS, much like what was done with the user policies.

An added benefit with ZENworks is that the Microsoft Group Policy can be associated with any group, container, or user in the NDS tree. In Microsoft's Active Directory the Group Policy can only be associated with a container.

Terminal Server Management

ZENworks for Desktops 3 has added user policies to assist in managing Microsoft's Terminal Server and Citrix systems. These policies enable the administrator to configure how users connect to these systems and how their drives and connections are managed.

Automatic Workstation Import and Delete

ZENworks for Desktops 3 has introduced an automatic way to have workstations imported and removed from the NDS directory. Previously, once the user had logged into the system a cookie was placed in the directory. Then the administrator had to run a tool that would take these cookies and create the Workstation object. The workstation import manual method provided in ZENworks 2 has been dropped from the ZENworks for the Desktops 3 product.

With ZENworks for Desktops 3, a workstation import service exists that can be set up in your DNS domain that receives requests from workstations (when they are first brought up — even before a user has logged into the system) for Workstation objects. This service then follows a policy in the directory that directs it on how to name the Workstation object that it automatically creates and associates with the requesting workstation.

In addition to automatically creating workstations, the system also monitors Workstation objects in the tree and based on policies in the directory removes objects that have not been active for a defined period. This way the directory is constantly removing Workstation objects that have no connection to devices in the network.

Workstation Imaging

ZENworks for Desktops 3 now includes an imaging system for imaging your workstations. You can take an image of a golden workstation and have that image stored away on a server and referenced by an Image object in the directory.

You then associate that image to any Workstation object in the tree, or you can give rules to the imaging system that identifies the hardware type that should be associated with this image. Then when a workstation connects with the network it can be imaged (by booting with Linux floppies) automatically by being told the image or allowing the rules to determine the appropriate image. Also, a Workstation object can be told to cause a reimage of its workstation on the next boot-up. This way if the IS&T staff determines that a user's workstation needs to be reimaged, they can simply mark the Workstation object and ask the user to reboot their system. This causes the reimaging to occur, and the workstation to be repaired and up and running quickly.

With the ability to inject applications objects into these images, the users have not only their base image, but all other applications also, restored onto their system.

Workstation Hardware and Software Inventory

In ZENworks for Desktops 3 the hardware and software inventory systems have been revamped. Now they scan the software on a workstation, looking for the header information and reporting that into the software scan information rather than relying on a matched software database. This way you can list all the software on a system whether it is in your database or not.

Additionally, both the hardware and software inventories can now be rolled up in an enterprise into a single database. That database can either be a Sybase or an Oracle database. You can also have as many database rollup levels as you wish. For example, you can have a local database for the site and a master database at the enterprise that contains all the information from all sites.

Remote Management

The following enhancements have been made in the ZENworks for Desktops 3 product Remote Management portion.

Remote Control

The remote control software has been updated for the Windows 95 and Windows 98 environments to improve their performance on these platforms. The Remote Control software is still available for Windows 95/98, Windows NT, and now Windows 2000.

Wake on LAN

A limited functionality of Wake on LAN has been included in ZENworks for Desktops 3, should your desktop hardware support this feature. Once a workstation has been imported and an inventory has been run on the workstation, then the administrator can go to the Workstation object in the directory and make a request to send a Wake on LAN packet to that workstation.

▶ . . . . ◀

What Are the Benefits of Using ZENworks for Desktops?

Significant benefits exist in using the ZENworks for Desktops product in your NetWare and NT environments. The greatest benefit comes from effectively leveraging existing information that is currently in your directory, and combining this with the new components and tree extensions provided in ZENworks for Desktops. By building these relationships in the directory between users and their desktops, enormous management potential surfaces and is easily available to the administrator. Using the NDS tree, and its hierarchical nature, enables you to manage all the desktops in your tree from one place in the tree, or delegated to local administrators and containers in sub-trees.

ZENworks for Desktops also is an easy extension of the current administration system. All the administration requirements for ZENworks for Desktops may be administered via snap-ins that are provided and plug directly into the ConsoleOne Administration utility. Additionally, ZENworks for Desktops uses the familiar rights associated with your tree to govern how accessible the features are to each user in your system.

The cost of managing the desktops that you have in your network is the single largest cost of having your network at all. Some analysts estimate the desktop maintenance cost to be 78% of all network costs. ZENworks for Desktops helps reduce this cost and specifically make the administrator's life easier by enabling the administrator to manage most end-user's desktop needs from their office. From the office, one can deploy applications to any user in the tree, deliver printers and printer drivers, create NT workstation accounts, and configure Novell clients on any set, or all desktops across the network. While in the office, one can cite specific policies to be applied to each user's desktop, or desktop groups, that can lock down a system or just customize a background screen. Without leaving the office, one can receive help requests from the user, look at the desktop hardware and operating system information, remotely control and repair the problems, even reimage the workstation if necessary. Among the greatest costs in maintaining a workstation is involved in travelling from one desktop to the next. With ZENworks for Desktops that effort is largely minimized.

## CHAPTER 2

Installing ZENworks for Desktops

Among the biggest keys to using software tools effectively is to properly install them. Properly installing a software product enables you to get started faster and avoid problems later. This chapter focuses on helping you prepare to install ZENworks for Desktops and its components.

We have broken down the installation of ZENworks for Desktops into the following main sections. This breakdown helps you prepare and install the product fast and correctly:

- ▶ Prerequisite Steps for Installing ZENworks for Desktops
- ▶ Installing Server Components
- ▶ Installing Client Components
- ▶ Installing Documentation

Steps for Installing ZENworks for Desktops

The first step you should take to install ZENworks for Desktops is to make certain your hardware and software are correctly set up. Before installing ZENworks for Desktops you should spend some time making certain that the following criteria have been satisfied and that your environment is ready for the install.

Required Hardware

Prior to installing ZENworks for Desktops, you should make certain that your systems meet the minimum hardware requirements. The next few sections cover the following hardware requirements to install ZENworks for Desktops.

Server Hardware

You initially install the ZENworks for Desktops components to server(s) on your network. You must make certain that server(s) meet the following criteria for installation:

- ▶ 64MB of server memory for NetWare versions 4.11 or 4.2
- ▶ 128MB of server memory for NetWare 5.0 and later
- ▶ 160MBof disk space on install volume
- ▶ 24MB of disk space on SYS volume

Client Hardware

During the ZENworks for Desktops install, you install files to one or more clients. You should make certain that those clients meet the following minimum hardware requirements:

- **Pentium Processor** — Although this is the absolute minimum, we would recommend at least a Pentium II processor when using ZENworks for Desktops on a Windows NT/2000 client machine.

- **16 Megabytes of RAM** — Once again, this is the absolute minimum, however we would recommend at least 24MB of RAM to run the ZENworks for Desktops client utilities on Windows NT. If you choose to run other applications at the same time, we recommend that additional memory be added to the client to compensate for the memory those applications take up.

- **5 Megabytes of Disk Space (Minimum Install)** — The minimum install only takes 5MB of disk space; however, we recommend being prepared by having enough disk space to do a full install.

TIP

One of the hardest problems to deal with in installing software is running out of disk space. What usually happens is the install is stopped in the middle and you are left with a partially installed product. You must then free up disk space and re-complete the entire install. You should watch for this especially when installing on the C: drive. Windows usually has a swap file on the C: drive, and other applications such as Netscape create their caches to the C: drive as well. Windows often also spools print jobs to a file on the C: drive. For these reasons, the C: drive fills up quickly and unexpectedly, so you should make certain that the disk space is available immediately before installing ZENworks for Desktops.

Required Software

Prior to installing ZENworks for Desktops, you should also make certain that your systems meet the minimum software requirements. The next few sections cover the following minimum software requirements to install ZENworks for Desktops.

Network Software

The first step is to install the ZENworks for Desktops components to NetWare server(s) on you network. You must make certain that your network meets the following criteria for installation.

NetWare 4.11 Server   To install ZENworks for Desktops, you must have at least one available NetWare 4.11 or later server that meets the aforementioned hardware requirements. ZENworks for Desktops installs to a NetWare 4.11 or NetWare 5.x server equally well. During the installation process ZENworks for Desktops installs additional utilities and the client installs to the server(s) you choose.

NOTE   Make certain that you have applied the latest support pack for the operating system you are using.

NDS Connection   You must also have NDS installed on your NetWare server and an NDS connection to the server you wish to install ZENworks for Desktops to. We would recommend that you use the latest DS.NLM available from http://support.novell.com. There are fixes included in the new versions that solve a lot of unwanted DS problems.

JVM   ZENworks for Desktops also requires that you install/update the Java Virtual Machine (JVM) on the server. The correct version of the JVM is included on the companion CD and can be installed from there (see the readme on the companion CD). This resolves issues when loading the Automatic Workstation Import.

NOTE   To avoid an extremely long install of the JVM, rename the JAVA directory at the root of the SYS volume. The JVM does an extensively long version checking install if the files are already present.

Application Server   ZENworks for Desktops requires an application server available on the network as well. This can be a NetWare server, a Windows NT server with NDS for NT version 8, or a Windows 2000 server with NDS eDirectory applied. Users must have access to the server(s) because files they must use are stored there.

Client Software

During the ZENworks for Desktops install, you install files to one or more clients. Prior to installing ZENworks for Desktops, you should make certain that those clients meet the following minimum software requirements:

Windows NT/2000 or Windows 98/95 Client   The ZENworks for Desktops client installs to a Windows NT/2000 or Windows 98/95 workstation. It does not currently support UNIX or Macintosh clients.

Client32   The Windows workstation must also have at least the version of Client32 NetWare client that ships with ZENworks for Desktops installed on it. ZENworks for Desktops has the option to set up a client install to make this happen. Later in the book we discuss how to update the clients automatically.

NOTE   ZENworks for Desktops does not support Novell clients that are set up with IP/IPX gateway support.

ConsoleOne   To administer ZENworks for Desktops, you need to install ConsoleOne on the client. We recommend installing the version that is included on the ZENworks for Desktops companion CD (see the readme for installation instructions).

NDS Connection   The client in which you install ZENworks for Desktops must have an authenticated NDS connection to a server that has ZENworks for Desktops installed on it.

NOTE   The ZENworks for Desktops install must use an authenticated NDS connection to install components. Even though mapped drive using bindery emulation may give an administrator file access to the SYS: volume, the ZENworks for Desktops install is not complete without an NDS authentication.

Installation Prerequisite Checklist

Once you have verified that your network has the required hardware and software, you should run through the following prerequisite checklist prior to installing ZENworks for Desktops:

▶ Make certain that you are authenticated to the network as either Admin or equivalent.

- ▶ Make certain that there are no Java Runtime Environments loaded on NDS for NT servers.

- ▶ Make certain that you are authenticated to all servers you wish to install ZENworks for Desktops to.

- ▶ If you are running the install on a NetWare server make certain that Java is unloaded by typing "java –exit" at the console prompt.

- ▶ Exit any programs that use files in the SYS:\PUBLIC directory.

- ▶ If you are installing Sybase make certain that it is not running on the server during the install.

- ▶ If you are installing from a client, exit any applications currently being run.

- ▶ Set the screen resolution on the workstation from which ConsoleOne will be run to 800 × 600 or you will not be able to view the entire application screen.

Installing Server Components

Once you have verified the hardware and software prerequisites for the server(s) and network you plan to install ZENworks for Desktops to, you can begin the installation procedure to install the ZENworks for Desktops server components as outlined in this section. The following sections detail the steps to install the ZENworks for Desktops server components.

Login to Tree as Admin

The first step to installing the ZENworks for Desktops server components is to login to your NetWare tree as Admin or as a user with supervisor rights to the NetWare servers and NDS containers where you wish to install ZENworks for Desktops.

Launch Install from CD

Once you are logged in as Admin or an Admin equivalent, you are ready to launch the ZENworks for Desktops install. The ZENworks for Desktops installation CD-ROM is supplied with an auto-run feature, which is automatically launched when you insert the CD-ROM into your client.

Select Which Language to Install

Once you have launched the install, a screen appears. From this screen you must select the language of ZENworks for Desktops to install.

Currently the only language supported is English; however, there are plans to include other languages with later releases.

NOTE

Select ZENworks Install

Once you have selected the language, you are given the option to install ZENworks, view the readme, review the get started guide, or browse the online documentation. Before selecting the 'Install ZENworks' option as shown in Figure 2.1, you should do the following four checks:

1. Make certain that there are no other Windows applications running on your client. This can cause problems later on in the install, which may force you to restart the install.

2. Make certain that none of the files in sys:\public or its sub-directories are in use. This can cause problems for both the ZENworks for Desktops install and the applications using those files.

3. Unload Java on the servers you wish to install ZENworks to.

4. Make certain that ConsoleOne is installed on the servers you are installing ZENworks to.

Select Installation Type

Once you have selected the ZENworks install you get a window similar to the one in Figure 2.2. From this window you have the option of selecting one of the following installation options depending on your needs:

Typical Install

A typical installation installs all of the ZENworks for Desktops server-side components on the servers you select. It also extends the NDS schema and copies the appropriate files to the servers. New Application objects are also created in NDS by the typical install. This is the easiest and fastest way to install ZENworks for Desktops on your servers.

FIGURE 2.1 *Main installation screen for the ZENworks for Desktops install*

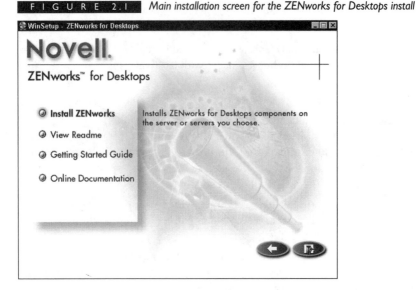

FIGURE 2.2 *Installation type screen for the ZENworks for Desktops install*

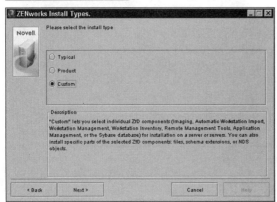

Product Install

The Product option installs selected groups of ZENworks for Desktops components on the servers you select. For each group you can select which components to install and which of the following part or parts of those components to include:

- ▶ File Copy
- ▶ Schema Extension
- ▶ Application Object Creation

This option gives the greatest control and is typically used by administrators for testing purposes to only install the components they wish to test.

Custom

The custom option enables you to specify which ZENworks for Desktops components to install. If you are comfortable with which options you need, you can use this option to select from the following products as shown in Figure 2.3:

- ▶ Application Management — Installs the software distribution piece (NetWare Application Launcher [NAL]) and extends the NDS schema to include Application objects.

- ▶ Automatic Workstation Import — Installs the programs and files necessary to complete the automatic workstation import to the servers.

- ▶ Workstation Management — Installs the workstation management pieces, and extends the NDS schema to include Workstation objects.

- ▶ Workstation Imaging — Installs the programs and files necessary to perform workstation management functions.

- ▶ Remote Management Tools — Installs the programs and files necessary to manage workstations remotely.

- ▶ Workstation Inventory — Installs the programs and files necessary to inventory workstations.

- ▶ Workstation Management — Installs the workstation manager on the selected servers.

- ▶ Sybase Database — Installs Sybase to the selected servers and sets up the database.

► . . . . ◄

F I G U R E   2 . 3   *Options in custom setup components screen for the*
ZENworks for Desktops install

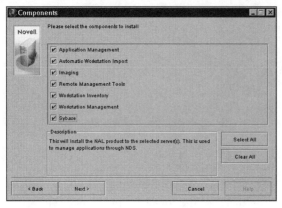

Once you have selected the product components you wish to install and
clicked next, you have the option of choosing which parts to install as shown
in Figure 2.4. You can select from the following available options by checking
the box next to it:

▶ Files

▶ Schema Extensions

▶ NDS Objects

► . . . . ◄

F I G U R E   2 . 4   *Component part filter screen for the ZENworks for*
Desktops install

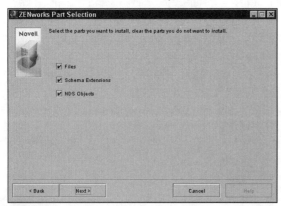

Select Tree for Installation

The next screen in the install enables you to specify which tree you wish to install ZENworks into. The ZENworks for Desktops install is only able to install ZENworks to one tree at time. Therefore, if you are authenticated to multiple trees, you must select one tree to update with ZENworks schema extensions, programs, and files.

Select Server(s) for Installation

Once you have selected the installation tree, you are given a list of servers to install ZENworks for Desktops to. You can select which server(s) to install ZENworks for Desktops to by checking the box to the left of the server name.

You do not need to install ZENworks to every server in your tree, just the ones that ZENworks applications will be used on. Once you determine which servers you wish to use, select the servers you wish to install ZENworks for Desktops to and click the 'next' button to continue.

Make certain that you have verified the server hardware and software prerequisites for installing ZENworks for Desktops on all of the servers you check in this menu before proceeding.

NOTE

Select Server for Inventory Database Installation

Once you have selected the servers to install ZENworks to, the workstation inventory option prompts you for a server to install the inventory database on. A list of servers is displayed and you can select one to install the database to.

You should consider the availability of the server when deciding which server to install the inventory database on. In other words, don't install the inventory database on a server that is in a separate location from most of the workstations. For example, if most of the users are in a New York office, you should select a server that is in New York as well.

Select Volume for Inventory Database Installation

Once you have selected the server to install the inventory database on, a list of volumes on that server is displayed. Select the volume that you wish to install the inventory database on and click the Next button.

You should consider growth. As you add more workstations to the inventory, the database grows. Make certain that you have enough disk space on the volume you select to accommodate the addition of new workstations.

NOTE

Select Languages for Installation

The next screen in the ZENworks for Desktops install is the language selection screen. A list of available languages is displayed. You must select English, but you can also specify any other additional languages that are available for you to install.

If some of your users have workstations in different languages, then ZENworks uses those languages for its applications when they are executed.

Select Import/Removal Type for Automatic Workstation Import

If you've selected to install the automatic workstation import option, a screen similar to the one shown in Figure 2.5 is displayed next. This screen lets you determine the role that this server is responsible for during automatic workstation import.

For each server you are installing ZENworks to you are able to define one of the following roles:

▶ **None** — This server plays no role in the automatic workstation import.

▶ **Import** — This server automatically imports workstations, but does not remove them. There must be at least one import server.

▶ **Removal** — This server removes workstations, but does not import them. This server type is optional. However, you should have at least one removal server if your workstation count changes very much.

▶ **Import/Removal** — This server acts as both an import and a removal server for automatic workstation import.

F I G U R E 2 . 5   *Server import/removal role selection screen for the ZENworks for Desktops install*

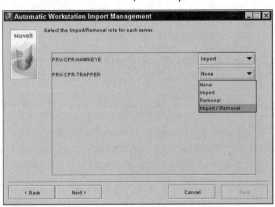

Select Inventory Roles for Inventory Servers

If you selected to install the inventory option, a screen similar to the one shown in Figure 2.6 is displayed next. This screen lets you determine the roles that each server you are installing ZENworks to will play as inventory servers.

For each server you are installing ZENworks to you are able to define one of the following server roles:

- ▶ **Root Server** — Highest level of server. Can have either leaf or intermediate servers attached to it.

- ▶ **Intermediate Server** — Intermediate server. Will act as an intermediate server between leaf servers and the root server.

- ▶ **Leaf Server** — Lowest level. Can attach to either a root server or an intermediate server.

- ▶ **Standalone Server** — Acts as a single entity. If there is only one server that is responsible for inventory, then you should select this role for the server.

For each of the servers in the database you are also able to determine the following two options:

- ▶ **Connected to Database** — This server connects directly to the database. Typically root servers or standalone servers.

- ▶ **Workstations Attached** — This server has workstations attached to it. Typically leaf servers.

F I G U R E   2 . 6   *Server inventory type selection screen for the ZENworks for Desktops install*

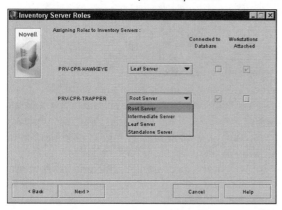

For more information about inventory server roles see the chapter on work-station import later in this book.

Select the ScanDir Volume to Store .STR files

Once you have configured the server roles you are given the option to deter-mine which volume on each server you want to act as a ScanDir location to store the .STR files, as shown in Figure 2.7. The .STR files contain the workstation scan data collected from workstations during the inventory process.

NOTE

Because the scan data files can grow large with every canning cycle, depending on the number of workstations that are scanned you should consider placing it on a volume other than SYS:.

► • ◄

F I G U R E   2.7   *Inventory ScanDir volume selection screen for inventory servers in the ZENworks for Desktops install*

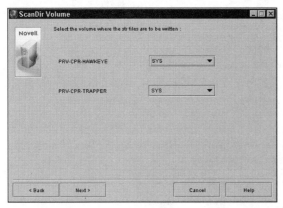

Select Site ID for Inventory Database

Once you have determined the storage location for the ScanDir, you are prompted to enter a unique site name and ID, if you selected to install the inventory database as shown in Figure 2.8. Identifying the databases uniquely enables you to query an individual database, report information, and view inventory information specific to the database.

For example, if there are Inventory databases at different geographical locations, you can query each site database and collect information specific to that site only.

NOTE

You must specify a unique site ID and site name for each database you install. ZENworks does not verify whether the site information is unique during the install. Do not use underscore characters in the site name.

FIGURE 2.8 *Database site ID screen for the inventory database in the ZENworks for Desktops install*

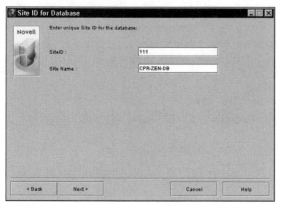

Complete the Install

Once you have completed the setup options you are given the summary screen as shown in Figure 2.9. This screen shows you the product components you selected and the size they take up on the server. If you need to make any changes you can click the Back button, otherwise click Finish and the ZENworks for Desktops install performs the tasks listed in the following sections.

Check File System

The ZENworks for Desktops installs check for available disk space on the servers you requested to install to. If there is insufficient disk space, you are given the option to proceed. The ZENworks for Desktops install installs some files that already exist on the server. The older files are overwritten. Therefore, there may be enough disk space to install ZENworks for Desktops even if the available showing is less than needed.

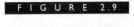

FIGURE 2.9   *Installation summary screen for the ZENworks for Desktops install*

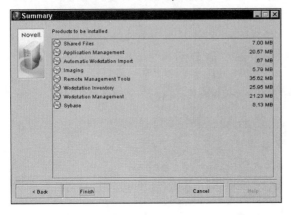

Check Schema

The ZENworks for Desktops install also checks the DS schema for problems prior to updating it. If no problems are found, then the schema is extended to include new objects and attributes necessary for the components you selected to install.

Copy Files

Once the file system, schema, and DS objects are checked and any problems are resolved, the ZENworks for Desktops install copies the files to each server selected in the previous menu in sequential order. A status screen lets you know which server is being installed and a percentage of progress to completion. Once the file copy is done you can click the 'Finish' button and the ZENworks for Desktops server component install is complete.

Create Workstation Inventory

Once the files have been copied, ZENworks creates a workstation inventory database on the server. Once this is done you are given the option to set the context to grant rights to Workstation objects. This is necessary for workstations to write a workstation entry to their container. It is not necessary to set the context during install; however, you need to set it later in ConsoleOne.

For the workstation inventory database to be created, TCP/IP must be set up on the target server.

NOTE

Log Problems

All problems with the file system, schema, or DS objects are reported in a log file and displayed on the screen. You are able to review the log file and correct any errors prior to continuing.

We highly recommend that you carefully review the log file for all errors and review the readme file (available from the same screen). If there are any errors, they are much easier to correct at this point than they will be later.

NOTE

## CHAPTER 3

Setting up ZENworks for Desktops in Your Tree

This chapter provides a quick overview of the ZENworks for Desktops system and a high-level view of the changes that occur within your tree. Try to follow and understand this system and how it impacts your current Novell Directory Services installations. Other chapters get into the details of installation and feature execution.

General ZENworks for Desktop Architecture

Novell ZENworks for Desktops requires some changes to your Tree structure in addition to installation and extensions to the new ConsoleOne administration tool. Additionally, a new client needs to be placed on the workstation with the addition of some agents. This section details the changes that need to occur to implement ZENworks for Desktops into your tree.

Objects in NDS and Their Impact on the Tree

When you install ZENworks for Desktops into your tree it not only copies the executable files necessary to run the software, but it also extends the schema in your tree. The schema extension in your tree introduces several new objects and attributes to your system. Following is a high-level list of the changes to your schema. For a more detailed view of the schema changes refer to Appendix A.

- ▶ **Container package object.** This object collects for your administration all of the policies that are available to be associated with a container. You create one of these objects when you wish to affect a container policy. One such policy is the search policy, which affects the order of searching for all policies in and below the container.

- ▶ **Server package object.** This object collects all of the policies that are available for servers. The policies for servers in the ZENworks for Desktops product include policies for automatic workstation import. Other server policies that are compatible with this object are also included in the ZENworks for Servers product. This object is introduced in ZENworks for Desktops 3.

- ▶ **Server group object.** This object enables the creation of a group of servers. This is useful when you want to apply a Server Policy package to a group of servers. This object is introduced in ZENworks for Desktops 3.

- **Service location package object.** This package collects the policies that are in the system that are related to locating services in the network. Currently these policies include the ZENworks Database Location policy. This object is introduced in ZENworks for Desktops 3.

- **User package object.** This object holds all of the policies that are associated with Users. This includes such policies as the Dynamic Local User, Help Desk, and Printer policies.

- **Workstation package object.** This package contains all of the registered policies for a workstation. These policies could be such items as client configuration policies and inventory policies.

- **Workstation image object.** This object represents an image that has been taken from a workstation. This image can then be applied to any workstation in the network from some commands in Novell's eDirectory or through a boot process with a floppy. This object is introduced in ZENworks for Desktops 3.

- **Workstation group object.** This object enables you to collect a set of workstations into a group. This is useful if you want to apply policies to a set of workstations that are not all in the same container.

- **Application object.** This is the object that is associated with an application that you want to have distributed or available on any desktop in the network.

- **Application folder object.** This object enables you to create a menuing/foldering system for the presentation of your applications on the user's start menu or windowed desktop.

- **Database object.** This object represents the database in the network where you are storing such information as logs of ZENworks activity and events, as well as hardware and software inventory information. This object is introduced in ZENworks for Desktops 3.

- **Inventory service object.** This object represents the inventory service that is configured and running in the network, collecting your hardware and software configurations of your workstations. This object enables you to configure the service; it is introduced in ZENworks for Desktops 3.

- **Several policy objects.** This is a set of Policy objects that represent policies that are contained in the User, Server, or Workstation policy packages. These may be such policies as the Help Desk policy, Remote Control policy, or Restrict Login policy, just to name a few. Currently in ZENworks for Desktops over 36 different policies are created and used in the ZENworks system.

The introduction of most of these objects to the tree is of minimal impact. The only objects that you need to consider because of their size are the application and the Workstation object.

The Application object can grow depending on the amount of registry settings that a particular application contains. You need to be careful where you place these objects because they can be large, especially for some applications such as Microsoft Office.

The Workstation object only introduces approximately 4KB of information. However, the culmination of all Workstation objects in your environment needs to be managed carefully and you must use good design techniques in placement of your partitions to make your tree most efficient.

ZENworks for Desktops 3 introduces the previously described new Policy objects but does not impact the previous ZENworks 2 policies. This is so that the ZENworks 2 system continues to function while you migrate your workstations and then portions of the tree (container by container) to the new ZENworks for Desktops 3 system. All ZENworks 2 functionality must still be administered through NWAdmin32. A tool is provided with ConsoleOne that migrates your ZENworks 2 policies to the new ZENworks for Desktops 3 system, should you decide to make a complete move.

Administration through Novell ConsoleOne

Previous versions of ZENworks for Desktops (such as ZENworks) delivered snap-ins into the Novell Administrator tool (NWAdmin32). This version of ZENworks for Desktops no longer delivers these snap-ins but provides the new ConsoleOne and the ZENworks for Desktops snap-ins into ConsoleOne to administer all of ZENworks for Desktop features.

Novell, Inc. has moved to ConsoleOne to provide a newer architecture for the administration of network resources. ConsoleOne provides a better programming interface for snap-in developers, easier management of plug-ins for administrators (no registry keys or memory problems), and because it is written in Java it facilitates the move of administration capabilities to non-Windows platforms. ConsoleOne is already available for NetWare, Linux, Solaris, and Windows environments.

The administration of ZENworks for Desktops follows the familiar method of administrating Novell Directories. ZENworks for Desktops leverages all of the features of the Directory including inheritance, rights, and standard associations.

Novell Client

ZENworks for Desktops required some enhancements to the Novell client and consequently the new client is included in the ZENworks for Desktops package. Future clients delivered from Novell continue to have support for ZENworks for Desktops, regardless of which bundled system is shipped. These enhancements include the addition of agents that are specific to ZENworks for Desktops and hook into specific events that occur on the workstation, such as user login, user logout, screen saver activation, and so on. These hooks allow ZENworks for Desktops agents to be notified when these events occur and begin doing their work.

When you install ZENworks for Desktops into your network, you have the option of copying the clients to the servers. If this is done, then your end-users can have their login scripts modified to include calls to the client's ACU (Automatic Client Update) system which checks their client to see if it is as new as the one on the server. If changes have been made to the client on the server, and it is newer than the client on the workstation, resulting in the need to have the workstation, then the new client is automatically installed on the workstation.

Some administrators install all of the parts of ZENworks for Desktops and then put the policies into place before they roll out the new client. When the new client is placed on the workstation, the new ZENworks for Desktops policies will be effective.

Novell Workstation Agents

For convenience, several ZENworks for Desktops agents that are necessary to interact with the Remote Control and Software Distributions system have been included with the client now being delivered from Novell. Specifically these items are Novell Workstation Manager, ZENworks for Desktops Remote Control, and the Novell Application Launcher service. Currently, the Novell Workstation Manager and Novell Application Launcher services can only be installed with the clients. The Remote Control facilities, in addition to being included with the clients, are also delivered as Application objects in the tree when ZENworks for Desktops is installed. Once delivered as Application objects, this service can then be installed independently on any workstation by associating the Application object with the User object in the tree and having the user run the ZENworks for Desktops Application Launcher.

Policy Packages and Policies

To help in the administration of all of the features and policies of ZENworks for Desktops, the various policies are conveniently grouped into policy packages. These policy packages are logical groupings of policies that are valuable for a user or device.

In previous versions of ZENworks for Desktops the system created policies packages for users, containers, and all of the various flavors of desktops (such as Windows 3.1, Windows 95/98, Windows NT/2000). In the new ZENworks for Desktops product the system now only creates policy packages for users, containers, and workstations. The individual desktop operating systems are identified within a single workstation policy package. This was to reduce the amount of redundancy in administration that was required for each of the different desktop flavors. The new system, however, still allows flexibility by enabling you to administer unique policies for each desktop version, should you desire to not use the general workstation policies.

Policy packages may be associated to the various appropriate objects. For example, user policy packages may be associated with a single user, a group of users, or a container. Workstation policy packages may be associated with a single workstation, a group of workstations, or a container. A single policy package may also be associated with several users, groups, and containers.

Because the system looks for policies by searching up the tree from the user or Workstation object (depending on the application), it is desirable to keep this search from proceeding too far up the tree. Therefore, ZENworks for Desktops included a search policy found in the Container policy package. This policy limits the number of levels and the search order that all ZENworks for Desktops systems use to discover and apply policies.

Various services are used by the ZENworks for Desktop system, and these services are located by the Services Location Policy package. This package is typically associated with a container and identifies where SNMP traps and the database is located. The applications in the system then use the database that is specified in the location policy.

► • ◄

ZENworks for Desktops Policy Package Wizard

In order to assist you in constructing policies, ZENworks for Desktop has included a wizard that is activated with the creation of a Policy Package object. The Policy Package Wizard is launched when you go to a container and request that a new Policy Package object be created. Previous versions of ZENworks had a wizard that could be executed from the tools menu of NWAdmin32; this is no longer supported in ConsoleOne.

Policy Package Wizard

The Policy Package Wizard is activated when you create a Policy Package from the Create menu choice or from the Policy Package Wizard icon on the ConsoleOne tool bar. The first screen, shown in Figure 3.1, presents you with the list of all available policy packages and the list of policies that are contained in each policy.

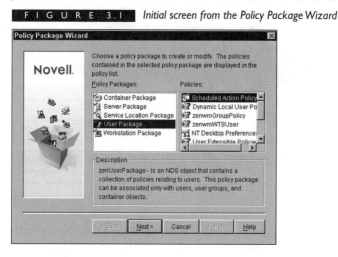

F I G U R E 3 . 1   *Initial screen from the Policy Package Wizard*

Once you select a policy package, the right side of the wizard fills in with the various policies that are available with the selected package. You need to press next in order to proceed in the creation of the policy package you have selected. This presents you the page that asks you to enter in the name of the policy package and the container where the package should reside. This screen is shown in Figure 3.2.

After selecting the name and container you are presented with a page that lets you go back to create another package or select the option to define additional properties for the package you are about to create. By selecting the additional properties option, and pressing next, the wizard creates the object and then opens the object properties, just as if you had browsed to the object and selected properties. Now you can modify and activate specific policies in the package.

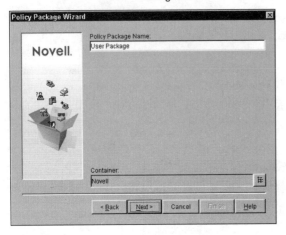

F I G U R E 3 . 2
Prompt for package name screen from the Policy Package Wizard

Setting up User Packages in the Tree

Once you have user objects in your tree and have the latest client agents installed on your user's workstations you can begin to manage your users in the tree.

The following describes at a high level some of the things that you can manage with the user policy package.

Creating User Policy Packages

You can quickly create a user policy package by using the following described steps. We get into the details of each policy in later chapters.

1. Launch ConsoleOne.

2. Browse in ConsoleOne to the container where you want to create the policy package. Remember that you can have the package reside in any container and still associate it with any other container in the tree; but you need to be aware of your partitions so as not to require large partitions to be replicated all over your tree, just to get to the policy packages.

3. Select the Container object and then press the right mouse button and select the Policy Package object. This opens the policy package create wizard to walk you through the creation.

4. Select User package and follow the wizard to identify the container and the name of the object. Pick Define additional properties in the last wizard page so we can activate some policies. If you didn't do this, then browse in ConsoleOne to the container that has your user policy package and select that object. You can double-click or do a right mouse click and choose properties on the menu.

5. You are presented with the property page for the user package you have defined. The screen should look like that described in Figure 3.3.

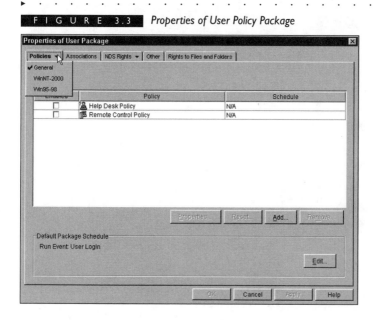

F I G U R E 3.3 *Properties of User Policy Package*

6. Under the general category you have both the Help Desk and the Remote Control policies that you can activate. The workstation specific policies can be accessed by pressing the small triangle next to the Policies tab and then selecting the desired workstation type from the drop-down menu. Once the workstation type is selected, then the policies tab for that specific workstation is displayed.

7. Select the Help Desk policy by clicking with the mouse on the check box beside the policy.

8. Go into Help Desk policy properties by either double-clicking to get to the properties or select the details button following (Figure 3.4).

9. Once in the properties of the Help Desk policy you can select various configuration options on the pages displayed to enable the user to see and run the Help Desk application. The Help Desk policy is described in detail in later chapters.

► . . . . ◄

F I G U R E 3.4   *Properties of Help Desk policy in the User Policy Package*

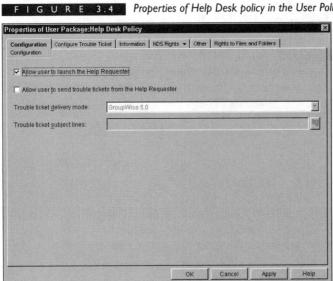

10. Press OK to complete the changes. If you have not associated this policy package with a container, group, or a User object, then a notification is displayed (Figure 3.5).

► . . . . ◄

F I G U R E 3.5   *Notification of unassociated User Policy Package*

11. Press Yes to associate this user policy package with a container in the tree. This once again brings up the property pages of the user policy package and displays the associations page (Figure 3.6). You need to then press the Add button and browse to the container, group, or user you wish to receive this policy package. Remember, every user below the identified container, within the specified group or the associated user, receives this policy package and all policies activated in this package.

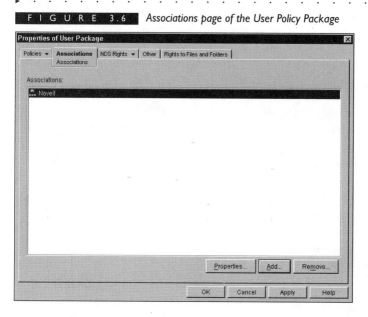

FIGURE 3.6 *Associations page of the User Policy Package*

12. Press OK to complete the change.

You have now created a simple user policy package and turned on the Help Desk policy for all of the users associated with this policy package. The Help Desk application is presented in the ZENworks Application Launcher package and is activated for the users with this policy.

Setting up Workstations in the Tree

Before you can start really managing the workstation you must create Workstation objects and associate them with physical workstations. This step is not necessary if you do not want to manage the physical device, but instead want to only manage the desktop. For example, if you only want to deliver applications to the workstation and apply Microsoft policies to the desktop when a user is logged into the workstation, then associating a user policy to the particular user does all this. However, if you want to manage the physical inventory and perform remote control functions in *addition* to managing the workstation accounts, then you must first have the Workstation object.

Previous versions of ZENworks for Desktops only provided a manual method for registering and importing workstations into the tree. The newer versions of ZENworks for Desktops provide an automatic way to have the system create and remove workstations. The manual methods from ZENworks 2 continue to work in the same tree. The automatic workstation import only works with Windows 95/98/NT/2000 workstations with the latest agents. You cannot manually import any Windows 95/98/NT/2000 workstations in ZENworks for Desktops 3. Legacy Windows 3.1 still requires the manual method in NWAdmin32 using your previously installed ZENworks 2 system.

The expected plan is to first update the workstations with the newer client and agents (which continue to function with ZENworks 2 policies). Then introduce ZENworks for Desktop 3 policies into the tree and the clients will automatically migrate over to the new policies. The client agents search for their policies and behaviors using the following logic.

1. See if the schema of the tree has been updated with ZENworks for Desktop 3 policies.

2. If schema is updated to ZfD 3, then look for a ZfD 3 search policy found in an associated container policy.

3. If a ZfD 3 search policy is found then assume you are working in a ZENworks for Desktop 3 system and use those policies.

4. If a ZfD 3 search policy is not found, then search for a ZENworks 2 search policy.

5. If a ZENworks 2 search policy is found, then assume you are working in a ZENworks 2 environment and use only those legacy policies, even though the schema was found to be a ZfD 3 schema (in Step 1).

6. If a ZENworks 2 search policy is not found, then assume you are working in a ZfD 3 system and use only those policies.

7. If the schema from Step 1 has not been updated from ZENworks 2, then assume you are in that environment and only look for ZENworks 2 policy packages.

Consequently, with this algorithm you can update your tree with ZENworks for Desktops 3 and update your clients. You will still be working with ZENworks 2 policies that were previously in the tree. Now you can go to a particular container and associate a ZfD 3 container policy, activating the search policy. This causes all desktops and users who are in that container to now switch over to using the ZfD 3 policies. Alternately, if the container has a ZENworks 2 container package with a search policy, you can also go to the container and deactivate a ZENworks 2 policy. This also causes all users and desktops to start using the ZfD 3 policies (assuming no other search policy is higher up in the tree path).

The following sections describe the automatic workstation methods of importing a workstation into the tree. Should you need to continue to manually import workstations through ZENworks 2, you need to refer to the system manuals or Novell's ZENworks Administrators Handbook (ISBN 0-7645-4561-2) from Novell Press for instructions on how to manually import workstations.

To get the system up and running you must first have an Import Policy active in your tree and the agents running on the server and workstations. You must do the following to get a functioning Import Policy in your tree:

1. Activate workstation agents.

2. Activate server agent. (Only for automated workstation import.)

3. Create a Policy Package (User package for manual, Server package for automated).

4. Turn on the Import Policy in the Policy Package.

5. Associate the Policy Package.

6. Enable login cycles to register the Workstation to the Tree and have the server agent automatically create the Workstation object and associate it to the device.

7. Associate other Policies to the Workstation objects to effect management.

Activate Workstation Agents

The workstation agents that are necessary for the creation and association of Workstation objects in the tree with a physical device are installed as part of the client that is associated with ZENworks. All future clients continue to provide and support these agents.

Therefore, before you can successfully import a workstation into the tree you must first have some version of the ZENworks for Desktop client on the workstation. Only the clients that are greater than version 4.8 support the automated workstation import; otherwise you need to perform the manual operations.

Activate Server Agents

If you want to have automated workstation import in your network, then you should have installed the automatic workstation agents onto the server as part of the installation process.

These agents on the workstation get into contact with the agents on the server through DNS services. You must either have a DNS server in your network with the DNS name of the automatic workstation import server registered (you gave the name at installation time) or each workstation must have the DNS name and address in the host file. The host name must be `zenwsimport`, because the agents will be doing a host name lookup with that name to find the IP address of the server with the service.

The agents must be running on the server. This is done by executing the zenwsimp.ncf file for NetWare or by having the install process install the automatic workstation import service on the NT servers.

NOTE

If you do not have the latest jncp.nlm and njcl.jar loaded on the server running the automatic workstation import agent, when workstations attempt to register the agent will throw an error stating that there was a NoSuchMethodError event. You can also look in the wsreg32.log file in the root drive of the workstation to give you some additional clues. The correct versions can be found on the ZENworks for Desktops 3 CD under the companionCD/ NJCL directory or from `www.novell.com`.

Creating a Policy Package

To start up the automatic workstation process you must have a workstation import policy activated and associated with the server that is running the import agents. This is done by creating a server policy package, activating the import policy, and then associating the server policy package with the server via a container, server group, or direct association.

1. Start ConsoleOne.

2. Select a container to hold the Server Policy Package object.

3. Create the Server Policy Package in the container.

4. Go through the Policy Package Wizard and select a Server Policy Package for the type of package and name the object. Follow the wizard along and associate the policy package with the container that has the Server object with the import agent running. Remember that these policies are effective in sub-containers as well, so you can associate the policy package high enough in the tree to affect as many servers as desired.

Creating a Workstation Import Policy

Now that you have created the Server Policy package and associated it with a container that holds the server, you need to activate the Workstation Import Policy in the package. To activate the Workstation Import Policy, do the following:

1. Start ConsoleOne.

2. Browse to the container that has the Server Policy Package you want to administer.

3. Select the Server Policy Package and bring up the properties on the object.

4. Select the Workstation Import Policy from the list of policies available. When you select and activate the import policy the check box to the side will be checked.

5. Perform details of the Workstation Import Policy if desired.

6. Select OK and close out the dialogs.

Once creating a Workstation Import policy, then the workstations that have not been registered with the tree attempt to contact the workstation import agent on the server when the workstation is booted. If a connection is made, then the agent receives information from the workstation (to help in the naming), and then creates the Workstation object in the tree and returns that object name back to the workstation. The workstation then stores that information in a secure portion of the registry and it is associated with that object in the tree.

In the preceding Step 5 you had the option of modifying the details of the Import Policy. Let's discuss briefly some of these options. If you decide to take the default Import policy, then workstations, when created, will be located in the same container as the Server object and will be named by the concatenation of the computer name and the MAC address of the network card. By going into the details of the Import Policy you can change the policy to identify under which container you want the Workstation object to reside (can be absolute or relative to server or policy container) and options on how to name the Workstation object.

Associations of Policy Packages

The ZENworks for Desktops system always starts with the relevant user, server, or Workstation object, depending on the feature being executed. Once the user, server (for agents), or Workstation object is located, then the system will walk-the-tree until it locates the first policy package it can find. Generally once a package is found the configuration set in that policy is applied to the system, and the ZENworks for Desktops feature activates. Some features exist, such as the Microsoft Windows desktop policies, that are an accumulation of several ZAW/ZAK policies to which the user may be associated. These policies require that the search proceed until the root of the tree.

Walking to the root of the tree for policy packages can be expensive in time, especially if the tree spans across a WAN link. Therefore, ZENworks for Desktops introduced the Search Policy that is contained in the Container Policy Package. This Search Policy limits the levels of containers that all processes search to find their policies.

Novell Workstation Registration and Object Creation

If the import policy has been created and associated with the Server object and the workstation import agents are running on the server, then, when a user logs into the system, it activates a workstation registration process. Based on the policy, it may take several logins before the registration occurs.

The registration process includes an agent running on the workstation attempting to resolve the DNS name of zenwsimport and uses that address to contact the automated workstation import process running on the server. The server process receives information about the workstation and the user and then, based on the naming description administered in the import policy associated with the server, it creates a Workstation object for the workstation. Once the object is created, it returns the distinguished name of the Workstation object back to the registration process on the workstation. The workstation then stores the workstation DN information in a secure portion of the registry and it becomes associated with the given Workstation object.

You can un-register a workstation by running the unreg32 in the SYS:\ PUBLIC directory on the workstation that you want to disassociate with an object. Then the initial rules of Workstation object creation go into effect and a new object is created at the proper time and given to the workstation.

Creating Other Policies

Once you have your users associated with their appropriate policy packages you can then create other policies in that package and have them affect the user's environment. This is also true with Workstation objects and their associated policy packages.

Remote Management Rights

A majority of the remote management features are available to users and administrators via rights in the NDS tree on the objects that represent the target device. For example, in order to remote control a target workstation you must have rights in the target Workstation object in order to perform the remote control function.

You must grant individuals rights in the tree in order to enable them to perform remote management functions on workstations and user desktops. The following objects in the tree may be granted remote management rights: user, group, organizational role, organization, organization unit, country, locality, [Root], [Public]. Two methods exist that you can use to set up these rights. The following subsections discuss these methods.

Remote Operators Page

A Remote Operators Page is associated with each Workstation object. Figure 3.7 displays this page.

From within this page you may add either users or groups to the list of operators. With each addition you can check which of the remote management utilities this addition has rights to perform. The three choices available are "Remote Control," "Remote View," "File Transfer," "Remote Execute," and "Remote Wakeup." By checking the box underneath the icon associated with each of these functions, you grant that user or group the rights to perform those functions on this particular workstation.

You can also discover who in the tree may have rights to perform some remote management on a specific workstation. This can be done by selecting a workstation in ConsoleOne and running the "Remote Management Rights" from the Tools menu, or by pressing the Display button on the remote operators page of the Workstation object. When this program is activated it examines those that have rights to this object and then displays a report on who has rights to which portions of rights management. A sample output report is shown in Figure 3.8.

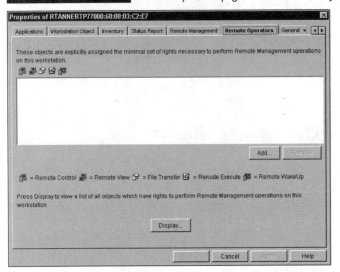

FIGURE 3.7 *Remote Operators page in a Workstation object*

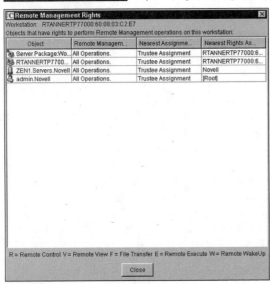

FIGURE 3.8 *Report of rights management on a specified workstation*

Inventory, Event, and Logging Databases

In order to keep track of the logging events generated by the workstation agents, other ZENWORKS server agents, SNMP events, and hardware and software inventories for your workstations, you need to install at least one database into your tree. This database holds off of the events, inventory, and reporting information. You can then generate reports against that database to display information about your workstations in the tree.

In ZENworks 2 you could only have a single site database (or one database for your tree), and if you had multiple site databases they could not be rolled-up together. In ZENworks for Desktops 3 you can have a wide variety of databases and inventory information across your tree.

You can have a server collect inventory information and then forward it on to a local database on that server, or another in the area. You can also have that information rolled up into another enterprise-level database. This allows you the ability to have a local site database that just contains local information and then have that information also included in an enterprise-level database that may contain information from many site databases.

When you installed the database on the server at installation time, a ZfD Database object was created in the same container where the server is located. This Database object represents the database that resides on that server. The object enables you to administer the server where the database is located and the passwords that are used by the agents to gain entry into the database. This object is also used in the Service Location Policy package that tells the workstation and server agents what database to use for storing their event and logging information.

To get the databases up and functioning for event and logging, you need to do the following:

1. Install the Sybase database onto a server. This places a blank database on the server and puts in the mgmtdbs.ncf file on NetWare to get it started.

2. Create a Service Location Policy Package and activate the database policy. You need to create the package and turn on the database policy that also needs to have a reference to the Database object in the database page.

3. Associate the Service Location Policy Package with a container. This enables agents of users or desktops in that container to locate the database.

4. Application objects that you want to track have a page that you can specify which events you would like logged in the database. See additional information in chapter 5, "Creating and Using Application Objects."

Additional administration needs to be accomplished in order to get workstation inventory data into the database. See the chapter on Workstation Inventory for additional information.

Reporting

ZENworks for Desktop 3 has changed the reporting capabilities of the system. Once you have set up an inventory database and identified what you wish to have stored in the database (such as inventory, application launching or failures, and so on), you can run reports against that database.

Previously ZENworks 2 relied on an ODBC driver application being installed on your workstation in order to be able to run your reports. ZENworks for Desktops 3 uses a JDBC interface to connect and query from the database. You can get to the reports by selecting the Tools ⇨ Inventory Reports from the ConsoleOne menu. You are asked to configure the database first, so the system knows which database to communicate with. When you configure the database by selecting Tools ⇨ Configure DB you are prompted for the IP address of the server containing the database. Under the advance options you can tell the system if the database is a Sybase or an Oracle server.

ZENworks for Desktops 3 introduces some semi-custom reports that are a step above the canned reports that were delivered in ZENworks 2. These semi-custom reports, when launched present you with a screen that lists the available reports and the items in the report that you can customize. When you select a report you are allowed to select a set of values that must match for the data to be included in the report. This enables you to create reports that are much more informative without the myriads of data that was printed out in prior versions. Figure 3.9 displays a sample screen from the Application launcher report selection.

Once you have selected a report, the system connects with the configured database and then queries the information with a JDBC connection. The results are then placed in a canned styled report and presented in the viewer that pops up to display the information. From the viewer you can save or print the report.

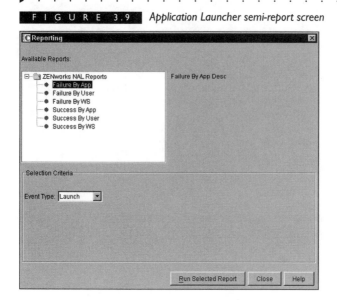

F I G U R E   3 . 9   *Application Launcher semi-report screen*

Setting up TED Distributions

ZENworks for Desktops 3 ships with some agents that plug into the Tiered Electronic Distribution system that was introduced with the ZENworks for Servers 1.0 product. These plug-ins only work with the ZENworks for Servers 2.0 version of TED, which has not been released yet.

These agents allow you to distribute Application objects and the installation files associated with them throughout the servers in your network. They also keep the files and objects up-to-date with the identified "golden" versions.

## CHAPTER 4

Creating Application
Packages Using snAppShot

One of the most useful tools provided in ZENworks for Desktops is the snAppShot utility. As an administrator installing and updating applications on client workstations, the snAppShot utility saves you an extensive amount of time by enabling you to create a template during a single install that can be used to easily distribute applications and upgrades to several workstations on your network.

This chapter familiarizes you with the snAppShot utility and how to use it to create application packages. To do this we first discuss the following topics:

- ▶ What is snAppShot
- ▶ When Should You Use snAppShot
- ▶ How snAppShot Works
- ▶ Advanced Features of snAppShot
- ▶ Limitations of snAppShot
- ▶ Using snAppShot
- ▶ snAppShot Application Packages versus .MSI Files

After covering the topics mentioned previously, the remainder of the chapter takes you through an extensive example of how to use snAppShot to package a common network application.

What Is snAppShot

The first step in using the snAppShot utility is to understand what it is. The snAppShot utility is an application used to create before and after images of a model workstation when installing or upgrading an application to it. So in effect, snAppShot takes a picture of the workstation before an application is installed or upgraded to it, and another picture after the application has been fully installed or upgraded.

Once snAppShot has the two pictures it is then able to discern the differences between the two pictures. It saves the differences and can use them later to upgrade or install applications to other workstations on the network.

When Should You Use snAppShot

Now that you understand what snAppShot is, you need to know when to use it. By default, snAppShot is generally used to package an application to distribute to several other users based on NDS and the Application properties.

However, since snAppShot captures changes made to a workstation during install, many situations exist in which you can use it to save time. This section describes how snAppShot is useful in three situations:

Complex Installations or Upgrades

Using snAppShot to aid in complex installations or upgrades can save you a considerable amount of time spent repeating the same steps over and over. By using snAppShot, you simply need to perform the complex installation or upgrade once, record the differences, and then apply those differences to the other workstations.

An example of where snAppShot is useful in a complex upgrade would be installing and configuring a printer driver on a Windows 2000 client. To do so we must follow these steps:

1. Enter the network path to the printer or browse the network to find the appropriate queue.

2. Use the Windows 2000 CD-ROM or the path to the CAB files that have the necessary files to install the printer driver.

3. Configure the printer drivers for the desktop.

4. Make the appropriate configuration changes also for the printer.

The preceding steps are tolerable if it is for one or two workstations, but if a hundred or more workstations need the printer set up, the task becomes monumental.

Using snAppShot on one Windows 2000 machine to "package" a printer installation enables you to create an Application Object template that you can use to create an Application object.

Once the Application object is created for the printer installation, other Windows 2000 clients can install the printer, with drivers, without having to use CAB files, Windows 2000 CD-ROM, or make the configuration changes!

Numerous Installations or Upgrades

Using snAppShot to aid in installations that must be done on numerous workstations can also save you a lot of time. Often, application upgrades or installations are very simple to perform and only take a short time on one workstation. However, that time is multiplied by the number of clients you have on your network. Many companies have thousands of clients and, though installing an application that takes only a few minutes on one client, the installation takes days to complete on *all* network clients.

snAppShot enables you to configure the upgrade or install to be automatically performed throughout the network. Instead of running the install or upgrade on workstation after workstation, you simply perform it once on the model workstation and use snAppShot to record the differences. Once recorded, the changes can be made to several other workstations easily and efficiently.

Using snAppShot to record the changes during the update and packaging into an Application object enables you to have the upgrade performed automatically as the users log in to the network. This saves a lot of time and effort in upgrading a large number of users. It also guarantees that every client has been upgraded.

To Verify Changes Made During an Install or Upgrade

Another situation where snAppShot is very useful is to verify or view the changes made by an application install or upgrade. Although snAppShot was not designed for this purpose, it works well because it captures the changes made during the install.

Several times I have installed an application that has created difficulties for other applications. Using snapshot enables you to detect what the application install did to your client and enables you to correct it without un-installing or re-installing an application.

A good example of where snAppShot can help with reviewing an application install is installing a new application that updates shared DLL's in the SYSTEM directory for Windows 98. The application replaces a working DLL with a newer DLL that has bugs.

Once the new DLL is installed, the new application works fine, but a previously installed application fails to load properly. Normally you would have two options to either re-install the application that is failing to unload, or to un-install the new application and hope that its un-install mechanism backed up the old DLLs before copying over them.

Using snAppShot, however, enables you to see which DLLs were replaced by the new application install so that you can simply replace them from a backup, CD-ROM, or other source.

How snAppShot Works

Now that you know what snAppShot is, and what it is for, you need to understand how it works. This section discusses how snAppShot is able to analyze and store the changes made by an installation or upgrade.

Files Created by snAppShot

When snAppShot is used to determine the changes made by an installation or upgrade, many files are created to store information. These files are used later when the installation or upgrade needs to be performed again. They contain all the information needed to update other clients without having to run the installation program or upgrade again.

The following sections describe the file types created by snAppShot when recording the changes during an installation or upgrade.

.AXT Files

AXT stands for Application Object Text template, meaning that the .AXT file is written in human-readable, text format. Therefore, you can open it in a text editor and edit the contents.

NOTE

The .AXT file takes longer to import into an Application object than an .AOT file, and it is prone to inaccuracies if certain .AXT file format standards are not followed.

An .AXT file is a collection of information about what happened on a workstation when an application was installed to it. You can also think of it as a "change log" that contains the differences between the pre- and post-application installation states of a workstation. snAppShot discovers these differences and records them in the .AXT file as shown in Figure 4.1.

You use the .AXT file when creating and setting up Application objects using Application Launcher for large-scale distribution. The .AXT file delivers the information about the application to the new Application object.

.AOT Files

AOT stands for Application Object template. The .AOT file is written in binary format and cannot be edited in a text editor.

NOTE

.AOT files import faster into an Application object and can be more accurate than their text-based counterpart, the .AXT file.

An .AOT file is a collection of information about what happened on a workstation when an application was installed to it. You can also think of it as a "change log" that contains the differences between the pre- and post-application installation states of a workstation. snAppShot discovers these differences and records them in the .AOT file.

F I G U R E 4.1   *Sample excerpt from a snAppShot .AXT file*

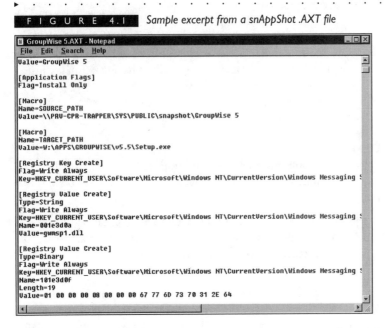

You use the .AOT file when creating and setting up Application objects using Application Launcher for large-scale distribution. The .AOT file delivers the information about the application to the new Application object.

.FIL Files

One .fil file represents one application file that was installed to a workstation. As there can be hundreds of files installed to a workstation during an application's installation or upgrade, there can also be hundreds of .fil files representing that application.

Think of .fil files as the Application object's copy of the originally installed application files.

For convenience later when you create Application objects, we recommend that you store .fil files in the same place as the .AOT file. If you place these files in a network location, it is easier to access them as you build and distribute the Application object.

A list of the .fil files that need to be copied to run an application is kept in the .AOT file. This list can be viewed from the Application Files property page in the Application object in NWAdmin.

FILEDEF.TXT

The filedef.txt file is a "legend" which compares originally named installed files with the newly named .fil files. snAppShot copies the filedef.txt file to the same directory where the .fil files are created. You then use it to compare .fil files to the originally installed files. A sampling from the filedef.txt file is shown in Figure 4.2.

FIGURE 4.2   *Sample excerpt from a snAppShot FILEDEF.TXT file*

```
filedef.txt - Notepad
File  Edit  Search  Help
1.fil=C:\Novell\GroupWise\DeIsL1.isu
2.fil=C:\Novell\GroupWise\grpwise.ins
3.fil=C:\Novell\GroupWise\gwatt1.ocx
4.fil=C:\Novell\GroupWise\GWMXLIB1.dll
5.fil=C:\Novell\GroupWise\GWWW1.DLL
6.fil=C:\Novell\GroupWise\GXMim1.dll
7.fil=C:\Novell\GroupWise\IMFMU2.FLT
8.fil=C:\Novell\GroupWise\IMGDF2.FLT
9.fil=C:\Novell\GroupWise\IMGEM2.FLT
10.fil=C:\Novell\GroupWise\IMMET2.FLT
11.fil=C:\Novell\GroupWise\IMPIF2.FLT
12.fil=C:\Novell\GroupWise\IMPS22.FLT
13.fil=C:\Novell\GroupWise\ISGDI32.DLL
14.fil=C:\Novell\GroupWise\USDIF.DLL
15.fil=C:\Novell\GroupWise\USDRW.DLL
16.fil=C:\Novell\GroupWise\USDX.DLL
17.fil=C:\Novell\GroupWise\USDXF.DLL
18.fil=C:\Novell\GroupWise\USEN4.DLL
19.fil=C:\Novell\GroupWise\USENS.DLL
20.fil=C:\Novell\GroupWise\USENW.DLL
21.fil=C:\Novell\GroupWise\USSDW.DLL
22.fil=C:\Novell\GroupWise\WPROF.DC
23.fil=C:\Program Files\Netscape\Users\me\prefs.js
24.fil=C:\WINNT\FORMS\FRMCACHE.DAT
25.fil=C:\WINNT\system32\GWAPPINT.INF
```

Information Saved by snAppShot

snAppShot is able to determine what changes have been made during an installation or upgrade by saving information before and after and then determining the differences. Installations and upgrades can change many different files and settings on a workstation; therefore, snAppShot saves many different types of information about the configuration of the workstation.

The following sections describe things that snAppShot stores before and after an installation or upgrade, and then uses to determine changes to the workstation:

Files and Folders

First and foremost, snAppShot saves a list of all files that were added or modified during the installation or upgrade. It also saves a copy of the file named as a .fil file to be used in later installations or upgrades.

INI Files

snAppShot also saves any changes to application or system .INI files, so that those files can be modified when the Application object is used later. The following are some of the files which snAppShot monitors for changes:

▸ **WIN.INI** — This file contains information about the Windows workstation setup, such as desktop settings, file types, and so on.

▸ **SYSTEM.INI** — This file contains information about device and driver setting for the Windows workstation.

▸ **PROTOCOL.INI** — This file contains information about the network settings for the Windows network protocols.

System Configuration Text Files

snAppShot records any changes to system configuration text files as well. That way any changes to drivers being loaded, paths being set, or environment variables being added or changed are recorded and can be applied to other systems when the Application object is used to install or upgrade the workstation.

The following are the two files which snAppShot monitors for system configuration changes:

▸ AUTOEXEC.BAT
▸ CONFIG.SYS

Windows Shortcuts

Any changes to Windows shortcuts are also recorded by snAppShot. Therefore, if an application installation or upgrade adds a new shortcut to the desktop or start menu, or modifies the path in an existing shortcut, those changes are applied to other systems as well along with the Application object.

Registry

snAppShot is also able to record any changes made to a Windows workstation's registry by an installation or upgrade. This is extremely important later because even if you copy all files installed by an installation or upgrade and make the appropriate changes to configuration files, the application often fails to run because registry settings have not been made.

Using snAppShot fixes that problem by saving the changes to the registry and then applying them when the Application object is used to install or upgrade the application on a new workstation.

Advanced Features of snAppShot

Although snAppShot is a relatively easy program to run, some advanced features make it an extremely powerful tool. This section discusses the following advanced features included in the snAppShot utility.

Using snAppShot Preferences

If you think of snAppShot as a camera, and the .AOT file as the outputted "picture," then you can think of snAppShot preferences as the adjustments you make to the camera (aperture settings, film speed, focus) before you take the picture.

snAppShot preferences let you control what snAppShot "sees" as it discovers the changes made to a workstation as a result of installing an application. In other words you can specify/control information recorded about the items described in the following sections during an installation or upgrade.

Files/Folders

Using snAppShot preferences, you can include or exclude the recording of certain changes to particular folders and files. This enables you to protect certain directories that you do not want altered on other workstations when the Application object is used on them to install or upgrade an application.

Windows Shortcuts

Using snAppShot preferences, you can exclude particular windows shortcuts files from being recorded. This allows you to protect certain application shortcuts from being created or altered on other workstations during the installing or upgrading of an application.

INI Files

Using snAppShot preferences, you can exclude particular application INI files from being recorded. This enables you to protect certain application INI files from being created or altered on other workstations when the Application object is used on them to install or upgrade an application.

System Configuration Files

Using snAppShot preferences, you can define which system configuration file changes are recorded. This enables you to set which system configuration changes should be recorded and created or altered on other workstations when the Application object is used on them to install or upgrade an application.

Registry Entries

Using snAppShot preferences, you can also include or exclude changes from particular portions of the Windows registry from being recorded. This enables you to protect certain areas of the Windows registry that you do not wish to be altered on other workstations when the Application object is used on them to install or upgrade an application.

Special Macros

Special macros are built-in machine and user specific values that the snAppShot utility is able to use to control how Application Object templates are created. These special macros read from the registry, enabling for the customization of Application objects in snAppShot. This customization enables you to distribute the same application to several machines that might have Windows installed or configured differently.

The following is a list of some common macros:

- ▸ **WinDir** — Directory containing the windows OS. Typically C:\Windows or C:\WINNT

- ▸ **WinSysDir** — Directory containing the windows system files (DLLs).

- ▸ **TempDir** — Windows temporary directory. Typically C:\Windows\temp.

- ▸ **Favorites** — File system directory that serves as a common repository for the user's favorite items.

- ▸ **Fonts** — Virtual folder containing system fonts.

- ▸ **Personal** — File system directory that serves as a common repository for personal documents.

NOTE

The online help that appears when you click the help button on the Application object macros property page in NWAdmin gives a detailed list and explanations of the macros available to snAppShot.

When snAppShot starts, it asks the client library for a list of the special macros. This list combined with the user macros (created in the custom mode) make up the complete list of macros, which are then placed in order from the longest value to shortest.

While snAppShot runs, it records the differences between the pre-installation scan and the second scan. It then creates an entry in the .AOT file, during which snAppShot calls the routine that searches and replaces data with the macro's name. Later, when the application launcher is used to distribute the object, it gets the macro values from the .AOT file.

The application launcher receives the values and names for these special macros by looking in the registry under the key:

```
HKEY_CURRENT_USER
+Software
+Microsoft
+Windows
+CurrentVersion
+Explorer
+Shell Folders
```

The application launcher client creates a special macro using the name and value.

 If the value does not exist, then the special macro is returned and the data value is set to blank.

NOTE

Let's say that a special macro is defined for a directory containing temporary files. The entry in the Windows registry would appear as:

```
HKEY_CURRENT_USER
+Software
+Microsoft
+Windows
+CurrentVersion
+Explorer
+Shell Folders
TempDir=C:\DATA\TEMP
```

This registry entry would correspond to the special macro:

```
%*TempDir%
```

Therefore, when snAppShot adds the creation information for the registry entry in the .AOT or .AXT file, it writes an entry similar to the following:

```
[Registry Value Create]
Type=String
```

```
Flag=Write Always
Key=HKEY_CURRENT_USER\Software\Microsoft\Windows\CurrentVe
rsion\Explorer\SHell
Folders
Name=TempDir
Value=%*TempDir%
```

When the application launcher tries to distribute the settings, it sees the special macro value and then, in an attempt to set this registry key, tries to read the value from this exact registry key.

If the registry value was set before the application is distributed then this works beautifully; however, if it is not set until after the application is distributed, then the application launcher tries to use data from the same registry entry that it is trying to create.

This problem can be remedied in two ways:

1. The first way to resolve this problem is to set the registry value before the user clicks on the icon (perhaps using ZENworks for Desktops workstation policies discussed later in this book). Then when the application launcher client reads the data for these special macros, it reads the correct value and knows how to replace the special macro correctly.

2. The second and better/more difficult solution is to manually edit the .AXT file created for the Application Object template. Instead of using the macro you are trying to create, add in an additional entry with a different macro name but the same value.

Partial Install Detection

If your application needs to reboot the workstation to finish the installation, snAppShot recognizes this and picks up where it left off before the reboot. All snAppShot data is stored in a hidden directory on the c: drive. Furthermore, snAppShot is automatically run after the machine is restarted. When snAppShot restarts, it detects a partial installation, and a window pops up and allows you to continue with the previous installation.

Limitations of snAppShot

Now that you know how snAppShot works and understand some of its advanced features, you need to know the limitations it has. snAppShot is a very powerful tool, however, it cannot be used for the tasks described in the following sections.

Capture Install Logic

snAppShot is unable to capture the "logic" of an installation involving choices based on existing hardware, software, or other settings. For example, if the application's Setup program installs a particular video driver or modem setting file to a workstation, these settings may not be valid when transferred to another workstation.

The following sections describe some of the things you should be aware of when you are using snAppShot to create application packages.

Hardware Specific Drivers

Some applications query the computer system to find out what hardware is installed and only install necessary drivers for the hardware that actually exists. This often results in problems if you distribute the application to clients that do not have the same hardware as the computer in which the application package was created. You can use the hardware inventory feature of ZENworks for Desktops, discussed later in this book, to quickly determine what specific hardware is installed on clients.

Available Disk Drives

Occasionally an application install prompts the user to input additional paths of locations to store files. When you use snAppShot to create an application package, make certain that any additional paths you specify, both local and network, exist on all clients you wish to distribute the application to. For example if you specify a path on the D: drive, all clients must have a D: drive on their computer. If necessary you can use macros and user prompts when distributing the application to handle this as well; however, that must be defined in the Application object itself.

Prerequisite Drivers and Applications

Another thing you should watch for when creating application packages using snAppShot is prerequisites for application installs. For example, if the application detects to see which version of DirectX is installed on the computer it may determine that the current version is correct and then not install needed DirectX drivers. This results in the drivers not being included in the Application object. If a client that is receiving the application from ZENworks for Desktops does not have the correct version of DirectX drivers, then the application may not function.

Guarantee Impact on ALL Workstations

Although, snAppShot can be used to install or upgrade applications on all workstations, it cannot guarantee the impact the application install or upgrade will have on all workstations. The following sections describe some rare occasions when an application distributed to a client might result in problems.

Conflicting Local Applications

It is possible that an application distributed with ZENworks from Desktops could conflict with a local application that was installed by the user of that workstation. An example of such an occurrence might be if you distribute a corporate virus scanner down to all workstations, and an existing application cannot open files correctly because the virus scanner believes it is a virus that is trying to modify the files.

Most companies have at least some sort of standard for applications that can be installed on clients. This standard usually ensures that applications being distributed with ZENworks for Desktops do not conflict with any other applications on the user's systems.

Specialized Shared DLLs

When an Application object is delivered to a workstation, it can be configured to copy files only if they are newer. This usually protects shared DLLs because the older functionality is usually available in newer versions.

However, some applications have DLLs which have functionality written specifically for them. This functionality does not exist in newer versions and, if they are overwritten with a newer file, then the application they supported may no longer function.

Hardware Requirements

Many applications are written for computer systems that have a high level of CPU speed, RAM, video memory, disk speed, and so on. If this type of application is distributed down to a client workstation that does not have the hardware capability to support them, then they will not function properly.

This can be controlled somewhat by configuring the Application object to check for hardware levels before installing (discussed in the next chapter). You can use the hardware inventory feature of ZENworks for Desktops, discussed later in this book, to quickly determine what hardware is installed on clients.

Image Entire Workstation

snAppShot is designed to record changes made by a single application install, and therefore, it cannot image an entire workstation for disaster recovery purposes. When snAppShot discovers a workstation it only saves some information about the files, such as the date, time, and size of the files. It does not save a copy of all the files on the workstation.

If you have a need to image an entire workstation you should refer to the section on imaging a workstation discussed later in this book.

Using snAppShot

Once you are familiar with when and why to use the snAppShot utility and some of its advanced features, you are ready to begin using it to create Application objects. When you start snAppShot you see a screen similar to the one in Figure 4.3.

This is the startup screen for snAppShot which allows you to select one of the following options depending on your needs and if you already have a preference file ready.

Standard

You should use the Standard Mode in snAppShot to discover the application installation changes on a workstation using default settings. If you have never run snAppShot before, and are unfamiliar with the available settings, this is the best option. It requires little intervention.

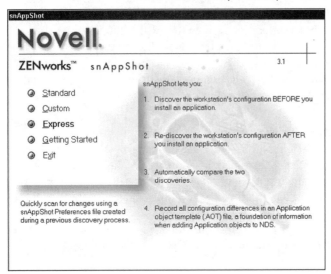

To use the Standard Mode simply selects it and perform the following operations to create the needed files:

Name the Application Object Icon Title

Once you select the Standard Mode installation from the main screen in snAppShot, a window similar to the one shown in Figure 4.4 is displayed. From this screen you need to input the name that the Application object has in the DS tree and a title for the icon which represents the Application object.

We recommend that you choose names for the object and its icon that are descriptive enough to distinguish which application and often which version. This saves confusion and time later.

NOTE

Specify the Network Location of the Application Source (.fil) Files

Once you have set the name for the Application object and title for its icon in the Standard Mode install, a screen similar to the one in Figure 4.5 enables you to set the network location to store the application source files (.fil).

FIGURE 4.4 *snAppShot window for naming the Application object and the application's icon*

FIGURE 4.5 *snAppShot window that allows the user to specify the location to store the application source files*

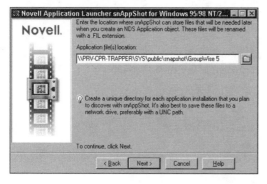

When setting this location you should remember the following two things:

1. Make certain that you select a location that all users who must use the Application object have access to.

2. Make certain that there is enough disk space, in the network location that you set, to store the entire application.

Specify the Network Location of the Application Template (.AOT and .AXT) Files

Once you have specified a network location for the .fil files, snAppShot enables you to set a network location for the application template (.AOT and .AXT files). Set the network location by either entering it into the text window or by clicking on the folder button and navigating to the appropriate directory.

Specify the Drives That Will Be Discovered

Once you have selected the network location to store the Application object support files, you are given the option to select which disk drive to scan on the workstation to determine changes as shown in Figure 4.6.

You can add drives to the list by clicking on the Add button and selecting the drives you wish to scan. Conversely, you can remove drives from the list by selecting the drive and then clicking on the remove button.

You are able to select network drives as well, but only if they are mapped. This allows you to install applications to a larger network drive if needed and still discover the changes.

NOTE

► • ◄

F I G U R E   4 . 6   snAppShot window for specifying which disk drives, network and local, are scanned during discovery

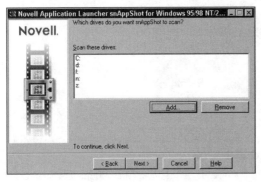

Make certain that you select all drives that the application install or upgrade affect. If you do not select a drive and the application install or upgrade adds, removes, or modifies files on that drive, the changes will not be discovered.

NOTE

Read the Pre-discovery Summary to Check Settings

Once you have all the drives you wish to select added to the list of drives to be scanned, click Next and a summary of the preferences are displayed in the next window, as shown in Figure 4.7. The information displayed includes:

- ▶ Application Object Name
- ▶ Application Icon Title
- ▶ Template Filename
- ▶ Application Files Directory
- ▶ Snapshots Working Drive
- ▶ Scan Options
- ▶ Disks to Scan
- ▶ Directories to Exclude
- ▶ Files to Exclude
- ▶ System Text Files to Scan

F I G U R E   4.7   *snAppShot window that allows review of the summary of the current preference setting before starting the first discovery*

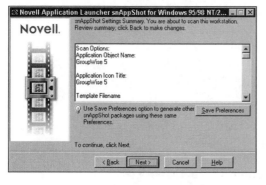

NOTE

Click Save Settings to save the snAppShot preferences you have defined thus far to a file. Later, during a similar snAppShot session, you can choose the preferences you save now to accelerate the process.

Run the First snAppShot Discovery

The first snAppShot discover is run when you click Next from the Preference summary window. A screen shows the status of the discovery and a count of the following items that have been discovered:

- Folders and Files
- Windows Shortcuts
- INI Files
- System configuration Files
- Registry Entries

Run Application's Installation or Upgrade

Once the first snAppShot discovery is completed, a Run Application Install button is available. When you select the Run Application Install button, a file pop-up menu appears and you are able to navigate to the application install executable and execute it.

Once the application install is complete, you are able to continue on with the discovery process of the snAppShot application.

NOTE

Write down where the installation program installs the application's executable file. It will be useful later when creating and distributing the Application object.

Enter the Path to the Application's Executable

Once you have completed the application install, snAppShot gives you the option to specify a path to the application's executable on this workstation. You can enter the location of the installed application files on this workstation in the text field.

Of course, if you do not want snAppShot to set a target distribution location, then leave this field blank and continue.

Run the Second snAppShot Discovery

Once you are finished with setting the path to the applications executable and click the Next button, snAppShot runs the second discover. Once again you are able to monitor the status of the discovery by noting the count of the following items:

- Folders and Files
- Windows Shortcuts
- INI Files

- System Configuration Files
- Registry Entries

Once the discovery is finished, snAppShot begins generating an object template. This is where the actual differences between the two discoveries are discerned and the template files created.

Depending on the number of folders, files, and registry entries on your workstation, the second discovery process can take a considerable amount of time. However, both the discovery and the template generation screens have status counters to let you know how far along they are.

Read the Completion Summary

Once the second snAppShot discovery is completed, and the template files generated, a completion summary of what took place is displayed in the following window, as shown in Figure 4.8. The completion summary contains information about the application template creation including:

- The location of the new Application Object template (.AOT)
- The location of the new .FIL files
- The location of the textual version of the Application Object template (.AXT)
- Listing of the steps to take to create the Application object
- Statistical totals from the second discovery
- Statistical totals from entries added to the Application Object template (.AOT)

F I G U R E 4 . 8 *snAppShot window that allows the user to review the summary of the Application Object template generation*

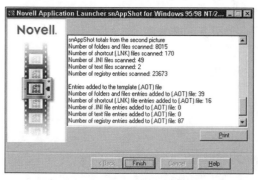

You have the option from this window to print out the summary. We recommend doing so and keeping it as a record to aid in troubleshooting future problems if they happen to occur.

Custom

You should use the Custom Mode in snAppShot to set specific options when discovering the application installation or upgrade changes on a workstation. Custom Mode is much like Standard Mode except that it gives you the added opportunity to specify the drives, files, folders, Registry hives, and shortcuts that you want to include or exclude in the discovery process. You can save these settings in a preference file for later use if you need to run snAppShot for a similarly configured application.

Only in Custom Mode are you able to see and use all of snAppShot's features. To use the Custom Mode, simply select it and perform the following operations to create the needed files:

1. Choose the snAppShot Preferences File

2. Name the Application Object and Icon Title

3. Specify the Network Location of the Application Source (.fil) Files

4. Specify the Network Location of the Application Template (.AOT and .AXT) files

5. Specify Which Parts of the Workstation to Include or Exclude

6. Specify the Drives That Will Be Discovered

7. Read the Pre-Discovery Summary

8. Run the First snAppShot Discovery

9. Run the Application's Installation or Upgrade

10. Specify How to Handle the Creation of Files, Folders, .INI File Entries, and Registry Settings

11. Enter the Path to the Application's Executable File

12. Define Macros for Distribution Automation

13. Run the Second snAppShot Discovery

14. Read the Completion Summary

Choose the snAppShot Preferences File

The first window that comes up after you select the custom mode in snAppShot is the choose snAppShot Preferences window. From this window you have the option of either using a previously saved preference file, or using the snAppShot default settings.

If you have previously created and saved a preferences file in a previous custom mode, you can navigate to that file or enter the path to it into the text field as shown in Figure 4.9.

F I G U R E   4 . 9   *snAppShot window for specifying a pre-created preference file or to use the default settings*

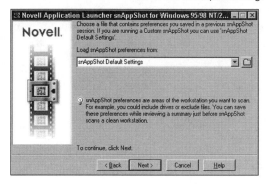

Name the Application Object and Icon Title

Once you select the preference file option in express mode in snAppShot, a window is displayed. From this screen you need to input the name that the Application object will have in the DS tree and a title for the icon which represents the Application object.

Specify the Network Location of the Application Source (.fil) Files

Once you have set the name for the Application object and title for its icon in the Standard Mode install, a screen enables you to set the network location to store the application source files (.fil).

When setting this location you should remember the following two things:

1. Make certain that you select a location that all users who must use the Application object will have access to.

2. Make certain that there is enough disk space in the network location that you set to store the entire application.

Specify the Network Location of the Application Template (.AOT and .AOT) Files

Once you have specified a network location for the .fil files, snAppShot enables you to set a network location for the application template (.AOT and .AXT files). Set the network location by either entering it into the text window, or by clicking on the folder button and navigating to the appropriate directory.

NOTE

If files already exist with the same object name, then you are given the option of whether or not to overwrite the older ones.

Specify Which Parts of the Workstation to Include or Exclude

Once you have selected the network location to store the Application object support files, you are given the option to select which of the following parts of the workstation you wish to include or exclude as shown in Figure 4.10:

FIGURE 4.10   *snAppShot window for specifying which parts of the workstation to include or exclude*

Files and Folders   From the workstation scan customization menu in snAppShot, you can modify which files and folder you wish to include or exclude. Simply select the files and folders option and click the customize button. A window similar to the one in Figure 4.11 pops up and you are able to select which files and folders to ignore.

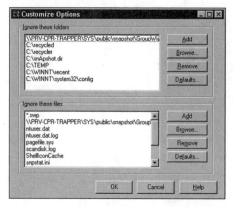

F I G U R E   4.11   *snAppShot window for specifying how and which files and folders are created in the Application Object template*

NOTE

Wild Cards are completely valid here. Therefore if you wish it exclude all .DAT files you could specify *.DAT in the list of files to ignore.

INI Files   From the workstation scan customization menu in snAppShot, you can modify which INI files to exclude. Simply select the INI files option and click the customize button. A window pops up and you are able to select which INI files to ignore.

System Configuration Text Files   From the workstation scan customization menu in snAppShot, you can modify which system configuration text files you wish to include in the scan. Simply select the system configuration text files option and click the customize button. A window similar to the one in Figure 4.12 pops up and you are able to select which system configuration text files you wish to include.

Windows Short Cuts   From the workstation scan customization menu in snAppShot, you can modify which Windows short cuts to exclude. Simply select the windows short cuts option and click the customize button. A window pops up and you are able to select which Windows short cuts to ignore.

F I G U R E   4 . 1 2   *snAppShot window that allows the user to specify which system configuration files are created in the Application Object template*

Registry   From the workstation scan customization menu in snAppShot, you can modify which registry hives you wish to include or exclude. Simply select the registry option and click on the customize button. A window similar to the one in Figure 4.13 will pop up and you will be able to select and deselect from a list of hives to include.

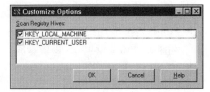

F I G U R E   4 . 1 3   *snAppShot window for indicating which Windows registry hives will be created in the Application Object template*

Specify the Drives That Will Be Discovered

Once you have specified which parts of the workstation to include or exclude, you are given the option to select which disk drive to scan on the workstation to determine changes.

You can add drives to the list by clicking on the Add button and selecting the drives you wish to scan. Conversely, you can remove drives from the list by selecting the drive and then clicking on the remove button.

NOTE

You are able to select network drives as well, however, only if they are mapped. This enables you to install applications to a larger network drive if needed and still discover the changes.

Read the Pre-Discovery Summary

Once you have all the drives you wish to select added to the list of drives to be scanned, click Next and a summary of the preferences are displayed in the next window. The information displayed includes:

- ▶ Application Object Name
- ▶ Application Icon Title
- ▶ Template Filename
- ▶ Application Files Directory
- ▶ Snapshots Working Drive
- ▶ Scan Options
- ▶ Disks to Scan
- ▶ Directories to Exclude
- ▶ Files to Exclude
- ▶ System Text Files to Scan

NOTE

Click Save Settings to save the snAppShot preferences you have defined thus far to a file. Later, during a similar snAppShot session, you can choose the preferences you save now to accelerate the process.

Run the First snAppShot Discovery

The first snAppShot discover is run when you click Next from the preference summary window. A screen shows the status of the discovery and a count of the following items that have been discovered:

- ▶ Folders and Files
- ▶ Windows Shortcuts
- ▶ INI Files
- ▶ System Configuration Files
- ▶ Registry Entries

Run the Application's Installation or Upgrade

Once the first snAppShot discovery is completed, a Run Application Install button is available. When you select the Run Application Install button, a file pop-up menu appears and you are able to navigate to the application install executable and execute it.

Once the application install is complete, you are able to continue on with the discovery process of the snAppShot application.

NOTE

Write down where the installation program installs the application's executable file. It is useful later when creating and distributing the Application object.

Set Options for Creating Files, Folders, .INI File Entries, and Registry Settings

Once the application's installation or upgrade is complete, snAppShot enables you to specify how to handle the creation of entries for the Application object. From the screen shown in Figure 4.14, you can set the addition criteria for the following entries:

► . . . . ◄

F I G U R E   4 . 1 4   *snAppShot window for specifying how snAppShot handles the creation of file, folder, INI file, and registry entries in the Application Object template*

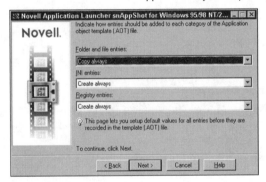

Folder and File Entries   From the Application object entry addition window in snAppShot, you can choose whether or not files and folders will be added to the Application object, by clicking the down arrow under the Folders and files option and selecting one of the following addition criteria as shown in Figure 4.15:

- ► Copy always
- ► Copy if exists
- ► Copy if does not exist
- ► Copy if newer

- ▶ Copy if newer and exists
- ▶ Requests confirmation
- ▶ Copy if new version
- ▶ Copy if different

snAppShot window that allows the user to specify how
snAppShot handles the creation of file and folder entries
in the Application Object template

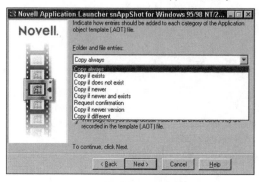

INI Files   From the Application object entry addition window in
snAppShot, you can configure whether or not INI files are added to the
Application object by clicking the down arrow under the INI files option and
selecting one of the following addition criteria as shown in Figure 4.16:

- ▶ Create Always
- ▶ Create if does not exist
- ▶ Create if exists
- ▶ Create or add to existing section

Registry Entries   From the Application object entry addition window in
snAppShot, you can configure whether or not registry entries will be added to the
Application object by clicking the down arrow under the registry entries option
and selecting one of the following addition criteria as shown in Figure 4.17:

- ▶ Create always
- ▶ Create if does not exist
- ▶ Create if exists

FIGURE 4.16 snAppShot window for indicating how snAppShot handles the creation of INI file entries in the Application Object template

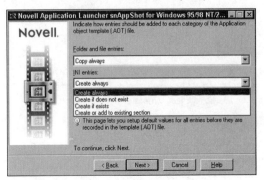

FIGURE 4.17 snAppShot window that allows the user to specify how snAppShot handles the creation of registry entries in the Application Object template

Enter the Path to the Application's Executable File

Once you have defined the addition criteria for entries into the Application object, snAppShot gives you the option to specify a path to the application's executable on this workstation. You can enter the location of the installed application files on this workstation in the text field.

Of course, if you do not want snAppShot to set a target distribution location, then leave this field blank and continue.

Define Macros for Distribution Automation

Once you are finished with setting the path to the applications executable and click the Next button, you have the option to define macros to control the distribution of Application objects. A screen similar to the one shown in Figure 4.18 enables you to add, edit, or remove macros to control automation of application distribution.

F I G U R E   4.18   *snAppShot window that allows the user to add, edit, or remove macros to be used in the Application Object template*

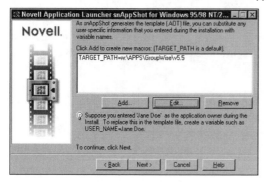

When you click the add button in the macro definition window, you are given the option to specify a variable name and a string that it is replaced within the template data as shown in Figure 4.19.

F I G U R E   4.19   *snAppShot window for specifying a variable name and string in macros*

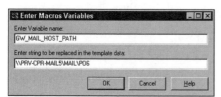

Run the Second snAppShot Discovery

Once you are finished with defining macros to automate Application object distribution, click Next and snAppShot runs the second discover. Once again you are able to monitor the status of the discovery by noting the count of the following items:

- Folders and Files
- Windows Shortcuts
- INI Files
- System Configuration Files
- Registry Entries

Once the discovery is finished, snAppShot begins generating an object template. This is where the actual differences between the two discoveries are discerned and the template files created.

Read the Completion Summary

Once the second snAppShot discovery is completed and the template files generated, a completion summary of what took place is displayed in the following. The completion summary contains information about the application template creation including:

- The location of the new Application Object template (.AOT)
- The location of the new .FIL files
- The location of the textual version of the Application Object template (.AXT)
- Listing of the steps to take to create the Application object
- Statistical totals from the second discovery
- Statistical totals from entries added to the Application Object template (.AOT)

Express

You should use Express Mode when you've already saved a snAppShot preference file from a previous discovery process. By choosing this file, you can skip over most of the Standard or Custom Mode settings which enables you to discover a new application installation much more quickly than in Standard or Custom Mode.

To use the Express Mode simply select it and perform the following operations to create the needed files.

Choose the snAppShot Preferences File from a Previous Session
The first window that comes up after you select the express mode in snAppShot is the choose snAppShot Preferences window. From this window you have the option of using a previously saved preference file.

If you have previously created and saved a preferences file in a previous custom mode, you can navigate to that file or enter the path to it into the text. If you have not previously created and saved a preference file, you must do so before selecting the express mode.

Read Summary Page to Verify snAppShot Discovery Settings
Once you have selected a preference file from a previous application package, click Next and a summary of the preferences are displayed in the next window. The information displayed includes:

- Application Object Name
- Application Icon Title
- Template Filename
- Application Files Directory
- Snapshots Working Drive
- Scan Options
- Disks to Scan
- Directories to Exclude
- Files to Exclude
- System Text Files to Scan

Run the First snAppShot Discovery
The first snAppShot discover is run when you click Next from the Preference summary window. A screen shows the status of the discovery and a count of the following items that have been discovered:

- Folders and Files
- Windows Shortcuts
- INI Files
- System configuration Files
- Registry Entries

Run Application's Installation Program

Once the first snAppShot discovery is completed, a Run Application Install button is available. When you select the Run Application Install button, a file pop-up menu appears and you are able to navigate to the application install executable and execute it.

Run the Second snAppShot Discovery

Once the application install or upgrade is finished, click Next and snAppShot runs the second discovery. Once again you are able to monitor the status of the discovery by noting the count statistics of the following:

- Folders and Files
- Windows Shortcuts
- INI Files
- System Configuration Files
- Registry Entries

Once the discovery is finished, snAppShot begins generating an object. This is where the actual differences between the two discoveries are discerned and the template files created.

Read the Completion Summary

Once the second snAppShot discovery is completed and the template files generated, a completion summary of what took place is displayed in the following. The completion summary contains information about the application template creation including:

- The location of the new Application Object template (.AOT)
- The location of the new .FIL files
- The location of the textual version of the Application Object template (.AOT)
- Listing of the steps to take to create the Application Object
- Statistical totals from the second discovery
- Statistical totals from entries added to the Application Object template (.AOT)

Super Express (Command Line) Mode

You should use Super Express (Command Line) Mode to discover changes to a workstation in the fastest possible way. The Super Express Mode of snAppShot enables you to run snAppShot from a command prompt which enables you to discover changes to a workstation faster than the other available modes.

In order to use this mode of snAppShot, which you do exclusively from the command line, you must use a preferences file from a previous snAppShot session. To use the Express Mode simply select it and perform the following operations to create the needed files, follow the steps described in the following sections.

Change to the Directory Where snAppShot Is Located

The first step to use the super express (command line) mode in snAppShot is to enter DOS and change to the directory where the snAppShot utility is located.

Enter the snAppShot Command

Once you are in the directory of the snapshot utility, enter the following command from the DOS prompt.

```
snapshot /u:<filename>
```

<filename> is the name of a snAppShot preferences file that you defined and saved earlier when running snAppShot in Custom or Express Mode.

Specify Whether to Overwrite a Previous snAppShot Discovery

Once you have executed the snapshot command from the DOS session, a window appears which gives you the option to overwrite the existing Application Object template, as shown in Figure 4.20. You must select yes to continue.

F I G U R E   4.20   snAppShot window that allows the user to overwrite the previous snAppShot discovery when using the super express mode

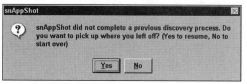

Once you select yes, the Application Object template creation continues the same as in the regular express mode by displaying the pre-discovery summary screen, followed by the first discovery.

snAppShot Application Packages versus .MSI Files

Now that we have discussed the creation of Application Object Packages using snAppShot, it is useful to discuss how they compare to Microsoft Windows installer package files (MSI).

Description of .MSI Files

An .MSI file is a storage file containing the instructions and data required to install an application. MSI files are used by the Microsoft Windows Installer to deploy and install applications to computers with 32-bit versions of Windows on them.

Description of .MSM Files

A merge module (.MSM) file, referred to as merge package file, is a single package that includes all files, registry changes, and setup logic to install a shared component. Merge modules are contained inside MSI files.

How .MSI Files Are Created

The information .MSI files contain depends on how they are created. The following sections describe the ways that .MSI files are typically created.

Development Tool Method

The most complete way of creating .MSI files is by using development tools to create MSM and MSI files and then configure them with the files, registry changes, resources, and logic to perform a complete install of the application.

This method is preferred by most application developers because it gives them the greatest control of how and what information and logic actually goes into the .MSI file.

Discovery Method

The discovery method of creating .MSI files is very similar to the way snAppShot creates its Application Object templates. The discovery method works by using a double discovery process to accumulate changes made by an install. Most third-party application installs are created by this method. The following steps describe how this method is accomplished:

1. Start with a clean PC, or one that is representative of the computers in your network.

2. Start Discover to take a picture of the representative PC's software configuration. This is the Before snapshot.

3. Install a program on the PC on which you took the Before snapshot.

4. Reboot the PC.

5. Run the new program to verify that it works.

6. Quit the program.

7. Start Discover and take an After snapshot of the PC's new configuration. Discover compares the Before and the After snapshots and notes the changes. It creates a Microsoft Installer package with information about how to install that program on such a PC in the future.

8. Clean the reference computer to prepare to run Discover again.

How do .MSI Files Work with ZENworks for Desktops

Now that you understand what .MSI files are and how they are created, you need to understand what role they can play in creating Application Objects instead of using .AOT or .AXT files.

The ZENworks snap-ins to ConsoleOne allow for you to use .MSI files to create Application Objects in exactly the same way that .AOT or .AXT files are used. Therefore, if an .MSI file is already available for an Application object, you can save yourself time and effort by simply using the .MSI file to create the Application Object (discussed in the next chapter).

## CHAPTER 5

Creating and Using
Application Objects

Now that you have an understanding of how to create an Application object template from Chapter 4, we need to discuss how to use that template to create an actual Application object and distribute it to users. Chapter 5 covers the following main points in taking you through the process of Application object creation and distribution:

- ▶ Creating the Application object
- ▶ Setting Properties for the Application object
- ▶ Setting up Application Distribution
- ▶ Distributing the Application

Creating the Application Object

The first step in using ZENworks for Desktops to distribute applications to users is to create an Application object. The Application object is an actual object in the NDS tree. ZENworks for Desktops uses this object to distribute the application to users based on the properties the object is created with. This section guides you through creating an Application object using the following four methods: with an .AOT or .AXT file; with an .MSI file without an .AOT, .AXT, or .MSI file; and by simply duplicating an existing Application object.

NOTE

We highly recommend starting with an .AOT or .AXT file, or duplicating an existing Application object because it greatly simplifies the setup, distribution, and management of applications on users' workstations. You create .AOT and .AXT files using snAppShot, which is a component of Application Launcher.

With an .AOT or .AXT File

Creating an Application object with an .AOT or .AXT file usually creates more complex Application objects. In other words, objects that make changes to Registry settings, .INI files, text configuration files, and so on.

An example of when to use an .AOT or .AXT file would be the Netscape Communicator Application object template we created in Chapter 4. Installing Netscape made several changes to the registry and modified existing .INI files. Therefore it is better to use a template to create the Netscape Communicator object.

To use an .AOT or .AXT template file to create an Application object you should follow these steps:

1. Open ConsoleOne and browse the NDS tree and right-click in the container in which you wish to install the Application object. Then select create.

2. From the Create menu, select Application. This launches the Create Application Object wizard.

3. From the create Application Object wizard, select Create Application Object with .AOT or .AXT File, and then select Next as shown in Figure 5.1.

FIGURE 5.1   *Screenshot from the Application Object wizard showing the creation options*

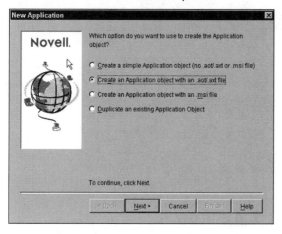

4. Browse for the .AOT or .AXT file, select it, and then click Open. A window appears that displays the path to the .AOT or .AXT file. From this window click Next.

5. Type the object name of the Application object in the Object Name text box.

6. Check (and change, if necessary) the target and source directories of the Application object as shown in Figure 5.2, and then click Next.

▶ · ◀

| F I G U R E   5 . 2 | Screenshot from the Application Object wizard showing the target and source directories |

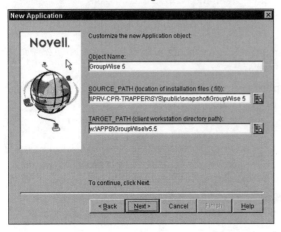

7. Review the information about the Application object (click the Back button to make any changes).

8. You have the option to select Display Details After Creation to access the property pages of this Application object. This is recommended to ensure that the Application object was correctly created.

9. You also have the option to select Create Another Application Object After This One if you want to create another after finishing with the current one.

10. Once you have made your selections from this window, click Finish and the Application object is created.

With an .MSI File

ZENworks for Desktops also enables you to create and administer an Application Object from an .MSI file. This makes it possible for you to use your existing .MSI files to roll out applications to users without having to create a fresh object or .AOT file.

Creating an Application object with an .MSI file is very similar to creating one with an .AOT or .AXT template file. Use the following steps to create an Application object for an MSI file:

1. Open ConsoleOne, browse the NDS tree, and right-click in the container in which you wish to install the Application object. Then select create.

2. From the Create menu, select Application. This launches the Create Application Object wizard.

3. From the Create Application Object wizard, select Create Application Object With .MSI File, and then select Next.

4. Browse for the .MSI, select it, and then click Open. A window appears that displays the path to the .MSI file. From this window click Next.

5. Type the object name of the Application object in the Object Name text box and then click Next.

6. Review the information about the Application object (click the Back button to make any changes).

7. You have the option to select Display Details After Creation to access the property pages of this Application object. This is recommended to ensure that the Application object was correctly created.

8. You also have the option to select Create Another Application Object After This One if you want to create another after finishing with the current one.

9. Once you have made your selections from this window, click Finish and the Application object is created.

Objects created from .MSI files are not managed exactly the same way other Application objects are. The following are ways that an Application object created from an .MSI file can be managed (they are discussed in more detail later in this chapter):

▶ **View Package Information** — Enables you to view specific information about the MSI package.

▶ **Set Properties for MSI Package** — Enables you to modify the public properties of the MSI package.

▶ **Set Transform File List** — Enables you to create of list of transform files to be applied to the MSI object prior to distribution.

▶ **Set Fault Tolerance Options** — Normal fault tolerance and load balancing options for applications can also be applied to Application objects that were created from an .MSI file.

Without an .AOT or .AXT File

The process of creating an Application object with an .AOT or .AXT file is usually employed to create simple Application objects that do not make any changes to Registry settings, such as .INI files, text configuration files, and so on.

A good example of when to use the process of creating an Application object *without* an .AOT or .AXT file is creating an Application object for a corporate calendar program. Many corporations have small home-grown calendar applications which contain information specific to their business. These programs rarely modify the registry or change system .INI files, and therefore are great candidates for this option.

To use an .AOT or .AXT template file to create an Application object you should use the following steps:

1. Open ConsoleOne, browse the NDS tree, and right-click in the container in which you wish to install the Application object, and then select create.

2. From the Create menu select Application. This launches the Create Application Object wizard.

3. From the Create Application Object wizard, choose Create Application Object Without .AOT or .AXT file, and then choose Next.

4. From this window, type the name of the Application object in the Object Name dialog box.

5. Then, use the browse button to specify the location of the executable in the Path to executable text box.

6. You have the option to select Display Details After Creation to access the property pages of this Application object. This is recommended to ensure that the Application object was correctly created.

7. You also have the option to select Create Another Application Object After This One if you want to create another after finishing with the current one.

8. Once you have made your selections from this window, click Finish and the Application object is created.

Duplicating an Existing Application Object

You should use the Duplicate an Existing Application Object method if the object you wish to create has already been created but you wish to create another, say to allow for different properties and distribution options.

A good example of when to use the Duplicate an Existing Application Object would be if you are setting up application fault tolerance and need several nearly identical Application objects. The fastest method to accomplish this is to create the primary Application object, then create as many duplicate Application objects as needed. You can then adjust each duplicated Application object as necessary (for example, specify different application source [.FIL] locations for each).

To use the Duplcate an Existing Application Object method to create an Application object you should use the following steps:

1. Open ConsoleOne, browse the NDS tree, and right-click in the container in which you wish to install the Application object. Then select create.

2. From the Create menu, select Application. This launches the Create Application Object wizard.

3. From the Create Application Object wizard, choose Duplicate an Existing Application Object, and then click Next.

4. From this window browse the NDS tree and identify the reference Application object by its Distinguished Name. Once the reference application is selected, click Next.

5. Specify a custom source path (where the .FIL files are stored) and target path (where the files are copied during a distribution, usually a workstation's c: drive).

6. Review the new, duplicated Application object's summary and click Back to make changes.

7. You have the option to select Display Details After Creation to access the property pages of this Application object. This is recommended to ensure that the Application object was correctly created.

8. You also have the option to select Create Another Application Object After This One if you want to create another after finishing with the current one.

9. Once you have made your selections from this window, click Finish and the Application object is created.

Setting Properties for the Application Object

Once you have created the Application object, you need to set the Application object's properties to define how it will behave. The following sections cover using ConsoleOne to define the identity, distribution behavior, run behavior, availability, fault tolerance, and existence of the Application Object.

Setting up the Application Object Identification

The first step in setting up the Application object in ConsoleOne is to access the Identification property page to control the application icon, description, folders, contacts, and notes that are used to define the application. Use the following steps to select which set of options you wish to modify:

1. Right-click the Application object and click Properties.

2. Click the Identification tab.

3. Click the down arrow on the Identification tab to access the available Identification property pages, as shown in Figure 5.3, and then click OK.

▶ • ◀

F I G U R E   5.3   *The Application Identification options tab in ConsoleOne*

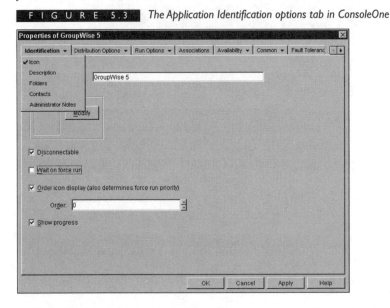

From the Application object's Identification property tab, you should access the individual property panels to configure the application identity options described in the following sections.

Setting Application Icon Properties

First, select the icon property panel from the Identification tab. A panel similar to the one shown in Figure 5.4 is displayed and you are able to configure the following options for the Application object.

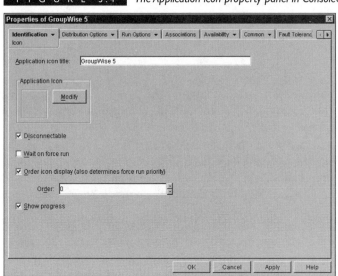

FIGURE 5.4 *The Application icon property panel in ConsoleOne*

Configure the Application Icon Title Type in the title you wish to use for the application in the application icon title box. The application icon title, which is mandatory, can be different than the Application object name (the name that NDS* uses to identify the application) and might contain periods and other special characters. You can also use the Description property page for longer descriptions of the application. The title you select here is what is displayed to a user when they access the Application object (for example the name that shows up in the Start menu if the application is set up to appear there).

TIP

If icon titles do not appear in their entirety, you might need to increase your icon spacing. Do this using Windows. After you have adjusted the icon spacing in Windows, exit Application Launcher or Application Explorer and restart for the changes to take effect. You can also use the Description property page for longer descriptions of the application.

Configure the Application Icon Title Next you should use the Application Icon option to assign an icon for the Application object. The icon you choose appears in Application Launcher or Application Explorer, depending on what you have specified on the Applications property page. If you do not specify an icon, a default Application Launcher icon is used.

Configure the Disconnectable Option   The disconnectable option enables you to control what happens to the icon when the user disconnects from the network. If this option is set then the icon remains present when the user disconnects, otherwise it does not appear.

Configure the Wait on Force Run Option   The wait on force run option enables you to specify whether or not the icon appears before the application has been run, if the force run option is set. If you enable this option then the icon won't appear until the force run is complete for the application.

Configure the Order Icon Display   From this window you also have the option to set the order icons and set the force run sequence. This option performs two very useful functions. First, it organizes the icons in Application Launcher and Application Explorer. Second, it dictates the order in which Application objects which are set as Force Run are used.

To set ordering, enter a numeric value into the Icon Order text box. All Application objects you wish to order must have a numeric value. The value of zero gives the icon the highest priority and thus the highest prominence in the list. The maximum value is 999. If you do not order Application objects, they are ordered alphabetically (the default order).

For example, suppose that you have ten icons (applications A, B, C, D, E, F, G, H, I, and J) that you want to organize in Application Launcher. You specify an order number of "0" for application G, "1" for application F, "2" for application E, and "3" for application D. You specify an order number of "4" for applications C, B, H, and I. You do not order the remaining applications, A and J.

The result is that the first four applications are ordered with G being the first in the list followed by F, E, and D. After this, applications C, B, H, and I are gathered together and arranged alphabetically. The last two icons, A and J, come at the end of the list and are arranged alphabetically (the default order).

If users (who have been associated with these Application objects) run Application Launcher they will see a list of icons according to this order. If these applications have all been set to force run, they will run in this order as soon as Application Launcher has loaded itself into memory.

Ordered and force run applications run in sequential order without waiting for the last force run application to terminate.

NOTE

Configure the Show Progress Option   The last thing you can configure from the icon property panel is the Show Progress option. You should select this option if you want an easy-to-read progress bar to be displayed to users the first time they distribute an application to their workstations.

TIP
Turn off this option if you are distributing only a small change to the application, such as a Registry modification. Turn it on if you are distributing a large application and want to give the user a general idea of how long the distribution will take. By default, this option is on.

Setting Application Description

The second setting available for Application object identification is the ability to enter text into the Description property panel to give users more complete information than the application icon caption allows. Select the description property panel from the Identification tab. A panel similar to the one shown in Figure 5.5 is displayed and you are able to set the description for the Application object.

FIGURE 5.5 *The description property panel for Application objects in ConsoleOne*

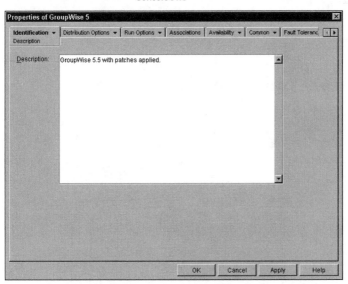

Once the description is set, users can right-click an Application object in Application Launcher or Application Explorer to see details containing both the descriptive name of the application and the more lengthy description that you provide here.

An example of when to use the description option for Application objects is if you have additional information about the application that users need. This might include information such as which new features are available in the application.

NOTE

The text you type in the Description property page is the same text the user sees if you have enabled the Prompt User Before Distribution option on the Distribution property page.

Setting Up Application Folders

The next setting available for Application object identification is the Folders property panel. The Folders property panel lets you specify the folder object you wish the application to reside in for the application launcher and start menu. Select the Folders property panel from the Identification tab. A panel similar to the one shown in Figure 5.6 is displayed and you are able to set up the application folder for the Application object.

F I G U R E   5 . 6   *The folders property panel for Application objects in ConsoleOne*

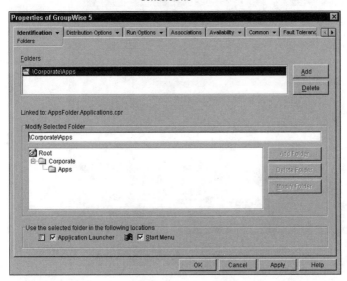

Once you are at the Folders property panel you can set up which folders the application Icon will reside in by using the following steps:

1. From the Folders property panel, click the Add button.

2. Navigate the NDS tree and select the application folder object you wish the Application to reside in.

3. In the Modify Selected Folder window, shown in Figure 5.6, Add, Delete, or Modify the folder which is selected. This controls the location where the application appears in the start menu and application explorer window.

4. Select whether you wish the application to appear in the folder for the application launcher, start menu, or both.

You can select multiple application folder objects for the application to reside in by following the previous steps. You may wish to do this if a difference exists in behavior or availability defined in different application folders. For example, you have an application folder for accounting, development, and sales but you only want the application to appear for accounting and sales. You handle this by adding the accounting and sales folders, but not the development folder, to the application. That way the application does not show up in the developers start menu, but it does show up for the accountants and sales persons.

Contact Setting for Applications

From the pull down list under Identification for Application objects you can also specify a contact list of people to contact for help if a problem occurs when deploying the application. To create the contact list, simply click the Add button and then type in the username or select the user object by browsing the NDS tree.

Adding Administrator Notes to Applications

From the pull-down list under Identification for Application objects you can also specify administrator notes for users to view when deploying the application. This can be very useful in describing to users why the application is being deployed, when it remains available, and other important information. To create administrator notes, simply type in the message you wish users to see if they view the information about applications available through the application launcher.

Viewing MSI Package Information for MSI Objects

Application objects that were created from an .MSI file enable you to select Package Option from the Identification drop-down menu. The package information panel for MSI Application objects displays the following information about the MSI package:

- ▸ The path to the MSI package
- ▸ The version of the MSI package

- ▸ The vendor who created the MSI package
- ▸ The locale (language) the MSI package is in
- ▸ Any help link that is associated with the MSI package

Setting Distribution Options for Application Objects

Once you have set up the Application objects identification, the next step in setting up the distribution options for the Application object in ConsoleOne is to configure the applications shortcuts, registry settings, files, INI settings, text files, distribution scripts, pre-install schedule, and general options. Use the following steps to select which set of options you wish to modify:

1. Right-click the Application object and click Properties.

2. Select the Distribution tab.

3. Click the down arrow on the Distribution tab, and a screen similar to the one in Figure 5.7 is displayed.

F I G U R E   5 . 7   *The distribution property panel in ConsoleOne*

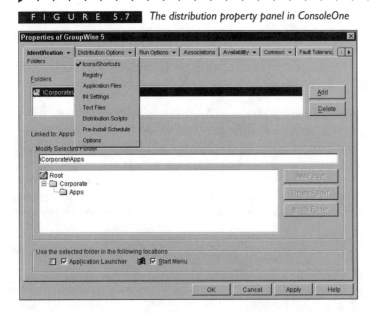

From the Application object's Distribution property tab, you should access the individual property panels to configure the application distribution options described in the following sections.

NOTE

If this Application object has been distributed previously, note that many of the changes on distribution will not go into effect until you change the Version Stamp value discussed later in this chapter. Changing the Version Stamp value signals Application Launcher to re-distribute the application.

Configuring Application Icons/Shortcuts

The top panel accessible from the distribution tab is the Icons/Shortcuts panel. The Icons/Shortcuts property panel enables you to add, change, or delete the Program Groups, Program Group Items, and Explorer shortcut icons that appear in Program Manager (Windows 3.*x*) and Windows Explorer (Windows95/98, Windows NT 4.*x*, and Windows 2000) when the application distributes to workstations.

One example of when you might modify the icons and shortcuts for an Application object is if you wished to use special icons for ALL applications that users run on their workstations. Using the Icons/Shortcuts property page for this Application object, you are able to change icons of other applications that might or might not have anything to do with this Application object.

Configuring Application Registry Settings

The next panel accessible from the distribution tab is the Registry Settings property panel. This panel enables you to add, change, and delete Registry keys and values when the Application object distributes to the workstation. Several Registry types are supported, including binary format, default strings, DWORD values, Expand Strings (REG_EXPAND_SZ), and Multi-Value Strings (REG_MULTI_SZ). You can import and export Registry settings, either as .AOT or .AXT files, or using the standard Registry (.reg) format.

Configuring Application Files

The next panel accessible from the distribution tab is the Application Files property panel. This panel is used to add, change, or delete application files and directories. You can also import new template information about files and directories. This lets you instruct the Application object what to do with the files and directories when the application distributes.

Configuring .INI File Settings for Applications

The next panel accessible from the distribution tab is the INI Settings property panel. This panel enables you to add, change, and delete .INI files, sections, and values when the Application object distributes to the workstation. Not only can you order the changes within the .INI file, you can also import or export .INI files and settings using the .AOT or .AXT file format or the standard .INI file format.

INI file configuration changes can be useful if you wish to add a specific version stamp that can be read later by the application to determine its current version. For example, Figure 5.8 shows that a specific version for the GroupWise Application object of 5.5 is made to the GW.INI file in the windows directory when the application is distributed. The next time GroupWise is run, it could use the version stamp to determine its current revision.

▶ • ◀

F I G U R E   5.8   *The INI settings property panel for Application objects in ConsoleOne*

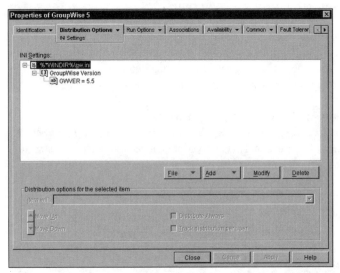

Configuring Text File Options

The next panel accessible from the distribution tab is the Text Files property panel. This panel enables you to add, change, or delete workstation text files (such as config.sys and autoexec.bat).

One example of when to use the Text Files properties page to modify the Application object is if users are experiencing problems due to an incorrect text string found in their workstation's config.sys file. Rather than visit and change each workstation or run the risk of users incorrectly and inconsistently implementing a change, you can set up a Text File that finds, deletes, modifies, or adds text strings to the text file of your choice. The Text File implements the changes the next time the application runs.

NOTE

If you set the Prompt user for reboot setting on the Distribution property page to Always, that setting overrides the setting you make here.

Configuring Application Distribution Scripts

The next available option to control distribution is setting up distribution scripts that are executed automatically each time the application is distributed to a workstation. Unlike environment parameters, scripts can overwrite existing drive mappings and printer ports.

The two types of distribution scripts are the Run before script and the Run after script. Run before distribution scripts are executed before the application is distributed. Run after distribution scripts are executed after the application is closed and before the network resources are cleaned up.

Distribution scripts enable you to provide dynamic mappings beyond those defined, run other applications, log in to other servers or NDS trees, and perform other tasks that must be done before and after an application is distributed. To set up distribution scripts use the following steps:

1. Right-click the Application object and click Properties.

2. Select the Distribution tab and select Distribution Scripts from the drop-down list.

3. Create the Run Before and Run After scripts in the text boxes shown in Figure 5.9.

▶ · ◀

FIGURE 5.9 *The distribution scripts property panel in ConsoleOne*

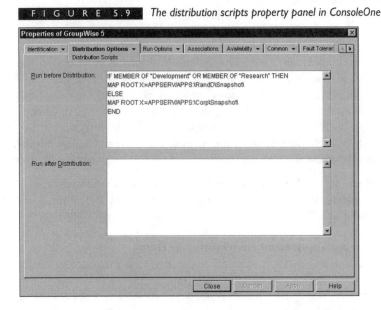

Configuring a Pre-Install Schedule for Application

The next available option to control distribution is setting up a pre-install schedule for local availability for the application. The pre-install can be extremely useful in deploying applications to a lot of workstations.

For example if you have an application that needs to go out to 1,000 workstations all on the same day, then having ZENworks for desktops deliver the application all at the same time could cause the network and server to be over utilized. If you know in advance that you need to deploy the application, then you can set up a pre-install schedule to deliver the application to the workstations over a period of time before the day it needs to be installed. After this, all 1,000 workstations can install the application at the same time, without causing network problems, because they have a local copy of the application to work from.

To configure an application pre-install, select Pre-Install Schedule from the Distribution tab drop-down list, and the schedule panel appears. If you wish to have the application pre-installed prior to having it deployed, then select the Pre-Install application box. The next step is to specify the schedule type you wish to use for the pre-install.

The None option is selected by default, however, you *can* configure the Application object to pre-install the application to workstations based on a set of specific days or a range of days as described in the following sections.

Set Schedule by Specified Days   You can schedule application pre-installs by specifying the Specified Days option as shown in Figure 5.10. This enables you to select specific dates during which you want the application to be available for pre-install.

F I G U R E   5.10 *The pre-install schedule availability for specified days property panel in ConsoleOne*

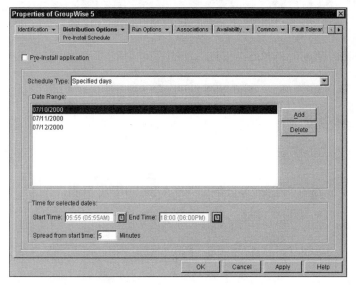

The application is only visible to be pre-installed to workstations on the specific dates and times you specify in this option. For example, if you select the dates June 7, 2000 and June 10, 2000, and start and end times of 8:00 a.m. and 5:00 p.m., the application is available to be pre-installed to a workstation from 8:00 a.m. to 5:00 p.m. on each of the days selected. The application is not available to be pre-installed to the workstation at any other time.

Set Schedule by Range of Days   You can set a schedule by specifying a range of days to make the application available for pre-install, as shown in Figure 5.11. An example would be if you select a start date of June 12, 2000 and an end date of June 16, 2000, with a start time of 6:00 a.m. and an end time of 6:00 p.m. The Application object icon would be able to be pre-installed to workstations from June 12th at 6:00 a.m. until June 16th at 6:00 p.m.

▶ . . . . ◀

FIGURE 5.11   *The pre-install schedule availability for a range of days property panel in ConsoleOne*

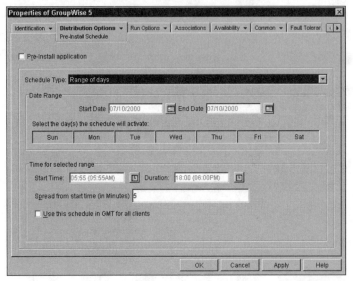

Spread from Start Time   You also have the option to specify a spread of time in which the application becomes available to users. This is useful if you don't want all users to run the application at the same time for fear that the load and traffic may bring down the network. The spread option literally "spreads out" user access times over the number of minutes specified so they don't all run the application at once.

An example of how to use the spread from Start Time option is to set it to 120 minutes; the application then becomes available, on a random basis, between the hours of 10:00 a.m. and 12 noon. This spreads the demand for the application out over a longer period of time and network traffic is minimized.

NOTE

If users access applications after the spread time is expired but before the end time of the Application object, they access the application at that time and the spread variable has no effect.

GMT (Greenwich Mean Time)   The final option you have available on the scheduling panels is to specify that all application scheduling that you do with the Application property page is based on the workstation's time zone.

In other words, if your network spans different time zones and you schedule an application to run at 4:00 p.m., it would normally run at 4:00 p.m. in each time zone. However, by selecting the GMT check box, workstations run applications at the same time worldwide (according to GMT). Although, you should be aware that GMT time is not available if you are filtering out days of the week when in the Specified Days mode.

Configuring General Application Distribution Options
The next panel accessible from the distribution tab is the Option property panel. This panel, shown in Figure 5.12, enables you to configure the following general distribution options for Application Objects.

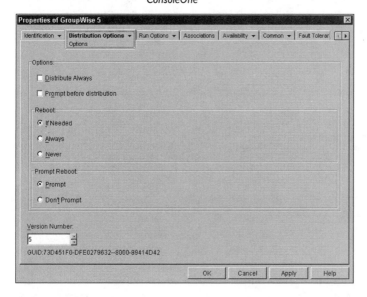

FIGURE 5.12   *The Options property panel for Application objects in ConsoleOne*

Distribute Always   Use the Distribute always option to force a distribution of the entire Application object every time the user runs the application or the application is set for a force run on the workstation (see the User or container object's Applications property page). This option is useful to ensure that all application settings are updated every time the application runs.

You can also update settings on a case by case basis. For example, if you want to always distribute a particular Registry key and value, you can set the Distribute Always option on the Registry Settings property page for that particular key and value. The Distribute Always option on the Distribution property page overrides the Distribute Always option on the Registry Settings, INI Settings, Application Files, Icons/Shortcuts, and Text Files property pages.

Prompt User Before Distribution   Next, use the Prompt Before Distribution option to display a message to users after they have clicked an Application Launcher-distributed application for the first time. This message asks them to confirm if they want to distribute the application to their workstation. This option is turned off by default.

TIP

To better inform users, the text that you write in the Application object's Description property page is displayed in this distribution confirmation dialog box. For example, you might write a note to the user such as "This is an essential application for your workstation that takes approximately ten minutes to distribute. Please answer Yes to distribute it now."

Prompt User for Reboot   Next, use the options in the Reboot group box to control how a workstation reboot should occur according to the following options:

- **If Needed** — The If Needed option (the default setting) only prompts for reboot if Application Launcher or Application Explorer needs to make changes that cannot occur while Windows is running (such as replacing open DLLs).

- **Always** — The Always option prompts the user to reboot every time a distribution takes place.

- **Never** — The Never option does not prompt the user to reboot. In this case, the changes take effect the next time the workstation reboots.

Use Version Stamp to Trigger Redistribution   Use the version Stamp option to trigger a redistribution of the application. A Version Stamp is simply text string representing the version of the application which is used to customize the Application object's GUID. In fact, any change you make to the Version Stamp is like changing the GUID.

NOTE

The Version Stamp might or might not have anything to do with the actual version of the software. It is a tool to help you upgrade applications. It helps you control the version of Application Launcher-delivered application.

If the Run Once option is checked and you change the Version Stamp, the Run Once option causes the application to run again once. This is useful when upgrading application software to a new or different version.

For example, suppose you purchased new application software and want to update an Application object. By changing the Version Stamp number and selecting the Run Once option, the application runs once after installation even though a previous version might have already run once.

View Application's GUID (Globally Unique Identification)   Finally, you have the option to view the applications GUID which is stamped in the workstations registry when ZENworks for Desktops distributes an application to a workstation. The GUID is a randomly generated number for tracking such as {5A0511440-77C5-11D1-A663-00A024264C3E}.

TIP

Use GUIDs to track and troubleshoot distributed applications. For example, if you want to ensure that a particular application has been distributed to a workstation, you can compare the GUID as recorded in the Application object's Distribution property page with the GUID that is currently stamped in the workstation's Registry.

Click the GUID to see the Application object's Distinguished Name (DN) among the Registry values. Note that GUIDs can be stamped on a per user and per workstation basis. See Track Distribution Per Workstation User for more information.

You can make several Application objects use the same GUID by using the Synchronize Distributed GUIDs option. This is useful if you are distributing a suite of applications. You can also "regenerate" or "re-randomize" the GUIDs for those same applications.

Setting Run Options for Application Objects

Once you have set up the distribution options for an application you need to set the run options. Setting the run options for an Application object enables you to control the behavior, environment, and licensing of an application as it is distributed to users. To access the options on the Run Options property tab, use the following steps to select which set of options you wish to modify:

I. Right-click the Application object and click Properties.

2. Select the Run Options tab.

3. Click the down arrow on the Run Options tab and a screen similar to the one in Figure 5.13 is displayed.

▶ · ◀

FIGURE 5.13 *The run options property panel in ConsoleOne*

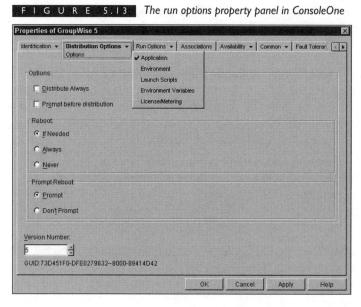

From the Application object's Run options property tab, you should access the individual property panels to configure the application run options described in the following sections.

Configuring Application Run Options

The top panel accessible from the run options tab is the Application panel. The Application property panel enables you to set the path, parameters, and behavior of an executable that needs to run when the application is distributed. Use this panel, shown previously in Figure 5.13, to configure the following options.

Install Only (No Executable Needed) If you just want users to install an application, but not run it, you should check the Install Only option. An example of this is if Application object's purpose is to just update some files on the workstation. When you select the Install Only option, the software is installed but not run.

Set Path to Executable File   If an executable file exists that needs to be run for the application distribution, then select this option. Next set the path in the Path to Executable text box to the executable that is to be run when an Application object icon is double-clicked in Application Launcher or Application Explorer. Use the Browse button to browse the file directory structure to find the executable you want. UNC pathnames are permitted. For example:

- `server\volume:path`
- `\\server\volume\path`
- `volume_object_name:path`
- `directory_map_object_name:path`
- `driveletter:\path`

NOTE   If you don't want to run an application (for example, this Application object's purpose might be to just update some files on the workstation), use the Install Only option and do not specify a path.

Run Applications Once   The final option you have from the object Identification properties window is to set the run once option. They run the application once and then remove the icon from the workstation.

You should check this option when an Application object's purpose is to install software to a workstation. It can be confusing and annoying to users if an install icon remains in the Application Launcher window or in Application Explorer after the software has already been installed

NOTE   If you selected Run Once and also specified a Version Stamp for this application, the application runs once until the next time you change the Version Stamp, whereupon the application runs once one more time. This latter method is useful for upgrading applications.

Configuring Environment Options for Running Application

The next run option configurable for Application objects is the Environment option. The Environment panel, shown in Figure 5.14, lets us set up information about the environment the application is run in.

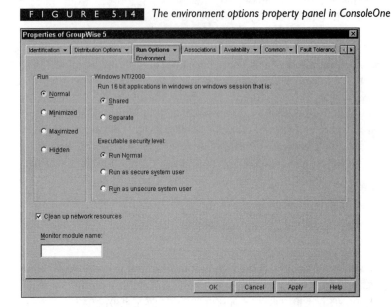

F I G U R E   5 . 1 4   *The environment options property panel in ConsoleOne*

The Run section on the environment options property panel enables you to select one of the following window types with which to deploy the application:

- **Normal** — Simply pulls up the default window and deploys the application in it.

- **Minimized** — Pulls up the window and begins the application deployment, then minimizes it so that it is out of the view of the user. This is the most commonly used option, because the user has access to the application deployment, however it is not cluttering up their screen.

- **Maximized** — Pulls up and maximizes the window for application deployment. This is used if you want the user very aware of the application deployment so that they wait until it is finished.

- **Hidden** — Hides the window that the application is deployed in from the user. This can be used for application you wish users not to know about as well as to seamlessly provide a silent update that users are not affected or aware of.

The Windows NT/2000 section of the environment property panel lets you specify whether 16-bit applications are run in Shared or Separate mode. It also enables you to configure the following application security levels:

▶ **Run Normal** — This is the default for applications being deployed to Windows NT/2000.

▶ **Run as secure system user** — This options makes the application run at a secure system level. Use this option if you need the application to be installed even on workstations that have a high security level setup.

▶ **Run as unsecure system user** — This options makes the application run at a non-secure system level. Use this option if you wish workstations that have a high security level setup to be protected from applications being deployed to them

The environment property panel also lets you select the Clean Up Network Resources option. If this is selected, then any mapped drives or ports that are made by the application deployment will be cleaned up when it is finished.

Configuring Application Launch Scripts

The next run option configurable for Application objects is launch scripts that are executed automatically each time the application is launched on a workstation. Unlike environment parameters, scripts can overwrite existing drive mappings and printer ports.

The two types of launch scripts are the Run before launch script and the Run after termination script. Run before launch scripts are executed before the application is launched. Run after termination scripts are executed after the application is closed and before the network resources are cleaned up.

Launch scripts enable you to provide dynamic mappings beyond those defined, run other applications, log in to other servers or NDS trees, perform special termination options, and perform other tasks that must be done before and after an application is launched. To create Launch scripts use the following steps:

1. Right-click the Application object and click Properties.

2. Select the Run Options tab and select Launch Scripts from the drop-down list.

3. Create the Run Before Launch and Run After Termination scripts in the text boxes shown in Figure 5.15.

The application run launch scripts option property panel in ConsoleOne

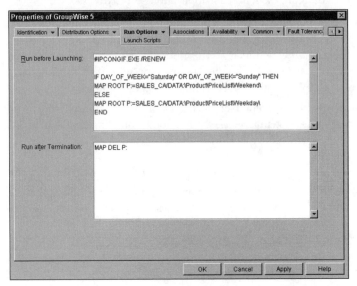

Configuring Environment Variables for Application Launch

The next run option configurable for Application objects is the environment variable option. The environment variable panel lets you add variables to be applied to the workstation environment when the application is deployed.

For example, if you have an application install that needs a temporary path variable name to be set to a specific location, you could add that variable name and path to the Application object. When the application is deployed the path variable is inserted to the environment on the workstation enabling the install to take place without any intervention from the user.

Configuring Licensing and Metering for Applications

The final run option configurable for Application objects is the licensing/metering variable option. The licensing/metering variable panel enables you to specify that you wish to use Novell licensing and metering to run the application. If you wish to use licensing, you can simply click the browse button and select the license certificate you wish to use from the NDS tree. You can also specify that you do not wish to run the application if NLS is not available.

Setting Application Object Associations

Once you have set up the run options for an application you need to set the Application object associations. Setting the associations for an Application object enables you to associate the application with a user, container, workstation, and control the behavior and visibility of the application as it is distributed to users. To access these options, select the Associations tab on the Application object and a screen similar to the one in Figure 5.16 is displayed.

FIGURE 5.16 *The run options property panel in ConsoleOne*

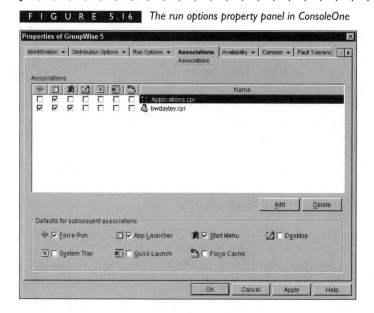

From the Application object associations panel, you can click the Add button then navigate the tree to add objects to which you wish to associate the application. Once the objects are added you can check the following items for each object to control the behavior and visibility of the application for that object:

▶ **Force Run** — The force run option specifies that once the application is available to the workstation, meaning that the user has logged in and meets the criteria specified, then the application is automatically deployed to the workstation.

▶ **App Launcher** — The App Launcher option specifies that the application should appear in the application launcher when the user runs it.

‣ **Start Menu** — The App Launcher option specifies that the application should appear in the start menu on the workstation.

‣ **Desktop** — The Desktop option means that when the application is available an icon is displayed on the desktop for the user to launch.

‣ **System Tray** — The Sytem Tray option specifies that when the application is available an icon is displayed in the system tray on the workstation for easy launch.

‣ **Quick Launch** — Puts the icon for the application in the quick launch menu for even faster and easier distribution of the object.

‣ **Force Cache** — Forces the application to be cached to the workstation, where it can be used later the next time it is run.

Setting Application Availability

Once you have set up the association options for an application you need to set the availability options. You can use the availability tab to access panels which are used to control when the application icon is available or when the users can install software.

This feature depends on the settings you have set up for the application launcher on a User, Workstation, Organizational Unit, Organization, or Country object. You should be aware of those setting before trying to set up scheduling for the Application object.

A good example of how to use the advanced feature is if you want to force run a virus detection application on user's workstations at a certain time, and only one time. You can force users to run the virus check by scheduling the appearance of the application using the Schedule property page and designating the application as "Force Run."

NOTE

Scheduling cannot deny access to an application outside of the schedule because file rights might still exist.

To access the options on the Availability property tab, use the following steps to select which set of options you wish to modify:

1. Right-click the Application object and click Properties.

2. Select the Availability tab.

3. Click the down arrow on the Availability tab and a screen similar to the one in Figure 5.17 is displayed.

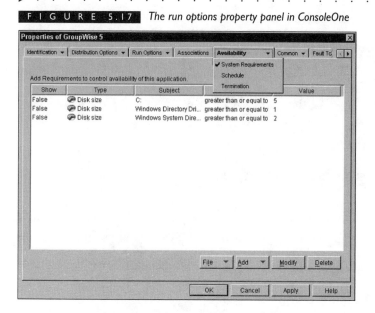

FIGURE 5.17 *The run options property panel in ConsoleOne*

From the Application object's Availability property tab, you should access the individual property panels to configure the application availability options described in the following sections.

Configuring System Requirements for Applications

The top panel accessible from the availability tab is the System Requirements panel. The System Requirements property panel enables you to choose which applications will be available to workstations by making certain that the workstation meets the certain criteria specified. The system requirements tab enables you to set requirements on installed applications, disk space, environment variables, memory, operating system, processor, registry entries, and file requirements. If workstations do not meet the criteria you specify, the icons do not appear on that workstation.

For example, suppose you want a GroupWise 5.5 application icon to appear only on workstations that have at least 32MB of RAM, a Pentium processor, 5MB of free disk space on the c: drive, and 100MB of free disk space on a temp drive. You can set up those options by clicking on the Add button, shown in Figure 5.18, to select and configure the requirement options described in the following sections.

F I G U R E   5.18   *The system requirements property panel for Application objects in ConsoleOne*

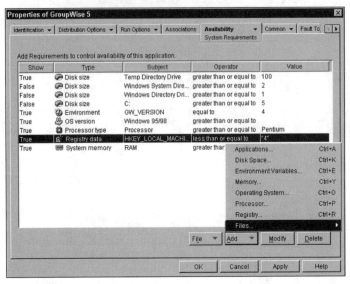

Applications   The system requirements tab for Application objects enables you to filter applications based on the existence of other applications on the client. To filter workstations by installed applications, click the Add button from the system requirements panel and then select Application from the pop-up menu. A window is displayed which enables you to navigate the directory services tree to find specific applications that should or should not exist.

To filter on a specific application, simply navigate to that Application object in the NDS tree and then select it. Next click either the Application object is installed or the Application object is NOT installed option. You want to use this option if an application is dependent on the existence of another one. For example if you wish to deploy an application update, you can check for the existence of the original application before making it available to the workstation.

Free Disk Space   The system requirements panel for Application objects enables you to filter applications based on the amount of free disk space available to the client. You can filter disk spaced on local drives and mapped network drives, as well as the following specific locations:

► Windows System Directory Drive

- ► Windows Directory Drive
- ► Temp Directory Drive

To filter workstations by disk space available, click the Add button from the system requirements panel and then select Disk Space from the pop-up menu. A screen similar to the one in Figure 5.19 appears. From this screen first select the location disk, in which space is needed, from the top drop-down list. Next type in the MB of disk space needed to install and run the application. Next you have the option of specifying one of the following logical requirements:

- ► Less than
- ► Less than or equal to
- ► Equal to
- ► Greater than or equal to
- ► Greater than

F I G U R E   5 . 1 9   *The memory requirements box from the system requirements property panel for Application objects in ConsoleOne*

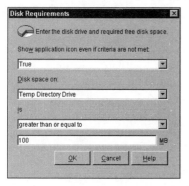

You can specify multiple locations that require disk space by performing the same steps again.

An example of when to use this is if the application requires a minimum of 5MB free on the Windows directory drive and 100MB free on the TEMP drive. If you specify these settings, the Application object icon will only appear on workstations that contain enough free disk space in all three locations.

Environment Variables   The system requirements panel for Application objects also enables you to filter applications based on specific environment variable settings on the client. To filter workstations by environment variables, click the Add button from the system requirements screen and then select Environment Variables from the pop-up menu. A screen similar to the one in Figure 5.20 appears. From this screen, first type in the name of the variable then select whether the name should or should not exist. You also have the option of filtering on the value of the variable by typing in a value and selecting a logic operation such as equal to.

FIGURE 5.20   *The environment variables box from the system requirements property panel for Application objects in ConsoleOne*

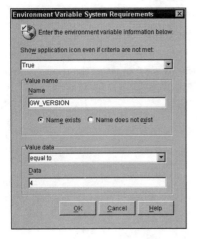

You can specify multiple environment variables to check for before displaying and installing the application by following the same process again.

One example of when to use this is if some users use Netscape as their browser and some use Internet Explorer. If you only want users that use Netscape to receive the Netscape object, you could set up a browser environment variable on the workstations and then specify that variable be present from the system requirements property panel.

Another example of when to filter on environment variables would be if you wanted to apply an update to users with GroupWise 4 on their systems. You could check the version environment variable on those systems to make certain that GroupWise is installed and that its version is equal to 4.

Memory The system requirements panel for Application objects enables you to filter applications based on the amount of memory installed on the client. To filter workstations by memory installed, click the Add button from the system requirements panel and then select Memory from the pop-up menu. A screen similar to the one in Figure 5.21 appears. From this screen first type in the MB of RAM needed to install and run the application. Next you have the option of specifying one of the following logical requirements:

- ► Less than
- ► Less than or equal to
- ► Equal to
- ► Greater than or equal to
- ► Greater than

FIGURE 5.21 *The memory requirements box from the system requirements property panel for Application objects in ConsoleOne*

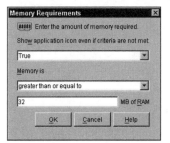

An example of when to use this option would be if the application requires 32MB of RAM; select true, memory is greater than, and then enter 32 in the text box. The Application object will not appear on workstations that do not have at least 32MB of RAM.

NOTE This field is valid only for Windows 95/98 and Windows NT/2000 workstations (Windows 3.*x* is ignored). Use it by entering the minimum amount of total installed RAM that the workstation must have to see and run this application.

Display Applications on a Particular Operating System The system requirements panel for Application objects enables you to filter applications based on the operating system installed on the client. To filter workstations by operating system, click the Add button from the system requirements panel and then select Operating System from the pop-up menu. A screen similar to the one in Figure 5.22 appears. From this screen first select true or false for availability based on your criteria. Next select the desired Windows platform. Then you have the option of specifying a specific version of the operating system by specifying a version number as well as one of the following logical requirements:

- ▸ Less than
- ▸ Less than or equal to
- ▸ Equal to
- ▸ Greater than or equal to
- ▸ Greater than

F I G U R E   5.22 *The operating system requirements box from the system requirements property Panel for Application objects in ConsoleOne*

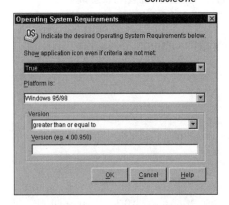

An example of when to use the operating system option would be if you create an Application object for an application that does NOT run on Windows NT 4.0 workstations. You can specify that specific criteria by selecting Windows NT, clicking the Version is box, and then typing 4.0 in the Version text box; then select the equal to option. Finally, select false for the availability option and the application will not show up on Windows NT 4.0 workstations.

Processor   The system requirements panel for Application objects enables you to filter applications based on the speed of the processor installed on the client. To filter workstations by processor, click the Add button from the system requirements panel and then select Processor from the pop-up menu. A screen similar to the one in Figure 5.23 appears. From this screen first select the minimum processor needed to install and run the application from the following list:

- ► 386
- ► 486
- ► Pentium
- ► Pentium Pro
- ► Pentium II
- ► Pentium III

F I G U R E 5.23   *The processor requirements box from the system requirements property panel for Application objects in ConsoleOne*

Next you have the option of specifying one of the following logical requirements:

- ► Less than
- ► Less than or equal to
- ► Equal to
- ► Greater than or equal to
- ► Greater than

NOTE

The Windows 3.*x* Application Programming Interface does not return values higher than 486. Therefore, if Application Launcher queries the processor type of a Windows 3.*x* workstation using a Pentium processor, Windows 3.*x* returns "486." In other words, even if you select the Pentium processor type for the Processor option, the application is displayed on **486** workstations running Windows 3.*x*.

Registry Entries   The system requirements panel for Application objects enables you to filter applications based on specific Windows registry settings on the client. To filter workstations by registry settings, click the Add button from the system requirements screen and then select Registry from the pop-up menu. A screen similar to the one in Figure 5.24 appears. From this screen, first navigate the registry to find the specific registry key to filter on. Type in the name of the registry entry or browse to find it. Then set the value of the entry, the data type (String or DWORD), and the logical operation to perform on it. Then you have the option to filter based on the following criteria:

▶ **Key exists** — Filter in if key exists in the registry, by selecting this radial button.

▶ **Key does not exists** — Filter in if key does not exist in the registry, by selecting this radial button.

▶ **Name** — You have the option to specify the name of the entry that associated with the key.

▶ **Value exists** — If the name box is filled out, then you can specify to filter the application in only if a name does exist for the selected key.

▶ **Value does not exist** — If the name box is filled out, then you can specify to filter the application in only if a name does not already exist for the selected key.

▶ **Value** — If a value is typed in and then ZENworks checks the value against the value of the entry based on the logical operation and data type specified in the value section.

You can specify multiple environment variables to check for before displaying and installing the application by following the same process again.

Files   The system requirements panel for Application objects enables you to filter applications based on specific files installed on the client. To filter workstations by files, click the Add button from the system requirements panel and then select 'Files' from the pop-up menu. Another pop-up menu appears which lets you select one of the following file filtering options:

▶ **File Existence** — The file existence option provides a window with two text boxes which enable you to specify the name of and location to the file to filter on. At the bottom two radial buttons are present, which enable you to specify whether to filter if the file exists or does not exist.

The registry settings box from the system requirements property panel for Application objects in ConsoleOne

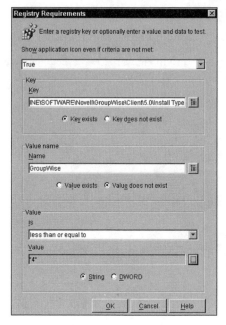

▶ **File Version** — The file existence option provides a window with two text boxes which enable you to specify the name of and location to the file to filter on. At the bottom of this window, you can input a specific version number to filter on as well as the following logical operations: less than, less than or equal to, greater than, greater than or equal to, and equal to.

▶ **File Date** — The file existence option provides a window with two text boxes which enable you to specify the name of and location to the file to filter on. At the bottom you can specify a specific date for the file bases on one of the following: before, on or before, on, on or after, and after.

Configuring Availability Schedule for Application

Once you have configured the system requirements for application availability, you can move on to setting up a schedule for availability for the application.

Select Schedule from the Availability tab drop-down list and the schedule panel appears. The none option is selected by default; however, you can configure the Application object to only be available to workstations based on a set of specific days or a range of days as described in the following sections.

Set Schedule by Specified Days   You can schedule application availability by specifying the Specified Days option as shown in Figure 5.25. This enables you to select specific dates during which you want the application to be available.

▶ • ◀

F I G U R E   5 . 2 5   *The schedule availability for specified days property panel in ConsoleOne*

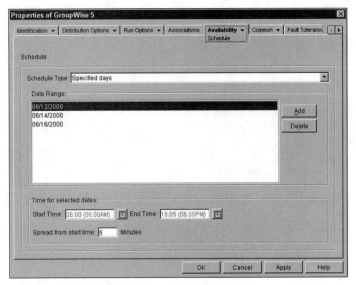

The application is only visible to users during the specific dates and times you specify in this option. For example, if you select the dates June 7, 2000, June 10, 2000, July 2, 2000, and July 7, 2000, and start and end times of 8:00 a.m. and 5:00 p.m., this makes the application available from 8:00 a.m. to 5:00 p.m. on each of the days selected. The application is not available on any other days or at any other time. You select no more than 350 specific dates for this option.

NOTE

When scheduling applications, you can also force them to run at the scheduled time (in addition to merely displaying them). Because the Force Run option is available on a per-association basis, you must select it from the Applications property page located on a User, Group, Organization, or Organizational Unit object. If the association is not set up for a Force Run, the application icon is displayed according to the location specified by the association.

Set Schedule by Range of Days   You can set a schedule by specifying a range of days to make the application available as shown in Figure 5.26. An example would be if you select a start date of June 12, 2000 and an end date of June 16, 2000, with a start time of 6:00 a.m. and an end time of 6:00 p.m. The Application object icon would be visible to workstations from June 12th at 6:00 a.m. until June 16th at 6:00 p.m.

F I G U R E   5 . 2 6   *The schedule availability for a range of days property panel in ConsoleOne*

Properties of GroupWise 5							
Identification ▾	Distribution Options ▾	Run Options ▾	Associations	**Availability** ▾	Common ▾	Fault Tolerance	◀ ▶

Schedule

Schedule

Schedule Type: Range of days

Date Range

Start Date 06/12/2000   End Date 06/12/2000

Select the day(s) the schedule will activate:

Sun	Mon	Tue	Wed	Thu	Fri	Sat

Time for selected range

Start Time: 06:00 (06:00AM)   Duration: 18:05 (06:05PM)

Spread from start time (in Minutes) 5

☐ Use this schedule in GMT for all clients

OK   Cancel   Apply   Help

Another useful way to use the range of days option is to make applications available only on certain days of the week within a given range of dates. You do so by combining Start and End Dates and Times with the Days Available buttons.

For example, suppose you select the dates June 2, 2000 and July 2, 2000, and start and end times of 6:00 a.m. and 6:00 p.m. You also select the Tuesday and Thursday buttons. This combination makes applications available on all Tuesdays and Thursdays that fall within the given date. Applications are available on Tuesdays and Thursdays beginning at 6:00 a.m. until 6:00 p.m.

Spread from Start Time   You also have the option to specify a spread of time in which the application becomes available to users. This is useful if you don't want all users to run the application at the same time for fear of load and traffic bringing down the network. The spread option literally "spreads out" user access times over the number of minutes specified so they don't all run the application at once.

An example of how to use the spread from start time option is to set it to 120 minutes; the application becomes available, on a random basis, between the hours of 10:00 a.m. and 12 noon. This spreads the demand for the application out over a longer period of time and network traffic is minimized.

NOTE

If users access applications after the spread time is expired but before the end time of the Application object, they access the application at that time and the spread variable has no effect.

GMT (Greenwich Mean Time)   The final option you have available on the scheduling panels is to specify that all application scheduling that you do with the Application property page is based on the workstation's time zone.

In other words, if your network spans different time zones and you schedule an application to run at 4:00 p.m., it would normally run at 4:00 p.m. in each time zone. However, by selecting the GMT check box, workstations run applications at the same time worldwide (according to GMT). Although, you should be aware that the GMT time is not available if you are filtering out days of the week when in the Specified Days mode.

TIP

Windows 3.x clients do not use a time zone concept. The only way Windows 3.x clients can use a time zone is if it is set in their environment. You can do this by putting the following command in the autoexec.bat file or login script:

SET TZ=<TIMEZONE> (for example MST7DST for Mountain Daylight Savings)

Configuring Application Termination Options

The final option you have available from the Availability tab is to set termination options for application availability. To configure the termination behavior select termination from the drop-down menu on the Availability tab. A panel similar to the one in Figure 5.27 appears.

F I G U R E   5.27 *The termination property panel for Application objects in ConsoleOne*

From this panel you can configure the following options which control the behavior terminating the application once it has been executed at the workstation.

None   This option (default) enables users to close the application on their own without any intervention from ZENworks. If you require the application to be closed for any reason (such as updates or database indexing) then you should not use this option because you will not be able to force users to close the application.

Send Message to Close Application   This option prompts users, at a specified interval, to close the application on their own until the application closes. For example, if you set an interval of five minutes, ZENworks sends a message (if one is active) to the user every five minutes until the application is closed or the message has been sent the configured amount of times.

To set this option:

1. Specify the number of times to send the message.

2. Specify the time interval between messages in the text box provided.

3. Click the message button and a message window is displayed. From this message window you can select to use the default message, no message, or a custom message. If you select custom message, you can type in a message to users which is displayed on their workstations asking them to close the application.

4. Choose OK.

Send Message to Close Then Prompt to Save Data   This option, send message to close then prompt user to save data, enables users a specified period of time to close the application on their own (this action is optional). When that period of time expires, the Application Launcher attempts to close the application. If users have not saved data, they are prompted to save it. Users can choose not to close the application. If users have no unsaved data, the application closes. Once the application has closed, users are not able to re-open it.

To set this option:

1. Select the check box next to Send warning and specify the warning interval and period in the text boxes provided (optional). If you want to specify a custom message, click the message button and a message window is displayed. Select Use Custom and then write one in the message text box.

2. In the next group box, specify the prompt message time interval in the text boxes provided. If you want to specify a custom message, click the message button and a message window is displayed. Select Use Custom and then write one in the message text box.

3. Choose OK.

Send Message to Close, Prompt to Save, Then Force Close   The send message to close, prompt to save, then force close option prompt users, for a specified period of time, to close the application on their own. When that period of time expires, ZENworks for Desktops can close the application that is prompting users, at specified intervals, to save their work. If users have still not closed within a specified period of time, the application is forced to close.

To set this option:

1. Select the check box next to Send warning and specify the warning interval and period in the text boxes provided (optional). If you want to specify a custom message, click the message button and a message window is displayed. Select Use Custom and then write one in the message text box.

2. In the next group box, specify the prompt message time interval and period in the text boxes provided. If you want to specify a custom message, click the message button and a message window is displayed. Select Use Custom and then write one in the message text box.

3. In the last group box, click the message button and write a note to users explaining why the application terminated and perhaps when it will be available again.

4. Choose OK.

Send Message to Close Then Force Close with Explanation   The send message to close then force close with explanation termination option prompts users, for a specified period of time, to close the application on their own. When that period of time expires, the application is forced to close.

To set this option:

1. Select the check box next to Send warning and specify the interval and period in the text boxes provided (optional). If you want to specify a custom message, click the message button and a message window is displayed. Select Use Custom and then write one in the message text box.

2. In the last group box, click the message button and write a note to users explaining why the application terminated and perhaps when it will be available again.

3. Choose OK.

Setting Common Options for Application Objects

Once you have set up the availability options for an application you need to set some common options to control some general behavior and configure the Application object. To access the options on the Common property tab, use the following steps to select which set of common options you wish to modify:

1. Right-click the Application object and click Properties.

2. Select the Common tab.

3. Click the down arrow on the Common tab and a screen similar to the one in Figure 5.28 is displayed.

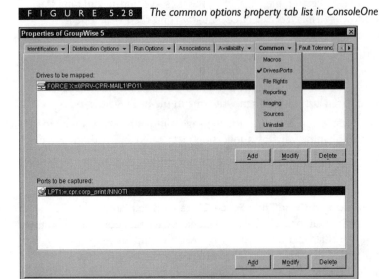

FIGURE 5.28   The common options property tab list in ConsoleOne

From the Application object's Common options property tab, you should access the individual property panels to configure some common options for the application as described in the following sections.

Configuring Application Drives and Ports

The first advanced option available for Application objects from the Common tab pull down menu is the Drives/Ports property panel. The Drives/Ports panel enables you to specify drives and ports that need to be mapped when the application is being launched on a workstation.

To add a drive to be mapped for the application launch, click the add button under the Drives to be mapped window to bring up the drive mapping box as shown in Figure 5.29. From this box you can perform the following options:

▸ Specify an Option (Drive, Search Drive 1 or Search Drive 16)

▸ Specify a Letter

▶ Specify a Network Path
▶ Specify if it Should be a Root Mapping
▶ Specify if it Should Overwrite Existing Mappings

F I G U R E 5.29 *The drive mapping box for common options in ConsoleOne*

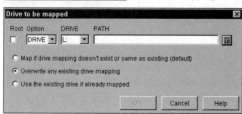

To add a port to be captured for the application launch, click the add button under the Ports to be captured window to bring up the port capturing box as shown in Figure 5.30. From this box you can perform the following options:

▶ Specify a Port to Capture
▶ Specify a Network Printer or Print Queue
▶ Specify to Use Notify Flag
▶ Specify to Use Form Feed Flag
▶ Specify to Use Banner Flag

F I G U R E 5.30 *The port capturing box for common options in ConsoleOne*

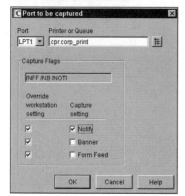

Configuring File Rights for Application Launch

The next advanced option available for Application objects from the Common tab pull-down menu is the File Rights property panel. The File Rights panel enables you to grant rights to files, directories, and volumes. This is used when this Application object is associated with a User object or with a Group, Organizational Unit, Organization, or Country object with which the user is already associated.

Use the following procedure to grant file rights to users when Application object is associated with them:

1. Right-click the Application object.

2. Click the File Rights button.

3. Click Add and specify the volume or directory to which users need access when they run the Application object.

4. Highlight the volume or directory and specify Supervisor, Read, Write, Create, Erase, Modify, File Scan, and Access Control rights as necessary then click OK.

5. Click OK, then associate this Application object with a User, Group, Organizational Unit, Organization, or Country object to grant the rights.

Configuring Application Reporting

The next advanced feature available from the Common tab pull down menu is the Reporting option. When an application is distributed to the workstation, the application launcher records if the application was properly distributed. A successful distribution is recorded as well, and if there were any errors with the distribution then this is recorded along with the reasons for the failure in the distribution.

This record of distribution is recorded on a local file, and results in an event being sent to the centralized database that is also used for hardware and software inventory. These distributions can be set up through the Reporting property panel in ConsoleOne.

To access the Reporting Property panel:

1. Right-click the Application object and click Properties.

2. Select the Common tab.

3. Click the down arrow on the Common tab and select the Reporting option.

4. Once at the Reporting property panel you have the option of performing changes to the Application object as shown in Figure 5.31.

The reporting property panel for Application objects in ConsoleOne

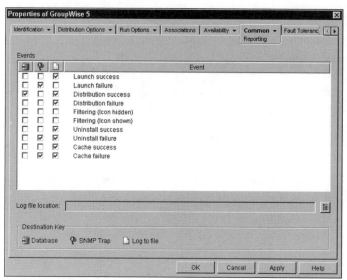

From the Reporting property panel you can select one of the three following keys for various events that occur during application deployment:

▶ **Enable Reporting** — Select the Enable Reporting box to enable distribution reporting for the Application object.

▶ **Specifying the location of the log file** — Select the Log File Path Box and specify a location in the text box to the location of where reporting should log events.

▶ **Enabling SNMP Traps** — Select the Send SNMP Traps box if you wish to use ManageWise to be notified of application distribution events.

You can specify these event keys for the following list of events:

▶ Launch Success

▶ Launch Failure

▶ Distribution Success

▶ Distribution Failure

▶ Filtering (Icon Hidden)

▶ Filtering (Icon Shown)

- ► Uninstall Success
- ► Uninstall Failure
- ► Cache Success
- ► Cache Failure

Configuring Launch Macros

One way to automate Application objects is to use the Macros property panel to set up special macros that can be used during object distribution and launch. These macros enable you to set up Application objects even when the user has a different system setup than what is expected by the administrator.

To access the Macro Property panel:

1. Right-click the Application object and click Properties.

2. Select the Common tab.

3. Click the down arrow on the Common tab and select the Macros option.

4. Once at the Macros property panel you have the option of adding special macros to the Application object as shown in Figure 5.32.

F I G U R E 5 . 3 2   *The macros property panel for Application objects in ConsoleOne*

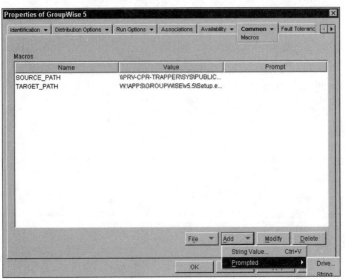

The following sections describe the special macros that can be added to an Application object for use in distribution and launching.

String Macros   The first type of macro available for Application objects is the string macro. The string macro can retain a value that remains static during application distribution and launching.

To set up a string macro, access the Macros property panel, using the steps described previously, from within ConsoleOne to select Add ⮑ String Value. You are able to set up the following options for the string macro:

▶ **Value name** — Name setup for the macro for install scripts, and so on.

▶ **Value data** — You can specify a value for the macro.

Prompted Drive Macros   The next type of macro available for Application objects is the prompted drive macro. The prompted drive macro enables you to prompt the user for a drive that will be used for application distribution and launching.

For example, users may want to put an application on a different drive than what was described in the Application object. Prompted macros enable the administrator the ability to request that the user be prompted for the information. By using the prompted macros feature, the administrator can have the destination drive requested of the end user and the resulting distribution goes to the specified drive.

To set up prompted drive macros and access the Macros property panel use the preceding steps from within ConsoleOne to select Add ⮑ Prompted ⮑ Drive. A window similar to the one shown in Figure 5.33 is displayed. From the prompted macro window, you are able to set up the following options for the prompted drive macro:

▶ **Prompt text** — Textual information to be displayed for the user when prompting for the macro.

▶ **Macro name** — Name setup for the macro for install scripts, and so on.

▶ **Default Value** — You can specify a default value for the drive macro for users to use if they have no need to specify otherwise. The available options are Windows System Directory Drive, Windows Directory Drive, Temp Directory Drive, or letters A..Z.

▶ **Minimum disk space** — You can specify a minimum amount of disk space required in setting the macro.

FIGURE 5.33 *The prompted drive macro information window for Application objects in ConsoleOne*

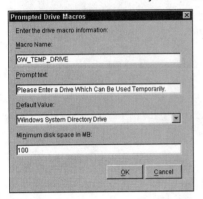

Prompted String Macros The next type of macro available for Application objects is the prompted string macro. The prompted string macro enables you to prompt the user for a string that is used for application distribution and launching.

For example, you want to ask the user for the user ID they use to access a corporate database; the macro can then be used by the application install later to access the database and retrieve information necessary for the install.

To set up prompted string macros, access the Macros property panel using the preceding steps from within ConsoleOne to select Add ⇨ Prompted ⇨ String; now you are able to set up the following options for the prompted string macro:

- **Prompt text** — Textual information to be displayed for the user when prompting for the macro.

- **Macro name** — Name setup for the macro for install scripts, and so on.

- **Default Value** — You can specify a default value for the macro for users to use if they have no need to specify otherwise.

- **Minimum disk space** — You can specify a minimum amount of disk space required in setting the macro.

- **Maximum String len** — You can use this option to specify the maximum number of characters allowed for string macros.

Configuring Application Object Imaging

The next advanced feature available from the common pull-down menu is the object imaging option. ZENworks enables you to create an image of the application by selecting the location of the image file, as shown in Figure 5.34, and then clicking the Create Image button. That image can later be applied to a newly imaged workstation as part of the imaging process discussed in the Imaging a Workstation chapter of this book.

F I G U R E   5.34   *The imaging property panel for Application objects in ConsoleOne*

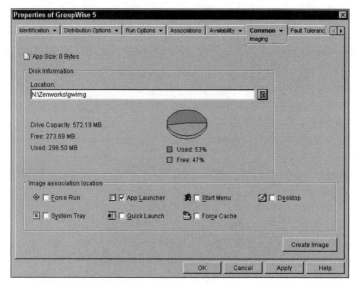

Configuring Application Sources

Another advanced feature available from the Common tab pull-down menu is the Sources option. The sources option enables you to specify network volumes and directories that ZENworks for desktops uses to find application packages for the application during distribution and launching.

You can add volumes or directories to the list by clicking on the add button and either typing in the UNC path, or using the browse button and navigating the NDS tree.

Configuring Application Uninstall

One of the most powerful features in ZENworks for Desktops application distribution is the ability to uninstall applications that were previously delivered. This provides administrators with control over which applications users have.

Use the following steps to access the application uninstall options panel for Application objects and configure the uninstall behavior:

1. Right-click the Application object and click Properties.

2. Select the Common tab.

3. Click the down arrow on the Common tab and select the Uninstall option as shown in Figure 5.35.

From the uninstall options panel you have the option to set the following options:

▶ **Enable Uninstall** — Determines if the application can be uninstalled or not.

▶ **Enable user to perform manual uninstall** — Determines if users are enabled to uninstall the application.

▶ **Prompt user before uninstall** — Prompts the user prior to performing an application uninstall, allowing the user to save any work being done by the application.

▶ **Terminate application before uninstall** — Forces the application to be terminated prior to uninstalling. This option should be used for any application that requires access to files, directories, or registry settings that are removed by the uninstall.

▶ **Uninstall application if not used within x days** — Enables you to specify a number of days the application remains available to users. If the user does not use the application within that number of days, the application is removed.

The following sections describe the options available to specifically control how the uninstall is performed on files, shortcuts, .INI files, and registry entries.

Files Uninstall   From the application uninstall panel you can specify the precise criteria of how files are uninstalled. Click the files tab and a screen similar to the one in Figure 5.35 is displayed. From this screen you can specify to uninstall files with any of the following attributes set:

▶ Copy Always

▶ Copy if Exists

- ► Copy if Does Not Exist
- ► Copy if Newer
- ► Copy if New And Exists
- ► Copy if Newer Version
- ► Request Confirmation
- ► Copy if Different

F I G U R E 5.35 *The files uninstall property panel for Application objects in ConsoleOne*

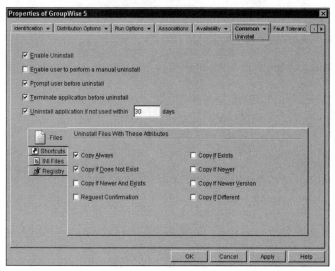

Shortcuts Uninstall   From the application uninstall panel you can specify the precise behavior of how shortcuts are uninstalled. Click the shortcuts tab and a screen similar to the one in Figure 5.36 is displayed. From this screen you can specify to uninstall shortcuts with any of the following attributes set:

- ► Create Always
- ► Create if Not Exists

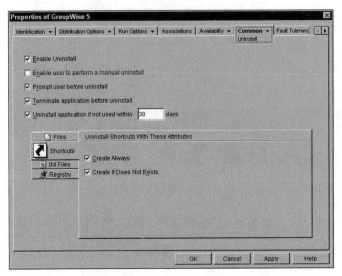

.INI Files Uninstall   From the application uninstall panel you can specify the specific behavior of how .INI files are uninstalled. Click the .INI files tab and a screen similar to the one in Figure 5.37 is displayed. From this screen you can specify to uninstall .INI files with any of the following attributes set:

- ▶ Create Always
- ▶ Create if Exists
- ▶ Create if Does Not Exist
- ▶ Create or Add to Existing Section
- ▶ Create or Append to Existing Section

Registry Uninstall   From the application uninstall panel you can specify the specific behavior of how registry entries are uninstalled. Click the how registry tab and a screen similar to the one in Figure 5.38 is displayed. From this screen you can specify to uninstall how registry entries with any of the following attributes set:

- ▶ Create Always
- ▶ Create if Not Exists
- ▶ Create if Exists

▶ · ◀

FIGURE 5.37 The .INI files uninstall property panel for Application objects in ConsoleOne

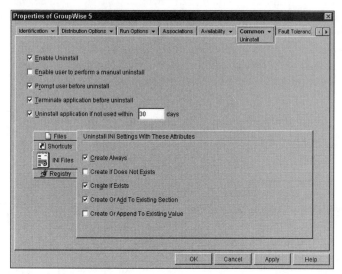

▶ · ◀

FIGURE 5.38 The registry uninstall property panel for Application objects in ConsoleOne

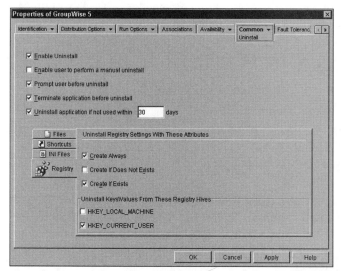

Configuring Properties for MSI Objects

If the Application object was created from an .MSI file, there will be a properties option available from the common pull-down menu. This option enables you to configure any public property that is configured inside the MSI package. Configuring these options enables you to control more tightly how the application is distributed to users. The properties can be anything configurable for an MSI package, for example an environment variable or a destination path.

Use the following steps to re-configure a property in the .MSI file:

1. Click the Add button from the properties panel and a window pop-up.

2. Click the down arrow to display a list of property names. All properties that are configurable are displayed in this list.

3. Select the property you wish to configure and add a value to the Value Data area.

4. Click OK and the property change is displayed on the properties panel along with the value you set.

Configuring Transform Files for MSI Object

If the Application object was created from an .MSI file, there will also be a transforms option available from the common pull-down menu. This option enables you to configure a list of transform files that will be applied to the MSI package before it is distributed to users.

Adding transform files to this list enables you even tighter control on the MSI Application object. These transform files modify the behavior of the MSI package install and therefore enable you more flexibility for application distribution. The transform file must be created using one of the approved methods.

Use the following steps to add a transform file to be applied to an MSI package prior to install:

1. Click the Add button from the transforms panel.

2. Type in the path to the transform file, or click the browse button and navigate the NDS tree to the file.

3. Once the transform file is selected, click OK and the transform file is displayed on the transform panel.

Setting up Application Fault Tolerance

Another powerful feature in ZENworks for Desktops application distribution is the ability to provide fault tolerance and load balancing to application delivery. The fault tolerance panel enables you to control the availability of applications to users.

Use the following steps to access the fault tolerance options panel for Application objects and configure the uninstall behavior:

1. Right-click the Application object and click Properties.

2. Select the fault tolerance tab.

The following sections describe setting up application fault tolerance and load balancing options from the fault tolerant panel.

Configuring Application Fault Tolerance Options

The first option available from the drop-down menu under the fault tolerance tab is to set up fault tolerance. The fault tolerant feature enables you to specify alternate forms of the Application object to make the application available even if a problem with the current one exists.

From the fault tolerance options panel you have the ability to enable fault tolerance and then set up the following fault tolerant options.

Use Source List   You can define a list of application package sources to use if the current Application object is unavailable for any reason. To add additional application package source locations, click the Add button. A window displays the sources that have been defined for this Application object (see "Configuring Sources" earlier in the chapter). Select the sources you wish to use and click OK to add them to the source section of the fault tolerant panel.

Use Application Objects   You can also define Application objects to be used as backup Application objects if the current object is unavailable. To add Application objects to the list click the Add button. Then navigate the NDS tree to add the additional backup Application objects.

Configuring Application Object Load Balancing

The next option available from the drop-down menu under the fault tolerant tab is to set up load balancing. The load balancing feature enables you to specify alternate forms of the Application object to balance the use for a number of users. This increases the reliability and availability of applications for busy networks.

From the load balancing options panel, shown in Figure 5.39, you have the ability to enable load balancing for the application and then set up the following load balancing options.

F I G U R E   5.39   *The fault tolerance load balancing property panel for*
Application objects in ConsoleOne

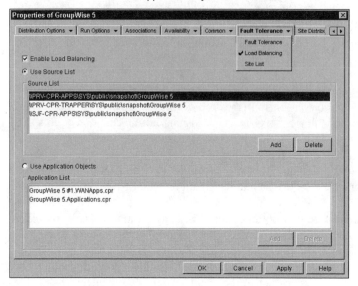

Use Source List   You can define a list of application package sources to
distribute the use of the current Application object. To add additional application package source locations, click the Add button. A window displays the
sources that have been defined for this Application object (see "Configuring
Sources" earlier in the chapter). Select the sources you wish to use and click OK
to add them to the source section of the load balancing panel.

Use Application Objects   You can also define Application objects to be
used as load balancing options for the current object. To add Application
objects to the list click the Add button; then navigate the NDS tree to add the
additional backup Application objects.

Configuring a Site List for Application Objects
The final option you can define additional sites for is the Application
object. If you need your application to be highly available for users, you
should create multiple copies of the Application object and link them to the
original object by clicking the link button in this window. That way you can
maintain a list of compatible application sources to use for fault tolerance and
load balancing.

## CHAPTER 6

Setting up Application Distribution

ZENworks for Desktops has a powerful application distribution engine that enables you to distribute your applications throughout your network. Once an Application object has been created in NDS, you only need to set up the application distribution environment to apply the application to several workstations on your network. This chapter covers using ConsoleOne to set up application users to receive applications and application foldering, as well as automating Application object distribution.

Setting up Application Foldering

The first step in setting up the application environment is to set up application foldering. ZENworks for Desktops offers powerful foldering capabilities that enable users to organize the applications that you deliver to them, using Application Launcher. These folders appear in the Application Launcher, Application Explorer browser view, and on the Start Menu.

NOTE

If two folders have the same name, their contents are merged together.

The following are the four types of folders available to users in Application Launcher:

- ▸ **Application Folder Object.** An Application Folder object is an independent object to which you associate Application objects. By linking many Application objects to one Application Folder object, you can manage the folder pathnames of many Application objects from one object. See "Create Application Folder Object and Associate with Application Objects" for more information

- ▸ **Custom Folder.** Custom folders are set up on the Application object's Folders property page and thus belong exclusively to the Application object. A custom folder cannot be shared with another Application object. You can name Custom folders any way you please and set up folders within folders (sub-foldering). Custom folders override any System folders that may exist as the result of Application object to container associations. See "Create Custom Folders for Application Object" for more information.

▶ **Personal Folder.** Personal folders let users create and name their own folders and place Application Launcher-delivered applications in them. See "Enable Users to Create Personal Folders" for more information.

▶ **System Folder.** System folders appear in Application Launcher or Explorer when you associate an Application object with a User, Group, Organizational Unit, Organization, or Country object, and you have not created any Custom folders for that Application object or associated the Application object with a Linked folder.

To set up application foldering to manage Application objects you need to perform the following tasks:

Create Application Folder Object and Associate with Application Objects

The first step in setting up application foldering is to create a folder object which can be linked to Application objects. Use the following steps from within ConsoleOne to create an application folder object:

1. Right-click the Organization Unit, Organizational, or Country object under which you want to create a Folder object.

2. Choose Create ➪ Application Folder, and then click OK.

3. Name the folder, select Define Additional Properties, and then choose OK.

Custom folders are tied to one Application object. Linked folders, however, may contain many Application objects. All folders appear in Application Launcher or Explorer browser view and also in the Start Menu.

Once the application folder has been corrected, use the Folders property panel on a folder object to create custom or linked folders in which to organize Application objects. To set up the Folder for applications, use the following steps to access and modify the Folders property panel from within ConsoleOne:

1. Right-click the application folder object and select Properties.

2. Click the Folders tab, and a screen similar to the one in Figure 6.1 appears.

3. Click Add ➪ Folder and then name the folder.

4. Click Add ➪ Folder and name the folder to put add additional folders within the folder you created in Step 3.

5. With a folder highlighted, click Add ➪ Application, browse to the Application object you wish to add, then choose OK. Repeat this process for all the Application objects you want to place in this folder.

6. Check the Application Launcher and/or Start menu boxes depending on whether you want to display the folders in Application Launcher/Explorer browser view or on the Start Menu.

FIGURE 6.1   *The folders property panel for application folders in ConsoleOne*

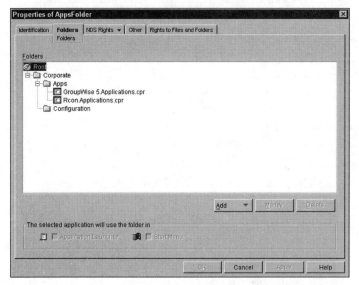

Create Custom Folders for Application Object

The next step in setting up application foldering is to use the Folders property panel for the Application object to create custom folders in which to organize Application objects, as described earlier in this chapter. A custom folder is tied to one Application object, however you can have multiple custom folders per Application object.

Using custom folders, you can achieve "sub-foldering" or placing folders within folders. This is often essential if you have numerous Application objects available to users. Custom foldering enables you to organize Application objects and control which users see which applications.

TIP

Suppose you have created a Folder object that contains several folders which are linked to several Application objects. You now would like to clear these folder-application links and start over. You could delete the Folder object, which converts all of the Linked folders to Custom folders, which are then saved in all the relevant Application objects. In this case you would have to open each Application object and delete the Custom folders in them. A quicker method is to delete the folders and the linkages to Application objects from the Folder object, but not delete the Folder object itself. When the Folder object is empty, you can decide if you want to start over with new folders and links to Application objects, or you can delete the Folder object.

Customize Application Launcher Configurations per User or Container

Once you have created the folder objects, you need to customize the application launcher configurations. ZENworks for Desktops enables you to customize the behavior of the application launcher at a User, Group, Organizational Unit, Organization, or Country object level.

Use the following steps to configure the application launcher for an object in ConsoleOne:

1. Right-click the object and select Properties.
2. Click the Application Launcher tab as shown in Figure 6.2.
3. From this screen select the View/Edit object's custom configuration from the drop-down menu.
4. Click the Edit button to bring up the Launcher configuration window as shown in Figure 6.2.

From the Launcher Configuration window you can set up the application launcher options for users, the application launcher, application explorer, and workstations as described in the following sections.

► • ◄

F I G U R E   6 . 2   *The Launcher Configuration panel for Application Folder*
objects

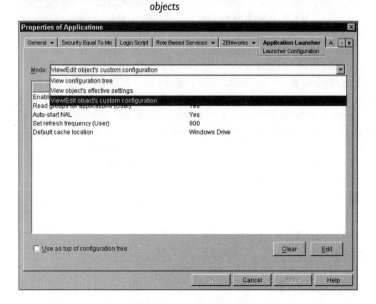

Setting up User Application Launcher Options

From the Launcher Configuration window you can specify configurations that dictate how users view and work with Application Launcher and Application Explorer desktop software by selecting the User tab as shown in Figure 6.3. From this screen you can set the following options that define how the Application Launcher behaves for users.

Allow Users to Exit (Default=Yes)

The Allow users to exit option determines whether or not users can exit Application Launcher or Explorer.

An example of when to use this would be if you are running software at a conference where workstations are available for the attendees of the conference to use. If you do not want users to exit Application Launcher and change settings on the hard disk drive, set this option to No.

The launcher configuration property page for user objects in ConsoleOne

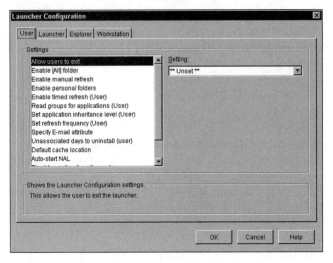

Enable (All) Folder

The folder view in Application Launcher might be confusing to some users. By setting Enable (All) folder to No, users see only the application icons available to them in Application Launcher.

Enable Users to Refresh Icons Manually (Default=Yes)

The Enable Manual Refresh lets users refresh Application Launcher or Application Explorer manually. This displays any Application objects that were delivered since the last refresh.

Enable Users to Set Up Personal Folders (Default=No)

If Enable personal folders is set to Yes, users can create their own folders and move the icons around in them as they see fit. However, the icons must originate from an application associated with the user. A user cannot add a new, unassociated Application object using personal folders.

The icons must originate from an application associated with the user. A user cannot add a new, unassociated Application object using personal folders.

TIP

Use caution when offering the option to create personal folders. Users might forget where they have placed applications and call you for help. Not allowing personal folders might be a way to exert more strict control and thus reduce support calls.

Enable Timed Refresh (User) (Default=No)

The Enable Timed Refresh option refreshes the application icons automatically without the user having to choose View ⇨ Refresh or press F5 to manually refresh icons. The Timed Refresh setting effects settings such as the Force Run feature.

Read Group Objects for Applications (User) (Default=Yes)

If a Group object has been associated with Application objects, users who are members of that Group can run Application objects by virtue of their membership. While this is a convenient way of indirectly associating users with applications, it can also decrease performance. If you want to increase performance, set this option to No.

Set Application Inheritance Level (User) (Default=1)

The set application inheritance level option specifies how many parent Organization or Organizational Unit objects up the NDS tree Application Launcher, or Application Explorer, to search for applications.

For example, if a user object's Distinguished Name is user1.dev.la.acme and this option is set to a value of 2, Application Launcher or Application Explorer would look at the Organization or Organizational Unit object dev and la for Application objects but ignore acme. A value of -1 instructs Application Launcher or Application Explorer to search all the way up the NDS tree.

Set Timed Refresh Frequency (User) (Default=3600 Seconds)

The Set refresh frequency option lets you specify the frequency in seconds.

For example, if you set the refresh to 300 seconds, Application Launcher or Application Explorer updates applications from the network automatically every five minutes and might even run some applications depending on how you have set them up.

NOTE

A short timed refresh interval is very useful in situations where you want changes to refresh quickly. However, a short timed refresh interval can cause higher network traffic. The Refresh Icons option and Timed Refresh options are not connected in any way except that they both control refresh. One option does not have to be selected for the other to work.

Specify E-mail Attribute (Default=Mailbox ID)

This option lets you specify the NDS attribute that you want to use to display an E-mail name in the Help Contacts tab (when the user right-clicks an application icon and chooses Properties). If users have problems with applications, they can contact people by e-mail to get help. The e-mail name that appears is pulled from the NDS attribute you specify here.

Unassociated Days to Uninstall

The Unassociated Days to Uninstall option enables you to specify the number of days to wait until after the user has been unassociated with an application before the application is uninstalled. The range can be from 0 to 730 days.

You can use this option if you do not want users to be immediately cut off from an application, but you also do not want them to have continual access; an example of this might be if a user is transitioning to a new job inside your company and still needs access to their old applications for a few weeks.

Default Cache Location

The default cache location enables you to specify a drive that ZENworks for desktops will use to cache applications that are configured for caching. The available options are either to specify the Windows Drive or drive letter A through Z.

If you are uncertain about the available local disk space for an application, you can add a specific drive mapping for this in a network location. First make a network volume available for ZENworks to cache applications. Next add a drive mapping to that network volume to the Application object. Then set the drive mapping to overwrite existing mappings. Finally set the default cache location to be that same drive letter.

Auto-start NAL

The Auto-start NAL option enables you to control whether the application launcher is automatically started when a user logs in; an example of this might be if you have a new application that needs to go out to users in a specific container. You could associate the application with the container and then specify this option so that the application launcher runs and the application is delivered to users when they log in to the container.

Disable Reading from the Cache

The disable reading from the cache option enables you to inhibit workstations from reading Application objects from cache. Enabling this option forces the workstation to retrieve the application from the network.

This option is extremely useful if you make changes to an Application object but do not wish to change its revision. For example you add some new data files to the Application object, but the application itself remains the same. You would use this option to force users to use a new Application object instead of the one in their cache.

Always Evaluate Referrals

The Always evaluate referrals option forces ZENworks for Desktops to always check the validity of protocol referrals, thus increasing the reliability of application deployment to users.

Setting up Application Launcher Options

From the Launcher Configuration window you can specify configurations that dictate how the Application Launcher behaves by selecting the App Launcher tab as shown in Figure 6.4. From this screen you can set the following options that define availability and behavior of the Application Launcher.

► . . . . ◄

FIGURE 6.4 *The launcher configuration property panel for the Application Launcher in ConsoleOne*

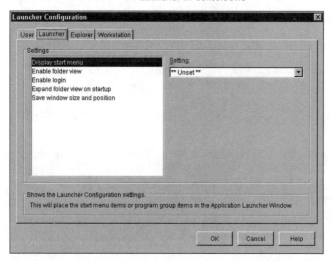

Display Start Menu

The Display Start Menu option copies the current Windows95/98 or Windows NT/2000 Start Menu organization (including Programs and above) into the Application Launcher. You can specify settings such as Never Show, Show Always, Show When Authenticated, or Show When NOT Authenticated.

Enable Folder View (Default=Yes)

For users to be able to see the folders you have created, you must make certain that this option is enabled. If Enable folder view is set to no, users see only the application icons available to them in Application Launcher.

Enable Login

Setting the Enable login option to Yes activates the Login option found on Application Launcher's File menu. The user can use this option to run the GUI Login software and log in to the network. This option is not available for Application Explorer.

NOTE

When this option is selected, and the user is not logged in, Application Launcher searches for the Login executable in the path and, if found, displays a Login icon in Application Launcher. If the Login executable cannot be found, or if the user is already logged in, the Login option is grayed. Ensure that Application Launcher can find the login program (login.exe or loginw32.exe) on the client workstation before you select the Login option.

Expand Folder View on Startup (Default=No)

The expand folder view on startup option enables you to specify if the user or container is enabled to view folders. The Expand Folder View on Startup option expands the entire tree of folder when the Application Launcher starts.

Save Window Size and Position

The save window size and position options enable you to set whether or not to save window size and position settings on a local drive. By setting this option to Yes, Application Launcher is always displayed in the same position for every user.

Setting up Application Explorer Options

From the Launcher Configuration window you can specify configurations that dictate how the Application Explorer behaves by selecting the Explorer tab as shown in Figure 6.5. From this screen you can set the following options that define availability and behavior of the Application Explorer.

► · ◄

F I G U R E 6 . 5	*The launcher configuration property panel for the Application*
	Explorer in ConsoleOne

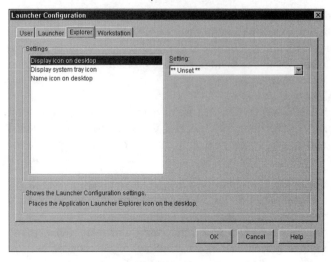

Display Icon on Desktop

The display icon on desktop enables you to specify whether or not you want the application explorer icon to appear on the users' desktop. When enabled, an Application Explorer icon appears on the desktop.

Display System Tray Icon

The Display system tray icon enables you to specify whether or not you want the application explorer icon to appear on the users' system tray. When enabled, an Application Explorer icon appears in the users System Tray, from which it is easily launched.

Name Icon on Desktop

The Name icon on desktop enables you to change the name of the icon that opens the Application Explorer browser view. For example, you could name it something such as "Corporate Applications."

Enable Manage Applications Dialog

The enable manage applications dialog option enables you to specify whether users have access to be able to control which applications will be cached locally.

This option provides much more control to users to manage their own application, but it also can create problems with application availability and network usage if you expect the application to reside in the workstation cache. It is a good idea to leave this option off, unless you have a specific reason to enable it.

Setting up Workstation Application Launcher Options

From the Launcher Configuration window you can specify configurations that dictate how workstations view and work with Application Launcher and Application Explorer desktop software by selecting the Workstation tab as shown in Figure 6.6. From this screen you can set the following options that define how the Application Launcher behaves for workstations.

FIGURE 6.6 The launcher configuration property page for workstation objects in ConsoleOne

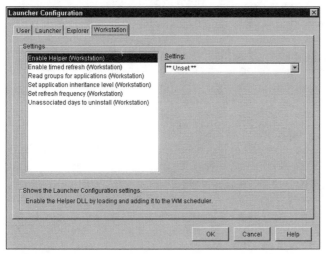

Enable Helper

The Enable Helper option enables the helper DLL by loading and adding it to the WM scheduler for the workstations.

Enable Timed Refresh

The Enable Timed Refresh option refreshes the application icons automatically without the user having to choose View ➪ Refresh or press F5 to manually refresh icons. The Timed Refresh setting effects also settings such as the Force Run feature.

Read Groups for Applications

If a Group object has been associated with Application objects, users who are members of that Group can run Application objects by virtue of their membership. While this is a convenient way of indirectly associating users with applications, it can also decrease performance. If you want to increase performance, set this option to No.

Set Application Inheritance Level

The set application inheritance level option specifies how many parent Organization or Organizational Unit objects up the NDS* tree Application Launcher, or Application Explorer, should be searched for applications.

For example, if a user object's Distinguished Name is user1.dev.la.acme and this option is set to a value of 2, Application Launcher or Application Explorer would look at the Organization or Organizational Unit object dev and la for Application objects, but ignore acme. A value of −1 instructs Application Launcher or Application Explorer to search all the way up the NDS tree.

Set Refresh Frequency

The Set refresh frequency option lets you specify the frequency in seconds.

For example, if you set the refresh to 300 seconds, Application Launcher or Application Explorer updates applications from the network automatically every five minutes and might even run some applications depending on how you have set them up.

Unassociated Days to Uninstall

The Unassociated Days to Uninstall option enables you to specify the number of days to wait until after the user has been unassociated with an application before the application is uninstalled. The range can be from 0 to 730 days.

You can use this option if you do not want users to be immediately cut off from an application, but you also do not want them to have continual access. This might happen if, for example, a user is transitioning to a new job inside your company and still needs access to their old applications for a few weeks.

Setting up Users to Receive Applications

Once you have set up application foldering, you need to set up users to receive applications via ZENworks for Desktops. This section covers using ConsoleOne to setup user objects to receive applications by: associating their object with an Application object, making application explorer and application launcher available to them, and setting application launcher configurations.

Associate a User, Group, Workstation, or Container Object to Application Objects

The first step in setting up users to receive applications is to use the Applications property panel to associate a User, Group, Workstation, Organizational Unit, Organization, or Country object to one or more Application objects. You could also use the Associations panel for Application objects to individually add users or containers; however, unless you associate applications using one of these two methods, applications are not available to users.

You should design your application associations to make it as easy as possible for you to administrate. For example, separating applications into company, division, group, and then users levels would enable you to make the fewest associations as possible and also reduce the cost of future administration.

In addition to associating applications with other objects, use the Applications property panel to specify where and how users access applications on their workstations. For example, you can display application icons in Application Launcher, Application Explorer, Windows Explorer, Start menu, Desktop, and System Tray (or in all of these areas). You can also force applications to launch when Windows starts.

NOTE

The default method of access is App Launcher, meaning that users see the application only in the Application Launcher and Application Explorer browser view (depending on what you have made available).

To add applications to a user or container to specify who sees the application and where it is displayed on workstations, use the following method:

1. Right-click the User, Group, Organizational Unit, Organization, or Country object, and then click Properties.

2. Click the Applications Tab.

3. Click Add, browse and select the Application object, and then click OK.

4. Select an Application object and then specify how and where you want the application to work by checking the appropriate check box, and then clicking OK as shown in Figure 6.7.

► • ◄

F I G U R E   6 . 7   *The application property panel for user, group, or container objects in ConsoleOne*

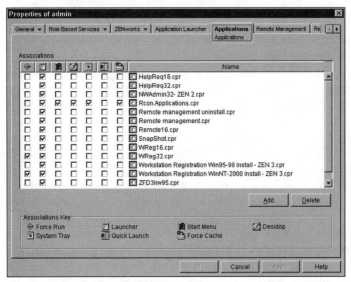

The following sections describe options that are available from the Applications panel to specify how the application is available to users.

Force Applications to Run

The Force Run option runs applications immediately when Application Launcher or Application Explorer starts and the application is available. You can use the Force Run option in conjunction with several other Application object settings to achieve unique behaviors.

For example, if you set an application as "Run Once" (on the Application object's Identification property page) and Force Run (on the User, Group, or container object's Applications property page), the application runs immediately one time (if available).

Put Applications in the Application Launcher or Explorer Browser View

The App Launcher option displays application icons in Application Launcher and Application Explorer (browser view) depending on which one you make available to your users.

Put Applications on the Start Menu

When Application Explorer is enabled, the Start Menu option displays icons on the Windows95/98 or Windows NT/2000 Start menu under Novell Application Launcher.

Put Applications on the Desktop

When Application Explorer is enabled, the Desktop option displays icons on the Windows 95/98 or Windows NT/2000 desktop area.

Put Applications on the System Tray

The System Tray option displays icons on the System Tray, an area on the Windows 95/98 or Windows NT/2000 Taskbar where small icons, representing applications, are placed for easy access. The Application Explorer can display or remove applications on the System Tray at any time.

Set Application for Quick Launch

The Quick Launch option puts the icon for the application in the quick launch menu for even faster and easier distribution of the object.

TIP

If you plan to add the application to the quick launcher then you should use an icon for the application that users can easily recognize.

Force Cache the Application

The Force Cache option forces the application to be cached to the workstation, where it can be used later the next time it is run. This can be extremely useful for applications that need to be run more than once. For example, you could use this option for a virus scanner that is run every time the user logs into the network. The workstation would only need to pull down the virus scanner object once and from then on it would be applied out of cache.

Make Application Explorer Available to Users

Once you have associated the Application object with the specific users you want receiving it, you need to make application explorer available to them. Application Explorer is software that runs on users' Windows 95/98 or Windows NT/2000 workstations. It displays the applications that you distribute to users using Application Launcher snap-in. You can specify to what degree users control the options in Application Explorer by using a User, Organizational Unit, Organization, or Country object's Launcher Configuration property page.

Application Explorer displays application icons in a special Application Explorer window, Windows Explorer, Start menu, System Tray, or Desktop. Use the Applications property page of the User, Group, Organizational Unit, Organization, or Country object to set up the different Application Explorer access points as we discussed earlier in this chapter.

To make Application Explorer available to users:

Ensure that nalexpld.exe is in a network directory (such as sys:\public) where users have rights and access. The Application Explorer is installed to the sys:\public directory when ZENworks for Desktops is installed on a server, but you may need to copy it to the public directory on other servers that do not have ZENworks for Desktops installed on them.

Because the application explorer can't run on Windows 3.x or Windows NT versions prior to 4.0, add the following command to the User or Organizational Unit object's login script to check for the windows version first:

```
if platform = "w95" then
    @\\servername\sys\public\nalexpld.exe
  end
if platform = "w98" then
    @\\servername\sys\public\nalexpld.exe
    end
if platform = "wnt" then
    if os_version = "v4.00" then
        @\\servername\sys\public\nalexpld.exe
    end
  end
```

Make Application Launcher Available to Users

Once you have associated the Application object with the users you wish to receive it, you also need to make Application Launcher available to them. Application Launcher is software that runs from a user workstation. It displays the applications that you distribute to them using Application Launcher snap-in. Using a User, Organizational Unit, Organization, or Country object's Launcher Configuration property page, you can specify to what extent users can control the options in Application Launcher.

For example, you can enable them to create personal folders (in which to store the applications you assign to them), refresh icons, or exit Application Launcher.

In addition to using these following steps, you also need to enable the Application Launcher option on a User, Group, Organizational Unit, Organization, or Country object's Applications property page so users can see applications in Application Launcher as discussed earlier in this chapter. This option is turned on by default.

To make Application Launcher available to users:

1. Ensure that nal.exe is in a network directory (such as sys:\public) where users have rights and access.

2. Add one of the following commands to the login script of the User object or the user's Organizational Unit:

```
#\\servername\sys\public\nal.exe
```

```
Or
```

```
@\\servername\sys\public\nal.exe
```

NOTE

The # command requires the external command to complete before executing the next line in the login script. The @ command enables the login script to continue processing while the external command is processed. We recommend using the @ symbol for faster script execution. Do not equate nal.exe, a "wrapper" executable that does not stay in memory, with nalwin32.exe. If you use # with nalwin32.exe, any scripts will wait until the user exits Application Launcher.

Automating Application Objects

The final step in setting up the application distribution environment is automating Application objects. Automating Application objects is the process of setting up scripting, scheduling, and macros to remove required interaction with Application object distribution. This step is completely optional; however, you may wish to use some of the following options to make the application distribution completely seamless for users.

Manage Application Object Macros

One way to automate Application objects is to use the Macros property page to manage the Application object macros that you create expressly for this Application object and that are used on other property pages of the Application object. You can use all types of macros (including Application object macros) in the following Application object locations:

- Path to Executable (Identification property page)
- Command Line (Environment property page)
- Working Directory (Environment property page)
- Mapping Path (Drives/Ports property page)
- Capture Port Path (Drives/Ports property page)
- Registry Settings Property Page: Key, Name, Value (String only)
- .INI Settings Property Page: Group, Name, Value
- Application Files Property Page: Source/Target, Directory
- Text Files Property Page: Find and Add String
- Icons/Shortcuts Property Page: All locations

TIP

You can put macros within macros. For example:

```
%TARGET_PATH%=%*WINDISK%\Program Files

EMAIL_ADDRESS=%CN%@acme.com.
```

To access the Macros property page use the following steps from within ConsoleOne:

1. Right-click the Application object and click Properties.

2. Click the Common tab and select Macros from the drop-down menu.

3. Click Import, browse and highlight the Application Object template (.AOT or .AXT) file that you created with snAppShot, and then click Open.

   Or Click Add and then String to create a new Macro template entry. Name the macro and include a value, and then click OK.

   Or Click Add Then Prompted and then either String or Drive to create a new Macro template entry. Name the macro and include a default value and prompt string, and then click OK.

TIP

For best results, we recommend using a UNC pathname for the source path rather than a mapped drive. If you use a mapped drive letter as the source drive, some files might not copy correctly.

Prompted Macros

One way to automate Application objects is to use the Macros property page to set up special prompted macros. Times exist in which the end-user has a different system setup than what is expected by the administrator.

For example, users may want to put an application on a different drive than what was described in the Application object. Prompted macros enable the administrator the ability to request that the user be prompted for the information. By using the prompted macros feature, the administrator could have the destination drive requested of the end user and the resulting distribution goes to the specified drive.

To set up prompted macros, access the Macros property panel, use these steps from within ConsoleOne to select Add ⇨ Prompted ⇨ String. A window similar to the one shown in Figure 6.8 is displayed. From the prompted macro window, you are able to set up the following options for the macro:

- **Prompt text** — Textual information to be displayed for the user when prompting for the macro.

- **Macro name** — Name setup for the macro for install scripts, and so on.

- **Default Value** — You can specify a default value for the macro for users to use if they have no need to specify otherwise.

- **Minimum disk space** — You can specify a minimum amount of disk space required in setting the macro.

- **Maximum String length** — You can use this option to specify the maximum number of characters allowed for string macros.

► . . . . ◄

F I G U R E   6 . 8   *The prompted string macro property window for Application objects in ConsoleOne*

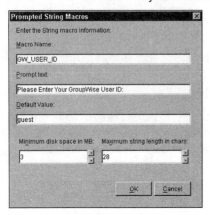

Special Windows Macros

Another way to automate application distribution is by using special Windows macros. A special Windows macro is one that defines Windows 95/98 and Windows NT/2000 directories. The typical paths, listed following, are based on default installations and may or may not match your specific setup. On Windows 95/98 workstations, macros behave differently if User Profiles are enabled.

The following macros are very helpful for redirecting application files that expect Windows directories to be in a particular location:

```
%*WinDir%   Windows directory, typically c:windows or
c:winnt

%*WinSysDir% Windows system directory, typically
c:\windows\system or c:\winnt\system32

%*WinDisk%  Drive letter (plus colon) for Windows
directory, typically c:

%*WinSysDisk%      Drive letter (plus colon) for Windows
system directory c:

%*WinSys16Dir%  Windows NT** 16-bit system directory
(c:\winnt\system)

%*TempDir%  Windows temporary directory (c:\windows\temp)
```

NOTE

The asterisk character (*) is a required syntax for these macros. Don't confuse these asterisk characters with the Novell trademark asterisk.

Login Script Variables

Another way to automate application distribution is by using login script variables. Application Launcher supports the familiar or traditional login script variables, however not all login script variables are supported.

Table 6.1 displays a list of supported login script macros and what they mean. Alternate macro names are shown in parentheses.

T A B L E   6 . 1   *Login Script Macros*

LOGIN SCRIPT MACRO	DEFINITION
DAY	Numeric day of the month. For example: 01, 10, 15, and so on.
FILESERVER (FILE_SERVER)	Name of the NetWare file server of NDS* monitored connection. For example: APPS_PROD.
FULL_NAME	Full name attribute of the User object. For example: Jane Doe.
HOUR24 (24HOUR)	Time of the day according to a 24-hour clock. For example: 02, 05, 14, 22, and so on.
HOUR (HOURS)	Hour of the day. For example: 0 = 12, 13 = 1, and so on.
LAST_NAME	Last name of the current user (also known as the user's NDS Surname attribute).
LOGIN_NAME	First eight bytes of the user's NDS object name. For example: jsmith.
MINUTE (MINUTES)	Current minute. For example: 02, 59, and so on.
MONTH	Current month number. For example: 01 for January, and so on.

(continued)

T A B L E 6 . I	Login Script Macros (continued)
LOGIN SCRIPT MACRO	DEFINITION
NDAY_OF_WEEK	Numeric day of the week. For example: I for Sunday, and so on.
NETWORK (NETWORK_ADDRESS)	Workstation network address. For example: 01010120.
OS_VERSION	Version of the OS. For example: v5.00. (Win3 shows DOS version, Win 95/98 and NT/2000 shows Windows version)
OS	OS type. For example: MSDOS, WIN98, WINNT, and so on. (Win3 shows MSDOS.)
PLATFORM	Platform running. For example: WIN, W98, WNT and so on.
PHYSICAL_STATION (P_STATION)	MAC address. For example: 0000C04FD92ECA.
REQUESTER_CONTEXT	Context of the requester (for the selected tree).
SECOND (SECONDS)	Number of seconds. For example: 03, 54, and so on.
SHORT_YEAR	Short year number. For example: 97, 00, and so on.
WINVER	Windows version. For example: v3.11, v4.00, and so on.
YEAR	Full year number. For example: 1997, and so on.

NDS Attribute Macros

Another useful tool in automating application distribution is using NDS attribute macros. Application Launcher supports macros that pull information from the attributes of the currently logged-in user, the current Application object, or from the attributes of other NDS objects.

An example of using NDS attribute macros would be a GroupWise* Application object that runs ofwin.exe with a command-line parameter:

```
/@U-@USERNAME@
```

USERNAME can be replaced with a macro that uses a user's NDS* common name (CN):

```
/@U-@%CN%@
```

If the NDS object name is the same as the e-mail login for GroupWise, every user that runs the application has the correct username passed into GroupWise.

Table 6.2 displays variables that are defined by an attribute in an NDS object that can be used as NDS attribute macros.

T A B L E 6 . 2	NDS Attribute Macros
ATTRIBUTE MACRO	**NDS OBJECT ATTRIBUTE**
%CN%	Common Name (user's object name or login name)
%DN%	User's Full Distinguished Name (used with Application Launcher only)
%Given Name%	Given Name
%Surname%	Last Name
%Full Name%	Full Name
%Telephone Number%	Telephone
%Home Directory%	Home Directory
%Email Address%	E-mail Address
%Mailbox ID%	Mailbox ID

Environment Variables

Another useful tool in automating application distribution is using environment variables. The following are some examples of environment variables that Application Launcher supports:

▶ %NWLANGUAGE%

▶ %TEMP%

▶ %PATH%

The value of the variable must not exceed the length of the Application object name; otherwise, the variable fails.

Schedule Application Pre-Install

Another useful tool in automating application distribution is to schedule application pre-install. Earlier in this chapter we discussed using the Pre-Install property panel for Application objects to set schedules of when the application will be pre-installed to the workstation. Set up large application distributions to be pre-installed in advance so that the objects are locally available to users. This provides you with the following safeguards:

▶ Low network bandwidth can't inhibit deployment of the application.

▶ You know for certain that all workstations are set up and ready to deploy the application.

▶ You don't need to stager workstation installs over a period of time, making the transition much easier for users.

Schedule Application Availability

Another useful tool in automating application distribution is to schedule application availability. Earlier in this chapter we discussed using the Scheduling property panel for Application objects to set schedules of when the application will be available. You can use this to help automate when users will be able to access the Application object.

Create Application Scripts

Another useful tool available to automate application distribution is the use of the Scripts property page to set up scripts that are executed automatically each time the application is launched and closed. Unlike environment parameters, scripts can overwrite existing drive mappings and printer ports.

The two types of application scripts are the Startup script and the post-termination script. Run before Launching (or Startup) scripts are executed after the environment is set and before the application is launched. Run after Termination (or post-termination) scripts are executed after the application is closed and before the network resources are cleaned up.

The following are some examples of what you can use application scripts for:

▶ Provide extra mappings beyond those defined on the Drives/Ports property page

▶ Provide a mapping to override another mapping

- ▶ Run other applications
- ▶ Log in to other servers or NDS* trees
- ▶ Terminate applications under certain circumstances

The following is an example of script syntax:

- ▶ #ipconfig.exe /renew — Run the ipconfig application to renew the DHCP configuration, pausing the script processing until Calculator returns control.
  - ▶ @ ipconfig.exe /renew — Run the ipconfig application to renew the DHCP concurrently with the remainder of the script processing.

To create Application object scripts use the steps listed in the creating pre-install scripts and launch scripts for Application objects section earlier in this chapter.

TIP

Commands for cleaning up the changes made by the pre-launch script should be placed in the post-termination script. The post-termination script is run after Application Launcher detects that the application has terminated.

The following is a list of scripting commands that Application Launcher does not support:

- ▶ CLS
- ▶ DISPLAY
- ▶ EXIT
- ▶ FDISPLAY
- ▶ INCLUDE
- ▶ LASTLOGINTIME
- ▶ NO_DEFAULT
- ▶ NOSWAP
- ▶ PAUSE
- ▶ PCCOMPATIBLE
- ▶ SCRIPT_SERVER
- ▶ SET_TIME
- ▶ SWAP
- ▶ WRITE

The following is a list of scripting commands that Application Launcher scripting does not do:

▶ Output anything to the screen

▶ Display errors

▶ Pause

Distribute the Applications

Once you have created the Application object, set up the properties for the object, and set up the distribution options, the final step is to actually distribute the Application object to the application users. To do this, do nothing. That is what ZENworks for Desktops application distribution is all about. Once you have it set up, ZENworks for Desktops automatically distributes the application for you according to your Application object settings.

## CHAPTER 7

Setting up User Policies

This chapter discusses the use and creation of User policies. User policies are associated with users and affect their working environment.

User policy packages in ZENworks for Desktops 3 may be created for any of the Windows 32 environments, namely Windows 95/98/NT/2000. The support for Windows 3.1 has been dropped from the product and is only available with the ZENworks 2 version.

Relationship of User Policies to Users

Users are associated with User Policies through associations with policies in any of three ways: 1) Policies can be associated with the user object directly; 2) Policies can be associated with a parent container of the user object; and 3) Policies can be associated with a group to which the user is a member.

When a user logs into the tree a ZENworks for Desktops 3 agent (Workstation Manager Service) walks up the tree looking for the first User Policy Package it can find that is associated with the user. Like all agents associated with ZENworks for Desktops 3, the order that the tree is searched is dependent on standard Novell Directory Services behavior and any Search Policies that may be in the tree. When a policy is being searched from the tree, the Workstation Manager agent walks the tree until it finds the root of the tree or a search policy that limits the searching. All of the applicable user policies are merged together and then the culmination is applied to the workstation. If any conflicts exist with the policies (such as two user policies both affecting the same parameter) then the parameter setting in the first policy found is applied.

The remote control policy can be created for both the user and the workstation. In the instances when a remote control policy exists for both the user and the workstation, the remote control subsystem takes the most restrictive combination of the policies. For example, if one policy says to prompt the user for permission and the other does not – then the system prompts the user.

General and Platform Specific Policy Advantages

ZENworks 2 provided administrators with a policy package for each distinct platform that was supported by ZENworks. In the new ZENworks for Desktops 3, these policy packages have been combined into a single user policy package. This gives you easier administration by being able to select policies in one place (the general page) and have them apply to all types of workstations that your users use. At the same time you do not loose the ability to have unique policies for each platform, because the general policies can be overridden by a platform specific policy (alternate platform page).

Regardless of the users that are logged into the system, each workstation finds the policies associated with it for that user, whether the policies come from the general policies or from the platform specific set, and execute the administrative configurations for that workstation.

In some occasions you may want to associate a particular, unique policy to a set of users that may be housed in containers along with other users of the same type. You can then create a group of users and associate specific policies to those users by associating the policy package to the user group. Consequently, these users receive the policies from this group rather than from the container.

Creating a User Policy Package

In order to have a policy that affects users who are logging into the tree through workstations, you need to create a user policy package. To create a User Policy package do the following:

1. Start ConsoleOne.

2. Browse to the container where you would like to have the policy package. Make sure you have the container where you want the policy package selected in ConsoleOne. Remember that you do not have to create the policy package in the container where you are doing the associations. You can associate the same policy package to many containers in your tree.

3. Create the policy package by pressing the right mouse button and choosing New ➪ Policy Package or by selecting the Policy Package icon on the toolbar.

4. Select the User Package object in the wizard panel and press Next.

5. Enter the desired name of the package in the Policy Package Name field and select the container where you want the package to be located. The container field is already filled in with the selected container so you should not have to browse to complete this field. If not, then press the browser button next to the field and browse to and select the container where you want the policy object stored. Press Next.

6. Select "Define Additional Attributes" field in order to go into the properties of your new object and activate some policies. Press Finish.

7. Check and set any policies you desire for this User Policy package and press OK.

The following subsections describe each of the fields and property pages that are available in the User Policy package.

Policies Property Page

All of the policies for users are activated within the policies property page. Initially the page is on the general policies. As other platforms are selected additional policies are displayed. You can select which platform to display by placing the mouse over the small triangle to the right of the word Policies in the tab. This activates a drop-down menu that allows you to select which platform specific page you wish to display. (See Figure 7.1.)

► · ◄

User Policy Package policies property page with drop-down menu

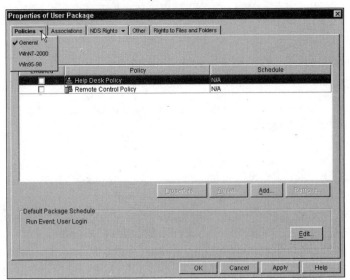

The following sections discuss briefly each of the policy pages, and then we cover the specifics of each policy.

General Policies

When you first go into the properties of the User policy package you are presented with the Policy Property page. The policy page first displays the general category. All of the policies that are activated in the general category are active for ALL platforms supported by ZENworks for Desktops 3 and associated to the logged in user.

Figure 7.2 is a snapshot of the initial property page of the user policy package.

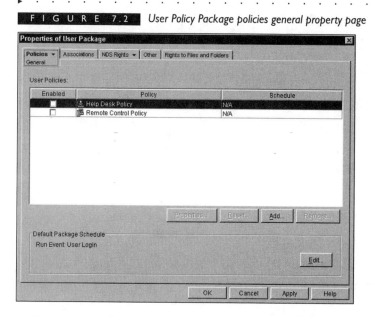

F I G U R E   7 . 2   *User Policy Package policies general property page*

As you can see from the image only two types of policies exist that are available to all of the platforms supported by ZENworks for Desktops 3. They include the Help Desk Policy and Remote Control Policy. These, as well as all of the other policies, are discussed later in this chapter.

In order to activate a policy you simply need to check the box to the left of the policy by clicking on the box with the left mouse button. You can then go into the details of the policy and set additional configuration parameters on that specific policy.

WinNT-2000 Policies

Within the policies tab you can select the Windows NT/2000 policy page. This page displays the policies that are available for your users of Windows NT and Windows 2000. These policies include the Dynamic Local User policy, Help Desk policy, NT Desktop Preferences policy, NT User Printer policy, Remote Control policy, User Extensible policies, Windows 2000 Group Policy, and the Windows Terminal Server Policy. See Figure 7.3 for a sample of the WinNT-2000 policies page.

F I G U R E 7.3 *User Policy Package WinNT-2000 policies property page*

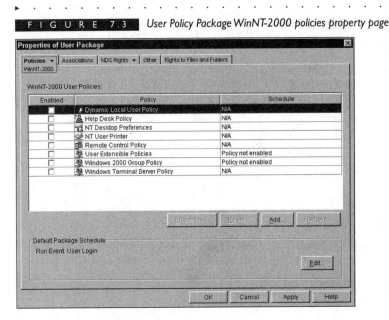

As you can see the Help Desk policy and the Remote Control policy are both under the general and the WinNT-2000 policies page. When you select a policy in the WinNT-2000 page it supercedes any selections that may have been on the general tab for that platform. The policies are not merged together; only the platform specific policy is used instead of the policy set in the general category. Also, only the policies selected in the platform specific tab are used in place of the general policies. For example, if the help desk policy is selected in the general tab, and the remote control policy is selected in the WinNT-2000 tab, then when an associated user logs into a Windows 2000 or Windows NT system the general help desk policy and the WinNT-2000 remote control policy are activated for that user.

Win95-98 Policies

Within the policies tab you can select the Windows 95-98 policy page. This page displays the policies that are available for your users of Windows 95 and Windows 98. These policies include the 95 Desktop Preferences policy, Help Desk policy, Remote Control policy, User Extensible policies, and the Windows Terminal Server Policy. See Figure 7.4 for a sample of the Win95-98 policies page.

F I G U R E   7 . 4   *User Policy Package Win95-98 policies property page*

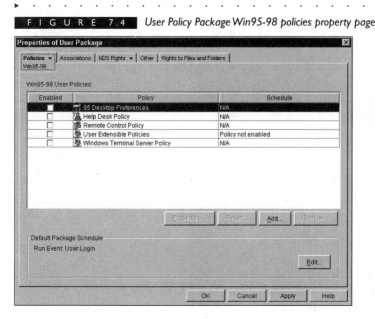

As with the WinNT-2000 properties page, you can see the Help Desk policy and the Remote Control policy are both under the general and the Win95-98 policies page. When you select a policy in the Win95-98 page it supercedes any selections that may have been on the general tab for that platform. The policies are not merged together; only the platform specific policy is used instead of the policy set in the general category. Also, only the policies selected in the platform specific tab are used in place of the general policies. For example, if the remote control policy is selected in the general tab and the help desk policy is selected in the Win95-98 tab (because you have a different help desk contact for that platform), then when an associated user logs into a Windows 95 or Windows 98 system then the general remote control policy and the Win95-98 help desk policy are activated for that user.

Associations Property Page

The "Associations Page" of the Windows User Policy Package displays all of the locations in the tree (containers) where the policy package has been associated. These associations do not necessarily reflect where the policy package is located in the directory. The Windows users that are in or below those containers have this policy package enforced. Pressing the Add or Remove buttons allows you to add or remove containers in the list that are associated with this policy.

NDS Rights Property Pages

The "NDS Rights" property page is made up of three pages. You can get to each of the pages by clicking on the small triangle to the right of the page name, and then selecting the desired page to be displayed.

These pages allow you to specify the rights that users have to this object in the directory. The following subsections discuss briefly each of these pages. These NDS Rights pages are displayed for every object in the tree.

Trustees of This Object Page

On this page you can grant objects rights as trustees of the User Policy Package. These trustees have rights to this object or to attributes within this object.

When you assign a container as a trustee of an object then everyone in that container or subcontainer has some rights to this object. To get into the details of any trustee assignment (in order to modify the assignment) you would need to press the "Assigned Rights" button.

When you press the "Assign Rights" button, after selecting the user you want to modify you are presented with a dialog box that allows you to select either [All Attribute Rights] (meaning all of the attributes of the object) or [Entry Rights] (meaning the object, not implying rights to the attributes).

From within the assigned rights dialog box you may set the rights for the object on this package. You can set those rights on the object as well as any individual property in the object. The rights that are possible are the following:

  ▸ **Browse** — Although not in the list this right shows up from time to time (especially in the effective rights screens). This represents the ability to view this information through public browse capabilities.

  ▸ **Supervisor** — This identifies that the trustee has ALL rights, including delete for this object or attribute.

- **Compare** — This provides the trustee with the ability to compare values of attributes.

- **Read** — This allows the trustee to read the values of the attribute or attributes in the object.

- **Write** — This provides the trustee with the ability to modify the contents of an attribute.

- **Add Self** — This right allows the trustee to add themselves as a member the list of objects of the attribute. For example, if this right were given to an attribute that contains a list of linked objects, then the trustee could add themselves (a reference to their object) into the list.

If you wish to add the object as a trustee to an attribute you would need to press the "Add Property" button to bring up a list of properties or attributes that are available for this object.

From this list you may select a single attribute. This attribute is then displayed in the assigned rights dialog box. From there you can select the attribute and then set the rights you want the trustee to have for that property. A user does not require object rights in order to have rights on a single attribute in the object.

Remember that rights flow down in the tree and if you give user rights at a container level then those rights continue down into that container and any sub-containers until that branch is exhausted or another explicit assignment is given for that user in a sub-container or on an object. An explicit assignment changes the rights for the user at that point in the tree. Inheritance Rights Filters may also be placed to restrict this flow of rights down into the tree.

Inherited Rights Filters Page

This page allows you to set the IRF (Inheritance Rights Filter) for this object. This filter restricts the rights of any user that accesses this object, unless that user has an explicit trustee assignment for this object.

You can think of the IRF as a filter that lets only items checked pass through unaltered. Rights that bump up against an IRF filter are blocked and discarded if the item is NOT checked. For example, if a user who had write privileges inherited at some point above (they were explicitly granted that right at some container at or above the one we're in) were to run into an IRF for an object or attribute that has the write privilege revoked (that is, unchecked), then when they got to that object their write privilege would be gone for that object. If the object were a container, then they would loose write privileges for all objects in that container or sub-container.

You can effectively remove supervisor privileges to a portion of the tree by setting an IRF with the supervisor privilege turned off. You must be careful not to ever do this without someone being assigned as the supervisor of that branch of the tree (given an explicit supervisor trustee assignment at the container where the IRF is done) or you make that part of the tree permanent (that is, you are never able to delete any objects in that branch of the tree). ConsoleOne helps keep you from performing this action by giving you an error dialog box that keeps you from putting an IRF on the [Entry Rights] of the object with the supervisor right filtered away without having first given an explicit supervisor assignment on the same container.

Effective Rights Page

Effective Rights property page allows you to query the system to discover the rights that selected objects have on the object you are administering.

Within this page you are presented with the distinguished name (DN) of the object whose rights you wish to observe. Initially, this will be your currently logged in user running ConsoleOne. You can press the browse button to the right of the trustee field and browse throughout the tree to select any object.

When the trustee object is selected you may then move to the properties table on the lower half of the screen. As you select the property, the rights box to the right changes its text to reflect the rights that the trustee has on that property. These rights may be via an explicit assignment *or* through inheritance.

Other Property Page

This page may or may not be displayed for you, depending on your rights to the plug-in that now comes with ConsoleOne. This page is particularly powerful and should not be used by those who do not have an intimate knowledge of the schema of the object in question and its relationships with other objects in the directory. The intention of this property page is to give you generic access to properties that you cannot modify or view via the other plugged-in pages. The attributes and their values are displayed in a tree structure, allowing for those attributes that have multiple types (are compound types that consist of, say, an int and a distinguished name, or postal code that has three separate address fields).

Every attribute in eDirectory is defined by one of a specified set of syntaxes. These syntaxes identify how the data is stored in eDirectory. For this page, ConsoleOne has developed an editor for each of the different syntaxes that are currently available in eDirectory. When an attribute is displayed on this page the editor is invoked to display the data and then modify it should the user click the specific attribute.

For example, if the syntax for an attribute were a string or an integer, then an in-line editor is launched allowing the administrator to modify the string or the integer value on the screen. More abstract syntaxes such as octet-string require that an octet editor be launched giving the administrator access to each of the bytes in the string, without interpretation of the data.

The danger with this screen is that some applications require that there be a coordination of attribute values between two attributes within the same object or across multiple objects. Additionally, many applications assume that the data in the attribute is valid, because the normal user interface checks for invalid entries and does not allow them to be stored in the attribute. If you should change a data value in the other page, then no knowledge of related attributes, objects, or valid data values are checked because the generic editors know nothing about the intention of the field. Should you change a value without making all the other appropriate changes or without putting in a valid value then some programs, and the system, could be affected.

Rights are still in effect in the Other property page and you are not allowed to change any attribute values that are read-only, or values that you do not have rights to modify.

Rights to Files and Folders Property Page

This page in the property book is present in all objects in the directory. This property page allows you to view and set rights for this object onto the volumes and specific files and folders on that volume.

You must first select the volume that contains the files and folders to which you are interested. You can do this by pressing the "show" button on the right and then browsing the directory to the volume object. Selecting the volume object places it in the volumes view. When that volume is selected you can then go to the "add" button to add a file or folder of interest. This brings up a dialog box allowing you to browse to the volume object and then clicking on the volume object moves you into the file system. You can continue browsing that volume until you select the file or directory you are interested in granting rights.

Selecting the file or folder in the lower pane displays the rights that the object has been granted on that file or folder. To modify the rights simply click on or off the rights that you want to have explicitly granted for the object.

You can also see the effective rights that the object has on the files by pressing the "effective rights" button. This displays a dialog box, allowing you to browse to any file in the volume and having the effective rights displayed (in bold) for the object. These effective rights include any explicit plus inherited rights from folders higher in the file system tree. Remember that anyone with supervisor rights to the server or volume objects automatically gets supervisor rights in the file system.

► · ◄

95/98 Desktop Preferences Policy

This policy allows you access to the ZAW/ZAK features that are exposed by the Microsoft Windows system. Within the ZENworks for Desktops 3 system these ZAW/ZAK policies are divided into their logical parts: Desktop Preferences, User System Policies, and Workstation Policies. This policy allows the administrator to set the desktop preferences for any Windows 95/98 system to which the user is currently connected. This policy follows the user as they move from workstation to workstation.

Microsoft provides a tool called "poledit" that allows an administrator to construct some registry setting (ZAW/ZAK features) and have those settings saved in a ".POL" file. This ".POL" file can then be applied to any workstation by having the system look for these files on the server. The problem here is that these policy files must be located on every server that any user may use as an initial connection. With ZENworks for Desktops 3, this information is stored in these policies and into Novell Directory Services, thus making it always accessible to every user that connects to the system without having you place these policy files on every server.

The 95/98 Desktop Preferences allows the administrator to set Control Panel features as well as Roaming Profile configurations.

Roaming Profile Page

The settings for any particular desktop such as the desktop icons, screen colors, task bar selections, and so on, are stored in profiles. These profiles can, with this Roaming Profile feature, be placed into the file system on the network. By doing this, when the user, who has a profile saved on the network, logs into any 95/98 workstation, their profile is retrieved from the network and brought to that workstation. This allows a consistent look and feel for the workstation to be presented to that user regardless of which actual workstation they are using. Any changes to the desktop, or preferences, are stored back up onto the network and therefore reflected the next time that the user logs into any 95/98 workstation. Figure 7.5 has a screen image from the Roaming profile page.

FIGURE 7.5 *Roaming Profile page of a Windows 95/98 Desktop Preferences policy of the User Policy package*

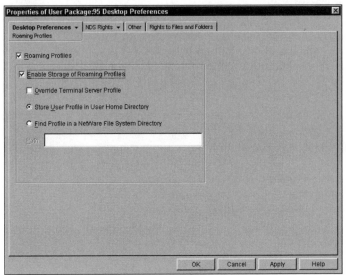

In the Roaming profile page the administrator can set whether Roaming profiles are available. If they are available then you want to also check the "Enable Storage of Roaming Profiles" check box. This allows the profiles to be stored on a network server for access from any 95/98 workstation.

The "Override Terminal Server Profile" option allows you, when checked, to have this user profile override any profiles that they may have received via the Terminal Server system available for NT servers.

Once the enabling of storage has occurred, then you have the choice of either allowing the profiles to be stored in the Users home directory or in a specified file system directory. By specifying that the profiles be stored in the User's home directory, a subdirectory called "Windows 95 Workstation Profile" is created in the home directory. Within that directory, the profile information is stored and maintained. If you identify a specific directory then all users that log into the 95/98 workstation with that policy store the desktop information directly into that directory, and have the profiles shared with all users that log into that workstation. This is why storage into a specific directory is recommended for mandatory profiles only.

NDS Rights, Other, *and* Rights to Files and Folders pages are described in the "Creating a User Policy Package" section.

Control Panel Page

By clicking on each of the icons presented in the Control Panel page of the Windows 95/98 Desktop Preferences policy, the administrator can configure the properties of each of these control panel items.

The standard scenario is that the agent searches the tree for this policy and applies it during the login of the user. This schedule can be changed in the policy package to be another scheduled time or event. To ensure that these preferences are always applied when the user logs into the tree, regardless of the schedule in the policy, you need to check the "Always update workstation during NDS Authentication" check box.

Accessibility Options

By clicking on this icon you are presented with a tabbed dialog with the ability to set the following properties:

► Keyboard page allows you to set the standard Windows 95/98 Accessibility Options for StickyKeys, FilterKeys, and ToggleKeys.

► Sound page allows you to set the following: SoundSentry, and ShowSounds.

► Mouse page allows you to configure the MouseKeys.

► General page allows you to configure Automatic reset, Notification, and SerialKey devices.

Console

This icon brings up the property page that allows you to configure the properties of the console window (such as, DOS box) for the Windows 95/98 system. The Console Windows properties allow you to set the following:

► Options tab allows the setting of console options such as Cursor Size, Display Options, Command History sizes and buffers, QuickEdit Mode, and Insert Mode.

- Layout tab provides the configuration for the Screen Buffer Size, Window Size, and the Window Position.
- Colors tab provides for the setting of the Console colors for the text and backgrounds.

From this policy you are not able to set the font properties of the Console window.

Display

Clicking on this icon brings up the property page that allows you to make the following configurations:

- Background tab allows setting of the wallpaper. You are able to specify that no wallpaper be presented or specify a file name of the .BMP file to be displayed for the wallpaper.
- Screen Saver page allows you to configure if a screen saver should be available. Also you may specify a particular .SCR or .EXE to be executed for the screen saver. In addition to the screen saver program you can specify if the screen should be password protected. Also on this page you may specify the ability to use the energy saving features of your monitor.
- Appearance tab allows you to specify the color scheme that you want applied for this user. You can set the color scheme to any of the following choices: Windows Standard, Brick, Desert, Eggplant, High Contrast Black, High Contrast White, Lilac, Maple, Marine (high color), Plum (high color), Rainy Day, Red White and Blue (VGA), Rose, Slate, Spruce, Storm (VGA), Teal (VGA), or Wheat
- Plus page allows you to set some basic features of the Plus! Package. These features include Use large icons, Show window contents while dragging, Smooth edges of screen fonts, Show icons using all possible colors, and Stretch desktop wallpaper to fit the screen.

Keyboard

This icon allows you to make the Speed setting for the user. You can specify character repeat rates and the cursor blink rate.

Mouse

This icon brings up the property page of the mouse system for the user. From this property page you can set the following features:

- ▸ Buttons tab provides you with the following features: Button configuration for left- or right-handed mouse; and Double-click speed.

- ▸ The Pointers tab allows you to configure the mouse cursor to be used: 3D Bronze, 3D-White, Conductor, Dinosaur, Hands 1, Hands 2, Magnified, Old Fashioned, Variations, Windows Animated, or Windows Default.

- ▸ The Motion property tab gives you the ability to set the pointer speed, snap to default, and the pointer trail speed.

Sounds

This icon allows you to specify the sound scheme as one of the following for these users: No Sounds, Jungle Sound Scheme, Windows Default, Musica Sound Scheme, Robotz Sound Scheme, or Utopia Sound Scheme.

► • ◄

Dynamic Local User Policy

Often, several users within a company have access to shared Windows NT workstations, and it would be an administrative nightmare to have to keep up accounts for all users of these shared systems. Consequently, ZENworks for Desktops 3 has the ability to dynamically create accounts on the local NT workstation while the user is logging into the system. The local account is literally created at login time.

By having the system automatically create the account at the time that the user is authenticated to the Novell Directory Services tree, any of these users can log into any Windows NT workstation and have a local account automatically created on that workstation. To prevent the system from allowing any user to log into a specific workstation you can administer the Restrict Login Policy in the Windows NT specific Workstation Policy Package. The Restrict Login Policy allows you to specify which users can or cannot log into the specific workstation. The following figure (Figure 7.6) displays the dynamic local user policy page.

NDS Rights, Other, and Rights to Files and Folders pages are described in the "Creating a User Policy Package" section.

Dynamic Local User page of a Dynamic Local User Policy within a User Policy Package

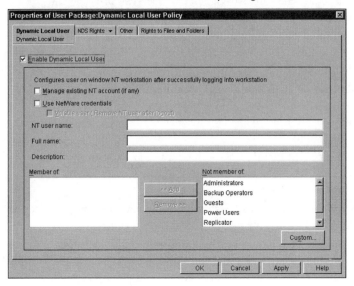

Checking the "Enable Dynamic Local User" allows the system to start creating accounts on the local system. The following options may be set in this policy:

▸ **Manage Existing NT accounts (if any)** — When checked this will allow the ZENworks for Desktops 3 agents to manage a previously existing account for this user through the Dynamic Local User system. If this is checked then any previously generated accounts are subject to the properties that you administer in this policy.

▸ **Use NetWare credentials** — When this is enabled the system uses the password that is used for Novell Directory Services as the password for the local account.

▸ **Volatile User (Remove NT user after logout)** — This check box is only accessible if you have previously checked the "Use NetWare credentials" box. This check box enables the system to remove the local account that was used for the dynamic user when the user logs out of the system. Having this feature enabled in conjunction with enabling the "Manage Existing NT account (if any)" options causes a previously created local account to become volatile and removed when that person logs out of the workstation.

► **NT username** — This field is only accessible if the "Use NetWare credentials" is disabled. The system uses the specified name for the local account when any Novell Directory Services user logs into the system.

► **Full name** — This field is only accessible if the "Use NetWare credentials" is disabled. The system uses the specified full name for the local account when any Novell Directory Services user logs into the system.

► **Description** — This field is only accessible if the "Use NetWare credentials" is disabled. The system uses the given description for the local account when any Novell Directory Services user logs into the system.

► **Member of/Not member of** — These lists allow you to specify which local accounts, created or used for these users, are members of which local NT groups.

► **Custom** — This button allows you to create new custom groups to the list in order to make the dynamic local users members of these groups.

If the NetWare credentials are not used for the Dynamic Local User policy — causing the NT username, Full name, and Description to be used — then this account will always be volatile and will be created and removed each time a user logs into and out of the workstation.

Additionally, if ANY password restrictions such as Minimum Password Age or Length or Uniqueness have been placed in the local workstation policy, then the Dynamic Local User system is not activated for that workstation. A dialog box notifying the user that Dynamic Local User features have been disabled is displayed whenever anyone attempts to log into the workstation.

► . . . . ◄

Help Desk Policy

The Help Desk Policy sets the features associated with the Help Request system that is provided with the ZENworks for Desktops 3 system. The Help Request system includes a program that can be presented to all users in the tree through the ZENworks for Desktops 3 Application Launcher. When ZENworks for Desktops 3 is installed it creates an Application Object that is associated with the Help Request program. By associating this application object to users, groups, or containers, the end-user is presented with this program on their desktop.

When the Help Request program is launched it checks to see that a policy package is associated with the currently logged-in user, and if a Help Desk policy is enabled. If a Help Desk policy is enabled, then the program launches on the desktop. The interface presented through the Help Requester is fully configured by the Help Desk policy and is described below with each page of the policy.

The Help Desk Policy is in the general category of the User Policy Package and therefore can be configured the same for all platforms. The Help Desk Policy is also located in each of the platform specific pages and can therefore be configured differently for each platform.

A Help Desk Policy is activated for this policy package by either double-clicking the Help Desk Policy or selecting the check box on the Help Desk Policy. Once this is selected and a check is displayed in the check box, then this Help Desk Policy is activated for all users of supported windows platforms.

NDS Rights, Other, *and* Rights to Files and Folders pages are described in the Creating a User Policy Package section.

Configuration Page

The Configuration Page of the Help Desk Policy allows you to administer the behavior of the Help Request system. By checking the "Allow user to launch the Help Requester" field you activate the Help Request system for all Windows 95 and Windows 98 users that are associated with this policy package. Until this box is checked, any user that launches the Help Request system is denied access, even though the application object associated with the Help Request application is associated with the user. Once this box is checked, the Help Request system is activated. The Configuration Page is reflected in Figure 7.7.

The Allow user to send trouble tickets from the Help Requester field is only activated when you check the box that allows the users to launch the Help Requester. Before checking this box, the user may only use the information and call buttons on the Help Requestor system. These buttons only provide information of the user and workstation objects and the contact information that was administered on the Information Page of the Help Desk Policy.

The Trouble ticket delivery mode identifies for the system the method that should be used by the Help Requestor application for the sending of generated trouble tickets. Currently the choices for this mode are Groupwise 5.x and MAPI. By checking the GroupWise 5.x system the Help Requestor application assumes that the GroupWise 5.0 or greater libraries are present on the end-users workstation and make the calls necessary to send the automatically created trouble tickets to the Contact Name e-mail address via these GroupWise calls. If the MAPI option is chosen then the same attempt is done only using standard Windows MAPI calls to activate the e-mail system.

► · ◄

F I G U R E   7 . 7   *Configuration page of the Help Desk Policy within a User Policy Package*

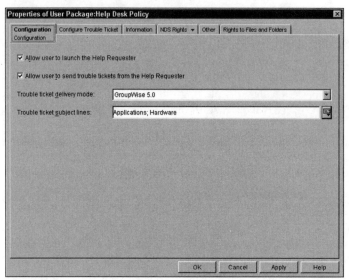

The Trouble ticket subject lines field allows you to enter as many trouble ticket subject lines as you wish. You can enter additional subject lines by selecting the field and simply typing in additional subject line values and pressing return. As you enter these subject lines they are added to the list of choices for the users. To remove a subject line just click the drop-down button to the right of the field, select the subject you wish to delete, and press the "delete" key. The subject lines that are stored in the policy are presented to the end-user via the Help Requestor system. The end-user may select which subject line to associate with the help request. This is also placed as the subject line in the e-mail message of the trouble ticket (so they can be helpful in routing the message to the appropriate person).

Configure Trouble Ticket Page

The Configure Trouble Ticket page is used to allow the administrator to specify the information that they want stored in the trouble ticket about the user and the workstation that is issuing the ticket.

The following fields can be checked in the Configure Trouble Ticket to signal that the information be included in the ticket. The information included is either related to the current user that is logged into the tree or the workstation.

- **User Context** — This includes the tree context (such as, .user1.novell) of the user object of the user who is logged into the workstation when the trouble ticket is sent.
- **User Tree** — This includes the tree name in the ticket.
- **User Location** — This includes the value in the location field of the user object for the current user.
- **User Phone** — This includes the phone number field of the user object for the current user.
- **Workstation ID** — This is the workstation object name of the workstation (such as .workstation1.workstations.novell).
- **Workstation Tree** — This specifies the tree name where the workstation object is located.
- **Workstation Inventory** — This includes inventory information about the workstation. This information includes the following: Computer Type, Computer Model, Serial Number, Asset Tag, OS Type, OS Version, Novell Client version, NIC Type, Video Type, BIOS Type, Processor, Memory Size, Disk Info, MAC Address, Subnet Address, and IP Address. This is basically the same information that is stored in the workstation object in the tree.

Information Page

The Information Page allows you to enter in a selected set of information to have displayed through the Help Request system presented to the end-user. When the Help Request system is launched on an individual's desktop, they are presented with this contact information

The Contact Name should be the name of the help desk personnel or service, such as PC Repair Services. The Telephone Number field is also presented to the end-user of the Help Request application and should be the help number that the user can call for assistance. The E-mail address is the electronic mail address of the person or organization to be contacted when the Help Request system is launched. Trouble tickets that are generated by the Help Request system are automatically sent to this e-mail address.

► · · · · · · · · · · · · · · · · · · · ◄

NT Desktop Preferences Policy

This policy allows you access to the ZAW/ZAK features that are exposed by the Microsoft Windows system. Within the ZENworks for Desktops 3 system these ZAW/ZAK policies are divided into their logical parts: Desktop Preferences, User System Policies, and Workstation Policies. This policy allows the administrator to set the desktop preferences for any Windows NT system to which the user is currently connected. This policy follows the user as they move from workstation to workstation.

Microsoft provides a tool called poledit that allows an administrator to construct some registry setting (ZAW/ZAK features) and have those settings saved in a .POL file. This ".POL" file can then be applied to any workstation by having the system look for these files on the server. The problem here is that these policy files must be located on every server that any user may use as an initial connection. With ZENworks for Desktops 3 this information is stored in these policies and into Novell Directory Services, thus making it always accessible to every user that connects to the system without having you place these policy files on every server.

The NT Desktop Preferences allows the administrator to set Control Panel features as well as Roaming Profile configurations.

Roaming Profile Page

The settings for any particular desktop such as the desktop icons, screen colors, task bar selections, and so on, are stored in profiles. These profiles can, with this Roaming Profile feature, be placed into the file system on the network. By doing this, when the user, who has a profile saved on the network, logs into any NT workstation their profile is retrieved from the network and brought to that workstation. This allows a consistent look and feel for the workstation to be presented to that user regardless of which actual workstation they are using. Any changes to the desktop or preferences are stored back onto the network and therefore reflected the next time that the user logs into any NT workstation. Figure 7.8 has a screen image from the Roaming profile page.

In the Roaming profile page the administrator can set whether Roaming profiles are available. If they are available then you want to also check the "Enable Storage of Roaming Profiles" check box. This allows the profiles to be stored on a network server for access from any NT workstation.

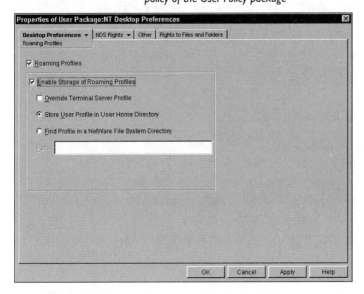

Roaming Profile page of a Windows NT Desktop Preferences policy of the User Policy package

The Override Terminal Server Profile option allows you, when checked, to have this user profile override any profiles that they may have received via the Terminal Server system available for NT servers.

Once the enabling of storage has occurred, then you have the choice of either allowing the profiles to be stored in the User's home directory or in a specified file system directory. By specifying that the profiles be stored in the User's home directory then a subdirectory called "Windows NT 4.0 Workstation Profile" is created in the home directory. Within that directory the profile information is stored and maintained. If you identify a specific directory then all users that log into the NT workstation with that policy store the desktop information directly into that directory, and share the profiles with all users that log into that workstation. This is why the storage into a specific directory is recommended for mandatory profiles only.

NDS Rights, Other, and Rights to Files and Folders pages are described in the "Creating a User Policy Package" section.

Control Panel Page

By clicking on each of the icons presented in the Control Panel page of the Windows NT Desktop Preferences policy, the administrator can configure the properties of each of these control panel items.

The standard scenario is that the agent searches the tree for this policy and applies it during the login of the user. This schedule can be changed in the policy package to be another scheduled time or event. To ensure that these preferences are always applied when the user logs into the tree, regardless of the schedule in the policy, you need to check the "Always update workstation during NDS Authentication" check box.

Accessibility Options

By clicking on this icon you are presented with a tabbed dialog with the ability to set the following properties:

▶ Keyboard page allows you to set the standard Windows NT Accessibility Options for StickyKeys, FilterKeys, and ToggleKeys.

▶ Sound page allows you to set the following: SoundSentry, and ShowSounds.

▶ Mouse page allows you to configure the MouseKeys.

▶ General page allows you to configure Automatic reset, Notification, and SerialKey devices.

Console

This icon brings up the property page that allows you to configure the properties of the console window (such as DOS box) for the Windows NT system. The Console Windows properties allow you to set the following:

▶ Options tab allows the setting of console options such as Cursor Size, Display Options, Command History sizes, and buffers, QuickEdit Mode, and Insert Mode.

▶ Layout tab provides the configuration for the Screen Buffer Size, Window Size, and the Window Position.

▶ Colors tab provides for the setting of the Console colors for the text and backgrounds.

From this policy you are not able to set the font properties of the Console window.

Display

Clicking on this icon brings up the property page that allows you to make the following configurations:

▶ Background tab allows setting of the wallpaper. You are able to specify that no wallpaper be presented or specify a file name of the .BMP file to be displayed for the wallpaper.

▶ Screen Saver page allows you to configure whether a screen saver should be available. Also you may specify a particular .SCR or .EXE to be executed for the screen saver. In addition to the screen saver program, you can specify if the screen should be password protected. Also on this page you may specify the ability to use the energy saving features of your monitor.

▶ Appearance tab allows you to specify the color scheme that you want applied for this user. You can set the color scheme to any of the following choices: Windows Standard, Brick, Desert, Eggplant, High Contrast Black, High Contrast White, Lilac, Maple, Marine (high color), Plum (high color), Rainy Day, Red White and Blue (VGA), Rose, Slate, Spruce, Storm (VGA), Teal (VGA), or Wheat

▶ Plus page allows you to set some basic features of the Plus! Package. These features include Use large icons, Show window contents while dragging, Smooth edges of screen fonts, Show icons using all possible colors, and Stretch desktop wallpaper to fit the screen.

Keyboard

This icon allows you to make the Speed setting for the user. You can specify character repeat rates and the cursor blink rate.

Mouse

This icon brings up the property page of the mouse system for the user. From this property page you can set the following features:

▶ Buttons tab provides you with the following features: Button configuration for left- or right-handed mouse; and Double-click speed.

▶ The Pointers tab allows you to configure the mouse cursor to be used: 3D Bronze, 3D-White, Conductor, Dinosaur, Hands 1, Hands 2, Magnified, Old Fashioned, Variations, Windows Animated, or Windows Default.

▶ The Motion property tab gives you the ability to set the pointer speed, snap to default, and the pointer trail speed.

Sounds

This icon allows you to specify the sound scheme as one of the following for these users: No Sounds, Jungle Sound Scheme, Windows Default, Musica Sound Scheme, Robotz Sound Scheme, or Utopia Sound Scheme.

► · ◄

NT User Printer Policy

This policy allows the administrator to set up network printers onto the local Windows NT desktop. In order to add printers to the policy you must have already set up some printers into your NetWare system and have corresponding printer and print queue objects in your Novell Directory Services tree. Figure 7.9 shows the policy screen.

NDS Rights, Other, and Rights to Files and Folders pages are described in the "Creating a User Policy Package" section.

► · ◄

F I G U R E   7 . 9   *Windows NT User Printer policy of the User Policy package*

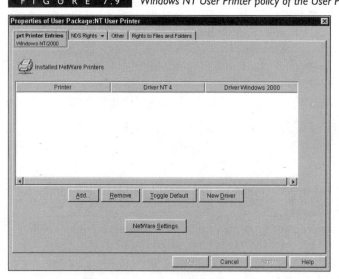

Perform the following steps to add a printer to the printer policy:

1. Press the Add button.

2. Browse through the dialog box and select the Printer or Print Queue object that you want to deliver to the users associated with the policy.

To remove a printer from the policy, simply highlight the printer from the list and then press the Remove button.

Any printers that have been added to this list are added to the user's desktop automatically when they first log into the system. When the printer is removed from this list, the printer is removed from the local system account the next time that user logs into the workstation.

Remote Control Policy

A Remote Management Policy is activated for this policy package by selecting the check box on the Remote Management Policy. Once this is selected and a check is displayed in the check box, then this Remote Management Policy is activated for all Users associated with the User Policy Package.

The Remote Management Policy controls the features of the Remote Management subsystem that is shipped with the ZENworks for Desktops 3 package and is not shipped with the ZENworks Starter Pack. The Remote Management system is comprised of two parts: Remote Management Session Manager that makes the connection and is used by the administrator, and the Remote Management Agents that are installed on the end-user's workstation. The remote control agents may be installed onto the workstation when the client that is shipped with ZENworks for Desktops 3 is installed, or the agents may be installed on the workstation through the remote control application objects that were added to your tree when you installed ZENworks for Desktops 3. You would need to simply associate these application objects to the users and then have the ZENworks for Desktops 3 Application launcher install these agents automatically on the workstation. For more information, see Chapter 5, "Creating and Using Application Objects."

The Remote Management system makes a peer-to-peer connection between the administrator's workstation and the remote workstation. This may be done using either the IPX or the TCP/IP protocol. In this policy you may specify the preferred protocol for the connection. This protocol is attempted first, but if the connection cannot be made, then the alternate protocol is used.

Remote controlling a workstation via ZENworks for Desktops 3 also requires rights within the Workstation Object that represent the workstation wanting to be controlled. Without these rights, the administrator is denied access to the remote control subsystem. Both the session manager and the agents validate that the user has rights to remote control the workstation. You assign the remote control rights through the Remote Management Rights wizard, or in the Workstation object in the Remote Operators page.

Remote Management Page

The Remote Management page identifies the features that you want to be activated with the Remote Management system. Figure 7.10 shows the Remote Management page of the policy.

NDS Rights, Other, and Rights to Files and Folders pages are described in the "Creating a User Policy Package" section.

► • ◄

F I G U R E   7 . 1 0   *Remote Management Policy page, General tab of a User Policy Package*

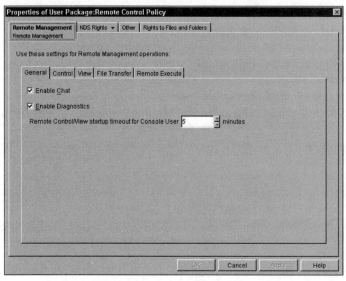

The following describes each of the options available under each tab of the Remote Management policy:

General Tab

This tab has options on general system functions.

► **Enable Chat** — This enables those who have this policy associated with them to accept a chat request. Chat sets up a communication system between the initiator and the receiver and allows them to type and send messages to one another.

▶ **Enable Diagnostics** — This allows the agent on the workstations to perform a diagnostics report. This can be done by selecting the workstation and then pressing the right mouse button and selecting Actions ⇨ Diagnostics of the menu. The Diagnostics utility performs some basic queries on the system and returns the information about the workstation. This information includes memory, environment, and processes running. Additionally, it would include NDS and Netware connection information, client information, network drives, and open file list, as well as printers, Network protocols, and network services active. You can also view the various event and error logs that have been recorded on that workstation.

▶ **Remote Control/View startup timeout for Console users** — This field allows the administrator to specify the number of minutes that they are willing to wait to establish a connection with the remote workstation. Once this time has expired, the connection attempt is abandoned. This does NOT have to do with the length of time that a connection is idle.

Control Tab

This tab describes the feature enabling of remote control functions.

▶ **Enable Remote Control** — When this option is enabled, then the remote control subsystem can be activated. Without this setting on no one may remote control the workstations where the currently logged in user has this policy associated with their user object.

▶ **Prompt user for permission to remote control** — This option causes a dialog box to be displayed on the end-user's machine when a remote control session is started. The end-user has the option of accepting or denying the remote control request. Within this dialog box the user is told who wants to remote control their machine and asks if this is approved. If the user denies the remote control session, then the session is terminated and the administrator cannot remote control the workstation.

▶ **Give user audible system when remote controlled** — This option provides the end-user a tone periodically while the remote control session is active. You can also set the number of seconds between each beep.

▶ **Give user visible signal when remote controlled** — This option displays a dialog box on the end-user's desktop while the remote control session is active. The dialog box displays that the workstation is being remote controlled and also displays the NDS name of the user that is remote controlling the workstation. You can set the number of seconds that you want to have between flashing the name of the user that is initiating the remote control session.

▶ **Allow blanking user's screen** — This option causes the screen on the remote desktop to be blanked, preventing the end-user from seeing what is being done by the administrator to their workstation. When you enable the blanking of the screen, the keyboard and mouse are automatically locked.

▶ **Allow locking user's keyboard and mouse** — With this option checked, when the administrator remote controls the workstation the keyboard and the mouse on the remote workstation are deactivated. The end-user may move the mouse or keyboard, but they will not function and any input from them will be ignored.

View Tab

This tab describes the feature enabling the remote view functions. Remote view is the ability for the administrator to view the remote Windows screen of the target machine but not be able to control the mouse or keyboard of the machine.

▶ **Enable Remote View** — When this option is enabled, the remote view subsystem can be activated. Without this setting on no one may remote view the workstations where the currently logged in user has this policy associated with their user object.

▶ **Prompt user for permission to remote view** — This option causes a dialog box to be displayed on the end-user's machine when a remote view session is started. The end-user has the option of accepting or denying the remote view request. Within this dialog box the user is told who wants to remote view their machine and asks if this is approved. If the user denies the remote view session, then the session is terminated and the administrator cannot remote view the workstation.

▶ **Give user audible system when remote viewed** — This option provides the end- user a tone periodically while the remote view session is active. You can also set the number of seconds between each beep.

▶ **Give user visible signal when remote viewed** — This option displays
a dialog box on the end-user's desktop while the remote view session
is active. The dialog box displays that the workstation is being remote
viewed and also displays the NDS name of the user that is remote viewing the workstation. You can set the number of seconds that you want to
have between flashing the name of the user that is initiating the remote
view session.

File Transfer Tab

This tab describes the feature enabling the file transfer system. This allows
you, the administrator, to send files to the remote workstation.

▶ **Enable File Transfer** — When this option is enabled, the file transfer
subsystem can be activated. Without this setting on no one may send
files to the workstations where the currently logged in user has this
policy associated with their user object.

▶ **Prompt user for permission to transfer files** — This option causes
a dialog box to be displayed on the end-user's machine when a file
transfer session is started. The end-user has the option of accepting or
denying the file transfer request. Within this dialog box the user is told
who wants to perform the file transfer from their machine and asks if
this is approved. If the user denies the file transfer session, then the
session is terminated and the administrator cannot send the files to
the workstation.

Remote Execute Tab

This tab describes the feature enabling of the remote execute system. This
allows you or the administrator to remotely execute a program on the remote
workstation. The output of the program is not displayed on the administrative
console.

▶ **Prompt user for permission to remote execute** — This option causes
a dialog box to be displayed on the end-user's machine when a remote
execute session is started. The end-user has the option of accepting or
denying the remote execute request. Within this dialog box the user
is told who wants to perform the request and asks if this is approved.
If the user denies the remote execution session, then the session is
terminated and the administrator cannot execute the program on the
workstation.

User Extensible Policies

Microsoft has required that software packages that bear the Windows approved logo provide abilities to be configured through .POL files. The poledit program allows you to edit these "extensible policies" and include them into the system .POL file. ZENworks also allows the policies that are stored in NDS to accept these additional "extensible polices" and provide them to all of the users that are associated with these policies.

The User Extensible policy allows you to import these special .ADM files into the NDS tree and have them administered and dispersed to the users associated with the policy package. Once these .ADM files have been imported into the tree they can be administrated and associated to users in the NDS tree. These settings are applied like the User System Policies.

User Extensible Policies Page

When you first bring up the User Extensible Policies dialog you are presented with the User Extensible Policies page. An example of this page is displayed in Figure 7.11.

FIGURE 7.11   *User Extensible Policies page of the User Extensible Policies policy*

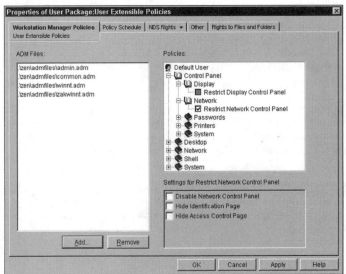

This page is split into three areas: ADM files, Policies, Policy specific window at the bottom-right corner.

The files listed in the ADM file list are the policies that are applied to the users associated with this policy. To add a policy file to the list simply press the "Add" button and you are presented with a file dialog box where you can browse and select the file. Remember that this file should reside on the server, as it is stored there for retrieval by the policy managers. When you browse and select a file make sure it is on the server, and that the drive that you use is mapped correctly for all users that would be associated with the policy. You can enter a UNC path in the file name field of the dialog box and thereby get a UNC path for the ADM file, however if you browse and then select, then the program puts a drive letter into the path necessitating that each user has the same drive mapping.

When this policy is initialized, four .ADM files are automatically pulled in by the plug-in into ConsoleOne. These include admin.adm, common.adm, winnt.adm, zakwinnt.adm. Each of these files are stored in the ConsoleOne\bin\zen\admfiles directory and are considered the default packages that will be used.

NOTE

The .ADM file must be stored on a server that users can access. The policy references the .ADM file and needs to retrieve it to apply it to the users and to allow the administrators to modify the settings. It would be recommended, therefore, to use a UNC path in specifying the location of the file.

You delete the .ADM file from the applied set by selecting the file and pressing the Remove button.

You can also modify the settings of the .ADM files by selecting the file in the ADM files windows. When you select the file, its registry content is displayed in the Policies window. The user interface for this window mimics the poledit program that is available from Microsoft. The small window underneath the Policies box displays information about the selected registry setting along with any subsetting categories that are available with the specific key. Selecting the key in the policies window populates the details fields.

You can browse through the ADM files and turn on (checked), turn off (unchecked and white), or leave as set in the registry (unchecked and grey) for each of the keys as you would in the poledit program. Once you have made your changes, then press "Apply" or "OK" to update the ADM files on the server.

NDS Rights, Other, and Rights to Files and Folders pages are described in the Creating a User Policy Package section.

Policy Schedule Page

The policy schedule page allows you to customize (outside of the package default schedule) when you want the ADM files applied to the workstation/desktop of the user.

This page allows you to select when the package should be applied: Event, Daily, Weekly, Monthly, or Yearly.

Once you have selected when you want the package applied, then you have additional fields to select in the lower portion of the screen. The following sections discuss the various options you have with scheduling the package.

Event

When you choose to have the ADM files applied upon an event that occurs in the workstation, then you have the additional need to select which event affects the changes.

The events that you can select are one of the following:

- ▶ **User Login** — This causes the policies to be applied when the user logs into the system. This happens after they enter their username and password, but before their desktop is shown and the user login scripts have started.

- ▶ **User Desktop is Active** — This runs the policies after the user has logged into the system and all login scripts have been completed, but before their desktop is displayed. This is available with Windows NT/2000 only.

- ▶ **Workstation is Locked** — This causes the policies to be applied when the workstation is locked (such as when the screen saver is activated and is locked awaiting a password). This is available with Windows NT/2000 only.

- ▶ **Workstation is UnLocked** — This runs the policies when the workstation becomes unlocked, after the user has supplied their password to unlock the system. This is available with Windows NT/2000 only.

- ▶ **Screen Saver is Activated** — This runs the policies when the screen saver is activated on an idle system.

- ▶ **User Logout** — This applies the policies when the user logs out of the system.

- ▶ **System Shutdown** — This applies the policies when a system shutdown is requested.

Daily

When you choose to have the ADM files applied daily on the workstation, you have the additional need to select when the changes are made.

This schedule requires that you select the days when you want the policy applied. You select the days by clicking on the days you desire. The selected days appear as depressed buttons.

In addition to the days, you can select the times the policies are applied. These times, the start and stop times, provide a range of time where the policies will be applied.

To keep all workstations from simultaneously accessing the servers, you can select the "Randomly dispatch policy during time period." This causes each workstation to choose a random time within the time period when they retrieve and apply the policy.

You can have the policy also reapplied to each workstation within the timeframe every specified hour/minute/second by clicking on the Repeat the action every field and specify the time delay. This results in a scheduled action being run on every associated user's workstation for the selected repeat time.

Weekly

You can alternately choose that the policies be applied only weekly.

In the weekly screen you choose on which day of the week you wish the policy to be applied. When you select a day, any other selected day is unselected. Once you have selected the day, you can also select the time range when the policy may be applied.

To keep all workstations from simultaneously accessing the servers, you can select the Randomly dispatch policy during time period. This causes each workstation to choose a random time within the time period when they retrieve and apply the policy.

Monthly

Under the monthly schedule you can select on which day of the month the policy should be applied, or you can select Last day of the month to handle the last day because all months obviously do not end on the same calendar date (thirty days hath September, April, June, and November, all the rest have thirty-one except for February . . .).

Once you have selected the day, you can also select the time range when the policy may be applied.

To keep all workstations from simultaneously accessing the servers, you can select the Randomly dispatch policy during time period. This causes each workstation to choose a random time within the time period when they will retrieve and apply the policy.

Yearly

You would select a yearly schedule if you want to apply the policies only once a year.

On the yearly page you must choose the day that you wish the policies to be applied. This is done by selecting the calendar button to the right of the Date: field. This brings up a monthly dialog box where you can browse through the calendar to select the date you wish to choose for your policies to be applied. This calendar does not correspond to any particular year and may not take into account leap years in its display. This is because you are choosing a date for each year that comes along in the present and future years.

Once you have selected the date, you can also select the time range when the policy may be applied.

To keep all workstations from simultaneously accessing the servers, you can select the Randomly dispatch policy during time period. This causes each workstation to choose a random time within the time period when they will retrieve and apply the policy.

Advanced Settings

On each of the scheduling pages you have the option of selecting the "Advanced Settings" button which allows you some additional control on the scheduled action that is placed on each user's workstation. Pressing the "Advanced Setting" button gives you a dialog page with several tabs to set the specifics details of the schedule.

When first displayed, the Completion tab is activated. The following sections describe each field on the tabs and how it relates to the action.

Completion   The completion dialog allows you to specify what should happen on the workstation once the scheduled action has completed. You can choose any of the following by selecting the check box next to the appropriate items:

▶ **Disable the action after completion** — This prevents the action from being rescheduled after completion. If you decide that the policy should be applied every hour, then choosing this turns off that action.

The policy will not be reapplied. This rescheduling only occurs and is reset when the user logs off and back onto the system.

▸ **Reboot after completion** — This causes the workstation to reboot after applying the policies.

▸ **Prompt the user before rebooting** — This allows the user to be prompted before rebooting. The user can cancel the reboot.

Fault   This dialog tab allows you to specify what should occur if the scheduled action fails in its completion.

The following choices are available to failed actions:

▸ **Disable the action** — This results in the action being disabled and not rescheduled or rerun.

▸ **Retry every minute** — This attempts to rerun the action every minute despite the schedule that may have been specified in the policy.

▸ **Ignore the error and reschedule normally** — This assumes that the action ran normally, and reschedules the action according to the policy.

Impersonation   These settings allow you to specify the account that should be used when running the action.

The following choices are available for the user type that is used to run the scheduled item:

▸ **Interactive user** — This runs the action with the rights of the currently logged in user. This should be used if it is acceptable to run this action and not have access to the secure portions of the registry, as most local users do not have access to the secured portions of the registry or file system.

▸ **System** — This runs the action in the background with administrative privileges. This impersonation level should be used only if the action has no user interface and requires no interaction with the user.

▸ **Unsecure system** — This runs the action as a system described above, but allows user interaction. This is only available on Windows NT and 2000 and should be used cautiously because normally NT does not allow a cross-over between user and system space.

Priority   This tab allows you to specify at which level you want the action to run on the workstation.

The following choices are available within the priority schedule:

- **Below Normal** — This schedules the actions at a priority that is below the normal user activity. This level does not interfere with the behavior of the system and gives the user a normal experience.

- **Normal** — This schedules the action at the same level as any user activity. This can cause the workstation to perform at a slower level because the service is competing with the user for resources.

- **Above Normal** — This level schedules the action at a higher priority than the user requests and results in being completed before user activity, such as mouse and keyboard input, is serviced by the system.

Time Limit   This tab of the scheduled advanced settings allows you to specify how long the service should be allowed to run before it is terminated. This can be used to protect yourself from having the action run for long periods of time on the workstation. This terminates the action, which may cause the action to not complete properly. This tab is not normally used because you usually want the action to fully complete.

Windows 2000 Group Policy

With Windows 2000 and Active Directory, Microsoft introduced the Group Policy to their servers. This policy can be applied to a set of users that are part of a container or a sub-container in Active Directory. Novell ZENworks for Desktops 3 has now incorporated this Group Policy into ZENworks and introduced a new policy to apply this policy to any group, user, or container in the tree.

The Microsoft Group Policy is nothing more than another .ADM file that is applied to all the users in the container — in Novell's case users associated with this policy via direct association, group association, or container association.

Figure 7.12 displays a sample screen of this policy.

This policy allows you to browse to the group policy ADM file (the default policy file for the Windows 2000 group policy is the default). You can then press the "Edit" button to launch the poledit program on the local administrator workstation to edit this group policy.

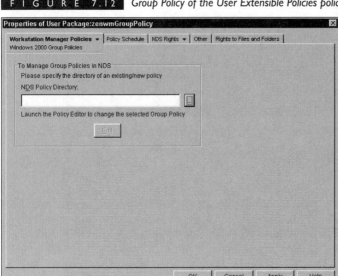

F I G U R E 7 . 1 2 *Group Policy of the User Extensible Policies policy*

NDS Rights, Other, *and* Rights to Files and Folders pages are described in the Creating a User Policy Package section. The Policy Schedule page is described in the User Extensible Policy section.

Windows Terminal Server Policy

For a greater compatibility between ZENworks for Desktops 3 and other systems, ZENworks has included a new policy that allows you to administer your users interaction and the behavior of Terminal Server available on Microsoft servers.

NDS Rights, Other, *and* Rights to Files and Folders pages are described in the "Creating a User Policy Package" section.

The following figure (Figure 7.13) displays a sample page of this policy.

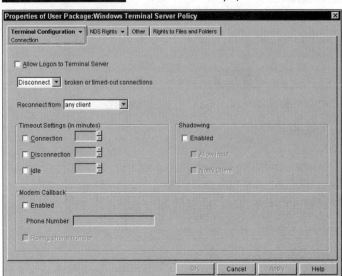

In this policy you may administer the various aspects of the Terminal Server. The following may be administered:

- ► **Allow login to terminal server** — This allows associated users the ability to log into the terminal server system.

- ► **Broken or timed-out connections** — You may cause the system to disconnect these broken connections or choose to reset the connection.

- ► **Reconnect from** — This allows you to choose if the reconnection should be done from any available client on the terminal server or from the previous client (the one that timed-out).

- ► **Timeout Settings** — Here you are able to set the time in minutes for each of the connection times, disconnect timeout and idle timeout times.

- ► **Shadowing** — These fields allow you to enable or disable shadowing on the terminal server along with the options to allow input and to notify the client when shadowing is enabled.

- ► **Modem Callback** — This allows you to enable modem callback and administer the phone numbers to use.

## CHAPTER 8

Setting up a Workstation Policy Package

This chapter discusses the use and creation of Workstation policies. Workstation policies are associated with workstations and workstation groups, and affect their working environment.

▶ • ◀

Relationship of Workstation Policies to Workstations

Workstations are associated with Workstation Policies through associations with policies in any of three ways: 1) Policies can be associated with the workstation object directly; 2) Policies can be associated with a parent container of the workstation object; and 3) Policies can be associated with a workstation group to which the workstation is a member.

The ZENworks for Desktops 3 Workstation Manager agent is activated on a workstation at user login time for Windows 95 and Windows 98 systems, and on Windows NT and Windows 2000 systems it is activated when the service is started. Once the ZENworks for Desktops 3 Workstation Manager agent is activated, it logs into the tree as the workstation and walks up the tree looking for the first Workstation Policy Package it can find that is associated with the workstation. Like all ZENworks for Desktops 3 agents, the order that the tree is searched is dependent on standard Novell Directory Services behavior and any Search Policies that may be in the tree. All of the applicable workstation policies are merged together and then the culmination is applied to the workstation. If any conflicts occur with the policies (such as two Workstation policies both affecting the same parameter) then the parameter setting in the first policy found will be applied.

The remote control policy can be created for both the user and the workstation. In the instances when a remote control policy exists for both the user and the workstation, then the remote control subsystem takes the most restrictive combination of the policies. For example, if one policy says to prompt the user for permission and the other does not — then the system prompts the user.

▶ • ◀

Advantages of Platform Specific Policies

ZENworks for Desktops 3 enables the administration of specific policies for each platform that is supported in the ZENworks for Desktops 3 system. By having a policy that is categorized for each type of platform, the administrator can make unique policies for each system. Regardless of the users that are logged into the system, each workstation finds the policies associated with it and executes the administrative configurations for that platform.

Occasions exist in which you may want to associate a particular, unique policy to a set of workstations that may be held in containers along with other workstations of the same type. You can then create a group of workstations and associate specific policies to those workstations. Consequently, these workstations receive the policies from this group rather than from the container.

Setting up a Workstation Policy Package

In order to have a Workstation policy package, you must first create the policy package. To create a Workstation policy package do the following:

1. Start ConsoleOne.

2. Browse to the container where you would like to have the policy package. Remember that you do not have to create the policy package in the container where you are doing the associations. You can associate the same policy package to many containers in your tree.

3. Create the policy package by clicking the right mouse button and choosing New ⇨ Policy Package or by selecting the Policy Package icon on the toolbar.

4. Select the Workstation Policy Package object in the wizard panel and press Next.

5. Enter the desired name of the package in the Policy Package Name field and select the container where you want the package to located. The container field is already filled in with the selected container so you should not have to browse to complete this field. If it is not, then press the browser button next to the field, browse to, and select the container where you want the policy object stored. Press Next.

6. Select the Define Additional Attributes field in order to go into the properties of your new object and activate some policies. Press Finish.

7. Check and set any policies you desire for this Workstation Policy package and press OK.

The following subsections describe each of the fields and property pages that are available in the Workstation Policy package.

Policies Property Page

All of the policies for users are activated within the Policies property page. Initially the page is on the general policies. As other platforms are selected additional policies are displayed. You can select which platform to display by placing the mouse over the small triangle to the right of the word Policies in the tab. This activates a drop-down menu that enables you to select which platform specific page you wish to display.

The following sections discuss briefly each of the policy pages and then we cover the specifics of each policy.

General Policies

When you first go into the properties of the Workstation policy package you are presented with the Policy Property page. The policy page first displays the general category. All of the policies that are activated in the general category are active for ALL workstation platforms supported by ZENworks for Desktops 3 and associated to the workstation.

Figure 8.1 is a snapshot of the initial property page of the workstation policy package.

FIGURE 8.1 *Workstation Policy Package policies general property page*

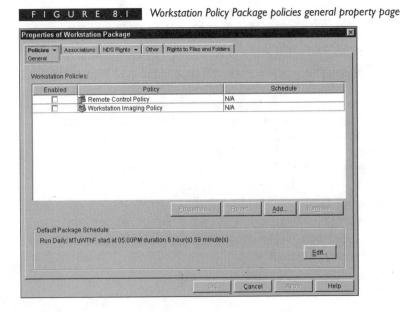

As you can see from the image, currently two policies exist that are available to all of the platforms supported by ZENworks for Desktops 3. They include the Remote Control Policy and the Workstation Imaging Policy. These, as well as all of the other policies, are discussed later in this chapter.

In order to activate a policy you simply need to check the box to the left of the policy by clicking on the box with the left mouse button. You can then go into the details of the policy and set additional configuration parameters on that specific policy.

Windows NT-2000 Policies

Within the policies tab you can select the Windows NT-2000 policy page. This page displays the policies that are available for Windows NT and Windows 2000 workstations. These policies include Computer Extensible Policies, NT Client Policy, NT Computer Printer policy, NT RAS Config Policy, Remote Control Policy, Workstation Imaging Policy, Workstation Inventory policy, WS Restrict Login Policy, and Windows 2000 Group Policy. See Figure 8.2 for a sample of the Windows NT-2000 policies page.

▶ · ◀

FIGURE 8.2 *Workstation Policy Package, Windows NT-2000 policies property page*

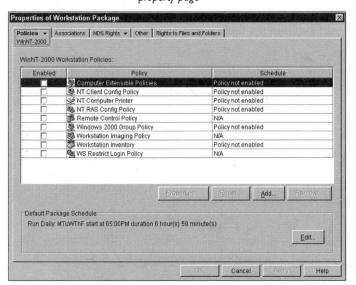

As you can see the same policies are both under the General and the Windows NT-2000 policies page. When you select a policy in the Windows NT-2000 page it supercedes any selections that may have been on the general tab for that platform. The policies are not merged together, and only the platform specific policy is used instead of the policy set in the general category. Also, only the policies selected in the platform specific tab are used in place of the general policies. For example, if the Workstation Import policy is selected in the general tab and in the Windows NT-2000 tab, then agents on a Windows 2000 system use the Windows NT-2000 Workstation Import policy rather than the policy in the general tab.

Win95-98 Policies

Within the policies tab you can select the Windows 95-98 policy page. This page displays the policies that are available for your Windows 95 and Windows 98 workstations. These policies include 95 Client Config Policy, 95 Computer Printer policy, 95 RAS Config Policy, Computer Extensible Policies, Remote Control Policy, Workstation Imaging Policy, Workstation Inventory policy, and WS Restrict Login Policy. See Figure 8.3 for a sample of the Win95-98 policies page.

▶ • ◀

FIGURE 8.3 *Workstation Policy Package, Win95-98 policies property page*

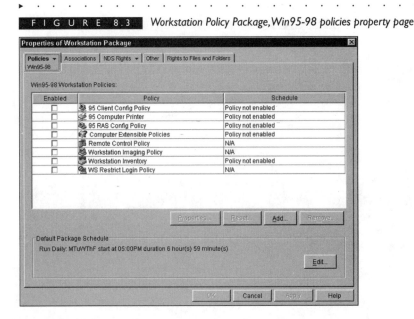

As you can see, the same policies are both under the General and the Win95-98 Policies page. When you select a policy in the Win95-98 page it supercedes any selections that may have been on the general tab for that platform. The policies are not merged together, and only the platform specific policy is used instead of the policy set in the general category. Also, only the policies selected in the platform specific tab are used in place of the general policies. For example, if the Workstation Inventory policy is selected in the general tab and in the Win95-98 tab, then agents on a Windows 95 and Windows 98 systems use the Windows 95-98 inventory policy and ignore the inventory policy under the general tab.

Associations Property Page

The Associations Page of the Workstation Policy Package displays all of the locations in the tree (containers) where the policy package has been associated. These associations do not necessarily reflect where the policy package is located in the directory. The agents that are associated with users or workstations that are in or below those containers have this policy package enforced. Pressing the Add or Remove buttons enables you to add or remove containers in the list that are associated with this policy.

NDS Rights Property Pages

The NDS Rights property page is made up of three pages. You can get to each of the pages by clicking on the small triangle to the right of the page name, and then selecting the desired page to be displayed.

These pages enable you to specify the rights that users have to this object in the directory. The following subsections discuss briefly each of these pages. These NDS Rights pages are displayed for every object in the tree.

Trustees of This Object Page

On this page you can assign objects rights as trustees of the Workstation Policy Package. These trustees have rights to this object or to attributes within this object.

If the user admin.novell has been added to the trustee list then this user has some rights to this object. To get into the details of any trustee assignment (in order to modify the assignment) you would need to press the Assigned Rights button.

When you press the Assign Rights button, after selecting the user you want to modify you are presented with a dialog box that enables you to select either [All Attribute Rights] (meaning all of the attributes of the object) or [Entry Rights] (meaning the object, not implying rights to the attributes).

From within the assigned rights dialog box you are able to set the rights the object may have on this package. You can set those rights on the object as well as any individual property in the object. The rights that are possible are the following:

- **Browse** — Although not in the list this right shows up from time to time (especially in the effective rights screens). This represents the ability to view this information through public browse capabilities.

- **Supervisor** — This identifies that the trustee has ALL rights, including delete for this object or attribute.

- **Compare** — This provides the trustee with the ability to compare values of attributes.

- **Read** — This enables the trustee to read the values of the attribute or attributes in the object.

- **Write** — This provides the trustee with the ability to modify the contents of an attribute.

- **Add Self** — This right enables the trustee to add themselves as a member to the list of objects of the attribute. For example, if this right were given on an attribute that contains a list of linked objects, then the trustee could add themselves (a reference to their object) into the list.

If you wish to add the object as a trustee to an attribute you would need to press the Add Property button to bring up a list of properties or attributes that are available for this object.

From this list you may select a single attribute. This attribute is then displayed in the assigned rights dialog box. From there you can select the attribute and then set the rights you want the trustee to have for that property. A user does not require object rights in order to have rights on a single attribute in the object.

Remember that rights flow down in the tree, and if you give a user or an object rights at a container level then those rights continue down into that container and any sub-containers until that branch is exhausted, or another explicit assignment is given for that user in a sub-container or on an object. An explicit assignment changes the rights for the user at that point in the tree. Inheritance Rights Filters may also be placed to restrict this flow of rights down into the tree.

Inherited Rights Filters Page

This page enables you to set the IRF (Inheritance Rights Filter) for this object. This filter restricts the rights of any user that accesses this object, unless that user has an explicit trustee assignment for this object.

You can think of the IRF as a filter that lets only items checked pass through unaltered. Rights that bump up against an IRF filter are blocked and discarded if the item is NOT checked. For example, if a user who had write privileges inherited at some point above (they were explicitly granted that right at some container at or above the one we're in) were to run into an IRF for an object or attribute that has the write privilege revoked (that is, unchecked), then when they got to that object their write privilege would be gone for that object. If the object were a container, then they would loose write privileges for all objects in that container or sub-container.

You can effectively remove supervisor privileges to a portion of the tree by setting an IRF with the supervisor privilege turned off. You must be careful to not ever do this without someone being assigned as the supervisor of that branch of the tree (given an explicit supervisor trustee assignment at the container where the IRF is done) or this action makes that part of the tree permanent (that is, you will never be able to delete any objects in that branch of the tree). ConsoleOne helps keep you from performing this action by giving you an error dialog box that keeps you from putting an IRF on the [Entry Rights] of the object with the supervisor right filtered away without having first given an explicit supervisor assignment on the same container.

Effective Rights Page

The Effective Rights property page enables you to query the system to discover the rights that selected objects have on the object you are administering.

Within this page you are presented with the distinguished name (DN) of the object whose rights you wish to observe. Initially, this is your currently logged in user running ConsoleOne. You can press the browse button to the right of the trustee field and browse throughout the tree to select any object.

When the trustee object is selected you may then move to the properties table on the lower half of the screen. As you select the property, the rights box to the right changes its text to reflect the rights that the trustee has on that property. These rights may be via an explicit assignment or through inheritance.

Other Property Page

This page may or may not be displayed for you, depending on your rights to the plug-in that now comes with ConsoleOne. This page is particularly powerful and should not be used by those who do not have an intimate knowledge of the schema of the object in question and its relationships with other objects in the directory. The intention of this property page is to give you generic access to properties that you cannot modify or view via the other plugged-in pages. The attributes and their values are displayed in a tree structure, enabling for those attributes that have multiple types (are compound types that consist of, say, an int and a distinguished name or postal code that has three separate address fields).

Every attribute in eDirectory is defined by one of a specified set of syntaxes. These syntaxes identify how the data is stored in eDirectory. For this page, ConsoleOne has developed an editor for each of the different syntaxes that are currently available in eDirectory. When an attribute is displayed on this page the editor is invoked to display the data and then modify it should the user click the specific attribute.

For example, if the syntax for an attribute were a string or an integer, then an in-line editor is launched, enabling the administrator to modify the string or the integer value on the screen. More abstract syntaxes, such as octet-string, require that an octet editor be launched giving the administrator access to each of the bytes in the string, without interpretation of the data.

The danger with this screen is that some applications require that there be a coordination of attribute values between two attributes within the same object or across multiple objects. Additionally, many applications assume that the data in the attribute is valid, because the normal user interface checks for invalid entries and does not allow them to be stored in the attribute. If you should change a data value in the other page, then no knowledge of related attributes, objects, or valid data values are checked, because the generic editors know nothing about the intention of the field. Should you change a value without making all the other appropriate changes, or without putting in a valid value, then some programs *and* the system could be affected.

Rights are still in effect in the Other property page and you are not enabled to change any attribute values that are read-only or you do not have rights to modify.

Rights to Files and Folders Property Page

This page in the property book is present in all objects in the directory. This property page enables you to view and set rights for this object onto the volumes and specific files and folders on that volume.

You must first select the volume that contains the files and folders in which you are interested. You can do this by pressing the Show button on the right and then browsing the directory to the volume object. Selecting the volume object places it in the volumes view. When that volume is selected you can then go to the Add button to add a file or folder of interest. This brings up a dialog box enabling you to browse to the volume object; then clicking on the volume object moves you into the file system. You can continue browsing that volume until you select the file or directory to which you are interested in granting rights.

Selecting the file or folder in the lower pane displays the rights that the object has been granted on that file or folder. To modify the rights simply click on or off the rights that you want to have explicitly granted for the object.

You can also see the effective rights that the object has on the files by pressing the Effective rights button. This displays a dialog box, enabling you to browse to any file in the volume and having the effective rights displayed (in bold) for the object. These effective rights include any explicit plus inherited rights from folders higher in the file system tree. Remember that anyone who has supervisor rights to the server or volume objects automatically gets supervisor rights in the file system.

95 Client Config Policy

A 95 Client Configuration Policy is activated for this policy package by selecting the check box on the Novell Client Configuration Policy. Once this is selected and a check is displayed in the check box, then this 95/98 Client Configuration Policy is activated for all Windows 95 and Windows 98 workstations that are associated with this policy package.

This policy enables you, the administrator, to control the client configurations for all of these workstations from a single policy. Previously one had to visit each individual workstation to make all of these settings. From this one policy all client configurations may be administered and made effective the next time that a user logs into the system.

From this policy you can administer all of the various components of the Novell Client. We are not discussing all of the various pages and the attributes you can administer. Suffice it to say that you can administer all of the parameters of the client, much like handling client properties on the workstation.

NOTE

You can administer the client configuration pages but they will NEVER be distributed until you mark fields as Distribute always. Some fields on each page have a right-mouse pop-up menu that displays choices such as Distribute always, Distribute never, Distribute always (replace), Distribute always (append). This pop-up menu can be on any field or value and signals to you that it is being distributed by bolding the field or value. We'll try to point out where these are as we describe the fields. This makes the policy very flexible and granular, but also makes the policy difficult to administer.

We discuss the Workstation Manage Page, as that is the agent that handles ZENworks for Desktops 3 tasks on the workstation.

NDS Rights, Other, *and* Rights to Files and Folders pages are described in the "Setting up a Workstation Policy Package" section. The Policy Schedule page is described in the "Computer Extensible Policy" section.

Workstation Manager Page

The workstation manager page enables you to manage the workstation manager agent that supports the ZENworks for Desktop 3 policies on the workstation. The following is a picture of this page (Figure 8.4).

Checking the Enable check box activates the Workstation Manager agent on the workstation and then begins the process of parsing policies and applying them to users and the workstation.

NDS refresh rate has to do with the number of minutes that the agent waits to start a cycle of refreshing its policies. The agent needs to connect to the NDS tree, as the workstation, and walk the tree to discover any workstation policies or actions that need to be scheduled for the workstation. You need to be aware that this time should be carefully considered. If you have a significant number of workstations and they are all attempting to walk the NDS tree every few minutes then the login and response times of the network are dramatically reduced. You should attempt to have this number be as large as is reasonable to pull policies down. Currently the default is every 9 hours (540 minutes).

▶ . . . . ◀

95 Computer Printer Policy

This policy enables the administrator to set up network printers onto the local Windows 95 desktop. In order to add printers to the policy you must have already set up some printers into your NetWare system and have corresponding printer and print queue objects in your Novell Directory Services tree (see Figure 8.5).

NDS Rights, Other, and Rights to Files and Folders pages are described in the "Setting up a Workstation Policy Package" section. The Policy Schedule page is described in the "Computer Extensible Policy" section.

Perform the following steps to add a printer to the printer policy:

I. Press the Add button.

2. Browse through the dialog box and select the Printer or Print Queue object that you want to deliver to the users associated with the policy.

To remove a printer from the policy, simply highlight the printer from the list and then press the Remove button.

Any printers that have been added to this list are added to the user's desktop automatically when they first log into the system. When the printer is removed from this list then the printer is removed from the local system account the next time that the user logs into the workstation.

F I G U R E 8.4 *Workstation Manager page of 95 Client Configuration Policy of a sample Workstation Policy Package*

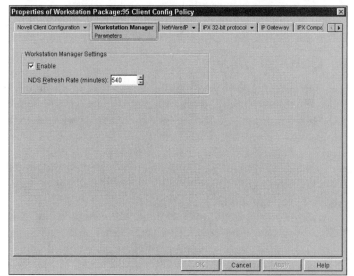

F I G U R E   8.5 *Windows 95 Computer Printer policy of the Workstation Policy package*

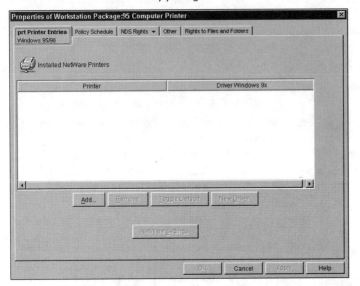

95 RAS Config Policy

The RAS Configuration Policy enables a workstation to dial into a network and establish a connection before any action is executed. The workstation itself may have some dial-up numbers that have already been defined with the local Windows Dial-up Networking utilities. These local numbers are not administered with this policy. Figure 8.6 displays the Dial-Up Networking page.

NDS Rights, Other, *and* Rights to Files and Folders pages are described in the "Setting up a Workstation Policy Package" section. The Policy Schedule page is described in the "Computer Extensible Policy" section.

This page enables the administrator to create numbers to be used in dialing up servers in the network. To create a new dial-up entry perform the following:

1. Select the New... button. This causes a dialog to come up that enables you to administer this new entry.

2. Within the Basic tab enter an Entry name and the phone number in the appropriate fields.

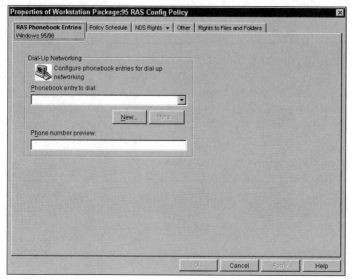

Dial-Up Networking page of a Windows 95/98 RAS Configuration Policy within the Workstation Policy package

3. If you wish to affect the Country code and Area codes, then check the Use Telephony dialing properties check box. This enables these fields so that you can select a country code and enter in the area code for the number.

4. Proceed to the Server tab and complete the administration by entering the fields for Dial-up server type, protocols, and so on.

The More button provides the ability to edit or delete the specific phonebook entries that have been entered into the policy. You must first select the entry in the phonebook that you wish to modify. This can be done by selecting the drop-down list under the entry to dial and selecting the entry to modify or delete. The number that is displayed in the preview is the number that has been administered for the current selection.

Computer Extensible Policies

Microsoft has required that software packages that bear the Windows approved logo provide abilities to be configured through .POL files. The poledit program enables you to edit these extensible policies and include them into the system .POL file. ZENworks also enables the policies that are stored in NDS to accept these additional extensible polices and provide them to all of the users that are associated with these policies.

The User Extensible policy enables you to import these special .ADM files into the NDS tree and have them administered and dispersed to the users associated with the policy package. Once these .ADM files have been imported into the tree they can be administrated and associated to users in the NDS tree. These settings are applied like the User System Policies.

NDS Rights, Other, *and* Rights to Files and Folders pages are described in the "Setting up a Workstation Policy Package" section.

Computer Extensible Policies Page

When you first bring up the Computer Extensible Policies dialog you are presented with the Computer Extensible Policies page. An example of this page is displayed in Figure 8.7.

F I G U R E   8 . 7   *Computer Extensible Policies page of the User Extensible Policies policy*

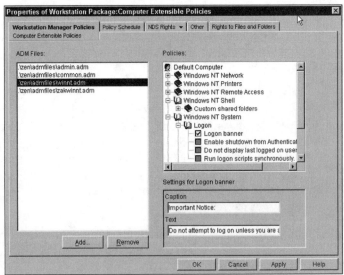

This page is split into three areas: ADM files, Policies, Policy specific window at the bottom-right corner.

The files listed in the ADM file list are the policies that are applied to the users associated with this policy. To add a policy file to the list simply press the Add button and you are presented with a file dialog box where you can browse and select the file. Remember that this file should reside on the server, as it is stored there for retrieval by the policy managers. When you browse and select a file make sure it is on the server, and that the drive that you use is mapped correctly for all users that would be associated with the policy. You can enter a UNC path in the filename field of the dialog box and thereby get a UNC path for the ADM file, however, if you browse and then select, then the program puts a drive letter into the path necessitating that each user have the same drive mapping.

When this policy is initialized, four .ADM files are automatically pulled in by the plug-in into ConsoleOne. These include admin.adm, common.adm, winnt.adm, zakwinnt.adm. Each of these files is stored in the ConsoleOne\bin\ zen\admfiles directory and they are considered the default packages to be used.

NOTE

The .ADM file must be stored on a server on which users have access. The policy references the .ADM file and needs to retrieve it to apply it to the users and to enable the administrators to modify the settings. It would be recommended, therefore, to use a UNC path in specifying the location of the file.

You delete the .ADM file from the applied set by selecting the file and pressing the Remove button.

You can also modify the settings of the .ADM files by selecting the file in the ADM files windows. When you select the file its registry content is displayed in the Policies window. The user interface for this window mimics the poledit program that is available from Microsoft. The small window underneath the Policies box displays information about the selected registry setting along with any subsetting categories that are available with the specific key. Selecting the key in the policies window, by double-clicking, populates this details field.

You can browse through the ADM files and turn on (checked), turn off (unchecked and white), or leave as set in the registry (unchecked and gray) for each of the keys as you would in the poledit program. Once you have made your changes, then press Apply or OK to update the ADM files on the server.

Policy Schedule Page

The policy schedule page enables you to customize (outside of the package default schedule) when you want the ADM files applied to the workstation/desktop of the user.

This page enables you to select when the package should be applied: Event, Daily, Weekly, Monthly, or Yearly.

Once you have selected when you want the package applied, then you have additional fields to select in the lower portion of the screen. The following sections discuss the various options you have with scheduling the package.

Event

When you choose to have the ADM files applied upon an event that occurs in the workstation, then you have the additional need to select which event affects the changes.

The events that you can select are one of the following:

► **User Login** — This causes the policies to be applied when the user logs into the system. This happens after they enter their username and password, but before their desktop is shown and the user login scripts have started.

► **User Desktop is Active** — This runs the policies after the user has logged into the system and all login scripts have been completed but before their desktop is displayed. This is available with Windows NT/2000 only.

► **Workstation is Locked** — This causes the policies to be applied when the workstation is locked (such as when the screen saver is activated and is locked awaiting a password). This is available with Windows NT/2000 only.

► **Workstation is UnLocked** — This runs the policies when the workstation becomes unlocked, after the user has supplied their password to unlock the system. This is available with Windows NT/2000 only.

► **Screen Saver is Activated** — This runs the policies when the screen saver is activated on an idle system.

► **User Logout** — This applies the policies when the user logs out of the system.

► **System Shutdown** — This applies the policies when a system shutdown is requested.

Daily

When you choose to have the ADM files applied daily on the workstation, then you have the additional need to select when the changes are made.

This schedule requires that you select the days when you want the policy applied. You select the days by clicking on the days you desire. The selected days appear as depressed buttons.

In addition to the days, you can select the times the policies are applied. These times, the start and stop times, provide a range of time where the policies will be applied.

To keep all workstations from simultaneously accessing the servers, you can select the Randomly dispatch policy during time period. This causes each workstation to choose a random time within the time period when they will retrieve and apply the policy.

You can have the policy also reapplied to each workstation within the timeframe every specified hour/minute/second by clicking on the Repeat the action every field and specify the time delay. This results in a scheduled action being run on every associated user's workstation for the selected repeat time.

Weekly

You can alternately choose that the policies be applied only weekly.

In this screen you choose which day of the week you wish the policy to be applied. When you select a day, any other selected day is unselected. Once you have selected the day, then you can also select the time range when the policy may be applied.

To keep all workstations from simultaneously accessing the servers, you can select the Randomly dispatch policy during time period. This causes each workstation to choose a random time within the time period when they retrieve and apply the policy.

Monthly

Under the monthly schedule you can select which day of the month the policy should be applied or you can select Last day of the month to handle the last day because all months obviously do not end on the same calendar date (thirty days hath September, April, June, and November, all the rest have thirty-one except for February ...).

Once you have selected the day, then you can also select the time range when the policy may be applied.

To keep all workstations from simultaneously accessing the servers, you can select the Randomly dispatch policy during time period. This causes each workstation to choose a random time within the time period when they will retrieve and apply the policy.

Yearly

You would select a yearly schedule if you want to apply the policies only once a year.

On this screen you must choose the day that you wish the policies to be applied. This is done by selecting the calendar button to the right of the Date: field. This brings up a monthly dialog box where you can browse through the calendar to select the date you wish to choose for your policies to be applied. This calendar does not correspond to any particular year and may not take into account leap years in its display. This is because you are choosing a date for each year that will come along in the present and future years.

Once you have selected the date, then you can also select the time range in which the policy may be applied.

To keep all workstations from simultaneously accessing the servers, you can select the Randomly dispatch policy during time period. This causes each workstation to choose a random time within the time period in which they will retrieve and apply the policy.

Advanced Settings

On each of the scheduling pages you have the option of selecting the Advanced Setting button which allows you some additional control on the scheduled action that is placed on each user's workstation.

When first displayed, the Completion tab is activated. The following sections describe each field on the tabs and how it relates to the action.

Completion   The completion dialog enables you to specify what should happen on the workstation once the scheduled action has completed. You can choose any of the following by selecting the check box next to the appropriate items:

- ▶ **Disable the action after completion** — This stops the action from being rescheduled after completion. If you chose to apply the policy every hour, then choosing this turns off that action. The policy is not reapplied. This rescheduling only occurs and is reset when the user logs off and back onto the system.

- ▶ **Reboot after completion** — This causes the workstation to reboot after applying the policies.

- ▶ **Prompt the user before rebooting** — This enables the user to be prompted before rebooting. The user can cancel the reboot.

Fault   This dialog tab enables you to specify what should occur if the scheduled action fails in its completion.

The following choices are available to failed actions:

- **Disable the action** — This results in the action being disabled and not rescheduled or rerun.

- **Retry every minute** — This attempts to rerun the action every minute despite the schedule that may have been specified in the policy.

- **Ignore the error and reschedule normally** — This assumes that the action ran normally and reschedules the action according to the policy.

Impersonation   These settings enable you to specify the account that should be used when running the action. The following choices are available for the user type that is used to run the scheduled item:

- **Interactive user** — This runs the action with the rights of the currently logged in user. This should be used if it is acceptable to run this action and not have access to the secure portions of the registry, as most local users do not have access to the secured portions of the registry or file system.

- **System** — This runs the action in the background with administrative privileges. This impersonation level should be used only if the action has no user interface and requires no interaction with the user.

- **Unsecure system** — This runs the action as a system described above but enables user interaction. This is only available on Windows NT and 2000 and should be used cautiously because normally NT does not allow a cross-over between user and system space.

Priority   This tab enables you to specify at which level you want the action to run on the workstation. The following choices are available within the priority schedule:

- **Below Normal** — This schedules the actions at a priority that is below the normal user activity. This level does not interfere with the behavior of the system and it gives the user a normal experience.

- **Normal** — This schedules the action at the same level as any user activity. This can cause the workstation to perform at a slower level because the service is competing with the user for resources.

► **Above Normal** — This level schedules the action at a higher priority than the user requests and results in being completed before user activity is serviced.

Time Limit   This tab of the scheduled advanced settings enables you to specify how long the service should be allowed to run before it is terminated. This can be used to protect yourself from having the action run for long periods of time on the workstation. Terminating the action, though, may prevent the action from completing properly. Therefore, because you usually want the action to fully complete, this tab is not normally used.

NT Client Config Policy

An NT Client Configuration Policy is activated for this policy package by selecting the check box on the Novell Client Configuration Policy. Once this is selected and a check is displayed in the check box, then this NT/2000 Client Configuration Policy is activated for all Windows NT and Windows 2000 workstations that are associated with this policy package.

This policy enables you, the administrator, to control the client configurations for all of these workstations from a single policy. Previously one had to visit each individual workstation to make all of these settings. From this one policy all client configurations may be administered and made effective the next time that a user logs into the system.

From this policy you can administer all of the various components of the Novell Client. We will not be discussing all of the various pages and the attributes you can administer. Suffice it to say that you can administer all of the parameters of the client, much like handling client properties on the workstation.

NOTE

You can administer the client configuration pages but they will NEVER be distributed until you mark fields as Distribute always. Some fields on each page have a right-mouse pop-up menu that displays choices such as Distribute always, Distribute never, Distribute always (replace), Distribute always (append). This pop-up menu can be on any field or value and signal to you that it is being distributed by bolding the field or value. We'll try to point out where these are as we describe the fields. This makes the policy very flexible and granular, but also makes the policy difficult to administer.

We will discuss the Workstation Manage Page, as that is the agent that handles ZENworks for Desktops 3 tasks on the workstation.

NDS Rights, Other, *and* Rights to Files and Folders pages are described in the "Setting up a Workstation Policy Package" section. The Policy Schedule page is described in the "Computer Extensible Policy" section.

Workstation Manager Page

The workstation manager page enables you to manage the workstation manager agent that supports the ZENworks for Desktop 3 policies on the workstation. The following is a picture of this page (Figure 8.8).

F I G U R E   8 . 8 *Workstation Manager page of an NT Client Configuration Policy of a sample Workstation Policy Package*

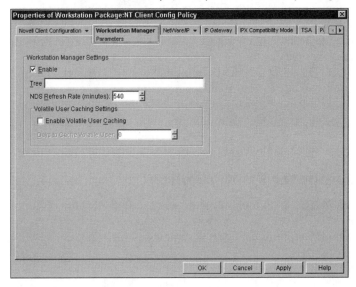

Checking the Enable check box activates the Workstation Manager agent on the workstation and then begins the process of parsing policies and applying them to users and the workstation.

The Tree field identifies the default tree for the workstation. It is expected that this tree is the tree where the workstation object is registered, or will be registered.

NDS refresh rate has to do with the number of minutes that the agent waits to start a cycle of refreshing its policies. The agent needs to connect to the NDS tree as the workstation and walk the tree to discover any workstation policies or actions that need to be scheduled for the workstation. You need to be aware that this time should be carefully considered. If you have a significant number of workstations and they are all attempting to walk the NDS tree every few minutes, then the login and response times of the network are going to be dramatically reduced. You should attempt to have the refresh rate be as large as is reasonable to pull policies down. Currently the default is every 9 hours (540 minutes).

Volatile use caching is the ability for the workstation to remove a local user account that was created automatically by the Workstation Manager agent when a user logged into the workstation. This account was created because of the Dynamic Local user capabilities of the WM agent (see Dynamic Local User Policy section in chapter 7, "Setting up User Policies."). This field enables you to activate volatile caching and then specify the number of days that an account should remain on the local machine before it is removed. The clock cycle starts over again the next time that the user logs into the machine. So basically, this is the length of time that an automatically created account remains idle on a workstation. You should take into account any security concerns you may have as you determine this time frame. Remember, while the local account is there the user may log into the workstation without connecting to the network.

► . . . . ◄

NT Computer Printer Policy

This policy enables the administrator to set up network printers onto the local Windows NT desktop. All workstations that are associated with this policy have these printers automatically set up in the Windows environment. In order to add printers to the policy you must have already set up some printers into your NetWare system and have corresponding printer and print queue objects in your Novell Directory Services tree. Figure 8.9 shows the policy screen.

NDS Rights, Other, *and* Rights to Files and Folders pages are described in the Setting up a Workstation Policy Package section. The Policy Schedule page is described in the Computer Extensible Policy section.

Perform the following steps to add a printer to the printer policy:

1. Press the Add button.

2. Browse through the dialog box and select the Printer or Print Queue object that you want to deliver to the users associated with the policy.

F I G U R E   8 . 9 *Windows NT User Printer policy of the Computer Policy package*

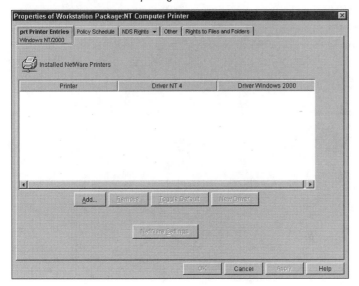

To remove a printer from the policy, simply highlight the printer from the list and then press the Remove button.

Any printers that have been added to this list are added to the user's desktop automatically when they first log into the system. When the printer is removed from this list, the printer is removed from the local system account the next time that the user logs into the workstation.

NT RAS Config Policy

The RAS Configuration Policy enables a workstation to dial into a network and establish a connection before any action is executed. The workstation itself may have some dial-up numbers that have already been defined with the local Windows Dial-up Networking utilities. These local numbers are not administered with this policy. Figure 8.10 displays the Windows 2000 Networking page.

You have the ability in this policy to configure separate RAS information for Windows NT and Windows 2000. Both pages are identical, but they only get applied to the specific type of workstations.

F I G U R E   8.10   *Dial-Up Networking administration page of a Windows NT/2000 RAS Configuration Policy within the Workstation Policy package*

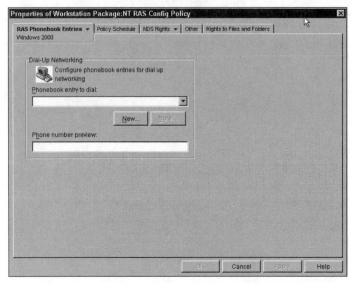

NDS Rights, Other, *and* Rights to Files and Folders pages are described in the Setting up a Workstation Policy Package section. The Policy Schedule page is described in the Computer Extensible Policy section.

This page enables the administrator to create numbers to be used in dialing up servers in the network. To create a new dial-up entry perform the following:

1. Select the New button. You are presented with a dialog box that enables you to administer this new entry.

2. Within the Basic tab enter an Entry name and the phone number in the appropriate fields.

3. If you wish to affect the Country code and Area codes, then check the Use Telephony dialing properties check box. This enables these fields so that you can select a country code and enter in the area code for the number.

4. Proceed to the Server tab and complete the administration by entering the fields for Dial-up server type, protocols, and so on.

The More button provides the ability to edit or delete the specific phone-book entries that have been entered into the policy. You must first select the entry in the phonebook that you wish to modify. This can be done by selecting the drop-down list under the entry to dial and selecting the entry to modify or delete. The number that is displayed in the preview is the number that has been administered for the current selection.

Remote Control Policy

A Remote Management Policy is activated for this policy package by select-ing the check box on the Remote Management Policy. Once this is selected and a check is displayed in the check box, then this Remote Management Policy is activated for all workstations associated with the Workstation Policy Package.

The Remote Management Policy controls the features of the Remote Management subsystem that is shipped with the ZENworks for Desktops 3 package and is not shipped with the ZENworks Starter Pack. The Remote Management system is comprised of two parts: Remote Management Session Manager that makes the connection and is used by the administrator, and the Remote Management Agents that are installed on the end-user's workstation. The remote control agents may be installed onto the workstation when the client that is shipped with ZENworks for Desktops 3 is installed or the agents may be installed on the workstation through the remote control application objects that were added to your tree when you installed ZENworks for Desktops 3. You would need to simply associate these application objects to the users or workstations and then have the ZENworks for Desktops 3 Application launcher install these agents automatically on the workstation. For more information, see Chapter 5, "Creating and Using Application Objects."

The Remote Management system makes a peer-to-peer connection between the administrator's workstation and the remote workstation. This may be done using either the IPX or the TCP/IP protocol. In this policy you may specify the preferred protocol for the connection. This protocol is attempted first, but if the connection cannot be made, then the alternate protocol is used.

Remote controlling a workstation via ZENworks for Desktops 3 also requires rights within the Workstation Object that represent the workstation wanting to be controlled. Without these rights the administrator is denied access to the remote control subsystem. Both the session manager and the agents validate that the user has rights to remote control the workstation. The way that you assign the remote control rights is through the Remote Management Rights wizard or in the workstation object in the Remote Operators page.

NDS Rights, Other, and Rights to Files and Folders pages are described in the "Setting up a Workstation Policy Package" section.

Remote Management Page

The Remote Management page identifies the features that you want to be activated with the Remote Management system. Figure 8.11 shows the Remote Management.

► · ◄

F I G U R E 8.11   *Remote Management Policy page, General tab of a Workstation Policy Package*

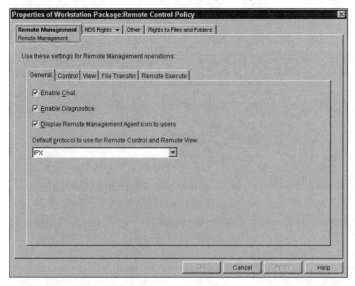

The following describes each of the options available under each tab of the Remote Management policy:

General Tab

This tab has options on general system functions.

► **Enable Chat** — This enables those who have this policy associated with them to accept a chat request. Chat sets up a communication system between the initiator and the receiver and enables them to type and send messages to one another.

▶ **Enable Diagnostics** — This enables the agent on the workstations to perform a diagnostics report. This can be done by selecting the workstation and then pressing the right mouse button and selecting Actions ⇨ Diagnostics of the menu. The Diagnostics utility performs some basic queries on the system and returns the information about the workstation. This information includes memory, environment, and processes running. Additionally, it would include NDS and Netware connection information, client information, network drives *and* open file list, as well as printers, Network protocols *and* network services active. Additionally, you can view the various event and error logs that have been recorded on that workstation.

▶ **Remote Control/View startup timeout for Console users** — This field enables the administrator to specify the number of minutes that they are willing to wait to establish a connection with the remote workstation. Once this time has expired, the connection attempt is abandoned. This does NOT have to do with the length of time that a connection is idle.

Control Tab

This tab describes the feature enabling of remote control functions.

▶ **Enable Remote Control** — When this option is enabled, then the remote control subsystem can be activated. Without this setting on, no one may remote control the workstations where the currently logged in user has this policy associated with their user object.

▶ **Prompt user for permission to remote control** — This option causes a dialog box to be displayed on the end-user's machine when a remote control session is started. The end-user has the option of accepting or denying the remote control request. Within this dialog box the user is told who wants to remote control their machine and asks if this is approved. If the user denies the remote control session, then the session is terminated and the administrator cannot remote control the workstation.

▶ **Give user audible system when remote controlled** — This option provides the end-user a tone, periodically, while the remote control session is active. You can also set the number of seconds between each beep.

▶ **Give user visible signal when remote controlled** — This option displays a dialog box on the end-user's desktop while the remote control session is active. The dialog box displays that the workstation is being remote controlled and also displays the NDS name of the user that is remote controlling the workstation. You can set the number of seconds that you want to have between flashing the name of the user that is initiating the remote control session.

▶ **Allow blanking user's screen** — This option causes the screen on the remote desktop to be blanked, preventing the end-user from seeing what is being done by the administrator to their workstation. When you enable the blanking of the screen, the keyboard and mouse are automatically locked.

▶ **Enable locking user's keyboard and mouse** — With this option checked, when the administrator remote controls the workstation the keyboard and the mouse on the remote workstation are deactivated. The end-user may move the mouse or keyboard, but they will not function and any input from them is ignored.

View Tab

This tab describes the feature enabling the remote view functions. Remote view is the ability for the administrator to view the remote Windows screen of the target machine but not be able to control the mouse or keyboard of the machine.

▶ **Enable Remote View** — When this option is enabled, the remote view subsystem can be activated. Without this setting on no one may remote view the workstations in which the currently logged in user has this policy associated with their user object.

▶ **Prompt user for permission to remote view** — This option causes a dialog box to be displayed on the end-user's machine when a remote view session is started. The end-user has the option of accepting or denying the remote view request. Within this dialog box the user is told who wants to remote view their machine and asks if this is approved. If the user denies the remote view session, then the session is terminated and the administrator cannot remote view the workstation.

▶ **Give user audible system when remote viewed** — This option provides the end- user a tone periodically while the remote view session is active. You can also set the number of seconds between each beep.

▶ **Give user visible signal when remote viewed** — This option displays a dialog box on the end-user's desktop while the remote view session is active. The dialog box displays that the workstation is being remote viewed and also displays the NDS name of the user that is remote viewing the workstation. You can set the number of seconds that you want to have between flashing the name of the user that is initiating the remote view session.

File Transfer Tab

This tab describes the feature enabling of the file transfer system. This enables you, the administrator, to send files to the remote workstation.

▶ **Enable File Transfer** — When this option is enabled, then the file transfer subsystem can be activated. Without this setting on no one may send files to the workstations where the currently logged in user has this policy associated with their user object.

▶ **Prompt user for permission to transfer files** — This option causes a dialog box to be displayed on the end-user's machine when a file transfer session is started. The end-user has the option of accepting or denying the file transfer request. Within this dialog box the user is told who wants to perform the file transfer from their machine and asks if this is approved. If the user denies the file transfer session, then the session is terminated and the administrator cannot send the files to the workstation.

Remote Execute Tab

This tab describes the feature enabling of the remote execute system. This enables you, the administrator, to remotely execute a program on the remote workstation. The output of the program is not displayed on the administrative console.

▶ **Prompt user for permission to remote execute** — This option causes a dialog box to be displayed on the end-user's machine when a remote execute session is started. The end-user has the option of accepting or denying the remote execute request. Within this dialog box the user is told who wants to perform the request and asks if this is approved. If the user denies the remote execution session, then the session is terminated and the administrator cannot execute the program on the workstation.

Windows 2000 Group Policy

With Windows 2000 and Active Directory, Microsoft introduced the Group Policy to their servers. This policy can be applied to a set of workstations that are part of a container or a sub-container in Active Directory. Novell ZENworks for Desktops 3 has now incorporated this Group Policy into ZENworks and introduced a new policy to apply this policy to any workstation group, workstation, or container in the tree.

The Microsoft Group Policy is nothing more than another .ADM file that is applied to all the users in the container — in Novell's case users associated with this policy via direct association, group association, or container association.

NDS Rights, Other, *and* Rights to Files and Folders pages are described in the Setting up a Workstation Policy Package section.

Figure 8.12 displays a sample screen of this policy.

F I G U R E   8.12
Windows 2000 Group Policy of the Workstation Policy package

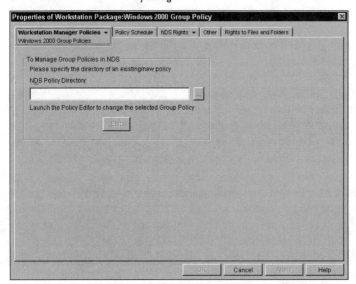

This policy enables you to browse to the group policy ADM file (the default policy file for the Windows 2000 group policy is the default). You can then press the Edit button to launch the poledit program on the local administrator workstation to edit this group policy.

Workstation Imaging Policy

New to ZENworks for Desktops 3 is the ability to image a workstation and then to apply that image back to the original or other workstations. See chapter 13, "Imaging a Workstation" for more detailed information on the functionality of the ZENworks for Desktops 3 imaging system.

The placement of an image, associated with an image object in the directory, onto a workstation may occur three different ways in ZENworks for Desktops 3.

1. Booting the workstation with a floppy disk that communicates with the imaging agent on the server.

2. Placing a special boot partition on an unregistered workstation that communicates with the imaging agent on the server.

3. Placing a special boot partition on a registered workstation and setting the Put an image on this workstation on the next boot field in the workstation object.

Each of these ways results in the workstation being imaged with the image associated with the workstation or determined by the imaging agent that resides on the server. The way that the workstation finds the imaging server is when the imaging boot diskettes are created, the administrator can specify either an IP or a DNS name for the server. This information is saved on the diskettes or in the special boot partition.

The Workstation Imaging Policy comes into effect if the workstation is to be imaged and there is NO image associated with the workstation object and the policy is activated.

This policy enables the administrator to create a set of rules that can govern when a particular image should be used, based on some basic information from the workstation. The imaging server follows the list of rules in the policy until one of the rules is satisfied. The rule that is satisfied results in an associated image that is then applied to the workstation.

Rules Page

This page enables the administrator to input the rules and associated images that the system uses to determine the image to place on a specific type of workstation. Figure 8.13 shows a sample of this page.

F I G U R E   8 . 1 3   *Rules page for a sample Workstation Imaging Policy of a Workstation Policy Package*

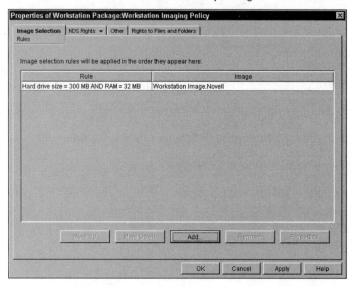

You must first press the Add button to add rules to the list. Once you have added several rules, you may then select a specific rule and change its order in the list, look at its properties, or remove the rule. When you press the Add button a dialog box is brought up to add the rule to the policy.

You first press the browse button next to the Use this Image field to browse to an image object in the tree that is associated with an image file on the image server. Once the image object is selected, then you may identify the rule that is associated with this image. You may currently only have six key/value pairs to compare about the workstation in order to determine what image to use.

In the middle of the dialog screen you can see the six potential equations that you can generate to determine if the image should be used. The equation is made up of a series of True/False statements that are put together with AND

and OR logic. You construct the statement by filling in the drop-down statements. (The resulting statement is displayed in a more English-like view to help you in understanding the equation.)

The logic for the AND and OR operators is strictly left to right in the equation. In the Rule Description box parentheses are added to the equation to help the administrator understand how the rule is evaluated. You cannot insert the parentheses, they are automatically inserted as part of the explanation of the equation and are not under user control.

You first select the key you wish to examine by selecting the key via a drop-down dialog box. The keys that you can choose from are the following:

▶ **Chipset** — This displays the reported processor. An example would be GenuineIntel Mobile Pentium MMX 233 MHZ.

▶ **Video** — This captures the type of video adapter that is in the workstation. An example of this would be Trident Cyber9397 (rev 243).

▶ **Network** — This is the network adapter for the workstation. An example would be "3Com."

▶ **Sound card** — This is the sound card that has been reported. Often this field results in No sound card detected. This is because the system sends out a PCI request and, if no sound cards respond, you get this even if a sound card is present.

▶ **Hard drive controller** — This is the type of hard drive in the system. If the hard drive is an IDE device, then the value for this field is IDE. If the hard drive is a SCSI device then you get the reported name of the device, such as FUJITSU MHJ2181AT.

▶ **MAC address** — This is the MAC address of the network card. An example of this value would be 00 60 80 03 C2 E7.

▶ **IP Address** — This would be the assigned IP address of the workstation. This would be reported as the traditional 137.65.237.5.

▶ **Hard drive size** — This reports the disk size in number of megabytes. Therefore and 8GB hard drive would be reported as 8192MB in this field. The imaging system may not always report the full disk capacity. It is advisable that you use a wide boundary when generating your rules. For instance if you want to look for 8GB drive put in the statement Hard drive size > 8000MB and not equal to an exact number.

▶ **RAM** — This is the reported amount of RAM in megabyte units. This would be reported as 64MB. This field also may not always report the exact amount of RAM space that you would expect on your workstation. It is advisable that you use a wide boundary when generating your rules. For instance if you want to look for 16MB RAM, put in the statement RAM > 15MB and not equal to an exact number.

When the workstation is booting the imaging system, it is in reality booting up the Linux operating system and running the tools that are included in the imaging system. The values for the keys described previously are values that the Linux system can report to the software. In order to discover what a system reports to Linux, you need to boot a sample workstation with the Imaging system boot disk and run the Img information command. This displays the information that is sent to the image server about the workstation. This information will be the data values that you put into the key comparison equations for your rules. You can also get this information from an image by opening the image in the ZENworks image editor, and choosing properties on the image root. See Chapter 13, "Imaging a Workstation," for more detailed information on the functionality of the ZENworks for Desktops 3 imaging system.

The next part of the equation is to specify the operator. Two types of operators exist: String and Integer operators. The Hard drive size and RAM fields are treated as integers whereas all of the other fields are treated as strings, where a case insensitive string compare is done to determine operator results. The string operators are contains, doesn't contain, begins with, equals. The integer operators are: =, <>, >, >=, <, <=.

These operators perform expected comparisons between the key value supplied by the workstation to the imaging server and the value that you place into the value field of the equation. The following meanings are placed with each operator:

▶ **contains** — The specified value is a substring anywhere in the reported value.

▶ **doesn't contain** — The specified value is not equal to or contained in the reported value.

▶ **begins with** — The specified value are represented in the initial character of the reported value.

▶ **equals** — The specified value is the same as the reported value.

- ► = — equals. The specified value is numerically equivalent to the reported value.
- ► <> — not equal. The specified value is not equal to the reported value.
- ► > — greater than. The specified value is greater than the reported value.
- ► >= — greater than or equal to. The specified value is numerically equal or greater than the reported value.
- ► < — less than. The specified value is less than the reported value.
- ► <= — less than or equal to. The specified value is numerically less than or equal to the reported value.

The next field in the operation is where you enter the value that you wish to compare. The far right field enables you to extend the operation to additional key/value comparisons. Your choices currently are AND and OR.

The Boolean operators are evaluated strictly from left to right. For example if the following rules were entered into the policy:

1. Hard drive size >= 600MB AND

2. RAM < 16MB OR

3. RAM > 31MB

Then the resultant evaluation would be (Hard drive < 60MB AND RAM < 16 MB) OR (RAM > 31MB). This would result in giving the image to any system that has a disk smaller than 200MB with less than 16MB of RAM. This would also give the image to any system that has more than 31MB of RAM regardless of the size of the hard drive.

You can view the precedence of the equation; complete with parentheses, on the bottom half of the screen as you introduce new key/value pairs into your rule.

Once your set of key/value pairs have been entered and you have reviewed your equation at the bottom of the screen, you press the OK button to include the rule into the imaging system and you are returned to the original Rules page with the rule that you had entered placed on the screen.

Once again, from this page, after you have entered some rules you can then specify the order that the rules are evaluated. After selecting a rule you can move that rule in the order by pressing either the Move Up or the Move Down buttons. As the imaging server is evaluating the rules, the first rule that results in a TRUE evaluation results in that imaging being supplied to the workstation.

▶ . . . . ◀

Workstation Inventory Policy

ZENworks for Desktops 3 has upgraded their workstation inventory process. In previous versions of ZENworks for Desktops, the system would scan for software components by looking for the file name, date, and file size and compare that to the set of known software components in the identified scan list. If an executable program was found on the disk but was not in the scan list, then the program was ignored.

Now in ZENworks for Desktops 3, the software scanning searches all executables on the workstation and pulls information from the headers of the binary files to discover the name of the program and the manufacturer. All found executables are reported for the workstation software inventory. The scan list is still used but now it is used to identify software that does not have information in the headers.

ZENworks for Desktops 3 additionally has upgraded the use of their databases for the hardware and software information. Previously you could only have a single database for a tree (although many just made different policies and segmented their tree into several databases); now you can have several databases holding information on portions of your tree and then an enterprise level database holding information about all workstations in the tree. This enables you to have local, smaller, databases and still have all the information in the enterprise database. Additionally, the enterprise database may be an Oracle database, although local databases must still be Sybase.

See the chapter on Workstation Inventory for more detailed information about the inventory system with ZENworks for Desktops 3.

With the Workstation Inventory policy you identify where the collector of the inventory information is located, whether software scanning is done, and the ability to customize the scan list to identify programs without identifying header.

NDS Rights, Other, *and* Rights to Files and Folders pages are described in the "Setting up a Workstation Policy Package" chapter.

Figure 8.14 displays the Workstation Inventory page of the Workstation Inventory Policy.

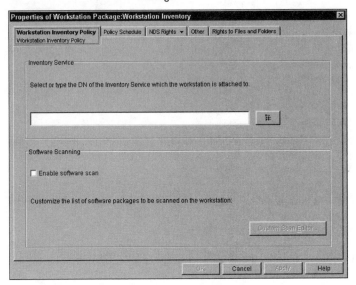

Workstation Inventory Policy within a Workstation Policy Package

Within the inventory policy the administrator has the ability to administer the following parameters:

▸ **Inventory Service** — This field represents the service object in the tree that represents the service module running on a server in the network. This server agent is responsible for receiving the information from the workstations and processing it, either by placing it in a local Sybase database, or forwarding it on to the next level of the inventory database hierarchy (see chapter 11, "Creating a Server Policy Package."). All workstations that have this policy associated with them send their scanned information to the specified server agent.

▸ **Software Scanning: Enable software scan** — This field turns on ZEN-works for Desktops 3 agents to perform a software scan in addition to the standard hardware scan.

▸ **Software Scanning: Custom Scan Editor button** — Pressing this button brings up a dialog that enables you to configure information about files that may be found on a workstation. You are able to store the Vendor Name, Product Name, Product Version, File name, File size into this list. When a file does not have header information then it is found in this table (by file name and size) and reported as the specified program. You can export and import these file lists into the NDS policy object.

Policy Schedule Page

This schedule determines when the hardware and software inventories for associated workstations are run. See the "Computer Extensible Policy" section, preceding, for a description of this page.

WS Restrict Login Policy

This policy enables the administrator to specify the users that may or may not log into the system from the workstations that are associated with this policy. This restricts all volatile users within the Dynamic Local User features of ZENworks for Desktops 3 from logging into the system including the local workstation. However, if an account for the user already exists on the workstation (non-volatile) then the user may still log into the machine locally even though they cannot log into the network.

The policy does not allow duplicates in both lists, and, if attempted, asks the administrator to choose whether the entry should be allowed to login to the system or not from this workstation policy.

You can specify within the list any user, group, or container that you want to grant or deny login privileges. If you specify a container then the agent only restricts users that are directly in that container and does not walk down into sub-containers. For example, should you specify the container Provo.Novell in the Deny login from: field, then all users with the context of Provo.Novell are denied access; if a user has the context of North.Provo.Novell then they are allowed to log into the system. Figure 8.15 displays the login restriction.

NDS Rights, Other, *and* Rights to Files and Folders pages are described in the "Setting up a Workstation Policy Package" chapter.

WS Restrict Login Policy within a Workstation Policy Package

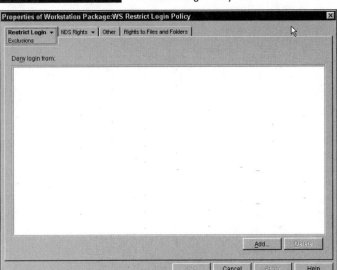

The policy is broken into two pages: Exclusions and Inclusions. In the Exclusions page you list the users, groups, or containers that you want to *not* have the ability to login to the associated workstations. In the Inclusions page you list the user, groups, or containers that you want to enable access to the associated workstations.

Do the following to add a user, group, or container to either of the Enable login from: or Deny login from: fields on these pages:

I. Press the appropriate Add... button for the field. This brings up a ConsoleOne browse dialog.

2. Browse within the tree to select the Novell Directory Services user, group, or container. Select the desired user, group, or container and press the OK button. This object is added to the list.

To remove an entry, simply select the object in the appropriate list and press the Remove... button.

## CHAPTER 9

Creating a Container
Policy Package

In addition to User and Workstation policies, a Container Policy Package also exists. This package is associated with a container and affects the understanding of policies below the container level. This chapter discusses the Container Policy package.

What Is a Container Policy Package?

A Container Policy Package contains a set of policies that are associated with only containers. These policies are expected to affect the behavior of other ZENworks for Desktops 3 user and workstation policies and are therefore only associated with containers.

Relationship of Container Policy Package to Other Policies

ZENworks for Desktops 3 agents work in a standard way to search out policies within a tree, starting at either the user or the workstation object depending on the application of the policy. Once the user or workstation object is located, then the ZENworks for Desktops 3 agents seek out a container policy package. The first container policy package that is found, while the agent is walking up the tree, is used to modify the behavior of the searching out of all other policies.

Once the container policy package is discovered, the agents use the information in the package to seek other user or workstation policy packages.

Setting up a Container Policy Package

In order to have a container policy package to affect the policies, you must first create the policy package. To create a Container Policy Package do the following:

1. Start ConsoleOne.

2. Browse to the container where you would like to have the policy package. Remember that you do not have to create the policy package in the container where you are doing the associations. You can associate the same policy package to many containers in your tree.

3. Create the policy package by clicking the right mouse button and choosing New ⇨ Policy Package *or* by selecting the Policy Package icon on the toolbar.

4. Select the Container Policy Package object in the wizard panel and press Next.

5. Enter the desired name of the package in the Policy Package Name field and select the container where you want the package to be located. The container field is already filled in with the selected container so you should not have to browse to complete this field. If not, then press the browser button next to the field, browse to and select the container where you want the policy object stored. Press Next.

6. Select Define Additional Attributes field in order to go into the properties of your new object and activate some policies. Press Finish.

7. Check and set any policies you desire for this Container Policy package and press OK.

The following subsections describe each of the fields and property pages that are available in the Container Policy package.

Policies Page

The policies page lists the set of available policies and those that are active. Figure 9.1 shows this policy page. Because no platform specific policies currently exist in the Container package, only the general page of the Policies tab is available.

FIGURE 9.1   *Container Package policy page*

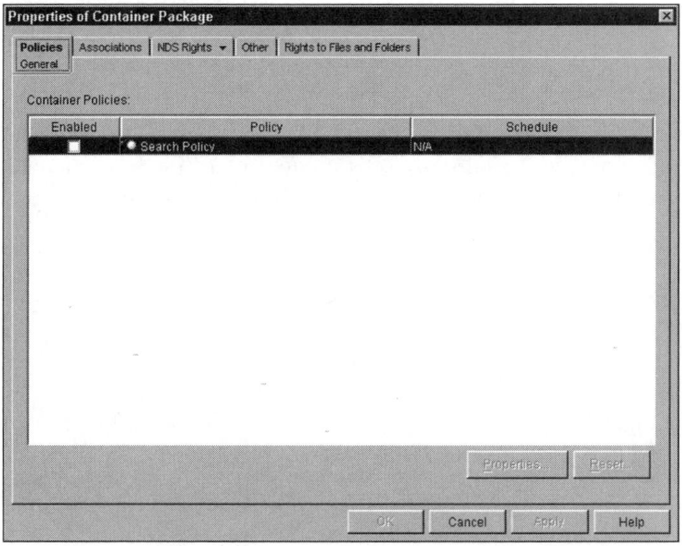

Once you have created a Container Package you can now activate policies. By clicking a policy within the policy package, that policy becomes active. An active policy is designated by a check in the check box. The details of any particular policy can be modified by selecting the policy and pressing the Properties button.

The Reset button on the policies page resets the selected policy back to the system defaults for that policy.

Associations Property Page

The Associations Page of the Container Policy Package displays all of the locations in the tree (containers) where the policy package has been associated. These associations do not necessarily reflect where the policy package is located in the directory. The agents that are associated with users or workstations that are in or below those containers have this policy package enforced. Pressing the Add or Remove buttons enables you to add or remove containers in the list that are associated with this policy.

NDS Rights Property Pages

The NDS Rights property page is made up of three pages. You can get to each of the pages by clicking on the small triangle to the right of the page name, and then selecting the desired page to be displayed.

These pages allow you to specify the rights that users have to this object in the directory. The following subsections discuss briefly each of these pages. These NDS Rights pages are displayed for every object in the tree.

Trustees of This Object Page

On this page you can assign objects rights as trustees of the Container Policy Package. These trustees have rights to this object or to attributes within this object.

If the user admin.novell has been added to the trustee list, this user has some rights to this object. To get into the details of any trustee assignment (in order to modify the assignment) you would need to press the Assigned Rights button.

When you press the Assign Rights button, after selecting the user you want to modify, you are presented with a dialog box that enables you to select either [All Attribute Rights] (meaning all of the attributes of the object) or [Entry Rights] (meaning the object, not implying rights to the attributes).

From within the assigned rights dialog box you may set the rights the object may have on this package. You can set those rights on the object as well as any individual property in the object. The rights that are possible are the following:

- **Browse** — Although not in the list this right shows up from time to time (especially in the effective rights screens). This represents the ability to view this information through public browse capabilities.

- **Supervisor** — This identifies that the trustee has ALL rights, including delete for this object or attribute.

- **Compare** — This provides the trustee with the ability to compare values of attributes.

- **Read** — This enables the trustee to read the values of the attribute or attributes in the object.

- **Write** — This provides the trustee with the ability to modify the contents of an attribute.

- **Add Self** — This right enables the trustee to add themselves as a member to the list of objects of the attribute. For example, if this right were given on an attribute that contains a list of linked objects, then the trustee could add themselves (a reference to their object) into the list.

If you wish to add the object as a trustee to an attribute you would need to press the Add Property button to bring up a list of properties or attributes that are available for this object.

From this list you may select a single attribute. This attribute is then displayed in the assigned rights dialog box. From there you can select the attribute and then set the rights you want the trustee to have for that property. A user does not require object rights in order to have rights on a single attribute in the object.

Remember that rights flow down in the tree and if you give a user or an object rights at a container level, those rights continue down into that container and any sub-containers until that branch is exhausted or another explicit assignment is given for that user in a sub-container *or* on an object. An explicit assignment changes the rights for the user at that point in the tree. Inheritance Rights Filters may also be placed to restrict this flow of rights down into the tree.

Inherited Rights Filters Page

This page allows you to set the IRF (Inheritance Rights Filter) for this object. This filter restricts the rights of any user that accesses this object, unless that user has an explicit trustee assignment for this object.

You can think of the IRF as a filter that lets only items checked pass through unaltered. Rights that bump up against an IRF filter are blocked and discarded if the item is *not* checked. For example, if a user who had write privileges inherited at some point above (they were explicitly granted that right at some container at or above the one we're in) were to run into an IRF for an object or attribute that has the write privilege revoked (that is, unchecked), then when they got to that object their write privilege would be gone for that object. If the object were a container, then they would loose write privileges for all objects in that container or sub-container.

You can effectively remove supervisor privileges to a portion of the tree by setting an IRF with the supervisor privilege turned off. You must be careful not to ever do this without someone being assigned as the supervisor of that branch of the tree (given an explicit supervisor trustee assignment at the container where the IRF is done) or you make that part of the tree permanent (that is, you are never able to delete any objects in that branch of the tree). ConsoleOne helps keep you from performing this action by giving you an error dialog box that keeps you from putting an IRF on the [Entry Rights] of the object with the supervisor right filtered away without having first given an explicit supervisor assignment on the same container.

Effective Rights Page

Effective Rights property page allows you to query the system to discover the rights that selected objects have on the object you are administering.

Within this page you are presented with the distinguished name (DN) of the object whose rights you wish to observe. Initially, this is your currently logged in user running ConsoleOne. You can press the browse button to the right of the trustee field and browse throughout the tree to select any object.

When the trustee object is selected you may then move to the properties table on the lower half of the screen. As you select the property, the rights box to the right changes its text to reflect the rights that the trustee has on that property. These rights may be via an explicit assignment or through inheritance.

Other Property Page

This page may or may not be displayed for you, depending on your rights to the plug-in that now comes with ConsoleOne. This page is particularly powerful and should not be used by those who do not have an intimate knowledge of the schema of the object in question and its relationships with other objects in the directory. The intention of this property page is to give you generic access to properties that you cannot modify or view via the other plugged-in pages. The attributes and their values are displayed in a tree structure, allowing for those attributes that have multiple types (are compound types that consist of, say, an int and a distinguished name, or postal code that has three separate address fields).

Every attribute in eDirectory is defined by one of a specified set of syntaxes. These syntaxes identify how the data is stored in eDirectory. For this page, ConsoleOne has developed an editor for each of the different syntaxes that are currently available in eDirectory. When an attribute is displayed on this page the editor is invoked to display the data and then modify it, should the user click the specific attribute.

For example, if the syntax for an attribute were a string or an integer, then an in-line editor is launched allowing the administrator to modify the string or the integer value on the screen. More abstract syntaxes such as octet-string require that an octet editor be launched giving the administrator access to each of the bytes in the string, without interpretation of the data.

The danger with this screen is that some applications require that there be a coordination of attribute values between two attributes within the same object or across multiple objects. Additionally, many applications assume that the data in the attribute is valid, because the normal user interface checks for invalid entries and does not allow them to be stored in the attribute. If you should change a data value in the other page, then no knowledge of related attributes or objects or valid data values are checked since the generic editors know nothing about the intention of the field. Should you change a value without making all the other appropriate changes, or without putting in a valid value, then some programs *and* the system could be affected.

Rights are still in effect in the Other property page and you are not allowed to change any attribute values that are read-only or that you do not have rights to modify.

Rights to Files and Folders Property Page

This page in the property book is present in all objects in the directory. This property page enables you to view and set rights for this object onto the volumes and specific files and folders on that volume.

You must first select the volume that contains the files and folders in which you are interested. You can do this by pressing the Show button on the right and then browsing the directory to the volume object. Selecting the volume object places it in the volumes view. When that volume is selected you can then go to the Add button to add a file or folder of interest. This brings up a dialog box enabling you to browse to the volume object; clicking the volume object moves you into the file system. You can continue browsing that volume until you select the file or directory to which you are interested in granting rights.

Selecting the file or folder in the lower pane displays the rights that the object has been granted on that file or folder. To modify the rights simply click on or off the rights that you want to have explicitly granted for the object.

You can also see the effective rights that the object has on the files by pressing the Effective rights button. This displays a dialog box, enabling you to browse to any file in the volume and having the effective rights displayed (in bold) for the object. These effective rights include any explicit, plus inherited, rights from folders higher in the file system tree. Remember that the person with supervisor rights to the server or volume objects automatically gets supervisor rights in the file system.

Search Policy

A Search Policy governs the behavior of the ZENworks for Desktops 3 agents as they search for user and workstation policies. With all of the ZENworks for Desktops 3 agents there could be some significant walking of the tree as it searches for the policies of the identified user and workstations, especially if the tree is of a significant depth. This is the reason why ZENworks for Desktops 3 has this search policy. Often the performance of your network searching with ZENworks for Desktops 3 is not significant until you cross a partition boundary. When you cross a partition boundary, the system must make a connection and authenticate to another server. This is particularly consuming should the system need to cross a WAN link.

The search policy tells the ZENworks for Desktops 3 agents how far up the tree it should search and what order (object, group, container) should be followed to find the policies. Remember that the order is significant because often the first policy found governs the behavior of the system.

Search Level Page

This page enables the administrator to identify how far up the tree the ZENworks for Desktops 3 agents should travel in their search for policies. Figure 9.2 shows this page.

FIGURE 9.2   *Search Level page of a Search Policy within a Container Policy Package*

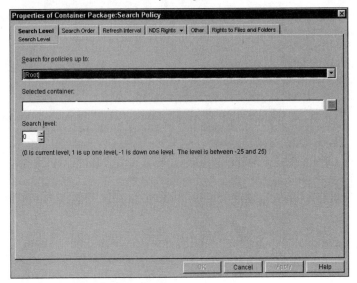

The following fields may be administered in the Search Level features of the Search Order policy:

▶ **Search for policies up to:** — This field enables you to specify the container in the tree at which searching will complete. The choices that can be made through the drop-down list may be any of the following:

- **[Root]** — Search up to the root of the tree.

- **Object Container** — Search up to the container that holds the object that is associated with the policy. For example, if we are searching for a user policy package the object container would be the context of the user object.

- **Partition** — Search up the tree to a partition boundary. Crossing a partition boundary causes connections to other systems in the tree. This option is available for performance considerations.

- **Selected Container** — This searches up to the specified container. When this option is chosen, then the Selected container field is activated and you can browse in this field to the desired container.

▶ **Search level:** — This field enables you to specify an additional level of container beyond that given in the Search for policies up to: field. A search level value of 0 causes searches to be limited to the specified container. A search level of a positive numerical value enables searching the number of containers specified. Should the search level be a negative number then the search proceeds at the specified level minus the number specified. For example, if the value of Object Container were selected, and the object is in the Provo.Utah.Novell container, and the search level is 0, then the searching stops at the Provo.Utah. Novell container. If the search level is 2 then the searching continues to the Novell container. If the search level is –1 then no policy will be found because the object container is already above the search level.

At first it may not be apparent why a negative search level exists, but this value does have a purpose. Suppose that your tree is set up as Organization. Region.Company, where the Organization is the container that is given to each organization in the company and the Region represents the area of the company. Now suppose that you want policies to only be effective for each organization, then you could set up one single search policy at the Region.Company level with a Selected Container as Region.Company and a search level of –1. This would enable each organization to have a customized policy and ensure that no one organization's policies would impact another's because the search would stop at the Organization level.

Search Order Page

This page enables the administrator to identify the order that the agents should go looking for policies. The default is always object, group, then container. This policy enables the administrator to change this order.

You can modify the search order by selecting the item in the search order list and then pushing the up or down arrows to rearrange the list. Pressing the Remove button removes the selected order. Pressing the Add button adds that search order item, if any have been previously deleted.

Because the first policy that is found has the greatest significance in the behavior of the system, you should be sure that you have the order set (from top to bottom) in the way that you want to find that first policy.

You should be aware of when it is a good idea to use the search order policy. Because many ZENworks for Desktops 3 features stop walking up the tree when a policy is found, it would be wise to make policies search in order of object, container, and then group. This is because the proximity of these objects in the tree is always going to be closer to the partition on the server.

The object is, obviously, always the closest in the tree to the Workstation or User object. Next the container is the closest in the tree-walking scenario because the container must be known in order for the object to be found in the tree. Consequently, the container is very close in the local replica to the object. Groups, however, can be stored in any container and they could be in a completely different part of the tree than the object. Therefore, the amount of walking of the tree that is potential with a group is significant. Any significant walk of the tree has a corresponding performance cost, and this should be considered as you manage your tree and search policies.

Refresh Interval Page

With ZENworks for Desktops 3 this page has been introduced into the search policy. This page is intended to eventually be part of the collaboration from ZENworks for Desktops and ZENworks for Servers.

This policy page is currently only effective for the ZENworks for Servers product and enables the administrator to identify if the policy manager should refresh the set of policies from NDS and how often to check NDS for new or changed policies. The policy manager in ZENworks for Servers is an agent that resides on the server and is responsible for getting ZENworks for Servers policies and enforcing them on the server. This page gives this refresh interval configuration to this agent. If the check box is off, meaning the agent should not refresh from NDS, then the agent only gets the policies at initialization time and only again should the server or the agent be restarted. If the check box is on, then the agent checks for any changes or new policies every time the interval has passed.

This same behavior is also available in Workstation manager, the agent that enforces policies on the workstation. It also looks for new policies and scheduled actions and only does that at boot time and at identified intervals. The Workstation Manager interval is specified in the workstation policy package under the NT/2000 Client Configuration and 95/98 Client Configuration policies.

## CHAPTER 10

Creating a Service Location Policy Package

In addition to User, Workstation, and Container policies a Service Location Policy Package also exists. This package is associated with a container and identifies where agents that are associated with objects below the associated container may locate services that they need, such as the database to record events or workstation inventory. This chapter discusses the Service Location Policy package.

What Is a Service Location Policy Package?

A Service Location Policy Package contains a set of policies that are associated with only containers. These policies are expected to identify the location of resources that other ZENworks for Desktops 3 agents, throughout the network, need. These resources are associated through the container to all agents that are working on behalf of the objects in the container or sub-container.

An example of this might be if you have set up a service location policy package associated with container A, and activated the database location policy specifying that the database is located on server A. Then all of the workstation agents that are on the PCs, whose workstation objects are located in or below container A, look in the tree and walk up the tree to find the service location policy package associated with container A. In this policy they would find that the database where they should store their events or inventory information is located on server A, because the database location policy in the service location package would be active. The agents would then contact the database on server A and send it their information.

Setting up a Service Location Policy Package

In order to have a service location policy package to identify resources in the network, you must first create the policy package. To create a Service Location Policy Package do the following:

1. Start ConsoleOne.

2. Browse to the container where you would like to have the policy package. Remember that you do not have to create the policy package in the container where you are doing the associations. You can associate the same policy package to many containers in your tree.

3. Create the policy package by pressing the right mouse button and choosing New ⇨ Policy Package or by selecting the Policy Package icon on the toolbar.

4. Select the Service Location Policy Package object in the wizard panel and press Next.

5. Enter the desired name of the package in the Policy Package Name field and select the container where you want the package to be located. The container field is already filled in with the selected container so you should not have to browse to complete this field. If not, then press the browser button next to the field, browse to and select the container where you want the policy object stored. Press Next.

6. Select Define Additional Attributes field in order to go into the properties of your new object and activate some policies. Press Finish.

7. Check and set any policies you desire for this Service Location Policy package and press OK.

The following subsections describe each of the fields and property pages that are available in the Service Location Policy package.

Policies Property Page

All of the policies for users are activated within the policies property page. Initially the page is on the General policies. Currently in the Service Location Policy no platform specific policies exist, so no drop-down menu is present on this page. The policies page lists the set of available policies and those that are active. Figure 10.1 shows this policy page.

Once you have created a Service Location Package you can now activate policies. By clicking on a policy within the policy package, that policy becomes active. An active policy is designated with a check in the check box. The details of any particular policy are modified by selecting the policy and then pressing the Properties button.

The Reset button on the policies page resets the selected policy back to the system defaults for that policy.

Service Location Package policy page

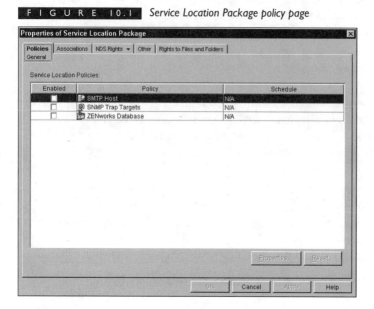

Associations Property Page

The Associations Page of the Service Location Policy Package displays all of the locations in the tree (containers) where the policy package has been associated. These associations do not necessarily reflect where the policy package is located in the directory. The agents that are associated with users or workstations that are in or below those containers have this policy package enforced. Pressing the Add or Remove buttons enables you to add or remove containers in the list that are associated with this policy.

NDS Rights Property Pages

The NDS Rights property page is made up of three pages. You can get to each of the pages by clicking on the small triangle to the right of the page name, and then selecting the desired page to be displayed.

These pages enable you to specify the rights that users have to this object in the directory. The following subsections discuss briefly each of these pages. These NDS Rights pages are displayed for every object in the tree.

Trustees of This Object Page

On this page you can assign objects rights as trustees of the Service Location Policy Package. These trustees have rights to this object or to attributes within this object.

If the user admin.novell has been added to the trustee list then this user has some rights to this object. To get into the details of any trustee assignment (in order to modify the assignment) you would need to press the Assigned Rights button.

When you press the Assign Rights button, after selecting the user you want to modify, you are presented with a dialog box that enables you to select either [All Attribute Rights] (meaning all of the attributes of the object) or [Entry Rights] (meaning the object, not implying rights to the attributes).

From within the assigned rights dialog box you may set the rights the object may have on this package. You can set those rights on the object as well as any individual property in the object. The rights that are possible are the following:

▶ **Browse** — Although not in the list, this right shows up from time to time (especially in the effective rights screens). This represents the ability to view this information through public browse capabilities.

▶ **Supervisor** — This identifies that the trustee has ALL rights, including delete for this object or attribute.

▶ **Compare** — This provides the trustee with the ability to compare values of attributes.

▶ **Read** — This enables the trustee to read the values of the attribute or attributes in the object.

▶ **Write** — This provides the trustee with the ability to modify the contents of an attribute.

▶ **Add Self** — This right enables the trustee to add themselves as a member of the list of objects of the attribute. For example, if this right were given on an attribute that contains a list of linked objects, then the trustee could add themselves (a reference to their object) into the list.

If you wish to add the object as a trustee to an attribute you would need to press the Add Property button to bring up a list of properties or attributes that are available for this object.

From this list you may select a single attribute. This attribute is then displayed in the assigned rights dialog box. From there you can select the attribute and then set the rights you want the trustee to have for that property. A user does not require object rights in order to have rights on a single attribute in the object.

Remember that rights flow down in the tree and if you give a user or an object rights at a container level, then those rights continue down into that container and any sub-containers until that branch is exhausted or another explicit assignment is given for that user in a sub-container or on an object. An explicit assignment changes the rights for the user at that point in the tree. Inheritance Rights Filters may also be placed to restrict this flow of rights down into the tree.

Inherited Rights Filters Page

This page enables you to set the IRF (Inheritance Rights Filter) for this object. This filter restricts the rights of any user that accesses this object, unless that user has an explicit trustee assignment for this object.

You can think of the IRF as a filter that lets only items checked pass through unaltered. Rights that bump up against an IRF filter are blocked and discarded if the item is NOT checked. For example, if a user who had write privileges inherited at some point above (they were explicitly granted that right at some container at or above the one we're in) were to run into an IRF for an object or attribute that has the write privilege revoked (that is, unchecked), then when they got to that object their write privilege would be gone for that object. If the object were a container, then they would lose write privileges for all objects in that container or sub-container.

You can effectively remove supervisor privileges to a portion of the tree by setting an IRF with the supervisor privilege turned off. You must be careful not to ever do this without someone being assigned as the supervisor of that branch of the tree (given an explicit supervisor trustee assignment at the container where the IRF is done) or you make that part of the tree permanent (that is, you will never be able to delete any objects in that branch of the tree). ConsoleOne helps keep you from performing this action by giving you an error dialog box that keeps you from putting an IRF on the [Entry Rights] of the object, with the supervisor right filtered away, without having first given an explicit supervisor assignment on the same container.

Effective Rights Page

Effective Rights property page enables you to query the system to discover the rights that selected objects have on the object you are administering.

Within this page you are presented with the distinguished name (DN) of the object whose rights you wish to observe. Initially, this is your currently logged in user running ConsoleOne. You can press the browse button to the right of the trustee field and browse throughout the tree to select any object.

When the trustee object is selected you may then move to the properties table on the lower half of the screen. As you select the property, the rights box to the right changes its text to reflect the rights that the trustee has on that property. These rights may be via an explicit assignment or through inheritance.

Other Property Page

This page may or may not be displayed for you, depending on your rights to the plug-in that now comes with ConsoleOne. This page is particularly powerful and should not be used by those who do not have an intimate knowledge of the schema of the object in question and its relationships with other objects in the directory. The intention of this property page is to give you generic access to properties that you cannot modify or view via the other plugged-in pages. The attributes and their values are displayed in a tree structure, allowing for those attributes that have multiple types (are compound types that consist of an int and a distinguished name, or postal code that has three separate address fields).

Every attribute in eDirectory is defined by one of a specified set of syntaxes. These syntaxes identify how the data is stored in eDirectory. For this page, ConsoleOne has developed an editor for each of the different syntaxes that are currently available in eDirectory. When an attribute is displayed on this page the editor is invoked to display the data and then modify it should the user click the specific attribute.

For example, if the syntax for an attribute were a string or an integer, then an in-line editor is launched enabling the administrator to modify the string or the integer value on the screen. More abstract syntaxes, such as octet-string, require that an octet editor be launched giving the administrator access to each of the bytes in the string, without interpretation of the data.

The danger with this screen is that some applications require that there be a coordination of attribute values between two attributes within the same object or across multiple objects. Additionally, many applications assume that the data in the attribute is valid, because the normal user interface checks for invalid entries and does not enable them to be stored in the attribute. If you should change a data value in the other page, then no knowledge of related attributes, objects, or valid data values are checked because the generic editors know nothing about the intention of the field. Should you change a value without making all the other appropriate changes or without putting in a valid value then some programs and the system could be affected.

Rights are still in effect in the Other property page and you are not allowed to change any attribute values that are read-only *or* that you do not have rights to modify.

Rights to Files and Folders Property Page

This page in the property book is present in all objects in the directory. This property page enables you to view and set rights for this object onto the volumes and specific files and folders on that volume.

You must first select the volume that contains the files and folders in which you are interested. You can do this by pressing the Show button on the right and then browsing the directory to the volume object. Selecting the volume object places it in the volumes view. When that volume is selected you can then go to the Add button to add a file or folder of interest. This brings up a dialog box enabling you to browse to the volume object; clicking the volume object moves you into the file system. You can continue browsing that volume until you select the file or directory to which you are interested in granting rights.

Selecting the file or folder in the lower pane displays the rights that the object has been granted on that file or folder. To modify the rights simply click on or off the rights that you want to have explicitly granted for the object.

You can also see the effective rights that the object has on the files by pressing the Effective rights button. This displays a dialog box that enables you to browse to any file in the volume and has the effective rights displayed (in bold) for the object. These effective rights include any explicit plus inherited rights from folders higher in the file system tree. Remember that anyone who has supervisor rights to the server or volume objects automatically gets supervisor rights in the file system.

SMTP Host Policy

Several of the features in ZENworks for Desktops 3 include the ability to have information and events e-mailed to identified users (see Chapter 5, "Creating and Using Application Objects"). In order to send the e-mail the agents must contact the SMTP server in your environment, communicate, and send the e-mail through that system. This policy enables you to specify the IP address of the SMTP host that the agents associated with this policy (through inheritance) use.

NDS Rights, Other, *and* Rights to Files and Folders pages are described in the "Setting Up a Service Location Policy Package" section.

SMTP Host Page

This page enables the administrator to identify the IP address of the SMTP mail server in their environment. Figure 10.2 shows this page.

F I G U R E   1 0 . 2 *SMTP Host page in the SMTP Host Policy of the Service Location Policy Package*

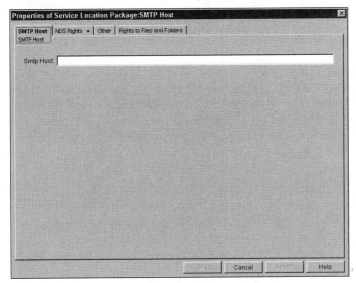

Just place your cursor on the SMTP Host field and enter the IP address of the SMTP mail host. You must enter the IP address and not the DNS name.

SNMP Trap Target Policy

In ZENworks for Desktops 3 the Application Launcher has been enhanced to send an SNMP message to a central server that stores these messages and enables you to print reports on the traps. These traps can identify whether an application was successfully distributed or not; if *not* it identifies the potential problem with the distribution.

This policy used to be in the Container Policy Package in previous versions of ZENworks for Desktops.

The SNMP Trap Target Policy is to identify the location of this service that is accepting and recording the SNMP messages from the Application Launcher. In previous versions of ZENworks for Desktops you had to place the database service as an SNMP Trap Target policy in order to get Application Launcher events. This is no longer necessary, as the Application Launcher can write directly to the database.

NDS Rights, Other, *and* Rights to Files and Folders pages are described in the "Setting Up a Service Location Policy Package" section.

SNMP Trap Policy Page

Figure 10.3 displays the trap target policy page. The service on the workstation walks the tree to find this policy and uses the service location stored in this policy as the destination of the SNMP messages.

Once you have brought up the policy page, you need to add as many trap targets as you desire. The service on the workstation sends the SNMP message to all of the specified trap targets. Press the add button and specify whether the destination can be achieved with an IP Address, an IPX Address, or a DNS name. After selecting the type, a dialog box comes up for you to enter either the address or the DNS name of the target service.

F I G U R E   1 0 . 3   *SNMP Trap Target Policy page of the Service Location Policy Package*

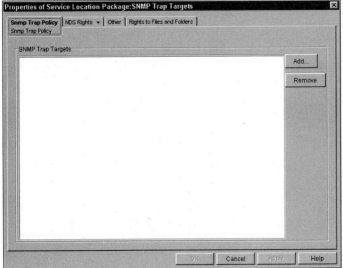

ZENworks Database Policy

Many of the agents in the system want to record information into the .ZENworks database that is installed on your system. Previously, agents such as the Application Launcher agent would get their event information into the database indirectly through SNMP messages. Now in ZENworks for Desktops 3 the Application Launcher agent and other agents write directly to the database and do not rely on the SNMP system to record events. In order for these agents to discover on which database they should place their information, they walk the tree, from the object representing the system they are supporting, until they find a Service Location policy package with a ZENworks Database policy active.

The database policy then refers to a ZENworks database object in the directory (that was created at installation time), which in turn contains the server or the IP address of the server that is supporting the database. The system uses other information in the database object as well.

Database Location Page

This page enables you to browse to the database object in the directory that represents the database that you wish to use. All agents associated with this policy then write their log information into this database. Figure 10.4 is a snapshot of this page.

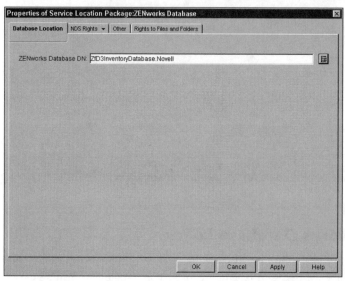

F I G U R E   I 0 . 4   *Database location page of the Database location policy in a Service Location Policy Package*

NDS Rights, Other, *and* Rights to Files and Folders pages are described in the Setting Up a Service Location Policy Package section.

To set the database, you must click the browse button to the right of the field, browse to, and select the database that you wish. This places the DN of the database object into the field.

## CHAPTER 11

Creating a Server Policy Package

In addition to User, Workstation, Service Location, and Container policies is a Server Policy Package. This package is associated with a container or a server and includes policies that are used by agents that reside on the server. This policy package is used by both ZENworks for Desktops 3 and ZENworks for Servers products, although some policies may be only effective for Desktops 3 and others for Servers. This chapter discusses the Server Policy package.

What Is a Server Policy Package?

A Server Policy Package contains a set of policies that are associated with agents that run on servers. These policies are expected to give policy information and configuration behavior to these agents and may be associated with the server, a group of servers, or a container.

The agents follow the expected walking of the tree to locate their server policy package. Namely they find the search policy and then use the order specified in the search policy, or they use the default. The default is to search for a server policy package associated with the server, then the group of servers, and lastly the container. The first policy package is the one that the agents use.

Setting up a Server Policy Package

In order to have a server policy package, you must first create the policy package. To create a Server Policy Package do the following:

1. Start ConsoleOne.

2. Browse to the container where you would like to have the policy package. Remember that you do not have to create the policy package in the container where you are doing the associations. You can associate the same policy package to many containers in your tree.

3. Create the policy package by pressing the right mouse button and choosing New ⇨ Policy Package or by selecting the Policy Package icon on the toolbar.

4. Select the Server Policy Package object in the wizard panel and press Next.

5. Enter the desired name of the package in the Policy Package Name field and select the container where you want the package to be located. The container field is already filled in with the selected container so you should not have to browse to complete this field. If not, then press the browser button next to the field and browse to and select the container where you want the policy object stored. Press Next.

6. Select Define Additional Attributes field in order to go into the properties of your new object and activate some policies. Press Finish.

7. Check and set any policies you desire for this Server Policy package and press OK.

The following subsections describe each of the fields and property pages that are available in the Server Policy package.

Policies Property Page

All of the policies for users are activated within the policies property page. Initially the page is on the general policies. As other platforms are selected additional policies are displayed. You can select which platform to display by placing the mouse over the small triangle to the right of the word Policies in the tab. This activates a drop-down menu that enables you to select which platform specific page you wish to display.

The following sections briefly discuss each of the policy pages, and then we cover the specifics of each policy.

General Policies

When you first go into the properties of the Server policy package you are presented with the Policy Property page. The policy page first displays the general category. All of the policies that are activated in the general category are active for ALL server platforms supported by ZENworks for Desktops 3 and associated to the server.

Figure 11.1 is a snapshot of the initial property page of the server policy package.

As you can see from the image currently four policies are available to all of the platforms supported by ZENworks for Desktops 3. They are Imaging Server Policy, Workstation Import Policy, Workstation Removal Policy, and zeninvRollUpPolicy. These, as well as all of the other policies, are discussed later in this chapter.

Server Policy Package policies general property page

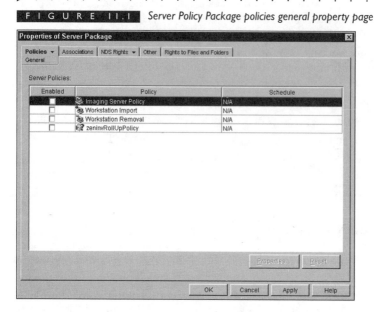

In order to activate a policy you simply need to check the box to the left of the policy by clicking on the box with the left mouse button. You can then go into the details of the policy and set additional configuration parameters on that specific policy.

NetWare Policies

Within the policies tab you can select the NetWare policy page. This page displays the policies that are available for NetWare servers. These policies include Imaging Server Policy, Workstation Import , Workstation Removal, and zeninvRollUpPolicy. See Figure 11.2 for a sample of the NetWare policies page.

As you can see the same policies are both under the General and the NetWare policies page. When you select a policy in the NetWare page it supercedes any selections that may have been on the general tab for that platform. The policies will not be merged together; only the platform specific policy is used, instead of the policy set in the general category. Also, only the policies selected in the platform specific tab are used in place of the general policies. For example, if the Workstation Import policy is selected in the general tab and the Workstation Removal policy is selected in the NetWare tab, then agents on a NetWare system use the general import policy and the NetWare removal policy is activated.

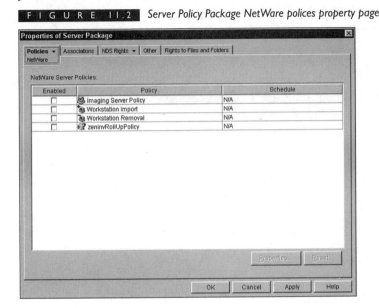

Server Policy Package NetWare polices property page

WinNT-2000 Policies

Within the policies tab you can select the Windows NT/2000 policy page. This page displays the policies that are available for your Windows NT and Windows 2000 servers. These policies include Imaging Server Policy, Workstation Import, Workstation Removal, and zeninRollUpPolicy. See Figure 11.3 for a sample of the WinNT-2000 policies page.

As you can see the same policies are both under the General and the WinNT-2000 policies page. When you select a policy in the WinNT-2000 page it supercedes any selections that may have been on the general tab for that platform. The policies will not be merged together; only the platform specific policy will be used instead of the policy set in the general category. Also, only the policies selected in the platform specific tab are used in place of the general policies. For example, if the Workstation Import policy is selected in the general tab and the Workstation Removal policy is selected in the WinNT-2000 tab, then agents on a Windows 2000 or Windows NT system use the general import policy and the WinNT-2000 removal policy is activated.

F I G U R E   I I . 3 *Server Policy Package WinNT-2000 polices property page*

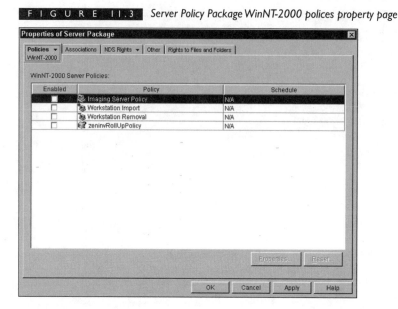

Associations Property Page

The "Associations Page" of the Server Policy Package displays all of the locations in the tree (containers) where the policy package has been associated. These associations do not necessarily reflect where the policy package is located in the directory. The agents that are associated with users or workstations that are in or below those containers have this policy package enforced. Pressing the Add or Remove buttons enable you to add or remove containers in the list that are associated with this policy.

NDS Rights Property Pages

The "NDS Rights" property page is made up of three pages. You can get to each of the pages by clicking on the small triangle to the right of the page name, and then selecting the desired page to be displayed.

These pages enable you to specify the rights that users have to this object in the directory. The following subsections briefly discuss each of these pages. These NDS Rights pages are displayed for every object in the tree.

Trustees of This Object Page

On this page you can assign objects rights as trustees of the Server Policy Package. These trustees have rights to this object or to attributes within this object.

If the user admin.novell has been added to the trustee list, then this user has some rights to this object. To get into the details of any trustee assignment (in order to modify the assignment) you would need to press the Assigned Rights button.

When you press the Assign Rights button, after selecting the user you want to modify you are presented with a dialog box that enables you to select either [All Attribute Rights] (meaning all of the attributes of the object) or [Entry Rights] (meaning the object, not implying rights to the attributes).

From within the assigned rights dialog box you may set the rights the object may have on this package. You can set those rights on the object as well as any individual property in the object. The rights that are possible are the following:

- **Browse** — Although not in the list, this right shows up from time to time (especially in the effective rights screens). This represents the ability to view this information through public browse capabilities.

- **Supervisor** — This identifies that the trustee has ALL rights, including delete for this object or attribute.

- **Compare** — This provides the trustee with the ability to compare values of attributes.

- **Read** — This enables the trustee to read the values of the attribute or attributes in the object.

- **Write** — This provides the trustee with the ability to modify the contents of an attribute.

- **Add Self** — This right enables the trustee to add themselves as a member of the list of objects of the attribute. For example, if this right were given on an attribute that contains a list of linked objects, then the trustee could add themselves (a reference to their object) into the list.

If you wish to add the object as a trustee to an attribute you would need to press the Add Property button to bring up a list of properties or attributes that are available for this object.

From this list you may select a single attribute. This attribute is then displayed in the assigned rights dialog box. From there you can select the attribute and then set the rights you want the trustee to have for that property. A user does not require object rights in order to have rights on a single attribute in the object.

Remember that rights flow down in the tree, and if you give a user or an object rights at a container level then those rights continue down into that container, and any sub-containers until that branch is exhausted, or another explicit assignment is given for that user in a sub-container or on an object. An explicit assignment changes the rights for the user at that point in the tree. Inheritance Rights Filters may also be placed to restrict this flow of rights down into the tree.

Inherited Rights Filters Page

This page enables you to set the IRF (Inheritance Rights Filter) for this object. This filter restricts the rights of any user that accesses this object, unless that user has an explicit trustee assignment for this object.

You can think of the IRF as a filter that lets only items checked pass through unaltered. Rights that bump up against an IRF filter are blocked and discarded if the item is NOT checked. For example, if a user who had write privileges inherited at some point above (they were explicitly granted that right at some container at or above the one we're in) runs into an IRF for an object or attribute that has the write privilege revoked (that is, unchecked), then when they get to that object their write privilege will be gone for that object. If the object is a container, then they will loose write privileges for all objects in that container or sub-container.

You can effectively remove supervisor privileges to a portion of the tree by setting an IRF with the supervisor privilege turned off. You must be careful not to ever do this without someone being assigned as the supervisor of that branch of the tree (given an explicit supervisor trustee assignment at the container where the IRF is done) or you will make that part of the tree permanent (that is, you will never be able to delete any objects in that branch of the tree). ConsoleOne helps keep you from performing this action by giving you an error dialog box that keeps you from putting an IRF on the [Entry Rights] of the object with the supervisor right filtered away, without having first given an explicit supervisor assignment on the same container.

Effective Rights Page

Effective Rights property page enables you to query the system to discover the rights that selected objects have on the object that you are administering.

Within this page you are presented with the distinguished name (DN) of the object whose rights you wish to observe. Initially, this is your currently logged in user running ConsoleOne. You can press the browse button to the right of the trustee field and browse throughout the tree to select any object.

When the trustee object is selected you may then move to the properties table on the lower half of the screen. As you select the property, the rights box to the right changes its text to reflect the rights that the trustee has on that property. These rights may be via an explicit assignment or through inheritance.

Other Property Page

This page may or may not be displayed for you, depending on your rights to the plug-in that now comes with ConsoleOne. This page is particularly powerful and should not be used by those who do not have an intimate knowledge of the schema of the object in question, and its relationships with other objects in the directory. The intention of this property page is to give you generic access to properties that you cannot modify or view via the other plugged-in pages. The attributes and their values are displayed in a tree structure, allowing for those attributes that have multiple types (are compound types that consist of, say, an INT and a distinguished name, or postal code that has three separate address fields).

Every attribute in eDirectory is defined by one of a specified set of syntaxes. These syntaxes identify how the data is stored in eDirectory. For this page, ConsoleOne has developed an editor for each of the different syntaxes that are currently available in eDirectory. When an attribute is displayed on this page the editor is invoked to display the data and then modify it should the user click the specific attribute.

For example, if the syntax for an attribute were a string or an integer, then an in-line editor is launched enabling the administrator to modify the string or the integer value on the screen. More abstract syntaxes, such as octet-string, require that an octet editor be launched giving the administrator access to each of the bytes in the string, without interpretation of the data.

The danger with this screen is that some applications require that there be a coordination of attribute values between two attributes within the same object or across multiple objects. Additionally, many applications assume that the data in the attribute is valid, because the normal user interface checks for invalid entries and does not allow them to be stored in the attribute. If you should change a data value in the other page, then no knowledge of related attributes or objects or valid data values are checked because the generic editors know nothing about the intention of the field. Should you change a value without making all the other appropriate changes, or without putting in a valid value, then some programs and the system could be affected.

Rights are still in effect in the Other property page and you are not allowed to change any attribute values that are read-only or that you do not have rights to modify.

Rights to Files and Folders Property Page

This page in the property book is present in all objects in the directory. This property page enables you to view and set rights for this object onto the volumes and specific files and folders on that volume.

You must first select the volume that contains the files and folders to which you are interested. You can do this by pressing the Show button on the right and then browsing the directory to the volume object. Selecting the volume object places it in the volumes view. When that volume is selected you can then go to the Add button to add a file or folder of interest. This brings up a dialog box enabling you to browse to the volume object, then clicking on the volume object moves you into the file system. You can continue browsing that volume until you select the file or directory you are interested in granting rights.

Selecting the file or folder in the lower pane displays the rights that the object has been granted on that file or folder. To modify the rights simply click on or off the rights that you want to have explicitly granted for the object.

You can also see the effective rights that the object has on the files by pressing the Effective rights button. This displays a dialog box, enabling you to browse to any file in the volume and having the effective rights displayed (in bold) for the object. These effective rights include any explicit plus inherited rights from folders higher in the file system tree. Remember that whoever has supervisor rights to the server or volume objects automatically gets supervisor rights in the file system.

Imaging Server Policy

New to ZENworks for Desktops 3 is the ability to image a workstation and then to apply that image back to the original or other workstations. See Chapter 13, "Imaging a Workstation" for more detailed information on the functionality of the ZENworks for Desktops 3 imaging system.

The placement of an image, associated with an image object in the directory, onto a workstation, may occur three different ways in ZENworks for Desktops 3.

1. Booting the workstation with two floppy diskettes that communicate with the imaging agent on the server.

2. Placing a special boot partition on an unregistered workstation that communicates with the imaging agent on the server.

3. Placing a special boot partition on a registered workstation and setting the Put an image on this workstation on the next boot field in the workstation object. (In this case the image is determined by an image association or the rules in the Workstation Imaging Policy; see Chapter 8, "Setting Up a Workstation Policy Package" for more details.)

Each of these ways results in the workstation being imaged with the image associated with the workstation, or determined by the imaging agent that resides on the server. The way that the workstation finds the imaging server is, when the imaging boot diskettes are created, the administrator can specify either an IP or a DNS name for the server. This information is saved on the diskettes or in the special boot partition.

The imaging policy becomes effective when the workstation is NOT associated with a workstation object. Because no image is associated with the specific workstation, the imaging server must determine, based on rules, what image to place on the workstation.

This policy enables the administrator to create a set of rules that can govern when a particular image should be used, based on some basic information from the workstation. The imaging server follows the list of rules in the policy until one of the rules is satisfied. The rule that is satisfied results in an associated image that is then applied to the workstation.

NDS Rights, Other, and Rights to Files and Folders pages are described in the "Setting Up a Server Policy Package" section.

Rules Page

This page enables the administrator to input the rules and associated images that the system uses to determine the image to place on a specific type of workstation. Figure 11.4 shows a sample of this page.

You must first press the Add button to add rules to the list. Once you have added several rules, you may then select a specific rule and change its order in the list, look at its properties, or remove the rule. When you press the Add button the following screen is displayed (see Figure 11.5).

You first press the browse button next to the Use this Image field to browse to an image object in the tree that is associated with an image file on the image server. Once the image object is selected, then you may identify the rule that is associated with this image. You may currently only have six key/value pairs to compare about the workstation in order to determine what image to use.

FIGURE 11.4 *Rules page for a sample Imaging Server Policy of a Server Policy Package*

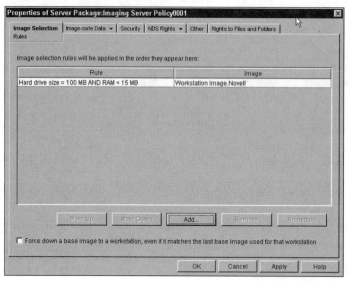

FIGURE 11.5 *Add rule dialog box for a sample Imaging Server Policy of a Server Policy Package*

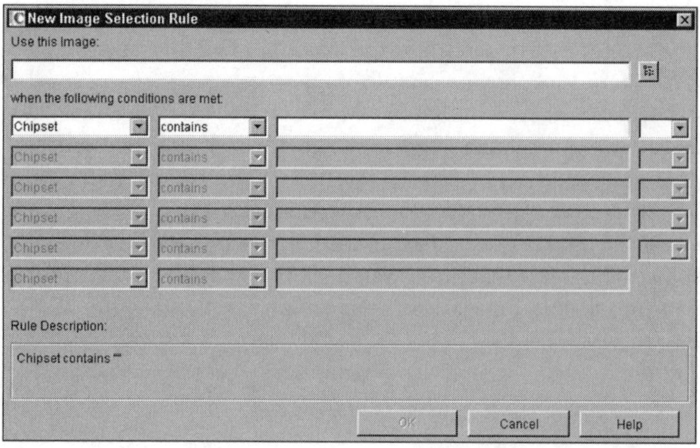

In the middle of the dialog screen you can see the six potential equations that you can generate to determine if the image should be used. The equation is made up of a series of True/False statements that are put together with AND and OR logic. You construct the statement by filling in the drop-down statements. (The resulting statement is displayed in a more English-like view to help you in understanding the equation.)

The logic for the AND and OR operators is strictly left to right in the equation. In the Rule Description box parentheses are added to the equation to help the administrator understand how the rule is evaluated. You cannot insert the parentheses, they are automatically inserted as part of the explanation of the equation and are not under user control.

You first select the key you wish to examine by selecting the key via a drop-down dialog box. The keys that you can choose from are the following:

▶ **Chipset** — This displays the reported processor. An example would be Genuine Intel Mobile Pentium MMX 233 MHZ.

▶ **Video** — This captures the type of video adapter that is in the workstation. An example of this would be Trident Cyber9397 (rev 243).

▶ **Network** — This is the network adapter for the workstation. An example would be 3Com.

▶ **Sound card** — This is the sound card that has been reported. Often this field results in no sound card being detected. This is because the system sends out a PCI request; if no sound cards respond you get this even though a sound card may be present.

▶ **Hard drive controller** — This is the type of hard drive in the system. If the hard drive is an IDE device, then the value for this field is IDE. If the hard drive is a SCSI device, then you get the reported name of the device, such as FUJITSU MHJ2181AT.

▶ **MAC address** — This is the MAC address of the network card. An example of this value would be 00 60 80 03 C2 E7.

▶ **IP Address** — This would be the assigned IP address of the workstation. This would be reported as the traditional 137.65.237.5.

▶ **Hard drive size** — This reports the disk size in number of megabytes. Therefore and 8GB hard drive would be reported as 8192MB in this field. The imaging system may not always report the full disk capacity. It is advisable that you use a wide boundary when generating your rules. For instance if you want to look for 8GB drive put in the statement Hard drive size > 8000 MB and not equal to an exact number.

▶ **RAM** — This is the reported amount of RAM in megabyte units. This would be reported as 64MB. This field also may not always report the exact amount of RAM space that you would expect on your workstation. It is advisable that you use a wide boundary when generating your rules. For instance if you want to look for 16MB RAM put in the statement RAM > 15MB and not equal to an exact number.

When the workstation is booting the imaging system, it is in reality booting up the Linux operating system and running the tools that are included in the imaging system. The values for the keys described previously are values that the Linux system can report to the software. In order to discover what a system reports to Linux, you need to boot a sample workstation with the Imaging system boot disk and run the Img information command. This displays the information that is sent to the image server about the workstation. This information is the data values that you put into the key comparison equations for your rules. You can also get this information from an image by opening the image in the ZENworks image editor and choosing properties on the image root. See Chapter 13, "Imaging a Workstation," for more detailed information on the functionality of the ZENworks for Desktops 3 imaging system.

The next part of the equation is to specify the operator. Two types of operators exist: String or Integer operators. The Hard drive size and RAM fields are treated as integers whereas all of the other fields are treated as strings where a case insensitive string compare is done to determine operator results. The string operators are contains, doesn't contain, begins with, equals. The integer operators are: =, <>, >, >=, <, <=.

These operators perform expected comparisons between the key value supplied by the workstation to the imaging server and the value that you place into the value field of the equation. The following meanings are placed with each operator:

▶ **contains** — The specified value is a substring anywhere in the reported value.

▶ **doesn't contain** — The specified value is not equal to or contained in the reported value.

▶ **begins with** — The specified values are represented in the initial character of the reported value.

▶ **equals** — The specified value is the same as the reported value.

▶ **=** — equals. The specified value is numerically equivalent to the reported value.

▶ **<>** — not equal. The specified value is not equal to the reported value.

- > — greater than. The specified value is greater than the reported value.

- >= — greater than or equal to. The specified value is numerically equal to or greater than the reported value.

- < — less than. The specified value is less than the reported value.

- <= — less than or equal to. The specified value is numerically less than or equal to the reported value.

The next field in the operation is where you enter the value that you wish to compare. The far right field enables you to extend the operation to additional key/value comparisons. Your choices currently are AND and OR.

The Boolean operators are evaluated strictly from left to right. For example, if the following rules were entered into the policy, then the resultant evaluation would be (Hard drive < 600MB AND RAM < 16MB) OR (RAM > 31MB).

1. Hard drive size >= 600MB AND

2. RAM < 16MB OR

3. RAM > 31MB

This would result in giving the image to any system that has a disk smaller than 200MB with less than 16MB of RAM. This would also give the image to any system that has more than 31MB of RAM regardless of the size of the hard drive.

You can view the precedence of the equation, complete with parenthesis, on the bottom half of the screen as you introduce new key/value pairs into your rule.

Once your set of key/value pairs have been entered and you have reviewed your equation at the bottom of the screen, you press the OK button to include the rule into the imaging system, and you are returned to the original Rules page with the rule that you had entered on the screen.

Once again, from this page, after you have entered some rules you can then specify the order that the rules are evaluated. After selecting a rule you can move that rule in the order by pressing either the Move Up or the Move Down buttons. As the imaging server is evaluating the rules, the first rule that results in a TRUE evaluation results in that imaging being supplied to the workstation.

Image-Safe Data Page

The Image-Safe data page is a tab that is composed of three pages. These pages represent information and data that is placed or retrieved from the system regardless of the image that is used. The following depicts the pages that are available by selecting the small triangle drop-down menu on the tab.

An agent exists that may be placed on the workstation called the Image-Safe Data agent. This agent has the responsibility of moving data between a special sector on the disk that is used to store configuration information such as IP address or DHCP configuration along with workgroup information. This information on the disk is not affected by an image taken or placed on the drive.

When the Image-Safe Data agent runs on the workstation it makes sure that the information in the special sector and the operating system are synchronized properly. For example, following an image placement the agent moves the data from the disk into the operating system, setting up the DHCP and computer name. On a workstation that has not just been imaged the agent moves the information from the operating system into the sector on the disk so the data can be restored should a new image be placed on the drive. Should the agent not run, then the workstation would be an exact mirror of the image (with the same IP and computer name configuration).

The Image-Save Data configuration page enables the imaging server to pass this configuration information to the agent via this disk sector.

IP Assignment Log Page

The IP Assignment Log page displays the IP addresses that the imaging server has assigned to any imaged or re-imaged workstations. The set of available IP addresses can be set in the IP Configuration Page described following.

The IP Assignment page displays the log of these addresses that have been assigned.

This page can also be used to place an IP address back into the pool of available addresses. If you have an address that you wish to place back into the pool then you can select it in the log list and then press the Remove button.

WARNING

When you remove a specific IP address it may not be properly represented in the IP Configuration range and therefore will not be reused.

If you have specified a range in the IP Configuration Page to be the set of IP addresses that you will make available for workstations, then when the imaging server uses a portion of the range (at the ends), the range is refreshed on the configuration page. For example, if the range 123.65.234.1 ... 123.65.234.100 were in the configuration and IP address 123.65.234.1-10 were assigned, then the range would be changed to 123.65.234.11 ... 123.65.234.100. Consequently, when you go to the log page and free up IP address 123.65.234.10, the range is not reconfigured and the freed IP address is not reassigned. You must manually go to the configuration page and modify the range to include the addresses that you have freed.

IP Configuration Page

The IP Configuration page enables you to specify whether the workstations that are imaged by the imaging server will obtain their IP address from a DHCP server or via a static assignment that is done as part of the imaging process.

If you select the DHCP option, then when the workstation is imaged the windows system is told to get IP addresses from a DHCP server. If, however, you select that you wish to specify an IP address, then the other fields on the page are activated.

To specify a static IP address you must first enter in the subnet mask and default gateway that you wish all of your imaged workstations (imaged via the image server using this particular policy) to receive. You must also specify the range of IP addresses that are used by the imaging server and assigned uniquely to each of the imaged workstations. You specify the set of IP addresses by using the Add and Add Range buttons.

When the imaging server is given a request for an image then, once the image has been placed onto the workstation, the IP address information is transmitted and assigned to the workstation. That address is then logged in the imaging server and not reused for another workstation.

To remove any address or ranges from the possible set, select the item and press the Remove button. These addresses will no longer be in the pool of available addresses for the imaging server to assign.

Windows Networking Page

In the Windows Networking page you can specify the computer name for the workstation and the workgroup for the system.

The computer name prefix that you enter in the field (maximum of 7 characters) is pre-pended to a randomly generated set of characters and numbers to construct the final 15 character computer name for the workstation.

The Make the computer a member of the following: fields enables you to specify the Workgroup that you want for the workstation. You select which you prefer by selecting the field and entering the Workgroup name.

Security Page

As part of the imaging system the administrator has the ability to request that the workstation have an image taken of itself and placed onto the server. This is done by checking some fields in the workstation object (See Chapter 13, "Imaging a Workstation," for more details), which causes the workstation to take an image of itself on its next reboot.

When the workstation takes an image of itself, or when an image is taken when a request is made through the Linux boot system, the image is transmitted to the image server. This image server then receives the .ZMG file and places it in the path that was specified. To protect the system from overwriting any files or by having users place the image files into inappropriate directories, the imaging server takes the information in the security page and restricts the placement of the image files.

When you check the Allow imaging to overwrite existing files when uploading you are enabling the system to overwrite any files that may have the same name as the one specified by the user, for the name of the image file.

The Restrict uploads to the following directories check box activates the requirement that all requested uploads must specify one of the directories identified. If the directory portion of the destination path, specified by the user, does not match one of the directories specified in the list on this page then the request to store the uploaded image is refused. To add paths to the list of accepted destinations, press the Add button and enter in the path that is acceptable.

Paths in the directories may be one of the following formats:

Driveletter:path

Volume\path

NTShare\path

The system does NOT, for example, take any UNC path. When the user enters the location of the file, including the path this information transmits to the imaging server, the server compares the directory portion of the path given with all of the strings in this list. If a match occurs (that is, the directory is listed) then the operation is accepted and the image is taken and stored, otherwise the operation fails and the image is not taken.

Workstation Import Policy

In previous versions of ZENworks for Desktops when a workstation registered with the tree, it would place a cookie into the container of the user. Then the administrator had to execute an import program on their workstation to take these registration records and create workstation objects. These workstation object DNs were then communicated back to the workstation via the same registration/reboot process. If your system was very large, it could become very uncomfortable having to keep running the import program. Often administrators got creative and scheduled the import process to run as a scheduled action on their workstations.

In ZENworks for Desktops 3 this is no longer necessary. A service that now runs on a NetWare or NT server automatically receives these requests and immediately creates the workstation object. Once the object is created it returns the DN to the workstation. The workstation no longer needs to perform a reboot in order to get its registered workstation DN. In order to perform these actions, the import service must be running on the server and must be accessible using the DNS name of zenwsimport either through the local host file on each workstation or via a DNS service. Additionally, the import service must have rights in the directory to be able to create the workstation objects. The pages in this policy enable the administrator to grant these create rights to the import service, to specify how to name the workstation objects and in which container to place the objects, and the ability to limit the number of requests that can be satisfied (to keep the system from overloading a server).

The import service can also be configured to ignore the first N requests from a workstation before it creates a workstation object. This can be useful if the workstation may need to pass through several hands to get properly configured and tested before it is actually given to the final end-user. This is to help this process settle before the workstation object is actually created.

NOTE Your desktops do not import automatically if the workstations are finding a ZENworks 2 search policy in the tree. They must see either no search policy or a ZENworks for Desktop 3 search policy in order to activate the automatic workstation import and other ZENworks for Desktop 3 features. See chapter 3, "Setting up ZENworks for Desktops in Your Tree," and the section, "Setting up the Workstation in the Tree" for more information.

The following describes each of the pages that are available with the Workstation Import process. NDS Rights, Other, *and* Rights to Files and Folders pages are described in the "Setting up a Server Policy Package" section.

Containers Page

This page enables the administrator to grant rights to the import service to containers where they must create workstation objects. When you add a container to the list, the system grants rights to the policy object. When the import service needs to perform an import it logs in as the policy being used, enabling it to obtain rights to create workstation objects in the specified container.

The process of adding and removing containers is familiar. You press the Add button and then you are presented with a dialog that enables you to browse through the tree to select the container you desire. Once selected, the container is added to the list and the import service is given a trustee assignment to that container and given the rights to Browse and Create objects.

To remove a container from the list, select the desired container and press the Remove button. This removes the trustee assignment that was given to the service and deletes it from the displayed list.

Platforms Page

The platforms page enables you to specify the naming of the workstation objects, the location of the object in the tree, and any workstation groups of which you want the workstation objects to be a member. This can be specified for each of the following categories: General, WinNT/2000, or Win 9x (for example, Windows 95/98).

Each of the pages within these categories is identical, with the exception that on the non-general pages you have the additional field: Enable platform settings to override general settings. When this field is checked, then the platform specific configuration parameters are used rather than the general. We only discuss the general pages because they apply to all of the other platform pages.

Figure 11.6 displays the first general page that is available.

Each page has three tabs that enable you to configure separate options of the import policy. These tabs are Location, Naming, and Groups. Each of the following subsections discusses these tabs.

Location Tab

This page enables the administrator to identify the container in the tree that should hold the workstation object when it is created during the import process. Figure 11.6 displays this screen.

The flag Allow importing of workstations enables or disables the ability to import workstations from this user. Once this flag is activated, then the other fields of the page are useable.

The Create workstation objects in drop-down box allows the administrator various options for locating the container in which to place the workstation objects. The options are as follows:

► **Server Container** — This option is new to ZENworks for Desktops 3 and when selected tells the system to place the workstation objects in the same container as the server that is running the import process.

General page of a sample Workstation Import Policy of a Server Policy Package

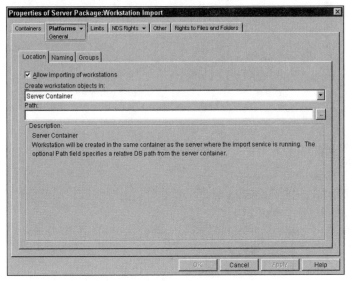

▶ **User Container**—This signals that the container that holds the user object, of the user that had logged into the system when the registration of the workstation occurred, is the container that also holds the workstation object. Remember it is the first user that connects to the system (after the number of ignored connections has passed) that has the association to the workstation. A path may be specified in the path field that would be considered to be relative to the User's container. The path field is constructed by entering a relative path. This relative path is constructed by a series of dots and container names. For each dot in the path, the system moves up one level from the associated object container. For example, the path of ..Workstations means for the system to go up two levels and then in a container called Workstations at that level. If an alternate user is desired then you must run the un-registration tool described in Chapter 13.

▶ **Associated Object Container** — This signals that the container that has the policy package associated with it is used as the starting container to place the workstation object. If a path is specified, then the associated container is used as the base and the path is considered a relative path. The path field is constructed by entering a relative path. This relative path is constructed by a series of dots and container names. For each dot in the path, the system moves up one level from the associated object container. For example, the path of ..Workstations means for the system to go up two levels and then enter a container called Workstations at that level.

▶ **Selected Container** — This identifies that the specified path is an absolute container path in the tree. The Path field is required with this selection and must identify the specific container that will hold the workstation object.

Workstation Naming Page

On this page the administrator can describe how the import process should use the information in the registration to craft the name of the workstation object.

The Workstation name field displays the final combination of registration information that is combined into the name. In the previous example, the workstation object name is the computer name followed by the MAC address. This is confirmed by the fact that the workstation name field has Computer+MAC Address. If the computer name was Rtanner and the MAC address of the NIC card were 12345, then the workstation object name would be Rtanner12345.

The Add name fields and place them in order: field displays the various components that are put together to form the workstation name. Each line that is displayed in this field represents a value that is part of the name. The order of the lines from top to bottom represents the order that they appear in the name. The options that can be placed in the names are as follows:

▶ **<User Defined>** — This represents an administrator defined string. When this field is chosen, then the administrator is prompted to enter a string into the dialog box. This string is placed into the name. This can be any combination of standard ASCII visible characters including white space characters.

▶ **Computer** — This represents the computer name that was given to the computer usually during installation of the operating system.

- **Container** — This represents the name of the container into which the workstation object is placed. This name is then included in the workstation name.

- **CPU** — This value represents the CPU type of the machine. The possible values are 386, 486, and PENTIUM.

- **DNS** — This represents the DNS (Domain Name Services) name of the computer.

- **IP Address** — This represents the IP address of the machine when it is first registered with the tree. In previous versions of ZENworks for Desktops this was retrieved through the Network Address request and a preferred protocol set to IP.

- **MAC Address** — This represents the address of the machine when it is first registered with the tree. In previous versions of ZENworks for Desktops this was referred to as the Network Address.

- **OS** — This represents the operating system type of the machine. The expected values would be WINNT, WIN95, for example.

- **Server** — This represents the name of the current server. If the user login has not occurred, and the preferred server has not been done, then this server could simply be the first server that responded with a connection. In WINNT systems, where the registration is running as part of a service, this server is the first server to respond to the request for the connection and not necessarily the preferred server of the user.

- **User** — This is the login name of the user that was connected to the tree when the registration process first executed.

As an example, let us assume that a workstation had been registered with the following values:

```
CPU = PENTIUM
DNS = zen.novell.com
MAC address = 00600803c2e7
IP address = 137.65.61.99
OS = WINNT
Server = ZENSERVER
User = rtanner
Computer = RonComputer
```

Then, if we were to administer the workstation import policy with the following naming attributes, the corresponding workstation name would be created, assuming pieces that are in quotes are a user-defined string:

```
UserOS = rtannerWINNT
DNSCPU = zen.novell.comPENTIUM
User" "MAC Address = rtanner 00600803c2e7
```

You must remember that these values are only used at workstation object creation time. Once the object is created its name never changes. So if you replace the NIC card, although the address of the workstation changed, the name of the workstation does not change; if the name includes the NIC address then the workstation retains the name with the old NIC address.

Workstations Groups

The workstation groups page enables you to specify into which groups you would like to place the workstation object when it is created. By placing the workstation object into a specific group you can automatically provide policies or rights to the workstation by group associations.

In the workstation groups page you may add and remove groups in the list and the workstation will be placed in as a member of each group. The following describes the behavior of each button on the screen:

▸ **Add** — Press this button to add a group to the list. When the button is pressed a dialog box is presented that enables you to browse the tree to identify the group. You browse the tree in the right pane and select the group in the left pane. Once a group is selected it is added and displayed to the list.

▸ **Remove** — This button is activated when a group in the window is highlighted by pressing the left mouse button when the cursor is over the desired group. When a group is selected and this button is pressed, the group is removed from the list.

▸ **Remove All . . .** — This button completely removes all groups from the list and cleans the set from consideration.

Remember that this policy is only activated when a new workstation is imported into the tree. If a workstation that was created with this policy is associated with a group and you go into the import policy and change the group memberships, the workstations that have already been created retain their group memberships. Only the new workstations created after the change are affected.

Limits Page

On the Limits page the administrator can have some control about when a workstation automatically registers and how the import service on the server behaves. The intention of these fields is to ensure that the performance of the service does not consume a significant amount of processing on the server.

The first portion of the page; the User login number field, enables you to configure how many times the workstation must be used (a user logs into the network via that desktop) before it is registered into the tree. This may be useful to use if your desktops must pass through several hands (that may connect to the tree) before it gets to its final user destination. Each time the workstation is used and a user is connected to the tree (or the Workstation Manager agents connects to the tree) the workstation communicates with the workstation import and requests a workstation object. If the number of login times has not been consumed, then the service reports that one is not created, and the workstation continues. This repeats until the number of login times has occurred, whereupon the service creates the workstation object and returns the DN of the workstation object to the workstation. The desktop then records this DN in its registry

The user login count is kept in the workstation registry and is transmitted to the import server who checks it against the policy. If the count is greater than the policy then the import is performed. This count on the workstation is NOT reset if the policy changes.

Limiting the number of workstations imported enables the administrator to throttle the number of workstations that are created. This keeps your NDS from overloading with a tremendous amount of objects and having to synchronize them around your tree. Imposing this limit forces the service to only create the specified number of workstations in an hour period. As soon as the maximum has been reached within the hour the workstations are told to proceed without a workstation object. The next time they log into the network, and the maximum has not been exceeded, then the service creates a workstation object for them.

Workstation Removal Policy

Along with the ability to automatically create workstations in the tree, ZENworks for Desktops 3 provides an automated way to have expired workstation objects removed from the tree. This is to keep the tree from being cluttered with workstations that are no longer associated with any physical device.

Each time a workstation is used and it has been registered in the tree, a service visits the workstation object and timestamps the last visit into the workstation object, along with refreshing several other pieces of information in the workstation object. This timestamp is what the Workstation Removal service is looking at when it determines if the workstation should be removed.

The following pages enable the administrator to configure how the system removes these expired workstation objects. NDS Rights, Other, *and* Rights to Files and Folders pages are described in the "Setting up a Server Policy Package" section.

Containers Page

This page enables the administrator to grant rights to the removal service to containers where they must remove workstation objects. When you add a container to the list, the system grants rights to the policy object. When the removal service needs to perform and delete a workstation object it logs in as the policy being used, enabling it to obtain rights to remove workstation objects in the specified container.

These containers are the only ones that the service monitors for stale workstation objects.

The process of adding and removing containers is familiar. You press the Add button and then you are presented with a dialog that enables you to browse through the tree to select the container you desire. Once selected, the container is added to the list and the import service is given a trustee assignment to that container, and given the rights to Browse and Delete objects.

To remove a container from the list, select the desired container and press the Remove button. This removes the trustee assignment that was given to the service and deletes it from the displayed list.

Limits Page

This page enables you to specify how stale a workstation object must be before it is considered for removal. Figure 11.7 is a snapshot of a sample limits page.

You can use the up and down spinner controls to specify the number of days the workstation should not be connected with a device before it is considered for deletion. Once the timestamp in the workstation object is older than the specified number of days on this page, then the removal service deletes the object from the directory.

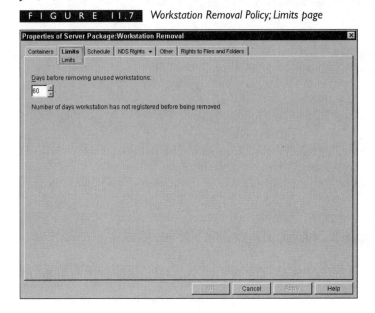

F I G U R E   11.7 *Workstation Removal Policy; Limits page*

Schedule Page

This page enables the administrator to identify how often and when the workstation removal service should run on the server.

On this page you may identify the following configuration schedules:

- ▶ **Year** — This is the year to begin the launch of the removal service.

- ▶ **Date** — This is the calendar date with the above year when the removal service will be launched.

- ▶ **Start Time** — This is the time of day when the removal service is available to run.

- ▶ **Duration** — This enables you to specify how long, after the start time, the removal service should run.

- ▶ **Repeat interval** — This enables you the ability to specify how often after the initial start date the removal service should re-run and be made available.

► **Limit number of workstations removed** — This enables you to specify in the session value the maximum number of workstations that should be removed while the removal service is available. When this maximum is reached the service quits removing workstations until the next specified execution time. This is to keep from consuming a significant amount of processing cycles for DS to refresh the partitions where the removal has occurred.

The service, when started, calculates based on the start date and how often it should come alive (interval) and which day it should work. If today's the day, then the service begins its workstation removal work. This is done so that even if the server were to need to be rebooted, the service still properly calculates the day it should run and not rely on being up the number of days in the interval.

zeninvRollUpPolicy

The Inventory RollUp Policy dictates to the services that are running on a specific server (such as, inventory server) where they should roll-up or transmit the inventory information that they have received from the various workstations. By doing this, the system provides the ability to receive local inventory information and then move it up in the tree hierarchy, consolidating inventory information from various remote locations, and constructing a more centralized database of inventory information (see Chapter 12, "Using ZENworks Workstation Inventory," for more detailed information).

When the inventory system is installed into the network, the system creates service objects that govern the behavior of the agents that are working on each of the inventory servers. These agents also respond to this policy to understand to which service agent they should transmit their inventory information. All service agents that are associated with this policy transmit their inventory information to the same target agent.

NDS Rights, Other, *and* Rights to Files and Folders pages are described in the "Setting up a Server Policy Package" section.

Figure 11.8 is a sample of this page.

As you can see in the sample screen (Figure 11.8) the policy simply requests the object DN of the service where the associated agents should transmit their inventory information. The local agents may keep a copy of the inventory data, if they are a designated database gathering location, but they still transmit an additional copy if they are configured to do so.

F I G U R E   1 1 . 8   *Inventory Roll-up Policy of a Server Policy Package*

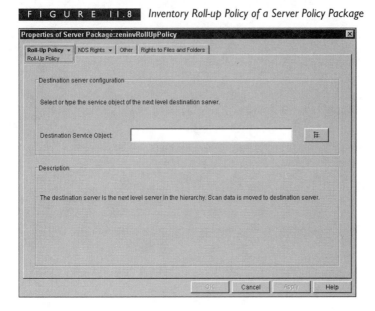

In this policy you press the browse button to the right of the field and browse the tree to select the service object of the inventory agent that you wish to receive the information.

The roll-up policy is only read by the service manager agent upon startup and then every 1000 minutes (this is not configurable). So if the policy change needs to be immediately effective, then the service manager agent on the server must be stopped and restarted.

CHAPTER 12

Using ZENworks
Workstation Inventory

ZENworks for Desktops includes powerful workstation inventory software that allows you to gather complete hardware and software inventory for all managed workstations on your network. Once workstations have been imported, the inventory software can be used to collect, store, and report information about the client workstations on your network. This information can be useful to help make business decisions on how to manage workstations. The following are some examples of business decisions that can be made from workstation inventory information:

- ► Which workstations need new applications
- ► Which workstations need updated hardware and drivers
- ► Which workstations should receive an application object
- ► Which workstations are running the corporate software standard
- ► Which workstations conform to the corporate hardware standard

The following sections describe the workstation inventory process, how to set inventory up in your environment, and what tasks can be performed once it has been properly installed and configured.

► · ◄

Understanding Workstation Inventory

To better help you understand how to make the most of the workstation inventory feature of ZENworks for desktops, you need to know how the process works and what components are involved. The following sections describe the inventory process, the servers that are involved, and the roles they play in various inventory database designs.

Understanding the Inventory Process

The inventory process is the act of acquiring hardware and software information from the workstation, relaying that information to the inventory server, and then storing it into a database for later retrieval. The following sections describe how workstations are scanned, how inventory data is rolled up to the database, what information is collected, and the files and directories involved.

Workstation Scanning

Workstation scanning is done by an application that runs on the client workstation. That application scans the workstation and collects data based on the configurations of the inventory settings. If the workstation is Desktop

Management Interface (DMI) compliant, then the scanner also queries the DMI service layer and collects data.

Once the scanner has collected information about the workstation, it stores it in an .STR file in the scan directory of the inventory server. The scanner tracks the changes in the scan data by storing it in the HIST.INI file. The scanner also stores a minimal amount of the scan data in the MINFO.INI file. The data in the MINFO.INI file is later used to update the NDS object for the workstation with a sub-set of the scan data for easier access and viewing. Any errors that the scanner reports are stored in the ZENERRORS.LOG file.

Workstation inventory scanning uses the following steps to update the inventory server and NDS:

1. The inventory policies in NDS define the inventory settings, such as scanning time, whether to include software scanning of workstations, and the location of the scan directory.

2. The Scanner reads the settings in the inventory policies and uses them to collect the workstation inventory information.

3. The Scanner stores the scan data of each workstation as an .STR file in the scan directory (SCANDIR) at the server.

4. The Scanner also stores a minimal sub-set of workstation inventory information of the workstation, in the NDS workstation object.

5. The Selector, running on the inventory server, validates the .STR file and places the file in the enterprise merge directory (ENTMERGEDIR). If a database is attached, the Selector places the files in the Database directory (DBDIR).

6. If a database is attached to the server, the server updates the database with the inventory information of the .STR file.

7. The network administrator is then able to view the inventory information, query the database, and generate inventory reports in ConsoleOne.

Inventory Data Roll Up

Now that you understand how the inventory scan process works, you need to understand how that information is rolled up to other servers and databases that are higher in the tree. In many networks, one server is not enough to collect and store inventory data for every workstation in the tree. For this reason, multiple servers can be configured to collect inventory data and roll that information up to other servers.

ZENworks uses the following steps to roll scanned data up once it has been collected on a server:

1. Once the Selector validates the .STR file and places the file in the enterprise merge directory (ENTMERGEDIR) for roll-up of scan data, the sending server uses a Roll-Up Policy to identify the server to which it will transmit the scan data. It also reads the roll up schedule to determine the specified time for roll-up of data.

2. The sending server compresses the .STR files as a .ZIP file and places the .ZIP file in the enterprise push directory (ENTPUSHDIR). The Sender then sends the .ZIP file to the Receiver on the next-level server.

3. The receiving server on the next-level receives the .ZIP file and places the file in ENTPUSHDIR. If this server has a database attached to it or if the server is a Root Server, the compressed files are placed in the database directory (DBDIR).

4. The receiving server extracts the .ZIP file containing the .STR files into a temp directory (DBDIR\TEMP) and updates the database with the inventory information of the workstation .STR file.

5. The network administrator is then able to view the inventory information, query the database, and generate inventory reports in ConsoleOne.

What Hardware Information Is Recorded

The scan program scans the workstation hardware for Desktop Management Interface (DMI) hardware. It collects device specific information for each DMI compliant device in the system including:

Floppy Disk Drive — Type/Capacity

Hard Disk Drive — Type/Size

Mapped Drives — Path/Size

CD-ROM — Type/Speed

Processors — Type/Speed

BIOS — Vendor/Version

Bus — Type/Speed

Mouse — Type/Port

Keyboard — Type/Port

Display Adapters — Vendor/Type/Memory

Network Adapters — Vendor/Type/Memory

Memory — Type/Speed

Serial Ports — Type

Parallel Ports — Type

Modems — Vendor/Type/Speed

What Software Information Is Recorded

The scan program also scans the workstation software for Desktop Management Interface (DMI) software. The software scan performs the following functions based on its setup and configuration:

▶ Check the existence of the software at the workstations and servers.

▶ Gather information about the application file.

▶ Report the information about the scanned software (such as Software Vendor, Software Title, File Size, and so on.).

▶ Check for the software specified in the inventory policy associated with the workstation object.

▶ Customize the software scanning based on the software list configured (discussed later).

▶ Collect configuration file information and report details and contents of the system files.

▶ Report information about the installed drivers.

Inventory Files and Directories

Workstation inventory uses several files and directories during the scanning and roll up process. You should be aware of the following files used during the scanning and roll up process:

▶ **HIST.INI** — Located in the Windows TEMP directory on the workstation. Contains the history of the scan data for each workstation.

▶ **MINIFO.INI** — Located in the Windows TEMP directory on the workstation. Contains a minimal sub-set of scan data that is used to update the workstation object in NDS for easier access.

▶ **.STR** — Formatted: *macaddress_gmt_sequencenumber*.STR. Located in the SCANDIR directory on the inventory server. Created by the scanning program. Contains all inventory information scanned from the workstation.

▶ **.ZIP** — Formatted: *scheduletime_inventoryservername_siteID_sitename*.ZIP Located in the EntPushDir and DBDir. Contains the compressed scan data for several workstations, up to 1000 .STR files, collected by a receiving inventory server. Used to transmit the data from one server to another.

▶ **.PRP** — Formatted: *scheduletime_inventoryservername*.PRP. Located in the .ZIP files. Identifies the information for roll up from the enterprise push directory to the next-level server. The properties file contains the schedule time, inventory server name, and signature which helps to authenticate the .ZIP file.

Once the scan program has run and the hardware and software information about the server has been recorded, that information is stored on the inventory servers in the following directory locations:

▶ **ScanDir** — Contains the .STR files which is the raw data collected by the scan programs which are run at the workstation.

▶ **DBDir** — Contains the .STR files for workstations that have been scanned on the network. The .STR files in the DBDir directory are used to update the workstation objects in the database.

▶ **EntMergeDir** — Stores the .STR and files created and transferred by the workstation scan programs.

▶ **EntPushDir** — Stores the .STR and .ZIP files used to roll inventory data up in an enterprise tree.

Understanding Inventory Database Server Types

Now that you understand how the scan process works, you need to understand what happens to the data that is scanned by the workstations. That data is stored in directories and databases located on inventory servers. The following are the types of servers that are used in the inventory process.

Root Server

The root server acts as the highest point in the inventory tree. A root server by default must have a database attached to it. The root server can collect data from intermediate servers, leaf servers, or from workstations attached to it. A root server can only be configured to receive data, not to roll it up to another level.

Intermediate Server

The intermediate server acts as a staging server to receive data from a lower server in the tree and send it to another intermediate server or to a root server. By default, the intermediate server does not have a database attached, nor does it have workstations attached. However, you can configure the intermediate server to have both workstations and a database attached to it. The intermediate server typically receives data from a leaf server or another intermediate server and then rolls it up higher in the tree, eventually to the root server.

Leaf Server

The leaf server acts as the gathering server of inventory information from workstations. By default, the leaf server must have workstations attached, but does not have a database attached to it. The leaf server simply gathers data and rolls it up higher in the tree. Typically the data is rolled up to an intermediate server, but a leaf server can also roll data up to a root server.

Stand-Alone Server

The stand-alone server acts as a single point of inventory data collection for workstations. The stand-alone server must have both a database and workstations attached to it. The data collected by a stand-alone server cannot be rolled up to another server, nor can information collected by a leaf server be rolled up to a stand-alone server. Typically the stand-alone server is used in small networks where only one inventory server is needed to collect data.

Understanding Inventory Server Roles

Now that you understand the types of servers that are used for workstation inventory, you need to know the roles they can provide. Depending on their types, each server can be configured to perform one or both of the following two roles.

Workstations Attached

The first role servers can perform is to have workstations attached. Setting this option for the server means that this server accepts data from the scan programs being run at the workstations. At least one server on the network must be performing this role, but usually most of the servers configured for workstation inventory will be performing the role of collecting data from the workstations. Leaf servers and stand-alone servers always have this option set, but you can configure root server and intermediate servers to have workstations attached as well.

Database Attached

The next role a server can perform is to have a database attached to it. Setting this option means that the server is configured to enter the information scanned by the workstation, either locally or up from a server below, into a local database. This means that a database must be running on the server to accept the information from ZENworks. Root servers and stand-alone servers always have this option set, but you can configure intermediate servers and leaf servers to have a database as well.

Workstation Inventory Design

Now that you understand the types of servers and the roles they play in workstation inventory, you need to design an inventory tree that matches your network. The following sections describe some common designs for generic networks.

Stand-Alone Inventory

The stand-alone inventory is the most simple design. Only one server is involved. That server acts as the collection and storage service for inventory data scanned from workstations. It has an inventory database installed on it and workstations attached.

This type of design is perfect for smaller networks with 5,000 or fewer workstations. It is easy to maintain and configure, however it is not scalable.

Centralized Inventory

The centralized inventory design, shown in Figure 12.1, is for large networks where all servers are connected on a LAN. In this approach allowance is made for a larger number of users by adding a number of leaf and intermediate servers for workstation scanners to send their data to.

The centralized inventory approach is still fairly easy to maintain; however, roll up policies must be configured for the intermediate and leaf servers.

FIGURE 12.1 *The centralized workstation inventory design*

Centralized Inventory

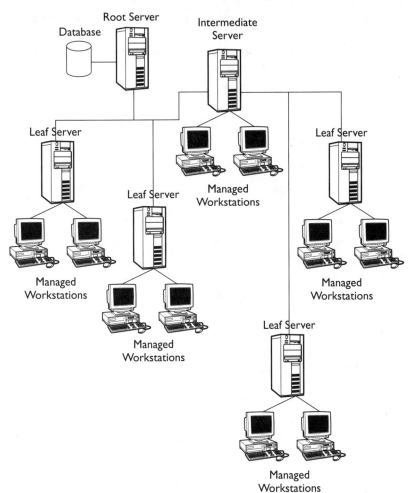

Distributed Inventory

The distributed inventory design, shown in Figure 12.2, is for large networks where several remote sites are connected through a WAN. In this approach allowance is made for a larger number of users by creating several root servers, one at each remote site, and then leaf and intermediate servers for workstation scanners to send their data to.

The distributed inventory approach is still much more difficult to maintain because you need to manage several inventory trees. However the distributed approach overcomes problems that can occur, rolling up large numbers of workstations from remote offices.

► . . . . ◄

F I G U R E   12.2 *The distributed workstation inventory design*

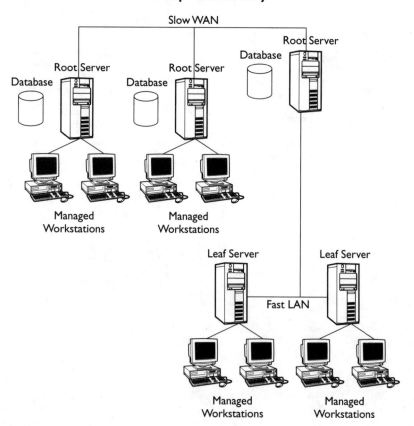

Enterprise Inventory

Enterprise Inventory

The final type of inventory design is the enterprise inventory design shown in Figure 12.3. Most enterprise networks take this approach in one form or another. In the enterprise design, accommodations for the large number of users, yet a single management point, is made by creating a single root server and then interlacing intermediate and leaf servers at strategic locations in the network to insure optimal performance.

FIGURE 12.3 The enterprise workstation inventory design

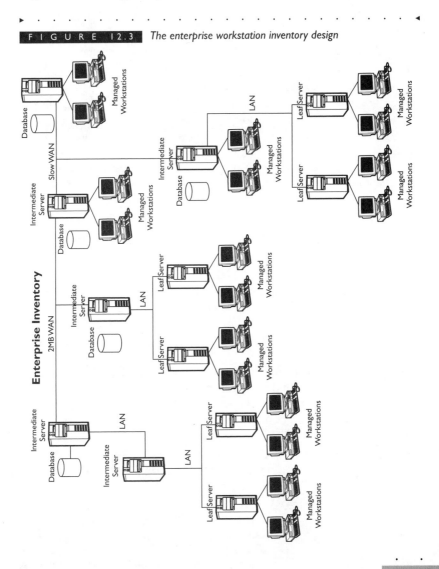

The best way to achieve an optimal enterprise design is to follow the steps outlined in the following sections.

List the Sites in the Enterprise   The first step in designing an enterprise workstation inventory tree is to describe the entire network of your company by doing the following:

▶ List the various sites in your company. (Buildings, cities, countries, and so on.)

▶ List the physical links between the various sites.

▶ Identify the type of links in terms of bandwidth and reliability.

Determine the Ideal Place for Root Server   Once you have listed the sites in you enterprise network, you need to determine the best place to put the root server. The inventory information stored in the inventory database of the Root Server consists of all lower-level sites on the network as well as the Root Server site.

The location of the root server determines the behavior and scalability of you inventory tree. You should consider the following factors when determining its location:

▶ The Root Server should be on the site with high network bandwidth.

▶ A Console administrator can collect Workstation Inventory information from any of the sites connected on high-speed links from the Root Server, or from the Root Server level site.

▶ A database server of suitable configuration can be provided for the Inventory server. For a network with 250,000 workstations, the recommended configuration for the Root Server is 25GB of disk pace and 1GB RAM.

Determine Requirements for Other Databases   Now that you have determined the location of the root server you need to determine if you need to maintain database servers at different sites. You may want to maintain additional databases if sites or sub-trees are managed for inventory at different locations over a slow link.

You should also consider specific reasons to have a separate database for a single site or a set of sites. There may be some organizational needs of your company to have the database server on different sites.

For a majority of enterprises, there may be no need to have any other database besides the enterprise-wide single database. All site-specific reports can be generated from this database easily.

If you determine that another database is required, consider the following to determine the appropriate location and setup:

▶ Identify the sites that need a database. Additionally, you need to examine whether the database will cater to the local site or a site of sites (sub-tree). Then identify the sites that require data in each inventory database.

▶ All the sites served by a single database should typically access this database instead of the database at Root Server for inventory management. This reduces the load on the database at Root Server.

▶ Database administrators should be available for these sites.

Identify the Route for Inventory Data   Once you have determined any additional databases needed you need to identify the routes for inventory data for all sites to the nearest database. From those routes you then need to determine the final the route to the database on the Root Server.

The route plan can become complex, so to help devise a route plan follow these guidelines:

▶ Each route can have an intermediate server at a staging site. The Intermediate Server receives and transmits the data to the next destination. These are application-layer level routes for inventory data. There can be various network-layer level routes between two adjacent servers, which is determined and managed by the routers in the network.

▶ The route answers the basic question: To which site will the inventory data travel from a particular site so that it eventually reaches the database at the Root Server, which is its final destination?

▶ There may be multiple routes. Choose the fastest and most reliable route. To determine the route, consider the physical network links.

▶ Routes identified once and made operational can be changed later; although there may be some cost in terms of management and traffic generation. If no intermediate database is involved, you can change the route by changing the NDS based policy only.

▶ Put Intermediate servers on sites where the link parameters change substantially. Criteria to consider is difference in bandwidth, difference unreliability of the links, and need for different scheduling.

▶ Availability of servers on the intermediate site for staging the inventory data should be considered in deciding the sites for Intermediate Servers. Provide enough disk space on these servers to store all the inventory data on the disk until the Roll-up policy asks to send them to the next destination.

▶ Workstations should not be connected to the Inventory server over WAN as the scanning of workstations should not happen across WAN.

Identify Servers on Each Site for Inventory, Intermediate, and Database
Once you have planned the routes that data will take to the root server, you need to identify servers on each site to perform the roles necessary to achieve the route. Specifically you need to identify servers to act as inventory, intermediate, and database server.

A single server can have different roles if it has sufficient resources. For example, an inventory server can be a Leaf Server with database. You could also designate a server as an Intermediate Server with Database, which receives inventory from the workstations and also has an inventory database.

When considering the roles of the server you should take into account the following factors:

▶ The number of workstations attached to the server also determines the load.

▶ Take an average of 50KB inventory data from each workstation to calculate the load.

▶ Any Inventory server that has workstations attached to it requires 100KB per workstation.

▶ The server that has the Inventory database requires 200KB per workstation.

▶ An Intermediate server that rolls-up data requires 5KB for roll-up of 50KB scan data.

Create the Tree of Servers for Workstation Inventory Once you have determined the roles that inventory servers will take at each site, you need to create the tree of servers that will be used for workstation inventory.

Once you have the inventory server tree designed, make certain that the following are true:

- ▶ The root of the tree is the Root Server.
- ▶ Servers on each site of the tree represent all the sites in the company.
- ▶ At least one server exists per site.
- ▶ Assuming that workstations to be scanned exist on each site, there is an inventory server role on each site.
- ▶ Optionally, database and intermediate servers exist at the appropriate sites.

Create an Implementation Plan   Once you have designed your inventory server tree, you need to create an implementation plan. The implementation plan should cover the phased deployment of inventory throughout the network.

To help with creating an implementation plan use the following guidelines:

- ▶ Start the deployment from the root server site and flow it down to the servers of other sites that connect to the Root Server.
- ▶ Use the number of workstations on each site and server as the main criteria for deployment.
- ▶ Deploy the product on approximately 5,000 workstations per day.

Setting up Workstation Inventory

Now that you understand how workstation inventory works, you need to know how to get it set up and configured for your network. This section covers installing the appropriate components for workstation inventory and configuring them to start your workstation inventory process.

Installing Workstation Inventory Components

The first step is to install the correct components. For workstation inventory to work you need to select the following options during the install process as outlined in Chapter 2:

- ▶ **Automatic Workstation Import** — This component installs the necessary objects and programs to import your workstations into the NDS tree. The workstation objects are necessary to collect and store the inventory data.

▶ **Workstation Inventory** — This component installs the necessary objects and programs to complete the inventory process.

▶ **Sybase** — This component installs the Sybase database and other database components to the server. You can only install the database to one server at a time; however, you must install a database on at least one server to begin workstation inventory. If you need to add additional databases simply run the install again and only select the Sybase option.

NOTE
Once the databases are installed you may wish to install and configure an Oracle database, or modify the setup of the Sybase database. Refer to the on-line documentation for ZENworks for Desktops and the readme file included on your installation CD for more information.

Setting Workstation Inventory

Once you have installed the appropriate components and you have your workstation inventory tree design completed, you are ready to begin configuring your network to start scanning workstation data and storing it into the inventory database. The following sections describe the configuration necessary to implement your tree design.

Configuring the Settings for the Inventory Service Object

The first step in configuring workstation inventory is to configure the settings for the inventory service object. The Inventory Service object settings configure the scanning for the associated workstations.

From within ConsoleOne, right-click the inventory service object ➪ click Properties ➪ click the Inventory Service Object Properties tab as shown in Figure 12.4. From the Inventory Service Object property page, you can configure the following:

Modify the Role for the Inventory Service Object   Based on the servers that you have deployed for scanning inventory, you must specify the role of the server. You can select Root Server, Intermediate Server, Leaf Server, or Stand-alone Server based on you inventory configuration.

The Inventory Service Object Properties tab for Inventory
Service objects in ConsoleOne

Discard Scan Data Files at the Specified Date and Time   Set the time
at which you wish any scan data files (.ZIP files) that have scan information
collected to be discarded. The scan data files are removed from the server at
the time specified in this field. This can be useful in keeping your servers from
running out of disk space.

Modify the Path for the Scan Files   When you install ZENworks for
Desktops, you specify the volume on the server for storing the scan data files.
If required, you can modify the volume or the directory of the Scan Directory
(SCANDIR) setting from the Inventory Service Object property page.

To modify the setting type in the location of the new SCANDIR directory
path on the server format the Scan Directory Path is as follows:

\\server_name\volumename\path

You cannot modify the server name specified in the SCANDIR path. If you modify the directory, the directory must already exist.

Enable Scanning of Workstations   To select the enable scanning of workstations option to scan the workstations associated with the policy, you must enable the scan option listed in the Inventory Service Object property page. By default, the scanners collect only hardware information of the workstations.

Enforce Full Scan   When scanning the workstation for the first time the Scanner collects the complete inventory of the workstation. A complete inventory scan of the workstation is referred as a *Full Scan*.

After the workstation is inventoried, the next time the Scanner runs, it compares the current inventory data to the history data that it maintains. If any changes to the workstation exist, the Scanner creates a *Delta Scan*, which collects the changes in inventory since the last scan was reported. The Delta scan setting is the default scan operation for each successive scan after the first scanning of the workstation.

If the Status Log reported by the inventory component indicates that the scanning on the workstation is not successful, you can enforce a Full Scan. This policy's settings are applicable for all workstations associated with it. To override this policy, you set this option for an individual workstation.

Configuring the Roll-Up Policy of Scan Data

If your workstation inventory tree design includes multiple levels, you need to configure roll-up of scan data in your inventory setup. You need to specify the details, such as the next-level server for roll-up in the Roll-Up Policy that is contained in the Server Package. Use the following steps to create and configure a role-up policy for scan data.

Create a Server Package That Contains the Roll-Up Policy for Identifying the Next-Level Server for Roll-Up.

1. In ConsoleOne, right-click the Policy Packages container ⇨ click New ⇨ click Policy Package ⇨ click Server Package ⇨ click zeninvRollUpPolicy ⇨ click Next.

2. Type the name for the Server Package ⇨ click Next ⇨ click Finish.

Enable the Roll-Up Policy in the Server Package and Associate the Server Package.

1. In ConsoleOne, right-click the Server Package ⇨ click Properties ⇨ click Policies ⇨ click one of the following sub-tabs: General, NetWare, or WinNT-2000.

2. Check the check box under the Enabled column for the zeninvRollup Policy.

3. Click Properties. The Roll-Up Policy tab should be displayed.

4. Browse to select the DN of the Inventory Service object ⇨ click OK.

5. Click the Associations tab ⇨ Add. The first time you enable the Roll-Up Policy, you are prompted to associate the policy package. The policy you configured and enabled earlier will not be in effect until you associate this policy package with a server.

6. Browse and select the server that you want to associate the Roll-Up Policy to ⇨ click OK.

Schedule the Roll-Up Time.

1. In ConsoleOne, right-click the Server Package ⇨ click Properties ⇨ click Policies ⇨ click one of the following sub-tabs: General, NetWare, or WinNT-2000.

2. Click the Roll-Up Policy row ⇨ Properties ⇨ Roll-Up Policy tab ⇨ Roll-Up Schedule. Modify the settings for scheduling the roll-up time ⇨ click OK.

NOTE

While scheduling the roll-up of data in the Inventory Policies, we recommend the roll-up frequency should be at least one day. It is likely that if the roll-up frequency is too low, for example less than one hour, there may be some performance degradation of the Inventory server.

Configuring the Policies for the Database

The installation program creates the database object for Sybase and configures the database server. However, you need to set up the associations for the database server.

If you are maintaining the Inventory database in Oracle, perform the following tasks before making the associations.

Create the Database object

1. In ConsoleOne, right-click a location in the tree for the Database object ➪ click New ➪ click Object ➪ click ZENworks Database ➪ click OK.

2. Type a name for the Database object ➪ click OK.

Configure the Database Server Options of the Database Object

1. In ConsoleOne, right-click the Database object ➪ click Properties ➪ click ZENworks Database.

2. Browse for the DN of the server or type the Server IP address. For a NetWare 4.x server, specify the IP address.

3. Type the values for the following options: Database(Read-Write) User Name: *MW_DBA*; Database(Read-Write) Password: *novell*

4. Click OK.

Ensure That the JDBC Driver Properties Are Correct as per Your Database Configuration.

1. In ConsoleOne, right-click the Database Object ➪ click Properties ➪ click Jdbc Driver Information.

2. Click Populate Fields and set the default settings for an Oracle database as shown in Table 12.1 ➪ click Populate Now.

3. Click OK.

T A B L E   12.1   *Database Settings for a Sybase Database and an Oracle Database*

DATABASE SETTINGS	FOR A SYBASE DATABASE	FOR AN ORACLE DATABASE
Driver	Com.sybase.jdbc.SybDriver	oracle.jdbc.driver.Oracle Driver
Protocol	Jdbc:	jdbc:
SubProtocol:	Sybase:	oracle:
SubName:	Tds:	thin:@
Port:	2638	1521
SID Service Name (Service ID of the Oracle database)		Orcl-

Once you have completed the steps for having the Inventory database in Oracle, or if you are simply using the Sybase database, then perform the following steps to do the associations for the server.

Create the Service Location Package to Associate the Database Object with This Package. You must set up the ZENworks Database Policy to establish the location of the database; otherwise, no information can be logged to the database. To establish the service location of the database, use the following steps:

1. In ConsoleOne, right-click the Policy Packages container ⇨ click New ⇨ click Policy Package ⇨ click Service Location Package ⇨ click ZENworks Database ⇨ click Next.

2. Type the name for the Service Location Package ⇨ click Next ⇨ click Finish.

Configure the Service Location Policy and Associate the Database with the Policy

1. In ConsoleOne, right-click the Service Location Package ⇨ click Properties ⇨ click Policies.

2. Check the check box under the Enabled column for the ZENworks Database Policy.

3. Click Properties.

4. Browse to the DN of the ZENworks Database object ⇨ click OK twice.

5. Click the Associations tab ⇨ Add.

6. Browse to select the container under which the Database Object is present ⇨ click OK twice.

Configuring the Inventory Policies for Workstations
Once you have configured the server database and service location policies you need to configure the inventory policies for the workstation. In the Workstation Inventory Policy, you configure the following settings for scanning workstations:

- Scanning time at the workstations
- Inventory server to which the workstations send scan data
- Include software scanning of workstations
- List of software applications for scanning

Use the following steps to configure the Workstation Inventory Policy

Create a Policy Package for the Workstations

1. In ConsoleOne, right-click the Container ⇨ click New ⇨ click Policy Package ⇨ click Workstation Package ⇨ click Next ⇨ click Workstation Inventory ⇨ click Next.

2. Type the name for the Workstation Package ⇨ click Next ⇨ click Finish.

Enable and Associate the Workstation Inventory Policy

1. In ConsoleOne, right-click the Workstation Package ⇨ click Properties ⇨ click Policies ⇨ click one of the following sub-tabs: Win95-98 or WinNT-2000.

2. Check the Enable the Workstation Inventory Policy ⇨ click OK.

3. Click the Associations tab ⇨ Add.

4. Browse to select the container object under which the workstations are registered ⇨ click OK twice.

Specify the Inventory Server to Which the Scanner Will Send the Workstation Scan Data.

1. In ConsoleOne, right-click the Workstation Package ⇨ click Properties ⇨ click Policies ⇨ click one of the following sub-tabs: Win95-98 or WinNT-2000.

2. Click the Workstation Inventory Policy row ⇨ Properties ⇨ the Workstation Inventory tab.

3. Browse to select the DN of the Inventory Service object. Check the Enable the Software Scan option to include software scanning of workstations.

4. Click the Custom Scan Editor button to select the software that you want to scan for at the workstations ⇨ modify the list. Click OK.

Schedule the Time for Activating the Scanning at the Workstations

1. In ConsoleOne, right-click the Workstation Package ⇨ click Properties ⇨ click Policies ⇨ click one of the following sub-tabs: Wind95-98 or WinNT-2000.

2. Click the Workstation Inventory Policy row ⇨ Properties ⇨ the Policy Schedule tab.

3. Modify the settings for scheduling the scan of the workstations ⇨ click OK twice.

Ensure That Scanning Is Enabled

1. In the Inventory Service Object property page, you enable the scan of the workstations associated with the selected Inventory server.

2. From ConsoleOne, right-click the Inventory Service object (servername_ ZENINVService) ⇨ click Properties ⇨ click the Inventory Service Object Properties tab.

3. Check Enable Scan of Workstations ⇨ click OK.

Once you have finished configuring the workstation inventory policies for workstations, make the following check in your environment to make certain that the inventory scanning process is able to complete properly:

▶ If you have configured the Inventory server that is a Windows NT/ 2000 server and Windows 95/98 workstations are present that will send their scan data to that Windows NT/2000 server, you must do the following for the scanners to collect data:

• If NDS users are present who are also Windows NT/2000 Domain Users, ensure that the users logged in are valid users of the Windows NT/2000 domain in the existing Share created by ZENworks.

• If users are logged in to a different domain, ensure that the users are Trusted users of the domain in the existing Share created by ZENworks.

• If NDS users are present who are not users of any Windows NT/2000 domain, ensure that the users do not log in to NDS during workstation start up. However, these users can log in to NDS later.

Workstation Inventory Tasks

Once you have installed, configured, and started the workstation inventory process for you network, you should be aware of several tasks. The following sections describe common tasks that you need to be aware of and perform to use and maintain your workstation inventory.

Optimizing Database Performance

One important task you should be familiar with is improving the database performance by improving database cache size. You can improve the performance of the Inventory database maintained in Sybase on NetWare or Windows NT/2000 servers. The default database cache size is 16MB; however, this database cache size may not be adequate for large databases with more than 10,000 workstations.

You should change the database cache size to an optimum size. We recommend a database cache size that is one-fourth of the database size. You must also consider server memory size while assigning a cache size. For example, if you have 128MB RAM, then a cache size of 32MB is recommended.

Use the following steps to change the database cache size on a NetWare server:

1. Close all connections to the Inventory database.

2. Quit the Sybase server.

3. Open the MGMTDB.NCF in SYS:\SYSTEM directory.

4. Modify the -c parameter. For example, -c 64M sets the cache size to 64MB.

5. Save the file.

6. On the server console, load the Inventory database. Enter MGMTDBS

Use the following steps to change the database cache size on a Windows NT/2000 server:

1. Run the file, NTDBCONFIGURE.EXE from PUBLIC\ZENWORKS.

2. Modify the -c parameter.

3. Save the file.

4. Restart the server so that the Inventory database service (Adaptive Service Anywhere - ZENworks for Desktops 3) starts up.

Backing up the Inventory Database

Another inventory task you should be aware of is backing up the inventory database. ZENworks for Desktops provides an option to back up the Inventory database from the server. We recommend that you back up the database on a weekly basis. However, if you are tracking the inventory of workstations frequently, increase the frequency of backup.

To run the backup tool on NetWare or Windows NT/2000 servers, enter the following command at the inventory server console: StartSer DBBACKUP

Use the following steps to restore the database:

1. If the Inventory database server is up, stop the database storing service. At the database server console, enter

   StopSer Storer.

2. Quit from the Sybase database.

3. On NetWare servers, at the database server prompt, enter q to stop the Sybase database.

4. On Windows NT/2000, stop the Sybase service (Adaptive Service Anywhere - ZENworks for Desktops 3).

5. Copy the backup files, overwriting the working database files.

6. Restart the database server.

NOTE

The backup tool creates a log file, BACSTATUS.TXT file located in ZENWORKS\DATABASE directory on NetWare and Windows NT/2000 servers. The log records the status of the backup operation. This file increases in size for every backup operation. Remove the existing contents of the file if you do not need the details.

These steps work for the Sybase database only. For detailed instructions on backing up the oracle database refer to the on-line ZENworks for Desktops documentation.

Synchronizing the Inventory Database with NDS

Another task you should be familiar with is synchronizing the inventory database with NDS. ZENworks for Desktops provides a tool to synchronize the workstation objects stored in the inventory database with the workstation objects in NDS. This tool removes the workstations that do not exist in NDS from the Inventory database.

The excess workstations in the inventory database exist because these workstations may have been deleted from NDS; however, the corresponding workstations were not removed from the database.

Use this tool regularly to maintain the database in a consistent state with NDS. You must run this tool for each Inventory database.

NOTE

You must ensure that the Service Manager is loaded when you run the Inventory database sync tool.

To synchronize the inventory database with NDS perform the following two tasks:

At the Inventory server console prompt, enter the following command to generate a lookup file from a comparison of the list of workstations in the database with those in NDS:StartSer NDSLookupForDB.

NOTE The default lookup filename (WSDELETE.LOK) file is located in PUBLIC\ZENWORKS\WMINV\LOG directory. The lookup filename in this section and the [DBDelete Service] section of the server property file should be the same.

At the inventory server console, enter the following command to delete workstations in the lookup file from the inventory database:

StartSer DBDelete

NOTE The log file WSDELETE.LOG located in the \PUBLIC\ZENWORKS\ WMINV\LOGS directory contains the status of deletion. This file contains information as to whether the database was synchronized successfully with NDS.

Customizing Software Scanning

Another important task you should be familiar with for workstation inventory is how to customize software scanning. You can customize the list of software applications that you want to scan for at the managed workstations by specifying the software scan settings in the Workstation Inventory Policy page.

By default, the Scanner does not scan for software applications at the workstation. You must enable the software scan option in the Workstation Inventory policy and configure the list of applications for scanning.

Use the following steps to add a new application for scanning:

1. In ConsoleOne, open the select the Workstation Inventory Policy and click Properties. Ensure that the Enable software scan option is checked.

2. Click the Custom Scan Editor button.

3. Click Add to specify the details of the application.

4. Fill in the details of the application: Vendor name, Product name, Product version, File name, File Size (in Bytes).

5. Click OK.

6. To save the application entry in NDS, click OK in the Custom Scan Editor dialog box.

You can also add application entries to the Custom Scan table by importing a file with the list of application entries by using the following steps:

1. Open a text editor.

2. Create a file with the format specified later in this section.

3. Save the application as a text file with any extension you prefer.

4. In ConsoleOne, select the Workstation Inventory Policy and click Properties. Ensure that the Enable Software scan operation is checked.

5. Click Custom Scan Editor.

6. Click Import. To save the application entry in NDS, click OK in the Custom Scan Editor dialog box.

The format of the Custom Scan file is as follows:

```
total_number_of_application_entries_in_Custom_Scan_file>;
total_number_of_columns_in_the_application_entry

vendor_name;product_name;product_version;file_name;file_
size(in Bytes)

vendor_name;product_name;product_version;file_name;file_
size(in Bytes)
```

You should keep the following guidelines in mind if you decide to create your own custom scan files:

▶ The default total number of columns in the application entry is 5.

▶ The separator between the columns is a semicolon (;).

▶ Fill in all the columns for each application entry.

▶ Do not use comma (,) in the file size parameter.

Exporting the Inventory Data to CSV Format

ZENworks for Desktops includes a tool which allows you to customize inventory data you want from the inventory database and export it to a file. Once you select the inventory components that you need and further filter the data, the export program exports the data into a Comma Separated Value (CSV) file format.

All workstations satisfying the filter you specify in the selected database are exported to a CSV file. If you save the settings, you can later reload the configuration file to export the data. The following sections describe how to set the filters and queries and export the data from both a client or a server.

Exporting Inventory Data from ConsoleOne

The Data Export tool can be run from ConsoleOne by clicking Tools ➪ Configure DB ➪ ZENworks Database object ➪ OK. Then click Tools ➪ Data Export.

Once the tool is open use the following steps to export the inventory data in to a CSV file:

1. Select to Create a New Database Query. This option lets you add a new query that defines the inventory fields such as hardware, software, network, and others that you want to export. You can also specify the criteria to limit the workstations and the database to be included in the query. Based on the inventory components and criteria you specify, the inventory data from the database is exported to a CSVfile. Click Next.

2. Select the database fields from the list of Database Fields ➪ click Add button. If you select a group component, all sub-components of the group are added. For example, if you select the Software component group, the sub-components of Software such as Vendor name, product name, and version are added. Click Next.

3. Specify the filter conditions for workstations, click Edit Query. Click Next.

4. View the data export settings. Click Save Configuration to save the configurations settings to an .EXP file, specify the filename for the EXP file ➪ click Save. The configuration file (.EXP) contains the settings such as the inventory components you selected, and also the query formed for filtering the workstation data export. You create an .EXP file so that you can reload the configuration settings and generate the .CSV files any time you need to. Click Next.

5. Click Perform the query from this Computer to run the data export processing from the workstation computer. This option accesses the Inventory database on the specified database server and exports the data in to a .CSV file. Click Finish.

6. Specify the .CSV filename ➪ click OK.

This generates the .CSV file in the specified directory. You can then open the .CSV file in any CSV-supported viewer to view the exported data.

Forming a Query and Setting Filter Conditions

To form the query and set the filter conditions select the Create a New Database Query from the Data Export tool and then set the following filter conditions:

Selecting the Database Sites   In the Find In option, select the names of the database sites from the list. The Data Export tool will export the data from the Inventory database sites you select. This tool locates all workstations satisfying the filter conditions within the selected database sites.

Click the Browse button to select one or more database site names from the list. In the Select Sites window, click one or more database sites. The selected site names are shown in double quotes.

To include all database sites for data export, check the Search Entire Database. The data export tool locates those workstations satisfying the filter conditions in all database sites.

Selecting the Attributes of the Inventory Components   Click the Browse Attribute button to select component attributes in the Select Attribute window. For example, to specify the version of Bios as a component in the data export, select Bios as the component, and select Version as the component attribute.

Components are as follows: Software, Hardware, Network System, DMI, General Information.

Operator   Relational operators show the relationship between the component and the value. Use the Matches option to specify the wildcard characters in the Value field.

Specifying the Values for the Inventory Attributes   Description values are the possible values of an inventory component. For example, 6.0 is a possible value for the DOS-Version attribute. Description values are not case-sensitive. Use the wildcard character % to substitute any number of characters, or the ? character to substitute one character in the Value field.

The list of description values displayed for an Inventory component is taken from the Inventory database corresponding to the component.

Specifying the Query Connectors and Controls   The connectors and controls available for building filter conditions include the following:

- ▸ **AND:** The expressions before and after the AND must be true.
- ▸ **OR:** Either the expression before the OR or the expression after the OR must be true.
- ▸ **Insert Row:** Lets you build the filter condition for this current row.
- ▸ **Delete Row:** Deletes the row.

▶ **New Group:** Lets you form a new filter condition group and specify the criteria for it. This group is combined with the previous group by using the relational operator specified between the groups.

▶ **End:** Ends the filter condition.

Exporting Inventory Data from the Server

Accessing the Inventory database from a server is recommended if you are exporting data from a large database or if you have specified complex queries for filtering the workstation.

Use the following steps to run the data export program from the server:

1. Ensure that you have generated the data configurations files. Then perform Steps 1 through 4 outlined earlier in this section. Also ensure that you save the settings in the .EXP file.

2. Click Perform the query on a Remote Server to run the data export program from any server that has Workstation Inventory components installed. Click Finish.

3. From the server console, run DBEXPORT.NCF on NetWare servers or DBEXPORT.BAT on Windows NT/2000 servers, by typing DBEXPORT configuration_filename.exp csv_filename.csv where configuration_filename.EXP is an existing file that contains the data export settings. The data exported from the database is stored in the csv_filename.csv. The corresponding .CFG file for the .EXP file should be in the same folder as the .EXP file. The .CFG file contains the list of the database attributes to be exported.

4. Choose the Inventory sites.

5. If you want to export the data from all database sites, satisfying the filter conditions, type 0.

6. To choose the database sites, type the numbers corresponding to the site names in the displayed list.

7. To select multiple site databases, separate the site numbers corresponding to the site names by commas.

8. The data export displays the number of workstations that satisfy the query and filter conditions for export.

9. Open the .CSV file in Microsoft Excel, or any other CSV-supported viewer to view the exported data.

Viewing Inventory Data

Another important inventory task you should be familiar with is viewing the information in the workstation inventory. The following sections describe how to view information about managed workstations.

Viewing Minimal Inventory Information from an NDS Object

Workstation inventory scanners store a sub-set of the scan data directly into the workstation object in NDS. You can view that information by right-clicking on the workstation object and selecting Properties ➪ ZENworks Inventory tab ➪ Minimal Information.

You are shown the following information about that workstation: Asset Tag, BIOS type, Computer Model, Computer Type, Disk Information, IP Address, IPX Address, Last Scan Date, MAC Address, Memory Size, Model Number, NIC Type, Novell Client, OS Type, OS Version, Processor, Serial Number, Subnet Mask, and Video Type.

Viewing the Workstation Inventory Summary of a Managed Workstation

If the minimal inventory information does not show all you need, you can see the complete listing from ConsoleOne by clicking Tools ➪ Configure DB and then right-clicking on the workstation object ➪ Actions ➪ Inventory.

This shows you an entire listing of the scan data for the workstation object.

Viewing the Workstation Inventory Summary of a Managed Workstation Formed by Query

If the entire listing for the workstation object is too much for you then you can view only the information that you requested by performing a query. Use the following steps to view the information that was formed by a query:

1. In ConsoleOne click a container.
2. Click Tools ➪ Configure DB.
3. Click Tools ➪ Inventory Query.
4. Specify the criteria for the query. Set the Find in, Search entire database, Find type, Attributes, Operator, Value and Save options for the query.
5. Click Find.

A query is run on the database and the results are displayed for you to view.

Creating Inventory Reports

Another inventory task that is useful to know is how to run inventory reports. You can run reports from a predefined list to gather inventory information from the Inventory database. Once you run the report it can be printed or exported as desired.

Use the following steps to generate the inventory report:

1. In ConsoleOne, click a server object.

2. Click Tools ⇨ Inventory Reports.

3. Click the report you want to generate. See Table 12.2 for a list of reports and their descriptions.

4. Specify the Selection Criteria. See Table 12.2 for a list of reports and their criteria.

5. Click the Run Selected Report button.

A status box appears displaying the progress of the report generation. When the report is generated, it appears in the viewer. Use the buttons on the toolbar to page through, print, or export the report.

T A B L E 12.2   *Report Types and Criteria for Inventory Reports*

NAME (SIMPLE/COMP)	CRITERIA*	DESCRIPTION
Workstation Scan Time Listing(S)		Data and time of the last inventory scan on each workstation
Workstation Operating System Listing(S)	OS Type, OS Version	List of all the workstations with an OS Type, an OS Version, and the total number of such workstations
Workstation BIOS Listing(S)	BIOS Install Date	List of all the workstations with a BIOS release date, and the total number of such workstations
Workstation Processor Family(S)	Processor Family	List of all the workstations with a processor family (such as Pentium* Pro), and the total number of such workstations

NAME (SIMPLE/COMP)	CRITERIA*	DESCRIPTION
Workstation Processor Speed(S)	Lower Bound, Upper Bound	List of all the workstations within a range of processor speed (such as 200-400 MHz), and the total number of such workstations
Workstation Video Adapter Listing(S)	Video Type	List of all the workstations with a video adapter (such as MGA 2064W), and the total number of such workstations.
Workstation Network Adapter Listing(S)	Adapter Name	List of all the workstations with a network adapter (such as 3Com* Fast EtherLink*) and the total number of such workstations
Workstation Software Listing(S)	Software Name and Version	List of all the workstations with a software name, version and the total number of such workstations
Workstation Memory Listing(S)	Lower Bound, Upper Bound	List of all the workstations within a range of memory, and the total number of such workstations
Software Summary Listing(S)	Software Name and Version	Lists of the total number of workstations with a particular software and version
General Workstation Inventory Report(C)	DN of Workstation	BIOS, computer description, OS description, display details, NIC, physical disk drive, IP address, and MAC address for each workstation
Asset Management Report(C)	DN of Workstation	BIOS, computer description, processor, and OS Description for each workstation

(continued)

349

T A B L E 1 2 . 2	Report Types and Criteria for Inventory Reports (continued)	
NAME (SIMPLE/COMP)	**CRITERIA***	**DESCRIPTION**
Hardware Inventory Report(C)	DN of Workstation	Memory, processor, display details, physical disk drive, and modem for each workstation
Networking Information Report(C)	DN of Workstation	OS Description, MAC Address, NIC Type, IP Address, and Network Drive mappings for each workstation
Software Inventory Report(C)	DN of Workstation	Software with product name, version, and vendor for each workstation
Software Inventory Report for the Entire Site(C)		All software with product name, version, and vendor for the entire database site

*The Database Site name can be used as a criteria for all reports.

View the Workstation Inventory Status Logs

Another valuable task that you should use frequently is viewing the status and scan logs generated by workstation inventory. The following sections list the logs, what they contain, and how to access them.

Workstation Scan Log

The workstation scan log monitors information from scan programs and the database storage process on the server. It contains the scanned workstation name, time of scan, inventory component, message type, and status message.

To access the workstation scan log from within ConsoleOne, select the container then click Tools ⇨ Workstation Scan Log.

Roll-Up Log

The roll-up log contains information collected from data sending servers, data receiving servers, and the database storage process. The roll-up log contains information about where the roll-up initiated from, roll-up start time, inventory component, message type, status message.

To access the roll-up log from within ConsoleOne, select the container for the Inventory Service Object then click Tools ⇨ Roll-Up Log.

Workstation Scan Status

The workstation scan status monitors information from the scan programs and the database storage process. It contains the time of scan and status message.

To access the workstation scan status from within ConsoleOne, right-click the workstation object and click Properties ⇨ ZENworks Inventory tab ⇨ Scan Status.

Status of Inventory Components on Server

The status of inventory components on the server contains information gathered from sending server, receiving servers, the selector on the server, the database storing process, the service manager, and the roll-up scheduler. It shows the time of log, source, message type, and a textual message.

To access the status of inventory components on the server from within ConsoleOne, right-click the Inventory Service object then click Properties ⇨ Status Report ⇨ Server Status.

Roll-Up Status

The roll-up status contains information gathered from sending server, receiving servers, and the database storing process. It shows the roll-up start time and message.

To access the roll-up status from within ConsoleOne, right-click the Inventory Service object then click Properties ⇨ Status Report ⇨ Roll-Up Status.

## CHAPTER 13

Imaging a Workstation

One significant feature added to ZENworks for Desktops 3 is the ability to create and deploy images of workstations throughout the network. With this capability you can provide an additional level of support and service to users of workstations by being able to take an image of a golden workstation for your organization and then apply that image to any workstation in the network. This can be used to initially set up workstations in your organization and to restore a workstation to properly functioning status should problems occur that are best repaired by getting the workstation to a known, beginning state.

Workstation Imaging System

The ZENworks for Desktop 3 system for imaging workstation is made up of the following components: Linux operating system, Linux imaging software, Imaging server agents, Windows workstation image-safe data agent. In addition to these components objects in eDirectory, and some administrative tools in ConsoleOne, are there to get the job done.

There may be a Linux partition placed on a workstation (minimum of 15MB) that can hold the Linux OS and the imaging engine. This is ideal to place on workstations that you may want to image on the fly (from Console-One) because, when requested, the workstation gets notified of this work and then performs the imaging task. If no work exists for the imaging system to perform, then the partition boots into the normal operating system. See the section on placing a Linux partition on a workstation for gotchas and instructions.

The ZENworks for Desktops 3 imaging system is designed to function in an automatic mode (although it does have a manual mode). The expectation is that you use the system to deploy images to your workstations in the network in order to set up initial systems or repair systems and get them back on-line as quickly as possible. Consequently, the system assumes that a workstation that is contacting the imaging server, but is NOT registered in the tree, is requesting an image; and a registered workstation is contacting the imaging server to see if any work (indicated by flags in the workstation object) is to be done.

Linux Operating System

ZENworks for Desktops 3 uses the free Linux operating system to take and apply images to workstations. The imaging process begins by booting the workstation with some boot floppies which contain the Linux operating system and several drivers to handle most network cards. If the boot disks cannot support your network card then you need to look for those resources on the Internet. The following sites may have the driver you're looking for:

```
cesdis1.gsfc.nasa.gov/linux/drivers/index.html
www.linuxvoodoo.com/drivers/cards/nics/index.html
www.scyld.com/network/index.html
```

Linux Imaging Software

This is the Linux software application that actually performs the taking and placing of the image. This software is automatically started with the boot disks and is launched when the workstation is told to take or receive an image.

This software is *not* writing bits and bytes on the sectors, but it has knowledge of the various supported file system types, and reads and writes the files. The supported file system types are FAT16, FAT32, NTFS 4 (Windows NT), NTFS 5 (Windows 2000). Because the imaging software is reading files, it also writes files. This means that if you take the manual approach to restoring the image and the partition is not empty then you have a mingling of currently existing files with the files from the restore — causing a very unexpected behavior (OS and driver files are intermixed, and so on).

Something else to note is that the images always have the suffix of .ZMG and are not compressed. You must have enough room on the destination server to store the entire image or the image transfer will fail and the partial image will be deleted.

The imaging software can function in one of two modes: automatic and manual. In the automatic mode the imaging software contacts the imaging server agent and requests any work. This work may be to take or receive an image (this is set in the workstation object). If an image must be taken or received, then the imaging software begins the process. If no work must be done, then the imaging software completes and the workstation reboots to the native operating system.

If the imaging software is in manual mode, then the software does not automatically communicate with the agent, but places prompts on the workstation screen that enables you to perform specific partitioning and imaging tasks including taking or receiving an image. See the section in this chapter under Advanced Imaging to understand the commands you can perform in the manual mode. When the imaging software is done, the user must manually request the reboot to the native operating system.

Imaging Server Agents

This is the agent that runs on the server and is responsible for communicating with the imaging software that is running on the workstation. These agents tell the workstation whether to take the image or to receive an image and are responsible for walking the NDS tree to find the image. This is the agent that is affected by the Imaging Server Policy in the Server Policy Package. It is responsible for receiving information from the workstation and processing the rules in the policy in order to find an image object that should be applied to the workstation.

Once the image is determined this agent gets the image file and transmits that image to the Linux image software residing on the workstation. It is also responsible for receiving any images that the workstation is sending it and storing them onto the server in the specified and approved locations.

The image server is loaded on the NetWare server as imgserv.nlm and the NT version is a service dll with the same name. The imaging server has a status screen that tells you some information on the number of requests and images it has received and served. It, unfortunately, does not have any information on the screen on currently receiving or delivering work. You can load the service with a debug option and get it to write a log file called ZIMGDBG.LOG on the server.

Windows Workstation Image-Safe Data Agent

This agent resides on the Windows workstation and is responsible for placing and receiving image-safe data from the disk and placing that into the Windows registry. It also makes sure that the information in the Windows registry is synchronized on the disk.

A special sector on the disk is reserved for placing information that is preserved despite having an image applied to the workstation. This way a workstation keeps its IP address, computer, domain, and group names.

EDirectory Objects

Several objects are introduced to the tree in order to support ZENworks for Desktops 3 imaging. These objects are the following:

▶ **Workstation Imaging Policy** — This policy is in the Workstation Policy package and represents the policy to determine, for the associated workstations, the image to be used if a re-image is requested. See Chapter 8, "Setting up a Workstation Policy Package" for more information about this policy.

▶ **Imaging Server Policy** — This policy is in the Server Policy package and represents the policy to determine for the associated imaging servers the image to be used if an image is requested for a non-registered workstation. See chapter 11, "Creating a Server Policy Package," for more information about this policy.

▶ **Image Object** — This object is an eDirectory object that represents an image that has been taken of a workstation and stored on the imaging server. See the following section to learn more about the image object.

▶ **Workstation Object: Imaging Configuration** — These are some configuration parameters that are part of the workstation object. In this page you can configure whether the workstation should take or receive an image on the next reboot.

Image Object

The Image object is created in the directory by the administrator and is associated with an image file (.zmg) that has been taken by the ZENworks for Desktops 3 imaging system. To properly configure an Image object you must do the following:

1. Take an image of a workstation and store that image on an imaging server. See the creating a workstation image section following.

2. Launch ConsoleOne and browse to the container where you want the image object to reside.

3. Create an Image object by selecting the container and then choosing the File ⇨ New ⇨ object menu and selecting Workstation Imaging object from the list of objects.

4. Once the object is created you want to go into the properties of the object by either selecting additional properties in the create process or selecting the object and choosing properties from the right-mouse menu.

5. Select the Image Files tab and administer the location of the .ZMG file by pressing the browse button on the Base Image File field. This brings up a dialog box enabling you to browse to the imaging server and to browse to the file system on that server to the .ZMG file.

6. Choose the file set to bring as part of the image by selecting the set in the Use File Set parameter at the bottom left side of the screen. You can have up to ten different file sets. See the Modifying an Image section following for more details.

7. You can also append additional images to this image by pressing the Add button and placing them in the Add on Image File: field. These additional images are included with the base image and placed on the workstation when it is imaged. These additional images could be Application Object images (see chapter 5, "Creating and Using Application Objects," for more information).

8. Press OK to save the administrative changes and get out of ConsoleOne.

Administrative Tools

Several tools exist that are available to perform the imaging operation. First are the snap-ins into ConsoleOne that enable you to create image objects and launch tools to create the imaging boot disks and to view and manipulate an image file.

The boot disk creator and the image explorer program are both windows programs that are launched from ConsoleOne from the Tools menu. The boot disk creator creates the Linux diskettes that are necessary to boot the workstations to communicate with the imaging server and to take and put the images.

The image explorer enables you to view the contents of the image file and to mark files in the image to be included in various sets of files, remove files, or add files to the image. See the "Modifying an Image" section later in the chapter for more details.

Creating Boot Diskettes

All imaging starts by booting the workstation up with the ZENworks for Desktops 3 Imaging boot disks. To create these diskettes you need to do the following:

1. Get two *newly* formatted floppy disks. The system does not work properly if you create image diskettes on previously used floppies without reformatting them first.

2. Launch ConsoleOne.

3. Launch the boot disk creator program (sys:\public\zenworks\imaging\zimgboot.exe) by going to the tools menu and selecting the correct option (Tools ➪ ZENworks Utilities ➪ Imaging ➪ Create or Modify Boot Diskettes).

4. Within the boot disk creator program choose the options that you wish. Figure 13.1 shows a sample of the boot disk creator window.

▶ • ◀

F I G U R E   1 3 . 1   *ZENworks Imaging Boot Disk Creator*

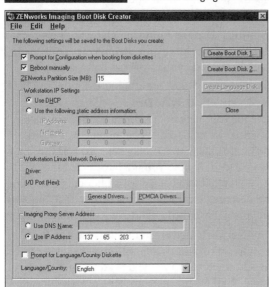

You can make the following choices in the program:

- **Prompt for Configuration when booting from diskettes** — After
  the boot process is done, this prompts the screen for the configuration information that is included on this screen (such as reboot
  manually, Proxy address, use DHCP, and so on). This enables you
  to change these values from the specified defaults given in this
  screen. You just press enter when running the imaging program on
  the workstation as you wish to keep the defaults that you specify
  on this screen.

- **Reboot manually** — This requires that the user request the reboot
  (Ctl-Alt-Del) manually at the completion of the imaging process
  (either take an image or receive an image) rather than having the
  program automatically reboot the workstation when done.

- **ZENworks Partition Size** — This enables you to specify how
  many megabytes you wish any Linux partition to be on the
  workstation, if you decide to create the partition.

- **Workstation IP Settings: Use DHCP** — Tells the Linux system to use DHCP to get the workstation's IP address to connect to the imaging server.

- **Workstation IP Settings: Use the following static address information** — Enables you to specify the address instead of using DHCP. This is the address used by the workstation to connect to the imaging server.

- **Workstation Linux Network Driver: Driver:** — Specify the special driver to use for your network card. The Linux boot disks come already configured for most of the common network cards. The known network cards are automatically detected and the appropriate driver is loaded. Should you not have a card that is part of the default set you need to go and get additional drivers to be included on the diskette. See the preceding section that contains a list of websites that may have the Linux drivers you want.

- **Workstation Linux Network Driver: I/O Port** — Identify the I/O port for access to your network card. In most cases this field can be blank because it is auto-detected. If not you need to enter the port number (for example, 300) for the interrupt for the network card.

- **Workstation Linux Network Driver: Drive buttons** — These buttons bring up a driver window that enables you to browse to the file system and find a Linux driver and then select it to be included on the diskettes. The driver selected in the field is attempted first, followed by the list of alternate drivers in the button lists, followed by the default drivers.

- **Imaging Proxy Server Address: Use DNS Name** — This flag enables you to select and enter the DNS name of the imaging server. Be sure and only choose this option if you have DNS enabled and have entered a record in the DNS system for this server. Be sure and put the full DNS name such as imgsrvr. novell.com.

- **Imaging Proxy Server Address: Use IP Address:** This flag identifies that the system should use the IP address to connect to the imaging server rather than DNS. The address specified should be the address of the server that is running the imaging service.

- **Prompt for Language/Country Diskette** — This is a flag requesting that the system should prompt for the language diskette at boot time. If this is on, the system waits for the language diskette to be inserted before it finishes. This is not necessary if you are using the default English system.
- **Language/Country** — Choose the country language. This results in these language files being placed on the system and used in the workstation imaging system.

5. Put a first floppy into the disk drive and press the Create Diskette 1 button. This writes a compressed file with the Linux boot system and portions of the Imaging engine.

6. Put a second floppy into the disk drive and press the Create Diskette 2 button. This writes a compressed file with the remainder of the Linux drives and imaging system.

7. If you chose to have a non-English version of the imaging system then you need to insert the third formatted diskette in the drive and press the Create Language Diskette button. This places the non-English language files on the floppy.

8. Press the close button.

Now these floppies can be used to boot the workstation and begin the imaging process.

If you have systems that are capable of booting from CD-ROM, then you can create a CD with the Linux boot system. With your CD writer software you need to create a CD using the ISO file called bootcd.iso from the public\zenworks\imaging directory or from the ZENworks for Desktops 3 Program CD. You also need the settings.txt file which holds the configuration for the boot CD, such items as prompt, size of Linux partition, and so on. You also need this settings.txt file on the CD. Your CD writer software is either able to include the settings.txt file into the ISO image, or needs to write a multi-session CD. Obviously, then your workstations need to support booting from a multi-session CD.

The session.txt file is an ASCII text file that holds key/value pairs that tell the boot system the configuration settings for the imaging engine. The following is a sample of the settings.txt file:

```
#  ZENworks Imaging settings.txt
#     denotes a comment
```

```
#PROMPT should be set to YES if you want to configure
# various parameters
#PROMPT=YES

#PARTITIONSIZE should be set to the Linux partition size
# in MB, to be created on install
PARTITIONSIZE=15

#IPADDR should be set to the desired ip address of the
# machine. To use DHCP comment out the line, or remove
# it from the file.
#IPADDR=137.65.138.128

#GATEWAY is the router address for this machine.  If
# using DHCP,remove this line, or comment it out.
#GATEWAY=137.65.139.254

#NETMASK is this machine's subnet mask.  If using DHCP,
# remove or comment out this line.
#NETMASK=255.255.252.0

#PROXYADDR is the address of the server running ZENworks
# Image Server nlm
PROXYADDR=137.65.203.1

#uncomment if you want to reboot manually.
#MANUALREBOOT=YES
```

▶ . . . . ◀

Creating a Workstation Image

Depending on your situation and setup, several ways exist to create a work-station image.

If the workstation is registered in the directory and has a Linux partition on it (see section following on placing a Linux partition on a workstation) then you can go to the workstation object in the tree and set a workstation flag (in the ZENworks Imaging Configuration tab) to take an image on the next boot. Then the next time that the workstation boots, the Linux partition boots and then the imaging engine on the workstation contacts the imaging server. The server notes that the workstation object has the flag set and requests that the workstation send an image. When the image is completed, the flag is reset in the workstation object and the workstation continues to boot into the native operating system.

Be sure to disable or remove any boot manager systems such as System Commander. You do not want them included in the image that you take, or when they are placed onto a workstation they overwrite the ZENworks boot system and the connectivity between the workstation and the imaging server does not occur, keeping you from having the features of automatic execution.

If the workstation is registered in the directory but does not have a Linux partition, then you need to boot from the floppies (or CD we made above). Once the system is booted you can let the Linux proceed in automatic mode. This contacts the image server and takes the image as described in the previous paragraph.

If the workstation is not registered in the directory and yet it has a Linux partition installed, then when the workstation boots into the Linux partition it contacts the imaging server who runs its rules attempting to discover a matching image. If one is found, then it images the workstation with the matching image. So you need to boot the workstation from the floppies to get the imaging engine into manual mode and to not connect to the imaging server.

If the workstation is not registered in the directory and does not have a Linux partition then you must boot from floppies (or CD) and then type manual when the Linux partition is booted. Then you type img mp <proxy address> <full path to image>. Don't forget that the path must use forward slashes and must include the server. The directories in the path must already exist. This takes an image of the workstation and places it on the imaging server.

NOTE

Whenever you take an image or place an image on a workstation the ZENworks Imaging engine does NOT take an image of the Linux partition or replace it with an image being brought down. The only way to place a Linux partition on a workstation is via the bootable floppies or another imaging program.

Because the imaging process understands FAT16, FAT32, NTFS 4, and NTFS 5 it reads the files from these systems and includes them in the image on a file by file basis. If the imaging system does not understand the partition type, then it does a sector by sector copy of the partition.

► . . . . ◄

Placing a Linux Partition on a Workstation

Unless you want to do all of your ZENworks for Desktops 3 imaging from floppy disks (2-3), you want to put a Linux partition on each of your workstations. This Linux partition is the boot partition, and upon boot-up of the workstation, contacts the imaging server to see if it has any requested work (based on administration in the workstation object). If it has work, then the imaging engine either gets or puts an image. If it has no work, then the imaging system continues the boot process, booting the workstation to the native operating system.

If you are placing a Linux partition on a previously functioning system then this process assumes that the workstation has already registered with the network and has an associated workstation object and that the Image safe data agent has run on the workstation. Having the workstation already registered prevents the imaging server from attempting to place a new image on the workstation. However, if you are placing the Linux partition on a new workstation this process can place a new, standard image on the workstation, preparing it for use in your organization.

The placing of the Linux partition and the ZENworks for Desktops 3 boot system does not function with such booting programs as System Commander. These systems need to be disabled or marked such that the Linux partition automatically gets booted. The ZENworks for Desktops 3 boot system functions properly with the Windows Boot manager by fixing up the boot.ini file to properly boot.

NOTE

The imaging system does some special recognition for Compaq systems and does not destroy the Compaq partition that is used to run machine configurations.

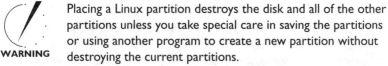

WARNING

Placing a Linux partition destroys the disk and all of the other partitions unless you take special care in saving the partitions or using another program to create a new partition without destroying the current partitions.

To place a ZENworks for Desktops 3 Linux imaging partition on a workstation you need to do the steps described following. Be sure to save any data on the workstation; any time that you are messing with partitions you must prepare yourself should a failure occur and the data is lost.

You could make sure that an empty place exists on the disk that is sufficient to hold the Linux partition (the size was identified in the creation of the boot disks and is 15MB minimum). This could be leftover space or created by some program such as Partition Magic to free up space. If sufficient free space is present on the hard drive, the Linux install process should consume that space ONLY IF THE FREE PARTITION IS PARTITION 0 (in other words, the first partition in the partition table) and thereby will not destroy any other partitions (although you have to be trusting, and you know how sometimes everything doesn't go perfectly). The following describes how to put the Linux partition on without loss of data and without any other tools.

1. Create your ZENworks for Desktops 3 Boot Diskettes with the proper configuration, including the setting to reboot manually. See the preceding section for tips on how to do that.

2. Boot the workstation with the ZENworks for Desktops 3 Imaging Boot Diskettes. Be sure to request manual mode when the system comes up. This is done by typing manual at the prompt following the boot to Linux. If you type nothing at the prompt in 60 seconds, then the system boots to automatic mode.

3. If this is a previously functioning workstation, than take an image of the workstation by entering the following command: **img makep <address/DNS of image server> <filename for image file>**. The address may be an IP address or the DNS name of the image server. The filename is the name of the image file you want to hold the image. The filename must include the following format: //servername/dir/ dir/../filename.img. The servername is actually ignored because the address of the server that is receiving the image stores the file on its disk. (Redirection of image servers does not work in manual mode.)

4. Enter **img dump** to view the list of known partitions on the disk. Remember the numbers of the partitions.

5. Enter **/bin/install.s** to install the Linux partition on the disk. This DESTROYS all data on the workstation's hard drive. It creates a new Linux partition on the disk the specified size and place of the Linux boot system on that partition. The ZENworks boot loader is automatically installed in this process. There should be a message that comes on the screen stating that the boot process could not fully function. This is because Linux creates logical partitions for all the partitions that are seen at boot time. You just added a new partition and it cannot create a logical partition for it. When it reboots the boot manager system automatically reinstalls itself when it is assumed that all partitions are now present.

6. Enter img dump to view the list of know partitions. There should be one less partition listed than in Step 4 because the Linux partition is hidden from this listing. You should also note that all the other partitions are destroyed (in other words, have no file system type associated with them).

7. Perform a reboot of the workstation to make sure the Linux partition is functioning properly. This can be done by typing, reboot, or by turning the workstation off and on. Make sure you have removed the Linux boot diskettes. This should boot to the Linux partition and get to the Linux prompt (because the system has been configured to not automatically reboot).

8. If you took an image in Step 3, then bring down the image that was taken by typing **image rp <address of image server> <image filename>**. The image is brought down to the disk. The image is then reduced in size sufficiently to take the remaining space on the disk (we had to take space for the Linux partition). If the image is too big to be reduced, then an error occurs. The installing of an image from ZENworks for Desktops 3 takes special care to not destroy or over-write the Linux partition. When the image is successfully down you have the same workstation data and environment with the exception of a new Linux partition.

9. Enter **img dump** to view the list of partitions again. There should be the same number as in Step 6 (one less than in Step 4) and there should now be file system types to the partitions that you have just restored.

10. Reinitialize the boot manager by running **/bin/lilo.s**. You should do this anytime you bring down any image to the workstation. In auto-matic mode the system performs this automatically.

11. Perform a reboot of the workstation. This can be done by typing **reboot** or by turning the workstation off and on. Make sure you have removed the Linux boot diskettes. This should boot to the Linux partition and get to the Linux prompt (because the system has been configured not to automatically reboot).

12. The workstation should now boot to the Linux partition that goes into automatic mode communicating with the image server. It should find no work if the workstation is registered and the image configuration flags are off. If the workstation is not registered and you did not lay down an image in Step 8, then the image server is contacted and goes through its rules processing (see Server Policy Package, Imaging Server Policy) and determine an image that should be placed on this workstation. If one is found, then that image is placed on the workstation. If you manually placed an image down on a workstation that had not been previously registered, then the imaging server compares the name of that image file with the image determined by the imaging server. If they are the same then the imaging server does not attempt to lay a new image down. This should result in the workstation having no work and again booting to its native operating system.

Modifying an Image

Once an image has been taken on the system and stored on the imaging server, then you can examine the contents of an image by running the ZENworks for Desktops 3 image explorer (public\zenworks\imgexp.exe). When you launch the image explorer you are placed in a windows program. From there you go to the file menu and open the .ZMG file that holds the workstation image. Figure 13.2 show a sample of an image in the image explorer.

FIGURE 13.2 ZENworks image explorer

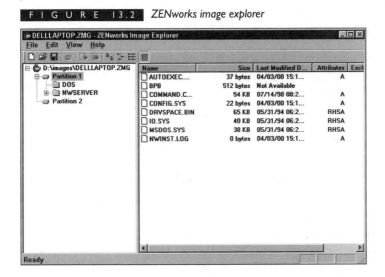

As you can see in the example, you can browse the image and discover the partitions in the image and all of the files in the image. You can also, using the image explorer, look at the information gathered from the workstation such as the hardware configuration. To look at this information, select the .ZMG file in the image editor and go to File ⇨ Properties or press the right mouse button and select Properties. When you do, the dialog box in Figure 13.3 is displayed.

► . . . . ◄

Image properties from an image in the ZENworks Image Explorer

As you can see this dialog displays the description of the image, all of the hardware information on the workstation where the image was captured. (You can use this information to help you construct your rules in the Image server policy.) Other fields include when created, the author, and any comments. If you want to modify any of the Description, Author, or Comments fields, just move the cursor to these fields and type in the information you desire.

From within the Image Explorer you can add files or directory of files to the image by selecting the partition and, optionally, the directory in the partition where you want the files. Then choose File ⇨ Add Files, or File ⇨ Add Directory, or File ⇨ Create Directory to create and add files individually or directories of files to the image.

You cannot remove files from an image, however, you can mark files and place them into image sets. These sets consist of a group of files that can then be referenced from the imaging server (for example, place all files in set 1 from image A onto this workstation). By default all files in the image are included in all sets.

NOTE

When the imaging engine requests an image from the imaging server it automatically requests all files from the image in set 1.

To exclude files or directory from a set you need to highlight the files or the directories and then click the right mouse button and select File Sets ➪ Edit to bring up the following dialog (see Figure 13.4) where you can select which sets to exclude from the identified files or directories. Or you can use the right mouse button and select File Sets ➪ Exclude from Set X to choose which set will not contain the selected files and directories.

F I G U R E   1 3 . 4   *Image Exclude from Set dialog in the ZENworks Image Explorer*

When you create a Workstation Image object in the directory, and associate it with the image file, you can specify in the object which set of files to use. See the discussion on image objects in the previous section, "Image objects."

Assigning an Image to a Workstation

Three ways exist in which the workstation automatically discovers the workstation image that it should place onto its hard drive.

1. The image may be chosen by the imaging server when an unregistered workstation boots the Linux system and contacts the imaging server. The imaging server goes through its rules to determine the image to place on the workstation. (See the chapter on Server Policy Packages for more details.)

2. The image may be chosen by the imaging server when a registered workstation boots the Linux system and contacts the imaging server and the workstation has an associated Workstation Imaging policy. (See the chapter on Workstation Policy Packages for more details.)

3. If the administrator has configured the workstation object to be associated with a specific image in the directory, then when the Linux system is booted and contacts the imaging server, the server looks into the workstation object to see if it should be re-imaged. If so, then it looks to see if a specific image file has been specified and sends that file. Otherwise, it performs as described in Step 2.

Workstation Object

In the workstation object properties, an Image page exists. Within this image page you have a couple of setting that you can administer in relationship to the Imaging system. The following settings can be applied on the Image page of the workstation object:

▶ **Take an image of this workstation on the next boot** — This flag enables you to specify that on the next reboot of the workstation, the Linux boot system contacts the imaging server and is told to take an image of the workstation. With this field you also get to specify the name of the image file. The image server saves the image to the specified file name.

▶ **Put an image on this workstation on the next boot** — This flag enables you to signal that the workstation should receive an image on the next boot. When the Linux boot system contacts the imaging server it is told that it should put down an image. In addition to this field you can specify the image object that represents the image you want put down on the workstation. Press the browse button to select the image object in the directory. If no image object is specified, then the image server looks for any Workstation Image Policy that may be associated with the workstation. If no Workstation Image Policy is associated with the workstation and no image is specified by the administrator, then no image is applied to the workstation.

After the workstation reboots and performs the requested action (make or restore an image) then these flags are reset so that upon the next reboot no work would be done. If the action is not successful, then these flags are *not* reset and continue to cause the action to be requested upon each reboot.

Applying Application Objects to an Image

One of the most significant advancements that ZENworks for Desktops 3 has over your standard imaging systems is the ability for you to include all the files and software associated with an application object into a workstation image. By performing this function, when the image is placed onto the workstation all of the included application object files are installed with the image. When the workstation boots into the native operating system, these application object files are treated as disconnected applications and are available from the workstation. See the chapter "Creating and Using Application Objects" to understand better how disconnect ZENworks Application Launcher works.

In order to apply the application objects to an image you need to perform the following steps. These steps assume that you already have an image object representing some base image and an application object in your tree.

1. Launch ConsoleOne.

2. Browse to and select properties on an application object that you wish to include in an image. This application object can be included in any number of images.

3. Go to the Common tab ⟿ Imaging property page.

4. On the Imaging proper page you can identify the name of the image file by browsing to an existing file (to be overwritten) or by typing in a new file name to be created. It is recommended that you type in a UNC path so that all machines can get to this image, rather than having to have a mapped drive to the identified volume.

5. Select the Application Object flags at the bottom of the screen that tell the ZENworks Application Launcher how to handle the application.

6. Press the Create an Image button to have the system create an image representation of the application into the specified image file.

7. Close the dialog boxes to get back to the main ConsoleOne screen.

8. Browse to and select the properties of the workstation image object that you want to include the application object.

9. Go to the Images tab.

10. Press the Add button on the screen and enter the server name and path to the image file you wish to have added to the image.

11. Press OK to save all the changes and exit ConsoleOne.

Now when the image is applied to a workstation either through the policy or direct association the base image plus the added image is placed on the workstation.

> If you update an application object you have to recreate the image file again. You do not have to re-add it to the base image as long as you kept the same image file name.

NOTE

▶ · ◀

Re-Imaging a Workstation

You can re-image the workstation (for example, apply a new image on top of the file system) through manual mode with the floppies or through the automatic method. The applying of an image does not overwrite the Linux partition or the Image safe data on the hard drive.

You can automatically apply an image by doing the following. This assumes that the workstation already has a Linux partition, that the workstation is associated with a workstation object and that an image exists in the tree.

1. Launch ConsoleOne.

2. Browse and select properties on the workstation object associated with the desktop.

3. Select the Images tab and select Put an image on this workstation on the next boot and press the browse button in the Image file field to select an image to apply.

4. Press OK and exit from ConsoleOne.

5. Request that the user reboot the workstation.

▶ · ◀

Advanced Imaging

When the workstation boots the Linux partition and you request to go into manual mode you have the following commands available. The commands only need to type enough to be unique. The following only describes the minimal keystrokes to get the command functional.

Remember that you are running on top of the Linux operating system and that any normal Linux command is valid on the command line. This enables you freedom to use any command to help in the setup and configuration of the workstation. For example, you can see a listing of files (ls — FC) or mount a drive (mount /dev/hdc /mnt/cdrom). Also any Linux utility that you may have can be run on the workstation.

Information Commands

The following commands are general purpose commands that display information about the system.

▶ **img h** — [image help] This displays a screen of help to assist in reminding you about some of the commands. It does not display an exhaustive list of available commands.

Example:

```
img h
```

▶ **img i** — [image information] This displays the detected hardware information. This is useful to determine the values for the rules in the policies. This information is sent by the engine to the imaging server.

Example:

```
img i
```

▶ **img i z** — [image information of ZENworks image-safe data] This displays the image safe data that is stored on the hard drive.

Example:

```
img info z
```

Automation Commands

The following commands deal with the process of having the imaging engine connect to the imaging server and perform any actions.

▶ **img a** — [image auto] This sends a request to the imaging server to see if any work needs to be performed. If work must be performed, then the imaging server immediately performs the work. The following codes are returned to the Linux shell upon completion: 0 — no work to perform; 0 — successful imaging task completed, no change to the hard drive; 1 — successfully received one or more images, the hard drive has been altered; n — other error codes.

Example:

```
img a
```

Partition Commands

The following commands deal with manipulation of the partitions on the workstation.

- ► **img d** — [image dump] This displays the partition information of the hard disk. With the additional 'g' the system displays the geometry of the disk. This command is important because the partition numbers displayed from this command are the partition numbers used as parameters to other advanced imaging commands.

  Example:

  ```
  img d
  ```

- ► **img dg** — [image dump geo] This displays the partition information of the hard disk. With the additional 'g' the system displays the geometry of the disk. This command is important because the partition numbers displayed from this command are the partition numbers used as parameters to other advanced imaging commands.

  Example:

  ```
  img dg
  ```

- ► **img pa<partition number> -** [image partition activate] — This command makes the specified partition the active partition. The partition number is the partition number returned from the 'img d' command.

  Examples:

  ```
  img pa2
  img pa1
  ```

- ► **img pc<partition number> <partition type> [partition size] [c<cluster size>]-** [image partition create] — This command creates a partition in an empty slot. The partition number is the partition number returned from the img d command. The command fails if the partition specified is not empty. The partition type must be one of the following: fat12, fat16, fat32, or ntfs. The partition size parameter is optional and represents the number of megabytes requested. If the size is not given then the largest partition size possible for the specified type is created. The cluster size is only supported for NTFS partition types, for the FAT partitions the cluster size is determined automatically by the size of the partition.

When a partition is created, the ZENworks imaging engine performs some low-level pre-formatting. This pre-formatting process is dependent upon the actual file system being created. It is usually a subset of the formatting process performed on new partitions by the various operating systems, but it is not enough to be recognized as a valid partition by those operating systems. It is only formatted enough to enable the imaging engine to start inserting files into the partition. At least one base image must be applied to the partition before it is recognized by the operating system.

Examples:

```
img pc2 ntfs 500 c8
img pc3 fat32
```

▸ **img pd<partition number>** — [image partition delete] This deletes the specified partition from the hard drive.

Examples:

```
img pd3
```

Creating Image Commands

The following commands deal with the creation of workstation images.

▸ **img ml[partition number] <path>** — [image make local image] This command makes an image of the disk and places it in the local file system. The optional partition number represents the partition where you wish to store the image. This specified partition is *not* included in the image. If no partition is specified then all partitions (except the Linux boot partition) are imaged and the image is stored on the Linux partition. The path must resolve to a valid path on the system — no directories are automatically created, and any existing file with the same name is overwritten.

By being able to specify the partition number used to store the image you can have an attached jaz drive, which shows up as a partition and then stores the image of the hard drive on your removable media.

Examples:

```
img ml2 imgdump.zmg
img ml fulldump
```

▶ **img mp <imaging server address> <UNCpath>** — [image make proxy image] This command takes an image of the workstation and sends that image to the specified imaging server. This imaging server address is the actual IP address (not the DNS name) of the imaging server. The UNC path is where the image is stored on that imaging server. The path must resolve to a valid path on the system – no directories are automatically created, and any existing file with the same name is overwritten. The UNC must have the format of //server name/dir/dir.../filename (make sure you use the forward slash). If the suffix .ZMG is not specified, then it is automatically appended to the filename. The server name is really ignored because the image is sent and stored on the imaging server specified by the IP address. The server name may be used at some future release.

Examples:

```
img mp 137.65.203.1 //zen1/vol1/images/dellb.zmg
img mp 137.65.203.254 //zen2/vol2/ibmlaptop
```

Advanced Create Image Commands

These advanced image creation commands include the ability to exclude specified partitions from the image.

▶ **img ml**[partition number] <path> [x<partition number>] — [image make local image] This command makes an image of the disk and places it in the local file system. The optional partition number represents the partition where you wish to store the image. This specified partition is *not* to be included in the image. If no partition is specified then all partitions (except the Linux boot partition) are imaged and the image is stored on the Linux partition. The path must resolve to a valid path on the system—no directories are automatically created, and any existing file with the same name is overwritten. The optional x<partition number> enables you to specify the partitions that should not be included (in other words excluded) from the image. This exclusion can include several partitions.

By being able to specify the partition number used to store the image you can have an attached jaz drive, which shows up as a partition, and then store the image of the hard drive on your removable media.

Examples:

```
img ml2 imgdump.zmg
img ml fulldump
img ml4 dosdump x2 x3
```

▶ **img mp <imaging server address> <UNCpath> [x<partition number>]** — [image make proxy image] This command takes an image of the workstation and sends that image to the specified imaging server. This imaging server address is the actual IP address (not the DNS name) of the imaging server. The UNC path is where the image is stored on that imaging server. The path must resolve to a valid path on the system—no directories are automatically created, and any existing file with the same name is overwritten. The UNC must have the format of //server name/dir/dir.../filename (make sure you use the forward slash). If the suffix .ZMG is not specified, then it is automatically appended to the filename. The server name is really ignored because the image is sent and stored on the imaging server specified by the IP address. The server name may be used at some future release. The optional x<partition number> enables you to specify the partitions that should not be included (in other words excluded) from the image. This exclusion can include several partitions.

Examples:

```
img mp 137.65.203.1 //zen1/vol1/images/dellb.zmg
img mp 137.65.203.254 //zen2/vol2/ibmlaptop
img mp 137.65.203.54 //zen3/d:/images/gx1.zmg x3
```

Restoring Image Commands

The following commands deal with the restoring of images onto the workstation. These commands may or may not destroy any previous data on the workstation.

▶ **img rl[partition number] path [s<set number>]** — [image restore from local] This restores an image from the partition and path specified onto the disk. All partitions on the hard disk, other than the Linux partition, are removed prior to the image being placed on the workstation.

The optional partition number specifies the partition (as displayed in the img d command) where the image is stored. The path must resolve to a valid image file on the system. If you are restoring from a removable media drive, then the partition number is the partition for the jaz or CD-ROM drive. The path must be a valid path and must represent an image file on the specified partition. The optional set number enables you to specify which set of files to include from the image. The sets can be specified in the ZENworks Image Editor program. If the set number is not specified it is assumed that it is set 1.

Examples:

```
img r12 myimage
img r13 theimage.zmg s2
```

▶ **img rp <proxy IP address> <UNCpath> [s<set number>]** — [image restore from proxy] This takes an image from the imaging server and puts it on the workstation. The proxy IP address must be the address of the imaging server where the image is stored. You cannot use a DNS name in this field. The UNC path must be a valid path that represents the image file. The path must be the format //server name/share/dir/ dir.../filename or //server name/volume/dir/dir.../filename. The optional set number enables you to specify which set of files to include from the image. The sets can be specified in the ZENworks Image Editor program. If the set number is not specified it is assumed that it is set 1.

Examples:

```
img rp 137.65.200.1 //zen9/image/delllaptop.zmg
img rp 137.65.200.1 //any/image/delllaptop.zmg s2
```

Advanced Restoring Image Commands

These advanced image restore commands enable you to specify that the partitions on the disk should not be destroyed and how to map the partitions in the image to the partitions on the disk. Additionally, when images are restored the partitions are automatically resized to fit the archived partition. In these commands the physical partition can remain larger than the archived partition.

▶ **img rl[partition number] path [s<set number>] a<archive partition>:p<physical partition>** — [image restore from local with partition mapping] This restores an image from the partition and path specified onto the specified partition on disk. This does not destroy the partition, but instead takes the archived partition and places its files into the specified partition. Any files already existing on the partition remain; files with the same name are overwritten. The optional partition number specifies the partition (as displayed in the img d command) where the image is stored. The path must resolve to a valid image file on the system. If you are restoring from a removable media drive, then the partition number is the partition for the jaz or CD-ROM drive. The path must be a valid path and must represent an image file on the specified partition. The optional set number enables you to specify which set of files to include from the image. The sets can be specified in the ZENworks Image Editor program. If the set number is not specified it is assumed that it is set 1.

The a<archive partition>:p<physical partition> enables you to create a mapping between the two drive spaces. You can take archived partition 1 and place it on physical partition 2, for example. You must specify at least one partition mapping to keep from having the default, wipe all partitions, behavior. You may specify as many mappings as are needed and you may map multiple archive partitions onto a single physical partition. An archive partition cannot be mapped to more than one physical partition.

Examples:

```
img rl2 myimage al:p2
img rl3 theimage.zmg s2 al:p2 a2:p2
```

▶ **img rp <proxy IP address> <UNCpath> [s<set number>] a<archive partition>:p<physical partition>** — [image restore from proxy onto mapped partitions] This takes an image from the imaging server and puts it on the workstation into the specified partition. The proxy IP address must be the address of the imaging server where the image is stored. You cannot use a DNS name in this field. The UNC path must be a valid path that represents the image file. The path must be the format //server name/share/dir/dir.../filename or //server name/volume/dir/dir.../filename. The optional set number enables you to specify which set of files to include from the image. The sets can be specified in the ZENworks Image Editor program. If the set number is not specified it is assumed that it is set 1.

The a<archive partition>:p<physical partition> enables you to create a mapping between the two drive spaces. You can take archived partition 1 and place it on physical partition 2, for example. You must specify at least one partition mapping to keep from having the default, wipe all partitions, behavior. You may specify as many mappings as are needed and you may map multiple archive partitions onto a single physical partition. An archive partition cannot be mapped to more than one physical partition.

Examples:

```
img rp 137.65.200.1 //zen9/image/delllaptop.zmg a2:p1
img rp 137.65.200.1 //any/image/dtop.zmg s2 a2:p2 a3:p2
```

Multi-Cast Commands

You can also set up the ZENworks Imaging system to perform multi-casting of the image. You can set up a single workstation to act as the master and send its hard drive contents to all the participating slave workstations.

You start the multi-cast session by entering the following on all workstations that are participating on the session:

```
img session <session name>
```

The session name must be a unique string to identify this multi-cast session. The session name string used must be identically entered on ALL workstations (both master and slave) that are going to participate in the session. This string is used to hash a multi-cast address, so a small chance exists that two different strings may result in the same multi-cast address. Multi-cast addresses are class D IP addresses. In order to ease wire sniffing, troubleshooting, and LAN traffic analysis, the imaging engine always uses 231 as the first octet in its address.

When started, by entering the img session <name> command, each workstation waits until the user determines which station will act as the master. The master workstation should be the SOURCE workstation; all slave workstation are DESTINATION workstations.

To designate the master workstation, go to the workstation that contains the SOURCE drive. The workstation should have already had the session command started and should be waiting just like all of the other workstations. Press the "m" key on the master workstation. This designates that workstation as the master. At this point all of the other workstations attempt to register with the master and receive a unique session identifier. If for some reason a slave station is rebooted before the session starts, it always receives the same identifier.

When the desired number of stations have registered with the master; the master displays a running count of the number of registered slaves, then starts the session by pressing "g" on the master workstation. Any station attempting to join the session after the session has started is denied access. This should now transfer the contents of the master to all of the slave workstations.

Once the session is over, the master workstation displays a list of the stations that did not successfully complete the image.

NOTE The multi-cast operations are dependent on the multi-cast features configured in your network equipment. Possible problems might include the routing of multi-cast packets not being allowed, stations outside of the defined scope of multi-cast on switches not receiving the packets, and so on.

Script Commands

The following commands perform some type of operation that would normally only be activated when the imaging engine is initially booted in manual mode. These are simple shell scripts that have been created for your convenience and use by the imaging system. Other script files exist, but these are the most useful to you.

▸ **/bin/cdrom.s** — This mounts the cdrom drive to /mnt/cdrom.

▸ **/bin/config.s** — This enables you to configure the settings.txt file for the Linux partition.

▸ **/bin/imaging.s** — This runs the imaging engine in auto mode, just like the img a command.

▸ **/bin/install.s** — This creates the Linux partition and installs it onto the hard disk. It removes all partitions *unless* the Linux partition already exists, then it just updates the files.

▸ **/bin/lilo.s** — this installs the ZENworks Imaging boot manager system, making sure that this system is booted first on the drive.

## CHAPTER 14

Maintaining a Workstation

Once the ZENworks for Desktops 3 system has been deployed across the network, the workstations have had the proper client installed, and the workstation is registered, then the workstation can be maintained and managed by the administrator from any location in the network. This provides obvious benefits as the administrator and support technicians rarely have to visit the individual workstation. This gives a significant cost improvement in maintaining your system.

Users and the Help Request System

The Help Request System is designed to function without the need of importing workstations. The intention of the Help Request System is to provide some immediate information to end-users about who to contact for problems with their workstations. In many cases, users do not know whom to contact for help in trouble situations, and when they finally get to the contact they often cannot provide simple information needed to help troubleshoot their system. The Help Request System provides this information to the user so they can contact the right person and provide this vital information, some of which cannot be easily discovered elsewhere. The Help Request System uses the information that is stored in the policy along with the data on the workstation to affect its user interface and data presented to the user.

In order for the Help Request System to be functional the following must have been completed:

1. A User Policy Package must have been created and associated with the users that are using the Help Request System.

2. The Help Desk Policy must be enabled within the User Policy Package.

3. Within the Help Desk Policy the check box, Allow user to launch the Help Requester, must be checked.

4. The Help Requester application object must be associated with the users that are using the system.

5. The users that launch the Help Requester must be running the ZENworks for Desktops 3 Application Launcher.

When the user logs into the system, and as part of their login script they start up the ZENworks for Desktops 3 Application Launcher, they are presented with the icon for the Help Requester for their operating system. The user can then double-click this icon in order to launch the Help Requester system. Figure 14.1 displays the initial screen of the Help Request application.

FIGURE 14.1 *Novell Help Requester application*

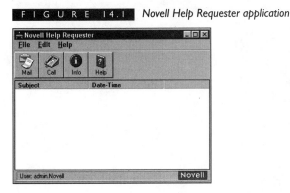

Based on the Help Desk Policy associated with the user, they may be presented with several task buttons within the Help Requester application. The users are not given the Mail taskbar button if the Allow user to send trouble tickets from the Help Requester feature is not enabled in the Help Desk policy. The user is always presented with the Call, Info, and Help taskbar buttons.

Mail Help Request Task

The Mail button on the Help Requester enables the user to send mail to the e-mail address specified in the Help Desk policy associated with the user. Figures 14.2 through 14.4 display the window displayed when the Mail button is pressed.

FIGURE 14.2 *Novell Help Requester Mail Dialog box, Message open*

Novell Help Requester Mail Dialog box; User tab pressed

Novell Help Requester Mail Dialog box; Workstation
tab pressed

The Message tab enables the end-user to enter a message to be sent to the
e-mail specified in the policy. The User tab displays the DN and information of
the currently logged in user to the workstation. The information in the user
tab is gathered from the user object in the NDS tree. The Workstation tab displays the DN, and tree of the workstation, along with the NDS hardware
inventory information. All of this information may or may not be sent in the
trouble ticket based on the options specified in the policy.

Call Button

When the user presses the Call taskbar button they are presented with the Call Dialog box (Figure 14.5). This displays the Help Desk data that was entered in the Information page of the Help Desk Policy. This contains the Contact name and number. In addition to the contact name, the dialog box also displays basic information about the user and workstation object and tree. The information in the tabs is the same information displayed and discussed in the preceding Mail Dialog section.

FIGURE 14.5 *Novell Help Requester Call for Help Dialog box; User tab pressed*

Info Button

The Info button presents the same information in the User and Workstation tabs as discussed in the preceding Call and Mail buttons sections. Figure 14.6 following displays the initial dialog box presented with the Info button. This additional information includes the help desk e-mail and the policy package that the Help Requester application is using.

F I G U R E 14.6 *Novell Help Requester Info Dialog box with the User tab highlighted*

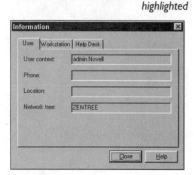

Help Desk Tab

The Help Desk tab shown in Figure 14.7 displays additional information about the Help Desk policy that is being used by the Help Requester program. This displays the contact information and the policy object that is being used.

F I G U R E 14.7 *Novell Help Requester Info Dialog box with the Help Desk tab highlighted*

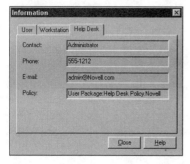

Remote Controlling a Workstation

On some occasions it is necessary to remote control a workstation from any other workstation in the tree. You may remote control a workstation via IP or IPX protocol and from any workstation in the network, however you must have Novell Directory Services rights to control the workstation. Before you can remote control a workstation the following must be completed:

1. The proper remote control agents must be present on the workstation. This can be accomplished by installing the ZENworks for Desktops 3 client that ships with the product. The client that comes with ZENworks for Desktops 3 always has the latest agents that are available.

   Additionally, You can deliver the agents to the workstation via the ZENworks for Desktops 3 Application Launcher. When ZENworks for Desktops 3 is installed into the tree, several application objects are created for the remote control agents for the Windows NT/2000 and Windows 95/98. If you have the Application Launcher launched from the login scripts of your user, you can force run the deployment of these agents to ensure that all workstations have the proper agent.

2. The workstation must have registered with Novell Directory Services and have a workstation object imported and associated with the workstation.

   A good way to test that you have got a good association is to modify some of the policies associated with the workstation and see if the changes take effect. One thing to do is to change the remote control policy so that the icon shows on the taskbar or the desktop and then see if this takes effect on the workstation. By doing this you know that the workstation is associated with the object and that the system is communicating properly with Novell Directory Services.

3. You must have rights to perform the remote control. When the remote control session starts, the session manager (program that runs from ConsoleOne) checks to see if you have rights to remote control the workstation. Additionally, the agent also verifies that you have rights to control the workstation.

   The rights to remote control a workstation can be given in several ways. One way is through the ZENworks Manage Remote Operators wizard launched from the tools menu. This wizard walks the tree starting at the specified container and makes sure that the users specified gain rights to remote control the workstations. Additionally, you can go to the workstation object itself and add users to the Remote Operators page. When they are added to this page they are given rights to remote control this workstation.

Once the system is set up with the workstation you may remote control any workstation that has registered and you have rights to remote control. To remote control a workstation you need to do the following:

1. Start ConsoleOne.

2. Browse in the tree to the particular workstation that you want to remote control. Highlight the workstation object. You may start remote controlling the workstation by pressing the right mouse and selecting Actions ⇨ Remote Control on the workstation object menu, or you may go into the details of the workstation and launch remote control from the Remote Management page, Remote Operations button.

3. The remote control session manager launches and verifies that you have rights and then attempt to connect to the remote control agents on the workstation that is associated with the object. The agent then responds and begins the remote controlling of the workstation, and you are presented with a window on your machine that represents the desktop of the remote machine. You now have control of the remote workstation and continue to until you exit the remote control session.

Workstation Diagnostics

There are occasions when it would be beneficial to perform some immediate diagnostics on a particular workstation. From the ConsoleOne utility, you may perform immediate diagnostics on the workstation. These diagnostics perform an immediate connection to the agent on the workstation and then deliver to the administrator information about the workstation. Figure 14.8 shows the output screen from the diagnostics.

The diagnostics information includes the amount of memory available and used, the environment information, device drivers, services information, and the event logs. In addition it displays the network connections, drives, and open files. Also it shows client information, printers, network protocols, and name space providers.

This tool provides you with some real-time information about the workstation as you debug the system and repair your user's problems.

F I G U R E   1 4 . 8 *Workstation Diagnostics of a Windows NT workstation*

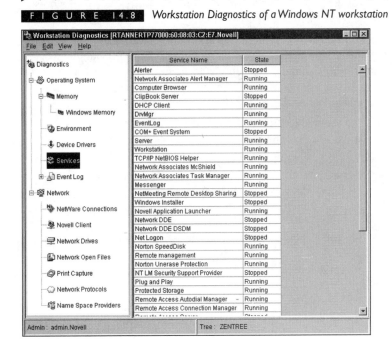

Un-registering a Workstation

In previous version of ZENworks for Desktops, the first user that logged into a tree registered the workstation into that tree. In ZENworks for Desktops 3, the system introduced into the automatic workstation import policy the ability to only import the workstation following a specified number of logins. This hopefully covers all of the needs that the IS department may have in logging into the tree and setting up the workstation prior to the final user. However, there may be some times when it is useful to reset the whole workstation importing process and get the workstation to re-register with the tree to get the entire process running from scratch. Fortunately, ZENworks for Desktops 3 provides a tool to assist you in un-registering your workstation so you can have it re-register with the tree the next time that a user logs into the tree from that workstation.

The following steps must be followed in order to un-register your workstation from the Novell Directory Services tree:

1. If a workstation object has already been imported for the workstation, then make sure that the workstation object is deleted from the tree. This is done by launching ConsoleOne and browsing to the container with the workstation object, highlighting, the object and pressing the delete key *or* choosing Object ⇨ Delete.

2. Log into the workstation with local workstation administrator privileges. You do not need to be the administrator for the tree.

3. Execute the program SYS:\public\unreg32.exe. This removes the registry keys that the ZENworks for Desktops 3 agents use to keep track of the workstation object.

4. The next user to log into the system starts the registration process again.

## CHAPTER 15

Using Software Metering with ZENworks for Desktops

A major advantage included in ZENWorks for Desktops is software metering. ZENWorks for Desktops software metering gives organizations the ability to manage software licenses and track software usage through using ZENWorks for Desktops application management and Novell's Licensing Services (NLS). Currently NLS cannot be administered in ConsoleOne, requiring that you administer the licensing in NWAdmin while managing ZENworks for Desktops 3 in ConsoleOne.

Once software metering is configured for an Application Launcher application, a license is used each time a user launches the application. In other words, every time a users runs the application one of the licenses is also in use.

NOTE
Applications must be delivered to the user through Application Launcher Explorer, or Application Launcher, in order to take advantage of Software Metering. Application objects must also be associated with license containers.

To set up and use ZENWorks for Desktops software metering you need to become familiar with the following procedures.

▶ · ◀

Using NLS Manager and NWAdmin to Install and Administer Licenses

The first piece of software metering you should be familiar with using is the NLS Manager or NWAdmin to install and administer licenses. The NLS Manager is a utility provided with Software Metering for NetWare versions 5.0 and previous. The functionality of the NLS Manager was rolled into NWAdmin starting with NetWare 5.1; therefore, we cover the different steps to complete each task for both.

You should use the NLS Manager or NWAdmin utility to create metered certificates as well as to add new ones to existing license containers. You can also use the NLS Manager or NWAdmin utility to generate reports and view information about software metering.

Once the NLS Manager is started, a window similar to the one in Figure 15.1 is displayed. From this window you are able to perform the tasks described in the following sections.

▶ . . . . ◀

FIGURE 15.1 *The main window in NLS Manager*

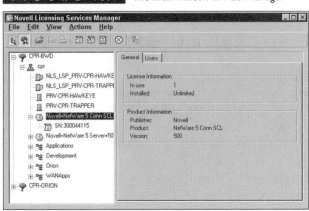

To access the licensing features from NWAdmin (on NetWare 5.1 or greater) select the Novell Licensing Services option from the Tools menu as shown in Figure 15.2.

▶ . . . . ◀

FIGURE 15.2 *The licensing options in NWAdmin for NetWare 5.1*

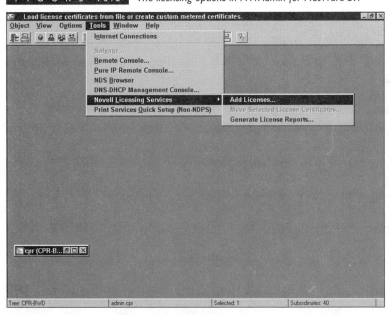

NOTE

The licensing functionality has also been added to the NWAdmin update for NetWare 5, which is distributed in Novell's Support Packs.

Installing a License Certificate Using NLS Manager and NWAdmin

The first procedure that you should be aware of is installing a license certificate. Installing a certificate for an NLS-aware application adds a License container object to the NDS database as well as a License Certificate object inside that container object.

To install a license certificate in NLS Manager use the following steps from NLS Manager:

1. From NLS Manager's main browser window, select View ⇨ Tree View.

2. Then select Actions ⇨ Install License Certificate, and a screen similar to the one in Figure 15.3 appears.

3. From that screen enter the path and filename of the certificate you wish to install.

4. Then select the NDS context where the certificate object should be installed.

5. Once both fields are entered, click OK to install the license certificate.

NOTE

A license certificate requires an activation key. If NLS Manager can't find one while you are installing a certificate, an Activation Key window allows you to enter one.

▶ · ◀

F I G U R E   15.3 *The install license certificate window in NLS Manager*

Install a License Certificate

Enter the path and file name of the License Certificate:

C:\LICENCES\NW5\62910433.CLS

Enter the NDS context where the License Certificate is to be installed:

O=cpr

Ok   Cancel   Help

To install a license certificate in NWAdmin use the following steps from the tree browse view:

1. First select the container you wish to install the license certificate into.

2. Then select Tools ⇨ Novell Licensing Services ⇨ Add Licenses as shown in Figure 15.2.

3. From the pop-up Window select License File and click OK. A window pops up enabling you to specify the license file you wish to install.

4. From this window navigate to the location of the license file you wish to install and select it. Click OK and a window similar to the one in Figure 15.4 appears.

5. From this window, browse to the NDS context where the certificate object should be installed. (The default is the currently selected container.)

6. Once both fields are entered, click the View button to see specific information about the license, or click the Add button to install the license certificate.

NOTE

A license certificate requires an activation key. If NLS Manager can't find one while you are installing a certificate, an Activation Key window enables you to enter one.

FIGURE 15.4 *The install license certificate window in NWAdmin*

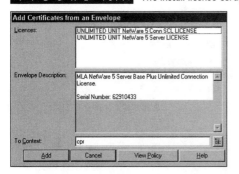

Creating a Metered Certificate Using NLS Manager or NWAdmin

The next procedure you should be familiar with is creating a metered certificate. Metered certificates enable you to track usage of applications. Using metered certificates enables you to track and manage the licenses for user applications even if they are not NLS aware.

To create a metered certificate using NLS Manager use the following steps from the main window:

I. First select View2 ⇨ Tree View.

2. Next select Actions ⇨ Create Metered Certificate, and a screen similar to the one in Figure 15.5 appears.

3. From that screen enter the name of the software publisher.

4. Then enter the product name.

5. Enter the version.

6. Next set the NDS context for the license certificate.

7. Then set the number of licenses for the certificate.

8. Enter or select the number of grace licenses you will allow.

9. Next set whether or not users will use a single license when launching an application multiple times from one workstation.

10. Click OK to finish.

NOTE The grace licenses option enables additional users to run. If you do not enter a number of grace licenses, users will not be allowed to open additional applications beyond the number specified in Number of Licenses.

F I G U R E   15.5 *The create metered certificate window*

Create a Metered Certificate

Publisher name: Novell
Product name: GroupWise
Version: 5.5
Create in context: cpr
Number of license units: 1

Options
Grace licenses units: 0
Update Interval (Min): 15
☐ Multiple launches at a workstation use just 1 license

☐ Create another certificate

OK   Cancel   Help

To create a metered certificate using NWAdmin use the following steps from a tree browse window:

I. First select Tools ⇨ Novell Licensing Services ⇨ Add Licenses.

2. From the pop-up Window select License Metering and click OK. A screen similar to the one in Figure 15.5 appears.

3. From that screen enter the name of the software publisher.

4. Enter the product name.

5. Enter the version.

6. Set the NDS context for the license certificate.

7. Set the number of licenses for the certificate.

8. Enter or select the number of grace licenses you will allow.

9. Set whether or not users will use a single license when launching an application multiple times from one workstation.

10. Click OK to finish.

NOTE

The grace licenses option enables additional users to run. If you do not enter a number of grace licenses, users will not be allowed to open additional applications beyond the number specified in Number of Licenses.

Assigning Licenses to Users Using NLS Manager or NWAdmin

Once you know how to install license certificates and create metering certificates you need to know how to assign licenses to users using NLS Manager or NWAdmin.

The NDS user who installs the license certificate is the owner. An owner can assign the following objects access to the licenses:

▶ User

▶ Group

▶ Organization

▶ Organizational Unit

▶ Server

For example, if an owner assigns a container object to use a certificate, all users in and below that container are able to use the certificate. Once license assignments are made, only those objects that have been assigned to the license certificates can use the license.

To assign and delete access to licenses using NLS Manager use the following steps through an Assignments property page:

I. Select View ⇨ Tree View.

2. Select the license certificate that you want users to access.

3. Select the Assignments property page.

4. Click Add to add objects.

5. Locate and select the object that allows the correct users to access the certificate's licenses.

Steps for deleting assignments to a license certificate in NLS Manager:

1. Navigate to the Assignments property page of the License Certificate object you wish to delete assignments on.

2. Select the object and click Remove.

To assign and delete access to licenses using NWAdmin use the following steps from a tree browse window:

1. Select the license certificate that you want users to access.

2. Right-click the license certificate and select details.

3. Select the Assignments property page.

4. Click Add to add objects.

5. Locate and select the object that enables the correct users to access the certificate's licenses.

Steps for deleting assignments to a license certificate in NWAdmin:

1. Navigate to the Assignments property page of the License Certificate object you wish to delete assignments on.

2. Select the user objects and click Remove.

Assigning a New Owner to a License Certificate Using NLS Manager

The next procedure you should be familiar with is assigning a new owner to a license certificate. Because the user who installs a certificate automatically becomes the owner of that certificate, you might want to reassign ownership at a later date.

NLS Manager enables you to assign a new owner to a license certificate at any time using the following steps:

1. Select View ➪ Tree View.

2. Select the license certificate.

3. Select the Owner property page.

4. Click the tree icon next to the License Owner field.

5. Locate and select the object you want to assign as owner of this certificate.

Only a certificate's owner can reassign ownership of the certificate.

NOTE

NWAdmin also enables you to assign a new owner to a license certificate by using the following steps:

1. Select the license certificate object from a tree browse window in the NWAdmin utility.

2. Right-click the object and select details.

3. Select the Installer property page.

4. From the Installer property page locate and select the object you want to assign as owner of this certificate.

Only a certificate's owner can reassign ownership of the certificate.

NOTE

Working with Reports in NLS Manager

The final procedure you should be aware of is the ability to create reports about licensed and metered products in the NLS Manager and NWAdmin utilities. Because these utilities track data about licenses and metered products, you can create reports that help you assess and monitor usage and compliance concerning these products for the past 15 months.

These reports can range in information about a single license certificate to information about all license certificates currently being used for a given product.

Creating a Report in NLS Manager

The first step in working with reports in NLS Manager is to create one of the following reports.

To create a report for a specific license certificate use the following steps from within NLS Manager:

1. Select View ⇨ Quick View.

2. Select a license container object's context.

3. Access the Usage Report Wizard by double-clicking the License container's context.

4. Follow the prompts.

To create a report for a product use the following steps from within NLS Manager:

1. Select View ⇨ Quick View.

2. Select the product you wish to create a report of.

3. Access the Usage Report Wizard by double-clicking the product.

4. Follow the prompts.

To create a report for license certificates use the following steps from within NWAdmin:

1. Select Tools ⇨ Novell Licensing Services ⇨ Generate License Reports.

2. From this Screen, Shown in Figure 15.6, you can select to scan either the tree or a pre-defined catalog to generate the report.

3. Select a license container you wish to begin the scan at and specify any specific publisher, product, or version filters you wish to use for the scan and click the OK button.

4. Once the scan is complete a list of license certificates and containers is displayed. To create a report simply select the license certificate you wish to report usage on and select Actions ⇨ Create License Usage Report. A screen similar to the one in Figure 15.7 appears.

► ◄

FIGURE 15.6 *The metered license certificate scan window in NWAdmin*

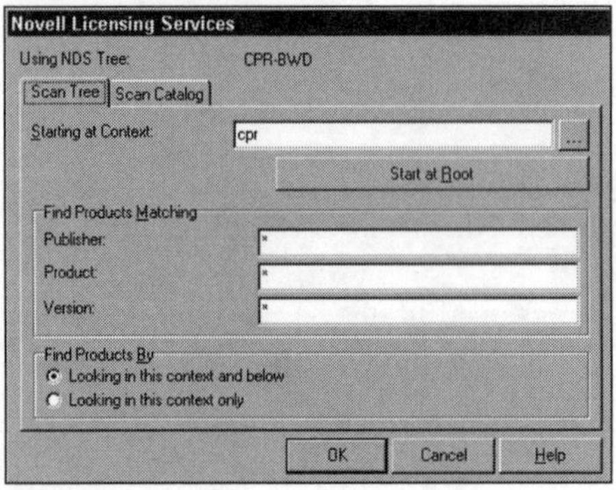

The metered license certificate reporting window in NWAdmin

```
Novell Licensing Services                                    _ □ ×
File   Edit   View   Actions   Help!

Product License Containers          In Use    Installed    Usage
  Netscape+Communicator+4.5           0         15          0.0 %
     Applications.cpr                 0         15          0.0 %
  Novell+NetWare 5 Cluster Server+500 2         Unlimited
     cpr                              2         Unlimited
  Novell+NetWare 5 Cluster User Access+51 0     0           0.0 %
     cpr                              0         0           0.0 %

This is a list of license containers found in NDS and grouped by product. License contexts are indented
beneath product names. For an aggregate report of a product's license usage, select a product name. For a
report of license usage within a context, select a single license container context.
```

Viewing a Report

Once you have created a report using NLS Manager or NWAdmin, you can toggle between a graphical view of the report and that report's text.

To use the graphical view click Graph, as shown in Figure 15.8, and a graphical representation of the data in the report is displayed on the screen. This view displays the number of license units installed and the number used. The dates along the bottom of the graph show the start and end dates that the report covers. You can change these dates to make the data more informational.

The metered License certificate usage report graph in NWAdmin

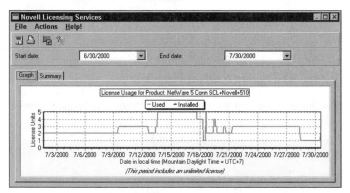

To use the textual view click Summary, as shown in Figure 15.9, and a textual representation of the data in the report is displayed on the screen.

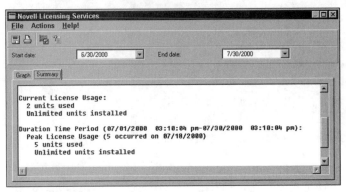

FIGURE 15.9
The metered License certificate usage report summary in NWAdmin

The textual view provides the following information:

▸ The date and time you created the report

▸ The product

▸ The location or NDS context of the object

▸ Current number of licenses being used and installed

▸ The range of dates being reported

▸ Peak usage of licenses including date the peak occurred

▸ The number of units used and installed during peak usage

▸ A list of possible dates out of compliance

Setting up Software Metering

Now that you are familiar with using the NLS Manager utility, you need to understand how to set up software metering. Setting up software metering involves using the following procedures to verify the metering requirements and setting up metering certificates.

Verify Setup Requirements

The first step in setting up software metering is to make certain that you have the correct system requirements met. The following are the current requirements for setting up software metering:

- ► You should have Supervisor rights to the [ROOT] of the NDS tree in which you install the Application Management portion of ZENWorks for Desktops.

- ► Users must have Read and File Scan rights to the directory in which you install NAL.

- ► Users must have sufficient rights to the directories in which you install the applications they can access.

Installed Locally or on the Network?

Once the system requirements are met you must make certain that the application is delivered to the user through the Application Launcher via the Application Launcher Window or the Application Explorer. Although software metering does not care where an application's executable file is located, it must be delivered to the user through the Application Launcher.

Ensure Users Have Access to NLS

The next step in setting up software metering is to ensure users have access to NLS. Users must always be attached to a NetWare server that provides licensing services.

TIP

By loading NLS on more than one server in your tree, and ensuring users have a connection to one or more servers with NLS loaded, you can ensure users have access to NLS. If a server running NLS goes down, NLS still works as long as it is running on another server and users have a connection to that server.

Assign Users to a License Certificate Object

Once you have verified that the system and setup requirements for software metering have been met, you need to assign users to a license.

If no object is specifically assigned to a license certificate object, anyone can use it. However, after assigning at least one user to a License Certificate Object, only the users, groups or containers who are assigned to that license can use it. This limits access to the licenses.

To assign users to a license certificate object use NLS Manager or the following steps in the NWAdmin utility:

1. First double-click a Product License container.

2. Next select a License Certificate object.

3. Then right-click and select Details to add users.

Create a License Container and Metered Certificate Object

To set up software metering, create a license container and metered certificate object. These objects enable ZENWorks for Desktops to track and control access to license objects.

The license container is a special container object in NDS to store metered certificate objects.

The Metered Certificate object contains the information you enter. License Containers can contain multiple Metered Certificate objects.

To create a metered certificate object and a license container use NLS Manager or the following steps in the NWAdmin utility:

1. Highlight the container where you want to create a Metered Certificate.

2. Select Tools ➪ Install License ➪ Create Metered Certificate; a screen similar to the one in Figure 15.10 appears. (For NetWare 5.1 or Greater and NetWare 5+Support Pack, select Tools ➪ Novell License Metering ➪ Add Licenses then License File.)

3. From that screen, enter information about the application that you want to meter, such as software publisher name, software product name, and version or revision.

4. Click OK.

► · ◄

FIGURE 15.10 *The create metered certificate window in NWAdmin*

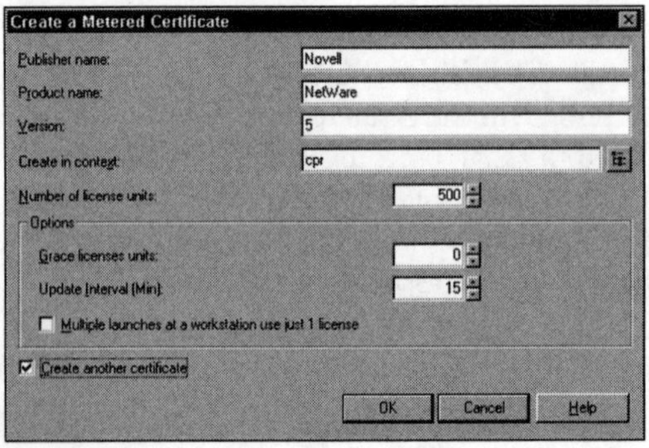

Add Additional Licenses (Metered Certificates)

The last procedure you need to be aware of when setting up software metering is adding additional licenses; for example, if you originally installed a 50-user license of an application and want to extend this to a 75-user license. To extend the license of the application, you need to create another Metered Certificate object.

The license container is a container class object in NDS and cannot be renamed. The metered certificate is a leaf object of the license container. The metered certificate basically represents the individual license count. To get a total license count, the license container totals up all leaf metered certificates beneath it.

To add additional licenses, add additional metered certificates using NLS Manager or the following steps in the NWAdmin utility:

1. Highlight the container where you want to add a license.

2. Select Tools ➪ Install License ➪ Create Metered Certificate. (For NetWare 5.1 or Greater and NetWare 5+Support Pack, select Tools ➪ Novell License Metering ➪ Add Licenses then License Metering.)

3. From that screen, enter the same name as the original license container to which you want to add licenses.

If you enter the same software publisher name, software product name, and same version number, a new Metered Certificate is created below the license container. This metered certificate is added to those already located in the license container to form a new license total.

## CHAPTER 16

Integrating ZENworks for Desktops with ZENworks for Servers

A major advantage included in ZENworks for Desktops is its ability to integrate into the tiered electronic distribution (TED) system that is included with the ZENworks for Servers product. This integration enables you to leverage the powerful TED engine for application distribution if you have both products.

The following sections describe what TED does and how to set up and use it to more effectively distribute applications to users on large networks.

How to Use TED with ZENworks for Desktops

The TED engine in ZENworks for Servers is comprised of distributor, subscriber, and proxy components hosted on NetWare servers throughout your tree. When you install ZENworks for Servers, the installation program creates objects for all TED components that you select.

Once you have installed TED you can configure and manage it from ConsoleOne, making it easy to distribute files by grouping them into data packages (distributions) and hosting them in distribution channels. Application objects can be added to the TED distribution system as data packages by adding a source distribution site (discussed later) to the application object.

TED then transfers the data package from single or multiple sources to the subscriber server nodes in your tree. TED lets you schedule distributions to take advantage of off-peak hours. It also sends notification of distribution statuses by sending e-mail messages, displaying real-time messages, logging events, database reporting, or sending SNMP Traps.

When application object distributions are placed in a channel, the distributor server notifies all subscriber servers of the availability of the distribution, or a subscriber server can be configured to poll the distributor server for any new distributions.

Once the subscriber server receives the data package, the application object is extracted into a directory, an application object is created on the subscriber server end, and it is available for normal application distribution from the new location.

(For more information about installing and using TED and ZENworks for Servers, refer to the ZENworks for Servers documentation on the Novell web site.)

Setting up Application Objects for TED Distribution

Now that you understand how TED and ZENworks for Desktops work, you need to understand how to set the application object up to be added to the TED channel and distributed to remote sites. This section covers the steps necessary to set up and add an application object to the TED distribution channel.

The first step in setting up the application object to work with TED is to right-click it in ConsoleOne and click properties. From the application properties window, select the Site Distributions tab as shown in Figure 16.1. The site distributions tab is only available if you have installed both ZENworks for Desktops and ZENworks for Servers.

F I G U R E   1 6 . 1 *Site distribution list window for application objects in ConsoleOne*

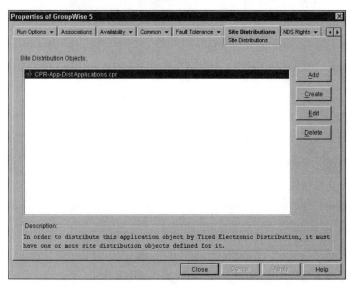

From this panel you must either add a site distribution object to the list or create a new one. The following sections describe how to create a new site distribution object by clicking the create button.

NOTE

The Site Distribution objects are hidden from view in the normal ConsoleOne tree view window.

Setting up Distribution Source Site

The first step in setting up a distribution site is to set up the site source and identification for the site distribution object. From the window in Figure 16.2, first type in a descriptive name for the site distribution object. Next, select a container in which to place the object. This container should be located in the same location or close to the location as the application object itself.

FIGURE 16.2 *Object source identification and location panel for site distribution in ConsoleOne*

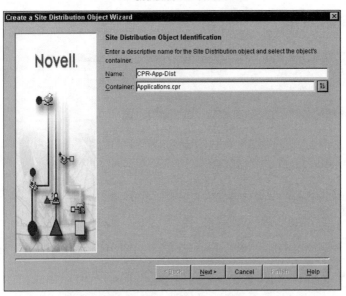

Setting up Distribution Destination Container

Once you have set up the source location and ID for the site distribution object you need to set up the destination container location, as shown in Figure 16.3. Either type in the location of the container *or* use the browse button to navigate the NDS tree to select the destination location.

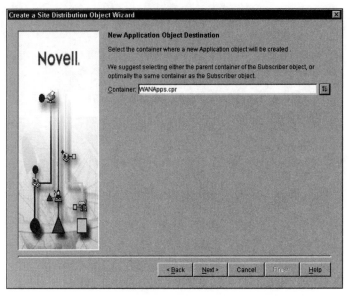

Application destination container panel for site distribution in ConsoleOne

The destination location should be located close to the users who need to have the application distributed to them. For example, if your main office is in New York, but you have one small office with 30 users in Detroit, then you would select the destination location to be in the same context as the Detroit users. That way the users are able to access the application object from the local copy on their server in Detroit.

Setting up Application Storage Volume

Once you have set up the destination container, you need to set up the destination volume where the application will be copied for distribution as shown in Figure 16.4. You can specify several volume names here. TED looks at the server for each volume starting with the first one. As soon as it finds a volume with that name on the server it copies the application package files to it.

Application destination volume panel for site distribution in ConsoleOne

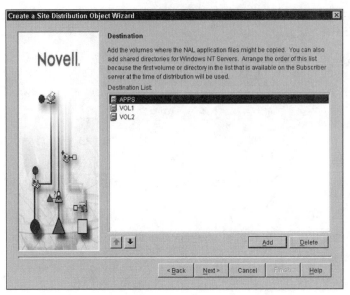

NOTE

TED looks at the volumes in the order they appear in this list. Make certain that you order the volumes so that the appropriate volume is selected each time. For example, always use an apps volume as the first one and create a large apps volume on most of your servers. Then only use the VOL1 volume if the apps is unavailable for any reason. That way you know there is enough room and you know where to find the applications.

Setting up Application Storage Directory

Once you have set up the destination volume list, you need to set up the destination directory path as shown in Figure 16.5. You have two options from this window. The first option is to accept the default path that is defined in the application object. The second option is to select a user-defined path and type in the path to create on the volume and copy the application object to.

FIGURE 16.5 *Application destination directory path panel for site distribution in ConsoleOne*

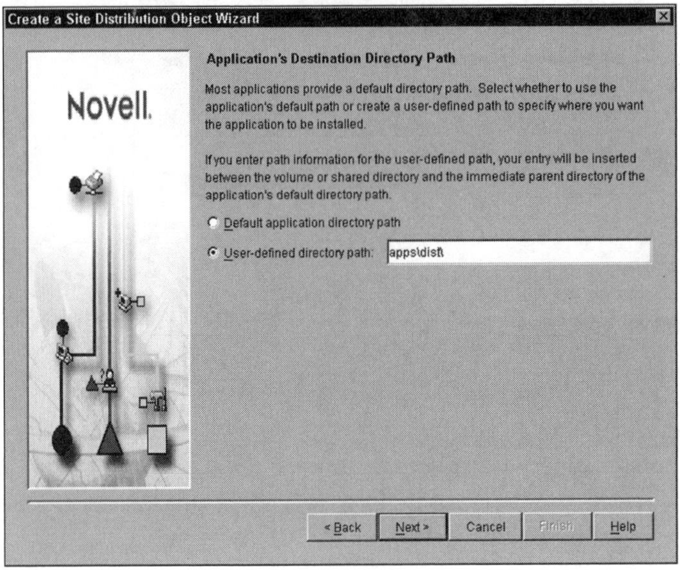

For example, if you want to keep all applications that are distributed remotely using TED in a single location then you should select the user-defined directory path option. Then for each object, type in similar paths such as 'apps\dist\GroupWise\' for the GroupWise application and 'apps\dist\Client\' for the Novell client install.

Associating Objects with Distribution Site

Once you have set up the distribution directory path for the application package, you need to associate objects with the distribution site. From the object association window in Figure 16.6, click the add button and select the objects in the application that you wish to be distributed at the remote location. If you select a container object, you are given the option to include users, workstations, or both inside that container.

Object association window for site distribution in ConsoleOne

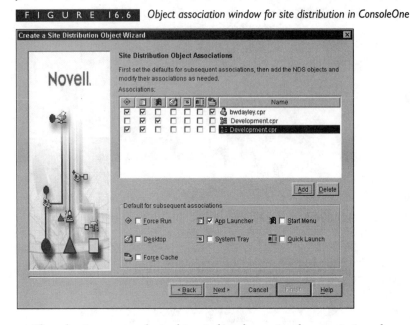

The selections you make in this window determine the associations the new application object receives when it is created once the package has been distributed by TED. You should plan these associations carefully to make certain that no users or workstations exist that would not be local to the site distribution destination.

From this window you can also configure the appearance behavior that the application object uses for distribution. You can configure the following options for each object association: Force Run, App Launcher Start Menu, Desktop, System Tray, Quick Launch, Force Cache. For more information on these options see Chapter 5.

Viewing Site Summary

Once you have set up the object associations of the application object for the site distribution object, a summary window similar to the one in Figure 16.7 is displayed. The summary includes the following information about the site distribution object:

▶ **Object Name** — Object name that represents the site distribution.

▶ **Object Container** — Location of the site distribution object in NDS.

► **Destination Container** — Container to which the distribution is completed and in which the new application object is created.

► **Destination Volume List** — List of volumes in order that TED tries to use them to copy the application package.

► **Destination Directory** — Directory that TED creates to copy the application package in.

► **Object Associations** — List of objects that are associated with the new application object.

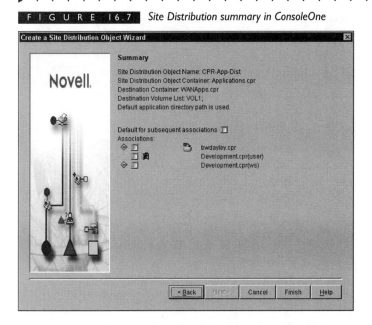

Site Distribution summary in ConsoleOne

Review the information carefully. If any problems exist then you can click the back button and make changes. Otherwise, click the finish button and the site distribution object is created and used to distribute the application, based on the distribution and run settings applied to the application object.

## CHAPTER 17

Troubleshooting
ZENworks for Desktops

ZENworks for Desktops is an extremely powerful tool which saves network administrators much needed time. However, because of the complexity of network environments, problems can occur that prevent ZENworks for Desktops from doing its job. This chapter covers how to troubleshoot and diagnose those problems in the following areas:

- ► Troubleshooting Desktop Management
- ► Troubleshooting Distributed Applications
- ► Troubleshooting Policies Packages
- ► Troubleshooting NetWare Errors

► . . . . ◄

Troubleshooting Desktop Management

The first area of troubleshooting we cover is desktop management. Desktop management is difficult to troubleshoot because several network components are involved; this includes the server, clients, NDS, and LAN.

The following sections discuss the most common areas to review when you are troubleshooting desktop management issues.

Reduce LAN Traffic

When troubleshooting desktop management issues, if LAN traffic is unacceptable after you create and associate Policy Packages with objects, you may need to reduce LAN traffic. One effective way you can reduce LAN traffic is by limiting how the system searches the tree for associations between Policy Packages and objects we discussed in earlier chapters. Limiting the searches should reduce LAN traffic.

To reduce LAN traffic by limiting how the system searches the tree for associations between Policy Packages and objects, use the following steps in ConsoleOne:

I. Create a Container policy package and choose Define Additional Properties ➪ Create.

2. Enable the Search Policy.

3. Highlight the Search Policy and choose Details ➪ Search Level.

4. Set the Search For Policies Up To field to Partition, and then choose OK. This limits how many directory levels are searched for associations between policy packages and objects.

5. Choose the Associations page, and associate this Container policy package to the container where you want to make the Search Policy effective. Remember that the Search Policy affects all containers below the associated container, because the workstation manager looks for the container package.

Troubleshoot Help Requester

When troubleshooting desktop management issues, if users are unable to run the Help Requester from a workstation, you may need to troubleshoot the following:

▶ From the User object, view the Effective Policies for the user and ensure you have an effective Help Desk Policy. If so, then highlight the policy, choose Details, and then check the settings.

▶ Ensure that you have associated a platform-specific User Policy Package containing a Help Desk Policy with that User object, a Group that the User object is a member of, or the container where the User object resides.

▶ Ensure that you have enabled a Help Desk Policy and that the Allow Users to Send Trouble Tickets field is checked.

Troubleshoot Import

When troubleshooting desktop management issues, if an attempt to import a workstation was unsuccessful, you may need to troubleshoot import by using the following suggestions:

NOTE

A workstation does not synchronize with NDS until after it has been imported and the Workstation Registration program is run again.

Verify Workstation Setup

The first step in troubleshooting workstation import issues is to verify that the correct client is installed on the workstation. This client can be installed from the ZENWorks for Desktops CD, or can be downloaded from Novell's web site.

Validate the Workstation Import Policy

The next step in troubleshooting workstation import issues is to validate the Workstation Import Policy. First verify that a search policy exists and that the user is enabled for the user logging in using the following steps:

1. From ConsoleOne, Right-click the user that is not registering their workstation and select Properties.

2. Click the Effective Policies tab.

3. Select the correct platform for the workstation that the user is logging into and then click Effective Policies.

4. There should be a Policy Package listed for the Workstation Import Policy. If not, you need to create and associate one.

Verify Workstation Registration/Syncher Agent

Once you have verified that the workstation is enabled for login, verify that the Workstation Registration/Syncher Agent is loading, by Right-clicking on the Novell Desktop Management icon in the System Tray and select Display Schedule.

There should be an entry for Workstation Registration/Syncher Agent. If not, then make sure the steps for "Validate that a Workstation Import Policy is enabled for the user logging in" were properly followed. You may have to reboot the computer and login twice before the policy becomes enabled.

Check Registry Keys for Workstation Manager

Next check the registry keys for Workstation Manager to ensure that the workstation is not already imported using the following steps:

1. Launch REGEDIT.EXE (or REGEDT32.EXE for NT/2000).

2. Browse to the following registry key:

    `HKEY_LOCAL_MACHINE\SOFTWARE\Novell\Workstation Manager\ Identification`

3. Workstation registration may be in three states (No WS Import Policy, Registration, or Imported).

4. If the workstation is in the No WS Import Policy state, then the Registered In, Registration Object, and Workstation Object values will be either NULL or will not exist.

5. If the workstation is in the Registration state, then the Registered In and Registration Object values will be populated, but the Workstation Object value will not exist.

6. If the workstation is in the Imported state, then the Registered In, Registration Object, and Workstation Object values will be populated.

NOTE

A good general troubleshooting step for registration is to delete the Registered In, Registration Object, and Workstation Object values. They will be recreated at the next boot up login attempt (except that the Workstation Object registry value is only created if the administrator imports the workstation NWADMN32).

Verify Trusted Tree for Workstation Manager

Once you have verified the registry keys, ensure that the Workstation Manager Trusted Tree is set to the correct Tree name by using the following steps:

1. Launch REGEDIT.EXE (or REGEDT32.EXE for NT).

2. Browse to the following registry key:

HKEY_LOCAL_MACHINE\SOFTWARE\Novell\Workstation Manager\
Identification

3. The Tree value must match the tree name the user is logging into *exactly*. ZENworks is enabled for one tree at a time, and this tree name is listed here. If the tree you are logging into does not match this registry value, then all of ZENworks is disabled (including the Workstation Import Policy).

Verify Workstation Is Already Registered in NDS

Then check the registry to see if the workstation is already registered in NDS by using the following steps:

1. Browse to the container listed in the Register In registry value from the following registry key:

HKEY_LOCAL_MACHINE\SOFTWARE\Novell\Workstation
Manager\Identification

2. Right-click the container and select Properties.

3. Click the Workstation Registration tab.

4. Look for an entry that matches the workstation the user is logging into.

Ensure the Container Is Ready for Workstation Registration

Once you have verified the workstation is registered in NDS, ensure that the container has been prepared for Workstation Registration using the following steps:

1. From ConsoleOne browse to the container listed in the Register In registry value from the following registry key:

   `HKEY_LOCAL_MACHINE\SOFTWARE\Novell\Workstation Manager\ Identification`

2. Click Tools ⇨ Workstation Utilities ⇨ Prepare Workstation Registration.

3. Determine whether or not you wish to register workstation in any sub-containers.

4. Then either check/uncheck Include subcontainers and click the OK button.

View the Error Log

When troubleshooting workstation import issues you can also view the error log from the Import Results dialog box that displays when you choose Tools ⇨ Import. From the dialog box look for errors and then continue troubleshooting from there.

Re-Register the Workstation

As a final option you can unregister the workstation by running the unreg utility from the following location and then reregister the workstation:

`SYS:\PUBLIC\UNREG32.EXE`

Troubleshoot Workstation Objects

When troubleshooting desktop management issues, if the Workstation object does not display in the tree after a registered workstation was imported, you should check the following:

1. From the User object, view the Effective Policies for the user and ensure you have an effective Workstation Import Policy. If so, then highlight the policy, choose Details, and then check the settings on both the Workstation Location and Workstation Naming pages.

2. Check the container where the User object resides to see if the Workstation object was created there.

3. Check the Workstation Registration page to see if the Workstation displays in the list.

Troubleshooting Distributed Applications

The next area of troubleshooting ZENworks for Desktops we cover is *distributed applications*. If users encounter problems using distributed applications, once you have created application objects and set up application distribution for them, you can use the following procedures to help diagnose and debug the issues.

Troubleshoot Application Launcher and Explorer

The first place to start when troubleshooting distributed applications is the Application Launcher and Explorer. You can obtain information about Application Launcher and Application Explorer to help you troubleshoot problems that your users may encounter.

Review Information About File Locations and Versions

When troubleshooting Application Launcher and Explorer, the best place to begin is to get information about file location and versions. This helps you determine if the correct files are being installed from the correct places.

To obtain information about file location and versions from the Application Launcher or Explorer use the following steps:

1. From Application Launcher or the Application Explorer window, select Help ⇨ About ⇨ More.

2. Read the information about file names, paths, and versions in use by Application Launcher. There may be later versions available from Novell's support web site.

Review Information About the State of Currently Running Applications

The next issue to consider when troubleshooting the Application Launcher is getting information about the state of currently running applications. This helps you determine if any resource conflicts or incompatibilities exist between different applications.

To get information about the state of currently running applications use the following steps:

1. Press and hold the Shift key when opening the About box (Help ⇨ About). The Applications Running text box gives the number of currently running Application Launcher-delivered applications running for the current user. The Resources In Use text box reports the number of resources (a server connection, a drive letter, or a printer port) in use.

2. Click Applications to display debug information about the applications running. Highlight an application and click Select to see the resources for that application.

3. Click Resources to display all resource information for all applications currently running.

4. Click Environment to read information about any environment variables in use for Application Launcher-delivered applications.

Review NDS Tree Specific Information

Once you have information about files and running applications you should look at NDS tree specific Information. For example, you may need to know the number of levels up the NDS tree the Application Launcher looks for applications.

To get the NDS tree specific information about the Application Launcher or Explorer use the following steps:

1. From Application Launcher or the Application Explorer window, choose Help ⇨ About ⇨ More.

2. While holding down Ctrl+Alt, double-click an Application object in the Login Information list.

3. Use the information in Table 17.1.

T A B L E 17.1	*NDS Specific Information About Application Launcher*
TEXT BOX	**ANSWERS THIS QUESTION**
Container Levels	What are the number of levels up the NDS* tree that the Application Launcher looks for applications? This number is specified on the Launcher Configuration property page of the User or container object to which the Application object is associated.

TEXT BOX	ANSWERS THIS QUESTION
Supports Application Objects	Are Application objects supported in this tree? Does this tree have the necessary schema extensions to support Application objects?
Schema Supported	What are the version numbers of supported schemas?
Rights to Group Membership	What rights does the user have to his or her group membership attribute on his or her User object?
Monitored Connection	What is the Distinguished Name (DN) of the server that is the monitored connection? This is important to know if you have set up an application site list so that users access applications from the server that is geographically closest to them.
Save Folders	Will personal folders be saved at exit if they have been changed?
NRD Support	Is NetWare Registry Database (NRD) supported? What is the path to the NRD.DLL? If No, NRD.DLL not found (NRDDLL16.DLL, NRDDLL95.DLL, NRDDLLNT.DLL). If Yes, No, NRD.DLL found but tree does not have the NRD extensions or user does not have rights to the NRD attributes on their user object. If Yes, Yes, NRD.DLL found and ready to go.
E-mail Attribute	What attribute on User object is used for e-mail address in Contacts page?
Login DLL version	What is the version and path to login DLL (used for script processing)?

Enable Error Logging File

Once you have reviewed information about the files, applications, and the NDS tree, you should enable error logging. This helps you troubleshoot issues because you specify the path to a file where any errors are logged if the application fails to install or launch.

NOTE

No other status is tracked here except for errors. Before users can run this Application object, they must be given rights to write to this file for this option to work correctly.

View and Edit User or Container's Application Launcher Configurations

Once you have looked at Application Launcher and Explorer you should view and edit user or container application launcher configurations. This helps you troubleshoot issues that are caused by problems with the setup of distributed applications in the user and/or container objects. To review the Application's Launcher configuration for user or container objects use the following procedures.

Use the Launcher Configuration Property Page

The first step in reviewing the Application Launcher configuration for user or container objects is to use the Application Launcher Configuration property page in ConsoleOne to view the following:

1. The effective Application Launcher and Application Explorer configurations for a User, Organizational Unit, Organization, or Country object

2. The Application Launcher configuration inheritance tree (where the current object gets configurations from objects higher in the tree)

3. Setup custom Application Launcher configurations for the currently selected container object

Review User or Container's Effective Application Launcher Configurations

Once you have reviewed the information above from the main Application Launcher page in ConsoleOne you should view the effective Application Launcher Configurations. Effective settings include custom configurations applied to the current object as well as configurations inherited from parent container(s). You can control how a container object inherits Application Launcher configurations by using the Use as Top of Inheritance Tree option.

To view the custom Application Launcher Configurations from within ConsoleOne use the following steps:

1. Right-click a User, Organizational Unit, Organization, or Country object and click Properties.

2. Click the Launcher Configuration tab.

3. Choose View Object's Effective Settings from the Mode drop-down list.

Review Application Launcher Configuration Inheritance Tree

Once you have reviewed the custom Application Launcher Configurations you should review the Application Launcher configuration inheritance tree for the user or container object by using the following steps:

1. Right-click a User, Organizational Unit, Organization, or Country object and click Properties.

2. Click the Launcher Configuration tab.

3. Choose View Configuration Inheritance Tree from the Mode drop-down list.

Review and Edit User or Container's Custom Application Launcher Configurations

Once you have reviewed the Application Launcher configuration inheritance tree you should review the container's custom Application Launcher configurations for the container object by using the following steps:

1. Right-click a User, Organizational Unit, Organization, or Country object and click Properties.

2. Click the Launcher Configuration tab.

3. Choose View/Edit Object's Custom Configuration from the Mode drop-down list. If no settings display in the list, no custom settings have been defined for this User or container object.

4. Click the Edit button to customize the settings for this object.

Use Object as Top of Inheritance Tree

Another procedure that may help in troubleshooting Application Distributing at a container level is to set the object as the top of the inheritance tree.

The Application Launcher searches the NDS* tree for configuration settings. Application Launcher starts at the lowest possible leaf object and navigates up the inheritance tree. It continues navigating this tree until it reaches a container object that has been designated as the top of the inheritance tree.

If the Application Launcher finds custom configurations in any of the objects while it is navigating the tree, they are the applied through inheritance. If it doesn't find any custom configurations, then the configuration is considered unset and the default configuration is applied. This allows control of when and where custom configurations are applied instead of the defaults.

To designate a User or container object as the top of the inheritance tree, select the Use Object as Top of Inheritance Tree option on the Launcher Configuration property page of that User or container object.

Backwards Compatibility

Newer versions of Application Launcher add new Launcher Configuration settings above those in older versions. It's possible that at any given time while you are rolling out the new Application Launcher or Application Explorer that you would like to preserve the old Launcher configuration settings. Make certain that this option is enabled in the Application Launcher screen in ConsoleOne if you wish to have backwards compatibility.

Review User Object's Inheritance Applications

The next step in troubleshooting distributed application launcher problems is to look at the applications inherited by user objects. You may find that the user inherits two applications that are incompatible or that combined take up too much of the client's resources, and so on.

Use the Show Inherited Applications option on the Tools ⇨ Application Launcher Tools menu to see the Application objects that have been associated with the User object, including all applications either associated with or inherited by the User object. The applications are listed by mode of delivery, such as Force Run, App Launcher, Desktop, Start Menu, and System Tray. These categories come from the Applications property panel, which is available for User, Group, Organization, and Organizational Unit objects.

Use the following steps to list the applications that the user has rights to use:

1. Highlight a User object.

2. Choose Tools ⇨ Application Launcher Tools ⇨ Show Inherited Applications.

3. Expand the user object to view all associated applications.

Set Timed Refresh Frequency

A useful setting when troubleshooting distributed applications is the Set refresh frequency option, which lets you specify the refresh frequency in seconds. For example, if you set the refresh to 300 seconds, Application Launcher or Application Explorer updates applications from the network automatically every five minutes and might even run some applications depending on how you have set them up.

Although a short timed refresh interval is very useful in situations where you want changes to refresh quickly, a short timed refresh interval usually causes higher network traffic.

TIP   If you are having problems with network traffic when distributing applications you should always increase the timed refresh frequency for Application Launcher and Explorer. You may need to play with the frequency value to match your specific environment.

Change Workstation Files in Use

Another useful step in troubleshooting distributed applications is to make certain that the workstation was properly rebooted with the appropriate files. Occasionally the workstation was not rebooted or a file was in use when the application was distributed, preventing it from being distributed properly.

When Application Launcher distributes applications, it might change workstation configuration files (for example, config.sys, autoexec.bat, or win.ini) depending on the settings in the Application object. The changes to these files do not take effect until after the workstation is rebooted. Application Launcher detects whether such changes are made, and prompts the user with a message stating that the workstation must be rebooted before the changes can take place.

Similarly, when application files are copied, the files they are replacing might be in use, and cannot be deleted or replaced. Application Launcher usually handles this situation. Generally, the new files are copied to a temporary area and then copied to their correct locations when Windows is restarted. However if a problem exists with the temporary area or the workstation was not rebooted then the correct files will not be properly installed.

Clean up Network Resources

The next step in troubleshooting distributed applications in ZENworks for Desktops is to make certain that network resources are being properly cleaned up.

The process of cleaning up means that the license for a particular network connection is removed. This prevents users from using a network connection when they don't need it. When the clean up Network Resources option is selected, drive mappings and printer ports associated with Application Launcher-delivered applications are removed.

NOTE

If the resource (a connection, map, or capture) is already in use when Application Launcher or Application Explorer is started, Application Launcher or Application Explorer uses it and does not clean it up. Otherwise, the resource is created and cleaned up when all other Application Launcher or Application Explorer applications are finished using it. The connection to the server containing the resource is removed as well. If the applications that Application Launcher or Application Explorer launched are still running when Application Launcher or Application Explorer is terminated, the allocated resources remain intact.

When an application is launched, Application Launcher or Application Explorer monitors the executable of the application. When the executable terminates, the process of cleaning up network resources begins. However, it's possible that the executable filename is actually a wrapper that sets up environments, runs other executables, and then terminates. If Application Launcher or Application Explorer monitors the wrapper executable, it might prematurely start cleaning up network resources before the application has terminated.

To prevent Application Launcher and Explorer from prematurely cleaning up an application's resources, consult your application documentation about whether the application uses a wrapper executable. If it does use a wrapper executable, find out the name of the module that remains running, then type this name, excluding the extension, in the text box provided.

Write Application Administrator Notes

As a network administrator it is particularly useful to keep records for use later. When troubleshooting issues with distributed applications you should use the Administrator Notes property page to create a section of notes that only you, as the administrator, can view and edit.

For example, you might want to remind yourself about some special settings for a particular application. This is true especially if your system is managed by several administrators. You could use the Administrator Notes property page to provide a history of application upgrades and file changes so that work is not duplicated.

To write administrator notes for an Application Object use the following steps:

1. Right-click the Application object and click Properties.

2. Click the Administrator Notes option from the Identification tab.

3. In the space provided, type the note, and then click OK.

Review Roll-Back Application Distribution

When troubleshooting application distribution you should be aware that if ZENworks for Desktops encounters an error during distribution, it rolls back or reverses all the changes made before the error and resets the workstation to the state it was in before the distribution began.

When you roll out or distribute a complex application using Application Launcher, changes are made to the targeted workstation. These changes might include text files (such as config.sys and autoexec.bat), Windows Registry entries, and .ini files. In addition, application files can be copied or deleted at the target workstation.

The method Application Launcher uses to roll back changes is simple. First, it creates temporary files and directories to store files and other rollback information on the workstation. If the distribution is successful, those files and directories are deleted. If the distribution encounters an error, Application Launcher uses the rollback information to restore the workstation to its original state. Once that is completed, the rollback information is deleted.

Problems rolling back can occur if a file is in use, the application is set to overwrite an existing application, and so on when the roll back occurs. Application Launcher is unable to roll back a file that is in use or does not exist.

Use Search and Replace Entire Application Object

A very useful tool in troubleshooting application objects is the search and replace entire application objects option in ConsoleOne. You can use the Search and Replace dialog box to search or search and replace the entire Application object for text strings.

For example, if a directory name is changed and the application object no longer functions, you could use this feature to correct the directory name every place it occurs in the application object.

To search and replace text strings in all property pages of application object, use the following steps:

1. Highlight the Application object that you want to search.
2. Choose Tools ⇨ Application Launcher Tools ⇨ Search and Replace.
3. Choose Options, and then choose the type of Application object settings you want to search.
4. Choose Match Case to make the search case sensitive.
5. Type the text you want to search for in the Search For text box, then click Find Next.

6. If you want to replace that text with other text, type it in the Replace With text box then click Find Next, then Replace or Replace All.

Use Search Specific Application Object Property Page

A very useful tool in troubleshooting application objects is the search specific application object property page in ConsoleOne. You can use the Find dialog box to search the current Registry Settings, INI Settings, or Application Files property page.

For example, if a specific registry setting was causing the application distribution to experience problems, then you could use this feature to find the registry setting in the application object.

To find specific application object settings use the following steps:

1. Right-click the Application object and click Properties.

2. Click the Registry Settings, INI Settings, or Application Files option panels from the distribution tab.

3. Choose the Find option (in most cases this might appear on the File button).

4. Type the text that you want to find, then choose Find.

Review Application Termination

When troubleshooting application distribution, make certain that the application was terminated properly. You can use the Termination property panel in ConsoleOne to view and modify how Application Launcher handles the termination of an application. If termination is improperly set up, then users may experience problems when the application runs.

Use the following steps to view and modify termination of the application:

1. Right-click the Application object and click Properties.

2. Click the Termination option panel from the Availability tab.

3. Select and modify the appropriate termination behaviors from the drop-down list.

Send Message to Close Application

If users should close the application, use the send message to close application option. For example, if you set an interval of 20 minutes, Application Launcher sends a message (if one is active) to the user every 20 minutes until the application is closed.

Send Message to Close Then Prompt to Save Data

Use the send message to close then prompt to save data if the application must be terminated, however, user data loss may occur. This option prompts users, for a specified period of time, to close the application on their own (this action is optional). When that period of time expires, the Application Launcher attempts to close the application. If users have not saved data, they are prompted to save it.

Send Message to Close, Prompt to Save, Then Force Close

Use the send message to close, prompt to save, then force close option when the application must be terminated, regardless of user data loss. This option prompts users, for a specified period of time, to close the application on their own. When that period of time expires, you can close the application prompting users, at specified intervals, to save their work. If users have still not closed within a specified period of time, the application is forced to close.

Send Message to Close Then Force Close with Explanation

Use the send message to close the force close with explanation when the application must absolutely be terminated and user data loss is not a concern. This option prompts users, for a specified period of time, to close the application on their own. When that period of time expires, the application is forced to close.

Enable Dial-Up Detection

When troubleshooting distributed applications for users who use dial-up connections, make certain that dial-up detection is enabled. Application Launcher and Application Explorer automatically detect a dial-up networking session. If such a connection is detected, the user is given the option to exit Application Launcher or continue to have Application read information from NDS.

For example, suppose that a network administrator puts a command in a user's login script to run nal.exe. The user goes home and, with a 56.6 kbps speed modem, dials and connects to the company's network. Application Launcher recognizes the dial-up connection. Instead of waiting a long time for Application Launcher to read the NDS tree for Application object information, the user can close Application Launcher and receive any Application Launcher-delivered applications.

Troubleshooting Policy Packages

Another area that you should be familiar with troubleshooting is the policy packages. No formal method exists for troubleshooting the workstation policy package; however, the following are some steps you can take to identify problems and resolutions to issues.

Review NDS Workstation Object

In the case of a workstation policy package, make certain a valid NDS Workstation Object has been created and is linked to workstations that use the policy package. This can be checked by viewing the values shown in Table 17.2 in the workstation's registry:

T A B L E 17.2	*Identification Key in Workstation's Registry*
KEY	**VALUES**
HKEY_LOCAL_MACHINE\ SOFTWARE\Novell\ Workstation Manager\ Identification	Registered In : REG_SZ : .OU=ZEN.OU=Site. O=Company Registration Object : REG_SZ : UserName, IPX_Network_Address, IP_ Network_Address, Station_Name, and so on... Workstation Object : REG_SZ : CN= StationName123456789012.OU= ZEN.OU=Site.O=Company

You are specifically looking for the Workstation Object value. It identifies which NDS Workstation Object the workstation is using when it is logged in. All Workstation Policy Packages need to be associated with this NDS Workstation Object or to a Workstation Group that has this NDS Workstation Object as one of its members.

If a Workstation Policy Package is not associated to the NDS Workstation Object listed in the Workstation Object registry value or a group it belongs to, then no Workstation Policy Packages are downloaded and applied. You can also check for effective policies on the effective policies panel of a container object's properties page.

Review Policy Package Type

Make certain that the appropriate type of Policy Package has been created. For example, if the workstation is running Windows NT/2000, make sure you have created a WINNT Workstation Policy Package.

Review Workstation Object Associations

In the case of a workstation policy package, make certain that NDS Workstation Objects have an association to the Policy Package. This can be verified by looking at the Details of the Policy Package within ConsoleOne by clicking on the Associations tab.

Make certain that all the workstations that use the NDS Workstation Object are listed there, are a member of a Workstation Group listed, or exist in a container listed.

TIP Make certain to look for potential problems with a Container Policy Package if you are only using the container to associate the NDS Workstation Object. If you are not sure, it is a good idea to associate the NDS Workstation Object directly (as a troubleshooting step, not as an implementation design).

Enable Policies

Make certain that at least one policy is enabled to download. If no policies are enabled, the user will not be able to detect any change to the user/workstation environment and may question if it is working properly.

Install Workstation Manager

Make certain that when the client for Win95/98 was installed, that the workstation manager component was installed also. You can verify if it has been installed by going into the control panel ➪ network configuration tab and looking for the service called Novell Workstation Manager.

Review Trusted Trees

Make certain that workstations have the active tree listed as a Trusted Tree. The Workstation Manager component of ZENworks uses the concept of Trusted Trees, and Windows 95/98 or NT/2000 Workstations only attempt to search for a ZENworks Policy Package if the tree is listed as a Trusted Tree. This feature gives greater administrative flexibility as to what workstations are controlled by ZENworks.

You can set the Trusted Tree by selecting the custom installation of the Novell Client for NT/2000 or 95/98. If Typical Installation is selected, it automatically sets the tree that you first log in to as the Trusted Tree.

To view the Trusted Tree property on a Windows NT workstation, go to the Control Panel ➪ Network ➪ Services ➪ Properties of Novell Workstation Manager. Make sure that the option for Enable Workstation Manager is checked and that the Tree field has the NDS Tree name spelled correctly.

To view the Trusted Tree property on a Windows 95/98 workstation, view the registry key directly at the following location:

```
HKEY_LOCAL_MACHINE\SOFTWARE\NOVELL\Workstation Manger\
Identification
```

Troubleshooting NetWare Errors

When troubleshooting ZENworks for Desktops you should always be aware of any NetWare error messages that are occurring. ZENworks for Desktops is heavily tied into the NetWare operating system, NDS and file system. Therefore, any error occurring in NetWare possibly effects ZENworks for Desktops as well.

NetWare Server File System Errors

When ZENworks for Desktops is having problems distributing applications you should always look for errors in the NetWare file system. These errors often help you narrow down the problem to a specific cause and resolution.

For example, if the ZENworks for Desktops client gives the user the following error, then you would suspect a connection problem with the server and could focus troubleshooting on finding the cause and fixing that problem.

```
918: This utility was unable to get connection
information. Error code: 89FF.
```

Table 17.3 contains common file system errors:

T A B L E 1 7 . 3 *Common File System Errors*

CODE	TEXT	DESCRIPTION
0x8901	INSUFFICIENT SPACE	The station does not have sufficient disk space. Make certain that the minimum free disk space requirements are set up for the application object being used.
0x8980	FILE IN USE	An attempt was made to open or create a file that is already open. Set the shareable attribute if you wish multiple users to access the file at the same time.
0x8983	DISK IO ERROR	A hard disk i/o error occurred on a NetWare volume. Typically a bad sector has been encountered and could not be migrated to the hotfix area. Replace the drive.
0x8999	DIR FULL	An attempt was made to write to a volume without available directory space. Make certain that you are not exceeding the maximum number of directory entries for the volume.
0x899C	INSUFFICIENT RIGHTS INVALID PATH	An attempt was made to access a path with invalid rights to the path or with an invalid path name. Make certain that the user has appropriate rights to the path and that the path name is correct.
0x89A8	ACCESS DENIED	Access has been denied. Make certain that the user has appropriate rights to the file.
0x89BF	NAME SPACE INVALID	An invalid name space was used. Make sure the correct namespaces are loaded on the volume being used.

NDS Errors

Another area you should always review when troubleshooting ZENworks for Desktops is the NDS error messages. ZENworks for Desktops uses NDS heavily not only for normal authentication and access, but as a service for controlling ZENworks for Desktops objects.

NDS errors can be categorized as follows:

NDS Operating System Error Codes

Some NDS background processes require the functionality provided by the NetWare operating system. These processes, such as communication and transaction servers, can return operating system specific error codes to NDS. These error codes are then passed on to the NDS background process that initiated a request. In NetWare 4.*x*, versions of NDS can also generate operating system error codes.

Usually operating system error codes that are generated by NDS have a negative numerical representation, while normal operating system error codes have a positive numerical representation. The numerical range for operating system error codes generated by NDS is –1 through –256, inversely the numerical range for operating system error codes is 1 through 255.

NOTE

NDS returns the positive numerical error code rather than the negative error code normally used by NDS to application to prevent any incompatibility. Therefore, any occurrence of an error code within the range of 1 to 255 or –1 to –255 should be treated as the same error.

NDS Client Error Codes

The next class of NDS error codes is the client error codes. Some NDS background processes require the functionality provided by other NDS servers. Use of these functions, such as bindery services, requires that an NDS server act as an NDS client to the server providing the functionality. Therefore, these functions often result in client-specific error codes being returned to the NDS background processes and operations.

NDS client error codes are generated by the NDS client that is built into NDS. The NDS client error codes fall in the range of codes numbered –301 through –399.

NDS Agent Error Codes

Another class of NDS error codes is the NDS agent error codes. NDS agent error codes represent errors that originated in the NDS Agent software in the server that are returned through NDS. These codes numbered – 601 through –799 (or FDA7 through F9FE).

NOTE Temporary errors are normal, because the NDS database is designed as a loosely consistent database. You should not be alarmed if NDS error conditions exist temporarily. However, some errors might persist until the error condition is resolved.

Other NDS Error Codes

Some NDS background processes require the functionality provided by other NLM programs, such as timesync.nlm or unicode.nlm. If any of these modules encounter an error, it can be passed on to the ds.nlm. Unicode.nlm and other errors in this category range from –400 to –599.

Tools to Troubleshooting NDS Errors

To effectively troubleshoot NDS errors that affect ZENworks for Desktops, you should be familiar with the tools available to troubleshoot NDS problems. The following tools are provided to monitor and repair error conditions with NDS:

The NDS Manager Utility   The NDS manager utility provides partitioning and replication services for the NDS database on a NetWare server. It also provides repair capabilities for repairing the database from a client workstation, which alleviates the network administrator's total dependence on working from the server console.

The DSREPAIR Utility   The DSREPAIR utility enables you to work from the server console to monitor and repair problems with the NDS database on a single-server basis. It does not correct problems on other servers from a single, centralized location. It must be run on each server that you want to correct NDS database errors on.

The DSTRACE Utility   The DSTRACE utility enables you to work from the server console to diagnose NDS errors. These errors might appear when you are manipulating NDS objects with the administration utilities. NDS errors also show up on the DSTRACE screen.

Table 17.4 contains common NDS errors.

T A B L E   17.4   *Common NDS Errors*

CODE	TEXT	DESCRIPTION
-601 FDA7	NO SUCH ENTRY	The specified NDS object could not be found on the NDS server that is responding to a request.
-603 FDA5	NO SUCH ATTRIBUTE	The requested attribute could not be found. In NDS, if an attribute does not contain a value, then the attribute does not exist for the specific object.
-625 FD8F	TRANSPORT FAILURE	The source server is unable to communicate with the target server. This error is almost always LAN-related.
-626 FD8E	ALL REFERRALS FAILED	The object could not be found, however it is still possible that the object does exist. It is likely that the server could not communicate with another server that is holding a copy of the object.
-634 FD86	NO REFERRALS	The source server has no objects that match the request and has no referrals on which to search for the object. This is not a serious error, just a response. This error usually resolves itself.

Understanding eDirectory Changes for ZENworks for Desktops

When ZENworks for Desktops 3 is installed on your network, it will make several extensions to your current eDirectory tree. These extensions allow new ZENworks for Desktops objects to be created and data linking those objects to existing objects to occur.

This appendix will identify the new objects that have been introduced to your tree and changes to existing base objects when ZENworks for Desktops 3 was installed.

► • ◄

New Objects for ZENworks for Desktops 3

Table A.1 lists the significant new objects that are introduced into eDirectory for ZENworks for Desktops 3. Additionally, this will describe all objects and not just objects that have been introduced since ZENworks for Desktops 2 (i.e., ZENworks).

T A B L E   A . I   *List of New Objects Added to the Tree for ZENworks for Desktops 3*

OBJECT	DESCRIPTION
95 Client Config Policy	This policy allows you to administer all of the aspects of the Novell Windows 95/98 client. All workstations that are associated with this policy will use these configurations in their client settings.
	This policy is administered as part of the Workstation Policy Package. See chapter titled "Setting up a Workstation Policy Package" for more information.
95 Computer Printer Policy	This policy allows you to specify printers and drivers that should be applied to associated, registered Windows 95 or 98 workstations. When the workstation connects to the tree, if it does not have the specified printers, then they will be added to the Windows systems.
	This policy is administered as part of the Workstation Policy Package (see chapter titled "Setting Up a Workstation Policy Package" for more details).

OBJECT	DESCRIPTION
95 Desktop Preferences Policy	This policy allows you the ability to control the Windows 95 and Windows 98 workstation desktop items such as desktop background, mouse, console, and sounds. This policy is associated to a user and will adjust any desktop that the user uses. This policy is administered as part of the User Policy package. See the chapter titled "Setting Up User Policies" for more information.
95 RAS Config Policy	This object holds add-on lists of phonebook entries for 95 configuration of the dial-up workstation system. This policy is administered in the Workstation Policy package and therefore is associated with registered workstations. See chapter titled "Setting Up a Workstation Policy Package" for more details.
Application	This object represents a Windows application that you want delivered to work-stations and to users. In this object are links to the files to run or installed and the administrative restrictions and configurations for how to present this application to the user. This object is created by the administrator and is associated with users, groups, workstations, workstation groups, and containers. See the chapter titled "Creating and Using Application Objects" for more details.

(continued)

T A B L E A . I	List of New Objects Added to the Tree for ZENworks for Desktops 3 (continued)

OBJECT	DESCRIPTION
Application Folders	This object allows the administrator to specify a foldering view that can be presented to the users as they are given appli-cation objects. These folder objects will allow you to specify the menu design that can be used on the start menu to get to the application.

This object is created by the administrator and is associated with Application Objects. See the chapter titled "Creating and Using Application Objects" for more details. |
| Computer Extensible Policies | This policy allows you to add-on additional .ADM policy files to the workstations in your system. In this policy you can import and administer these .ADM files and then associate them to the registered workstations, having them applied when the workstation comes up and logs into the tree. Unlike more policies, this policy is cumulative, meaning that the system will walk the tree (according to the search policy) and collect all of these associated policies and combine them. Most agents stop on the first policy they find.

The Computer Extensible Policies feature is administered as part of the Workstation Policy Package (see chapter titled "Setting Up a Workstation Policy Package" for more details). |

OBJECT	DESCRIPTION
Dynamic Local User Policy	This policy holds the configuration parameters, used by the Workstation Manager agent on the workstation, for the creation of local user accounts at login. These accounts are created on the fly in the local Windows user database and represent users in the tree that log into the workstation. This policy is administered in the User Policy Package and therefore is associated with users in the directory. See chapter titled "Setting Up User Policies" for more details.
Help Desk Policy	This object contains the configuration information used by the Help Desk Windows application. It holds the contact information and enables the user to run the application. This policy is administered in the User Policy Package and therefore is associated with users in the directory. See chapter titled "Setting Up User Policies" for more details.
Imaging Server Policy	This policy is used by the ZENworks Imaging agent that runs on the server. This policy holds configuration information that tells the agent the configuration and addresses to assign to workstations and the policy also holds rules that allows the agent to determine which image to place on an unregistered workstation that contacts the agent. This policy is part of the Server Policy package and is associated with the servers where the ZENworks for Desktops Imaging agent is located. See chapters titled "Imaging a Workstation" and "Creating a Server Policy Package" for more information.

(continued)

T A B L E   A . I   *List of New Objects Added to the Tree for ZENworks for Desktops 3 (continued)*

OBJECT	DESCRIPTION
NT Client Config Policy	This policy allows you to administer all of the aspects of the Novell Windows NT/2000 client. All workstations that are associated with this policy will use these configurations in their client settings. This policy is administered as part of the Workstation Policy Package. See chapter titled "Setting Up a Workstation Policy Package" for more information.
NT Computer Printer Policy	This policy allows you to specify printers and drivers that should be applied to associated, registered NT, or Windows 2000 workstations. When the workstation connects to the tree, if it does not have the specified printers, then they will be added to the Windows systems. Unlike more policies, this policy is cumulative, meaning that the system will walk the tree (according to the search policy) and collect all of these associated policies and combine them. Most agents stop on the first policy they find. This policy is administered as part of the Workstation Policy Package (see chapter titled "Setting Up a Workstation Policy Package" for more details).
NT Desktop Preferences Policy	This policy allows you the ability to control the Windows NT and Windows 2000 workstation desktop items such as desktop background, mouse, console, and sounds. This policy is associated to a user and will adjust any desktop that the user uses. This policy is administered as part of the User Policy package. See the chapter titled "Setting Up User Policies" for more information.

OBJECT	DESCRIPTION
NT RAS Config Policy	This is the policy that holds additional phonebook entries to apply to Windows NT and Windows 2000 workstations. This policy is administered in the Workstation Policy Package and is associated with registered workstations in the directory. See chapter titled "Setting Up a Workstation Policy Package" for more details.
NT User Printer Policy	This policy allows you to specify printers and drivers that should be applied to any Windows NT or Windows 2000 workstation that is used by an associated user. When the user logs into the tree, if their workstation does not have the specified printers, then they will be added to the Windows system. This policy is administered as part of the User Policy Package (see chapter titled "Setting Up User Policies" for more details).
Remote Control Policy	This policy will dictate the features that are activated in the remote control system. The remote control system includes remote control, file transfer, chat, remote diagnostics, and remote execute. This policy is a general policy and can be associated with either a registered workstation (any Windows version) or a user. If this policy is associated with both the workstation and the user of a desktop, then the most restrictive permissions of the two policies will be used. This policy is administered in both the User Policy package (see chapter titled "Setting Up User Policies" for more details) and the Workstation Policy package (see chapter titled "Setting Up a Workstation Policy Package" for more details).

(continued)

TABLE A.I	List of New Objects Added to the Tree for ZENworks for Desktops 3 (continued)
OBJECT	**DESCRIPTION**
Search Policy	This policy tells the workstation agents which order to process any policies found in the tree. The default order is object, group then container, and to search to the root of the tree. With this policy you can change the order and stop the searching up the tree to a container or partition level.
	This policy is part of the Container Policy Package and is associated with containers, which will impact any user and workstations in that container or sub-container. See the chapter titled "Creating a Container Policy Package" for more details.
Server Group	In order to facilitate the association of policies to a set of servers, ZENworks for Desktops introduces the Server Group object that allows you to create a list of servers.
	This server group is administered much like user groups and can be associated with Server Policy Packages.
SMTP Host Policy	This policy allows you to specify the IP addresses of the SMTP e-mail agent. There are several workstation and server ZENworks for Desktops agents that can be administered to send e-mail to an individual when particular events occur.
	This policy is part of the Service Location Policy package that identifies the resources in the network available for agents. See the chapter titled "Creating a Service Location Policy Package" for more details.

OBJECT	DESCRIPTION
SNMP Trap Target Policy	This policy allows you to specify the IP addresses of the SNMP monitors that will receive messages from the SNMP agents in the workstations. Unlike more policies, this policy is cumulative, meaning that the system walks the tree (according to the search policy), collects all SNMP policies, and combines them. Most agents stop on the first policy they find.

This policy is part of the Service Location Policy package that identifies the resources in the network available for agents. See the chapter titled "Creating a Service Location Policy Package" for more details. |
| User Extensible Policies | This policy allows you to add-on additional .ADM policy files to your users. These .ADM files are used by Microsoft in the policy editor — resulting in an .ADM file. In this policy you can import and administer these .ADM files and then associate them to the users.

The User Extensible Policies feature is administered as part of the User Policy Package (see chapter titled "Setting Up User Policies" for more details). |
| Windows 2000 Group Policy | This policy brings all of the attributes of Microsoft's Group Policy into ZENworks for Desktops. This policy, in ZENworks for Desktops, can be assigned to any group, user, or container. In Active Directory it can only be assigned to a container. This policy is only available for those on Windows NT/2000.

This policy is administered in both the User Policy package (see chapter titled "Setting Up User Policies" for more details) and the Workstation Policy package (see chapter titled "Setting Up a Workstation Policy Package" for more details). |

(continued)

TABLE A.1	List of New Objects Added to the Tree for ZENworks for Desktops 3 (continued)
OBJECT	**DESCRIPTION**
Windows Terminal Server Policy	This policy allows you to specify settings to manage your Windows Terminal Server NT/2000 system, user accounts.
	This policy is associated with users and is administered as part of the User Policy package. See the chapter titled "Setting Up User Policies" for more information.
Workstation	This object represents a registered workstation in the tree. A workstation registers with the tree through the ZENworks for Desktops Import agent that resides on a server. When the workstation registers with the agent, it will create a workstation object in an identified location and with a specified name (see Workstation Import Policy). The workstation will then save its workstation object name in the secure portion of the registry, and the Workstation Manager agent, on the workstation, will log into the tree as that workstation to gather policies and perform work for the administrator.
	This object holds such information as a history of the users that have logged into this workstation, the critical hardware inventory information, any remote control restrictions, associated application objects, and the IP and/or IPX address of the workstation.

OBJECT	DESCRIPTION
Workstation Group	In order to facilitate the association of policies to a set of workstations, ZENworks for Desktops introduces the Workstation Group object that allows you to create a list of workstations. This workstation group is administered much like user groups and can be associated with Workstation Policy Packages.
Workstation Image	This object represents a ZENworks for Desktop image that has been taken on a workstation. This object refers to an image file (.ZMG) that is stored on an imaging server. The object is used as a reference to that file in other objects and policies. This object must be manually created by an administrator.
Workstation Image Policy	This policy contains the configuration and rules for applying images for workstations that are registered. When the ZENworks for Desktops Imaging agent on the server is contacted, then it will look to see if the workstation is a registered workstation and if any imaging configuration has been set in the workstation object. If there is no configuration in the workstation object, then this imaging policy is applied for the workstation. This policy is administered in the Workstation Policy package; see chapter titled "Setting Up a Workstation Policy Package" for more information.

(continued)

T A B L E A . I	List of New Objects Added to the Tree for ZENworks for Desktops 3 (continued)

OBJECT	DESCRIPTION
Workstation Import Policy	This policy holds administered parameters for the naming of workstations, the container where workstation objects should be created, and the number of imports that should occur in a given timeframe (in order to not overload your server). The ZEN works for Desktops import agent that runs on the server uses this policy to determine how and when to create the workstation object. This agent logs in as this policy to do its work, so the policy is given rights in the containers where the workstation are to be created.
	This policy is administered in the Server Policy Package and is associated with the servers that run your ZENworks for Desktops import agent. See the chapter titled "Creating a Server Policy Package" for more details.
Workstation Inventory Policy	The Workstation Inventory policy allows administration of the inventory system for ZENworks for Desktops. In this policy you specify if hardware and software inventory should be taken on the associated workstations. You also specify the Inventory Service object which represents the inventory agent that is running on a server.
	This policy is part of the Workstation Policy package and is associated with workstations in the tree. See chapter titled "Setting Up a Workstation Policy Package" for more information.

OBJECT	DESCRIPTION
Workstation Removal Policy	This policy describes when the ZENworks for Desktops workstation removal agent should examine the administered containers to discover workstations that have not connected to the tree in a specified time-frame. These workstations will be automatically deleted from the tree. If these workstations later connect back to the tree the import agent will create a new workstation object. This policy is administered in the Server Policy Package and is associated with the servers that run your ZENworks for Desktops import agent. See the chapter titled "Creating a Server Policy Package" for more details.
WS Restrict Login Policy	This policy allows the administrator to specify the users that can and cannot use the associated workstations. The Workstation Manager agent on the workstation uses this to block or allow users to log into the workstation. This policy is administered through the Workstation Policy package that is associated with workstations, containers, or workstation groups. See the chapter titled "Setting Up a Workstation Policy Package" for more information.

(continued)

T A B L E A . I	*List of New Objects Added to the Tree for ZENworks for Desktops 3 (continued)*
OBJECT	**DESCRIPTION**
zeninvRollUp Policy	This policy will allow you to administer the next level up ZENworks Inventory Service that the local server agent should send their information. This is used to link ZENworks Inventory Service agents to other ZENworks Inventory Service agents in a hierarchical manner.
	This policy is part of the Server Policy Package and is associated with servers in the tree. See chapter titled "Creating a Server Policy Package" for more information.
ZENworks Database	This object represents the ZENworks database that is stored on the server. This database is used to store logging information from various agents as well as the hardware and software inventory of the workstations in your tree. This policy holds such information as the passwords into the database, the drivers, and the IP address of the server.
	This object is created by the install process, but can be created by the administrator as well.

OBJECT	DESCRIPTION
ZENworks Database Location Policy	This policy allows you to specify the ZENworks Database object that those associated with the Service Location Policy should use for storage. There are several workstation and server ZENworks for Desktops agents that will use this database to store inventory and logging information. This policy is part of the Service Location Policy package that identifies the resources in the network available for agents. See the chapter titled "Creating a Service Location Policy Package" for more details.
ZENworks Inventory Service	This object is normally created when you install, from the product CD, the inventory server agents. This object represents the inventory service agent that is running on a server. This agent will be contacted by the workstations and given the hardware and software inventory. It is this agent's job to place that information into the ZENworks database, and to move the information up the tree into a higher-level database, if so configured. This object is associated with a Workstation Inventory policy, telling those agents which service to contact.

Modified Objects for ZENworks for Desktops 3

Table A.2 lists the significant objects that will be modified to contain additional attributes following the installation of ZENworks for Desktops 3. It is assumed by ZENworks for Desktops 3 that these objects already exist in the eDirectory system. If not, then an error will result at install time.

T A B L E A . 2	List of Modified Objects in the Tree for ZENworks for Desktops 3
OBJECT ▬	**DESCRIPTION**
Country	This object is modified to allow a ZENworks for Desktop policy package and an application object to be associated with the object.
Group	This object is modified to allow a ZENworks for Desktop policy package and an application object to be associated with the object.
Locality	This object is modified to allow a ZENworks for Desktop policy package and an application object to be associated with the object.
Organization	This object is modified to allow a ZENworks for Desktop policy package and an application object to be associated with the object.
Organizational Unit	This object is modified to allow a ZENworks for Desktop policy package and an application object to be associated with the object.
Queue	This object is modified to provide an attribute to attach printer driver and printer information. In this manner, when one wants to work with the queue, they will automatically get the proper drivers for the printer.
Server	This object is modified to allow a ZENworks for Desktop policy package and an application object to be associated with the object.
User	This object is modified to allow ZENworks for Desktop policy packages and application objects to be associated with the user and to provide remote control administration capabilities and restrictions on the administrator for this user. Additionally the object is modified to link users to the current workstation object representing the desktop they are using.

Using snAppShot to Create an Application Object Package

In this Appendix we will discus an example of using the snAppShot utility to create an application object package for distribution to other workstations. This appendix is split into the following two sections:

▶ Using snAppShot to Package GroupWise

▶ Review of the Created Object Template

Using snAppShot to Package GroupWise

In this example, we will use the Custom Mode in snAppShot to set specific options for snAppShot and then use snAppShot to capture the changes made in an application object template package when installing GroupWise on a client workstation. This way we can use the created template later to distribute GroupWise to several other clients.

We will use the Custom Mode of snAppShot to perform the operations described in the following sections to create the application object template for GroupWise.

Launch snAppShot

The first step to create an application object template for GroupWise is to launch the snAppShot utility by double-clicking on the Snapshot icon located in the following directory as shown in Figure B.1:

```
SYS:\PUBLIC\SNAPSHOT
```

FIGURE B.I   Folder displaying the snAppShot utility icon

Choose Custom Mode from Main Menu

The next step is to select which mode we will use to create the application object template for GroupWise. In this example we will choose the custom mode so that we can use some specific preference settings as shown in Figure B.2.

FIGURE B.2 *Window in the snAppShot utility which allows user to specify which mode of discovery to use in application object template creation*

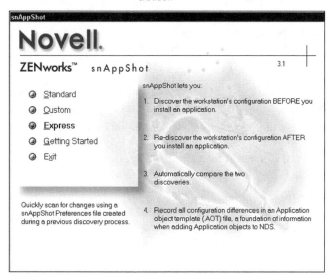

Choose the snAppShot Preferences File

The first window that comes up after you select the custom mode in snAppShot allows us to either choose a snAppShot previously saved preference file, or use the snAppShot default settings.

Because you have not previously created and saved a preferences file in a previous custom mode, we will use the default settings.

Name the Application Object and Icon Title

Once we have selected to use the default preference settings in snAppShot, we input the name that the application object will have in the DS tree (GroupWise 5.5) and a title for the icon which represents the application object (GroupWise).

Network Location of the Application Source (.FIL) Files

Once we set the name for the application object and title for its icon, we set the network location to store the application source files (.FIL) for the GroupWise object template to the following directory:

```
T:\Snapshot\GroupWise 5.5
```

Network Location of the Application Template (.AOT and .AXT) Files

Once you have specified a network location for the .fil files, , we set the network location to store the application template (.AOT and .AXT files) for the GroupWise object template to the following director:

```
T:\Snapshot\GroupWise 5.5\GroupWise.AOT
```

NOTE

By specifying a network location for these files, you can more easily access them when it comes time to create the Application object and distribute it to users. Notice that we set the network location for both the source files and the application template files to the same directory. This makes for easier handling of the application object package later.

Including or Excluding Parts of the Workstation

Once we have selected the network location to store the application object support files, we will use the snAppShot screen in Figure B.3 to select the following parts of the workstation to covered in the following sections.

► · ◄

FIGURE B.3 *Window in the snAppShot utility which allows user to specify which parts of the workstation to include or exclude*

Files and Folders

From the workstation scan customization menu in snAppShot, we can modify which files and folder you wish to include or exclude. However, we do not need to ignore any specific files or folder, so we leave the setting at the default shown in Figure B.4.

F I G U R E   B . 4   *Window in the snAppShot utility which allows user to specify how and which files and folders will be created in the application object template*

INI Files

From the workstation scan customization menu in snAppShot, you can modify which INI files to exclude. However, we do not need to ignore any specific INI files, so we leave the setting at the default.

System Configuration Text Files

From the workstation scan customization menu in snAppShot, we can modify which system configuration text files you wish to include in the scan. We do have NETWORK.BAT file that is executed when all workstations are booted, setting specific preferences. This file is specific to each workstation and even though the GroupWise install shouldn't effect it, we add it to the list to be safe.

Windows Short Cuts

From the workstation scan customization menu in snAppShot, we can modify which Windows shortcuts to exclude. However, we do not need to ignore any specific Windows shortcut files, so we leave the setting at the default.

Registry

From the workstation scan customization menu in snAppShot, we can modify which registry hives you wish to include or exclude. However, we do not need to specify any specific registry sections to ignore or exclude, so we leave the setting at the default.

Specify the Drives That Will Be Discovered

Once we have specified which parts of the workstation to include or exclude, we select which disk drive to scan on the workstation to determine changes. In this case, since we are installing GroupWise to the C drive, we only need to select the C drive for scanning.

Read the Pre-Discovery Summary

Now that we have set all the preferences for the first discovery, we are given a summary of the preferences in the next snAppShot window. The information displayed includes:

- ▶ Application Object Name
- ▶ Application Icon Title
- ▶ Template Filename
- ▶ Application Files Directory
- ▶ Snapshots Working Drive
- ▶ Scan Options
- ▶ Disks to Scan
- ▶ Directories to Exclude
- ▶ Files to Exclude
- ▶ System Text Files to Scan

NOTE

Notice that the file we selected as a system configuration text file to ignore is listed in the summary: C:\NETWORK.BAT. This is a good example of things to check for before proceeding with the first discovery.

You can click Save Settings to save the snAppShot preferences you have defined thus far to a file. Later, if we use snAppShot to create a template for a GroupWise upgrade, we can use that preference file in the express mode.

Run the First snAppShot Discovery

The first snAppShot discover is run when we click next from the preference summary window. The screen shown in Figure B.5 shows the status of the discovery and a count of the following items that have been discovered:

- ▶ Folders and Files
- ▶ Windows Shortcuts
- ▶ INI Files
- ▶ System Configuration Files
- ▶ Registry Entries

FIGURE B.5 *Window in the snAppShot utility which shows the user the current status and statistics about the first discovery scan currently running*

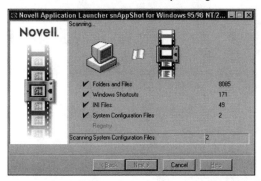

Run the Application's Installation or Upgrade

Once the first snAppShot discovery is completed, a Run Application Install button is available.

When we select the Run Application Install button, a file pop-up menu will appear and you will be able to navigate to the application install executable and execute.

Specify How to Handle the Creation of Files, Folders, .INI File Entries, and Registry Settings

Once the GroupWise installation is complete, snAppShot allows us to specify how to handle the creation of entries for the application object. From the screen shown in Figure B.6, you can set the addition criteria for the entries described in the following sections.

Window in the snAppShot utility which allows user to specify how snAppShot will handle the creation of file, folder, INI file, and registry entries in the application object template

Folder and File Entries

From the application object entry addition window in snAppShot, we can configure whether or not files and folders will be added to the application object by clicking the down arrow under the files and folders option and selecting the following addition criteria as shown in Figure B.7:

Window in the snAppShot utility which allows user to specify how snAppShot will handle the creation of file and folder entries in the application object template

We use the Copy if newer version because we do not want to overwrite any files that may have been added by the user in a local workstation specific installation.

NOTE

INI Files

From the application object entry addition window in snAppShot, we configure whether or not INI files will be added to the application object by clicking the down arrow under the INI files option and selecting the following addition criteria:

We use the Create if does not exist because we do not want to overwrite any existing INI files that may have been added by the user in a local workstation specific application installation.

NOTE

Registry Entries

From the application object entry addition window in snAppShot, we configure whether or not registry entries will be added to the application object by clicking the down arrow under the registry entries option and selecting the following addition criteria.

We use the create always because want to overwrite any registry entries that may be pointing to invalid file or directory locations that do not match the current application installation.

NOTE

Enter the Path to the Application's Executable File

Once we have defined the addition criteria for entries into the application object, we specify a path to the application's executable on this workstation. To do so we enter the following location of the GroupWise application installation files on this workstation in the text field as shown in Figure B.8.

F I G U R E   B . 8   *Window in the snAppShot utility which allows user to set the path for the application's executable file*

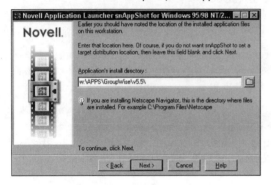

Define Macros for Distribution Automation.

Once we are finished with setting the path to the applications executable and click the next button, use the screen shown in Figure B.9 to define macros to control the distribution of application objects.

F I G U R E   B . 9   *Window in the snAppShot utility which allows user to add, edit, and remove macros to be used in the application object template*

Click the add button in the macro definition window and an option is given to specify a variable name and a string that it will be replaced with in the template data.

Run the Second snAppShot Discovery

Once we are finished with defining macros to automate application object distribution, we click next and snAppShot runs the second discover as shown in Figure B.10. Once again we are able to monitor the status of the discovery by noting the count of the following items as shown in Figure B.10:

- ► Folders and Files
- ► Windows Shortcuts
- ► INI Files
- ► System Configuration Files
- ► Registry Entries

FIGURE B.10 *Window in the snAppShot utility which shows the user the current status and statistics about the second discovery scan while it is running*

Once the discovery is finished, snAppShot will begin generating an object template. This is where the actual differences between the two discoveries are discerned and the template files created.

Read the Completion Summary

Once the second snAppShot discovery is completed and the template files generated, a completion summary of what took place is displayed in the next window. The completion summary contains information about the application template creation including:

- ► The location of the new application object template (.AOT)
- ► The location of the new .FIL files

- ► The location of the textual version of the application object template (.AOT)
- ► Listing of the steps to take to create the application object
- ► Statistical totals from the second discovery
- ► Statistical totals from entries added to the application object template (.AOT)

Review of the Created Object Template

Once we have reviewed the summary from running snAppShot, and clicked next, the process is complete and the application object template package has been created. We can now go to the network location where the application object template was created and review the items described in the following sections.

Directory Listing

Figure B.11 shows a directory listing of the files in the application object template directory. These files represent the packaged object ready for distribution. You can see the following files:

- ► .AXT File
- ► .AOT File
- ► FILEDEF.TXT File
- ► Various .FIL Files

FIGURE B.11   *Directory listing of the files located in the GroupWise application object template directory*

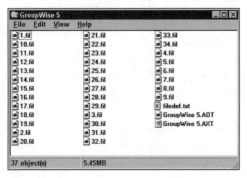

FILEDEF.TXT File

Looking at the filedef.txt file in Figure B.12, we can see the mappings of .fil files to the actual GroupWise application files.

F I G U R E   B . 1 2   *FILEDEF.TXT file for the GroupWise application object package*

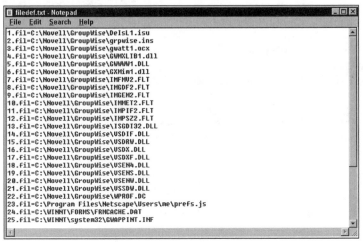

```
filedef.txt - Notepad                                    _ □ ×
File  Edit  Search  Help
1.fil=C:\Novell\GroupWise\DeIsL1.isu
2.fil=C:\Novell\GroupWise\grpwise.ins
3.fil=C:\Novell\GroupWise\gwatt1.ocx
4.fil=C:\Novell\GroupWise\GWMXLIB1.dll
5.fil=C:\Novell\GroupWise\GWWWW1.DLL
6.fil=C:\Novell\GroupWise\GXMim1.dll
7.fil=C:\Novell\GroupWise\IMFMV2.FLT
8.fil=C:\Novell\GroupWise\IMGDF2.FLT
9.fil=C:\Novell\GroupWise\IMGEM2.FLT
10.fil=C:\Novell\GroupWise\IMMET2.FLT
11.fil=C:\Novell\GroupWise\IMPIF2.FLT
12.fil=C:\Novell\GroupWise\IMPSZ2.FLT
13.fil=C:\Novell\GroupWise\ISGDI32.DLL
14.fil=C:\Novell\GroupWise\VSDIF.DLL
15.fil=C:\Novell\GroupWise\VSDRW.DLL
16.fil=C:\Novell\GroupWise\VSDX.DLL
17.fil=C:\Novell\GroupWise\VSDXF.DLL
18.fil=C:\Novell\GroupWise\VSEN4.DLL
19.fil=C:\Novell\GroupWise\VSEMS.DLL
20.fil=C:\Novell\GroupWise\VSENV.DLL
21.fil=C:\Novell\GroupWise\VSSDW.DLL
22.fil=C:\Novell\GroupWise\WPROF.DC
23.fil=C:\Program Files\Netscape\Users\me\prefs.js
24.fil=C:\WINNT\FORMS\FRMCACHE.DAT
25.fil=C:\WINNT\system32\GWAPPINT.INF
```

Application Object Template File (Text Version .AXT)

Looking at the text version of the GroupWise object template, shown in Figure B.13, we can see all the changes that snAppShot recorded from the GroupWise installation that took place. These changes can be applied to other workstations when the application object is distributed.

Looking at the filedef.txt file in Figure B.13, we can see the mappings of .fil files to the actual GroupWise application files.

F I G U R E   B.13   *Textual version of the application object template file for the*
GroupWise application object

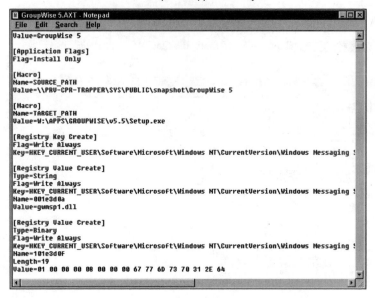

```
GroupWise 5.AXT - Notepad                                        _ □ ×
File  Edit  Search  Help
Value=GroupWise 5

[Application Flags]
Flag=Install Only

[Macro]
Name=SOURCE_PATH
Value=\\PRU-CPR-TRAPPER\SYS\PUBLIC\snapshot\GroupWise 5

[Macro]
Name=TARGET_PATH
Value=W:\APPS\GROUPWISE\v5.5\Setup.exe

[Registry Key Create]
Flag=Write Always
Key=HKEY_CURRENT_USER\Software\Microsoft\Windows NT\CurrentVersion\Windows Messaging

[Registry Value Create]
Type=String
Flag=Write Always
Key=HKEY_CURRENT_USER\Software\Microsoft\Windows NT\CurrentVersion\Windows Messaging
Name=001e3d0a
Value=gwmsp1.dll

[Registry Value Create]
Type=Binary
Flag=Write Always
Key=HKEY_CURRENT_USER\Software\Microsoft\Windows NT\CurrentVersion\Windows Messaging
Name=101e3d0F
Length=19
Value=01 00 00 00 08 00 00 00 67 77 6D 73 70 31 2E 64
```

Other ZENworks for Desktops Resources

Many other resources are available concerning ZENworks for Desktops. This appendix describes a few of the other resources that are available to assist you in your discovery and implementation of ZENworks for Desktops.

Novell Support and On-line Documentation

Novell has set up a website that you can get to through the Internet that is the product home for ZENworks. This website is www.novell.com/products/zenworks. From this website you can find Novell's on-line documentation and announcements for updates to the product.

Additionally, from this page you can follow the links to support.novell.com/products where you can find any patches and fixes that may be released for the product. ZENworks products are found under the NetWare and the Management Products categories.

ZENworks Cool Solutions

Many more uses of ZENworks for Desktops exist than can ever be described in a book like this. Many customers use ZENworks for Desktops every day and get very creative in their use of the system.

Novell has set up a location on the Internet where customers can go to ask their questions of the actual ZENworks for Desktop engineers and see what solutions other customers have come up with for ZENworks for Desktops.

The website for ZENworks Cool Solutions is www.novell.com/coolsolutions/zenworks.

This site changes often and features articles from real customers or insiders on how to make ZENworks for Desktops hum in your network. They also include a list of frequently asked questions and their answers and articles from other deployment specialists that are in the trenches. You can often find a white paper at the cool solutions site that will have the information you need for your issues.

From time to time this site also posts software that is not supported by Novell, but provided by some internal Novell engineers, Novell consultants, or customers. These tools can help you in your ZENworks for Desktops deployment and management.

Once on the ZENworks Cool Solution site, the webmaster had a set of ZENworks for Desktops engineers come and have a live, ask the experts session where customers from the Internet were able to ask their questions and get real-time answers to their issues. Now, you might even see some job postings for companies that are looking for ZEN Masters to come and implement ZENworks in their environments.

Novell Consulting Services

Novell Consulting Services has many good engineers that are familiar with ZENworks for Desktops and how it can help Novell customers in their environments. They can assist you, beyond support, in getting ZENworks for Desktops to do exactly what you want for your network. Novell Consulting Services can help you with field consulting and with any custom developments you may need, tailoring ZENworks for Desktops to your organization's needs.

ZENworks Inventory Database Schema

ZENworks for Desktops comes with several views to retrieve information from the inventory database. However, those views may not always give you the information you need exactly how you want it. If you are familiar with the Common Information Model (CIM), Desktop Management Interface (DMI), and have a solid understanding of Relational Database Based Managed Systems (RDBMS), then you can access the ZENworks inventory database directly by creating your own queries and views.

Accessing the inventory database can be a powerful tool for you to create metrics to measure company growth, user and workstation status, product usage, and so on. This appendix lists tables that define the schema and associations in the ZENworks inventory database. Also included in this appendix are sample queries that give you a jump start at accessing the database.

Database Class Associations and Attributes

The first concept you must understand when accessing the ZENworks inventory database is what is available and how is it available. Tables D.1 through D.5 help you understand the schema structure for inventory classes, class associations, association attributes, and class attributes for the following types of inventory objects:

- ▶ Miscellaneous Computer System objects
- ▶ ZENworks Site objects
- ▶ Client Software objects
- ▶ Network objects
- ▶ Disk objects

TABLE D.1 *Computer System Objects in ZENworks Inventory: Associations and Attributions*

LOOKUPCLASS	TARGET CLASS	ASSOC. CLASS	ASSOC. ATTRIBUTE 1	ASSOC. ATTRIBUTE 2	CLASS ATTRIBUTES
ZENworks.Bus	CIM.Unitary ComputerSystem	SystemDevice	PartComponent	GroupComponent	BusVersion, Protocol supported
ZENworks.BIOS	CIM.Unitary ComputerSystem	SystemBIOS	PartComponent	GroupComponent	Manufacturer, InstallDate, BIOSBytes, Caption, SerialNumber, Version, PrimaryBIOS, Size
ZENworks. Motherboard	CIM.Unitary ComputerSystem	ComputerSystem Package	Dependent	Antecedent	HostingBoard, Description, Version
ZENworks. ZENKeyboard	CIM.Unitary ComputerSystem	SystemDevice	PartComponent	GroupComponent	Delay, TypematicRate, Layout, NumberOf FunctionKeys, Description, subtype

(continued)

TABLE D.1 Computer System Objects in ZENworks Inventory: Associations and Attributions (continued)

LOOKUPCLASS	TARGET CLASS	ASSOC. CLASS	ASSOC. ATTRIBUTE 1	ASSOC. ATTRIBUTE 2	CLASS ATTRIBUTES
ZENworks.ParalellPort	CIM.Unitary ComputerSystem	SystemDevice	PartComponent	GroupComponent	Name, DMASupport, Address
ZENworks.SerialPort	CIM.Unitary ComputerSystem	SystemDevice	PartComponent	GroupComponent	Name, Address
CIM.PointingDevice	CIM.Unitary ComputerSystem	SystemDevice	PartComponent	GroupComponent	PointingType, Name, NumberOfButtons
ZENworks.PointingDevice Driver	CIM.Pointing Device	Device Software	Dependent	Antecedent	Name, Version
CIM.DMA	CIM.Unitary ComputerSystem	Computer SystemDMA	PartComponent	GroupComponent	DMAChannel, Availability, Description, BurstMode
CIM.IRQ	CIM.Unitary ComputerSystem	Computer SystemIRQ	PartComponent	GroupComponent	IRQNumber, Availability, TriggerType, Shareable
CIM.PowerSupply	CIM.Unitary ComputerSystem	SystemDevice	PartComponent	GroupComponent	Description, TotalOutputPower

LOOKUPCLASS	TARGET CLASS	ASSOC. CLASS	ASSOC. ATTRIBUTE 1	ASSOC. ATTRIBUTE 2	CLASS ATTRIBUTES
CIM.Battery	CIM.Unitary ComputerSystem	SystemDevice	PartComponent	GroupComponent	Name, Chemistry, DesignCapacity, DesignVoltage, SmartBattery Version
CIM.Card	CIM.Unitary ComputerSystem	Computer SystemPackage	Dependent	Antecedent	Description
CIM.Slot	CIM.Card	CardInSlot	Dependent	Antecedent	MaxDataWidth, ThermalRating
CIM.CacheMemory	CIM.Unitary ComputerSystem	SystemDevice	PartComponent	GroupComponent	Level, WritePolicy, Error Methodology, CacheType, LineSize, ReplacementPolicy, ReadPolicy, Associativity
CIM.Physical Memory	CIM.Cache Memory	RealizesExtent	Dependent	Antecedent	Speed, Capacity

(continued)

TABLE D.1 Computer System Objects in ZENworks Inventory: Associations and Attributions (continued)

LOOKUPCLASS	TARGET CLASS	ASSOC. CLASS	ASSOC. ATTRIBUTE 1	ASSOC. ATTRIBUTE 2	CLASS ATTRIBUTES
ZENworks. SoundCard	CIM.Unitary ComputerSystem	Computer SystemPackage	Dependent	Antecedent	Name, Description, Manufacturer
CIM.POTSModem	CIM.Unitary ComputerSystem	SystemDevice	PartComponent	GroupComponent	Name, Description, Caption
ManageWise.User	CIM.Unitary ComputerSystem	ManageWise. ObjectContact	Owner	Client	LastLoginName, CurrentLogin Name

TABLE D.2 Site Objects in ZENworks Inventory: Associations and Attributions

LOOKUPCLASS	TARGET CLASS	ASSOCIATION CLASS	ASSOCIATION ATTRIBUTE 1	ASSOCIATION ATTRIBUTE 2	CLASS ATTRIBUTES
ZENworks.Site	CIM.Unitary ComputerSystem	SystemSite	SystemSite	ComputerSystem	SiteID, SiteName
ManageWise. NDSName	CIM.Unitary ComputerSystem	Designates	Designation	Host	Label, Tree
ZENworks. SystemInfo	CIM.Unitary ComputerSystem	Computer SystemPackage	Dependent	Antecedent	Tag, Model, Serial Number, Manufacturer, Description

TABLE D.3 ZENworks Client Software Objects in ZENworks Inventory: Associations and Attributions

LOOKUPCLASS	TARGET CLASS	ASSOCIATION CLASS	ASSOCIATION ATTRIBUTE 1	ASSOCIATION ATTRIBUTE 2	CLASS ATTRIBUTES
ZENworks. NetWareClient	CIM.Unitary ComputerSystem	InstalledSoftware Element	Software	System	Version
ZENworks. InventoryScanner	CIM.Unitary ComputerSystem	InstalledSoftware Element	Software	System	Version, LastScanDate, InventoryServer, ModificationTime
CIM.Product	CIM.Unitary ComputerSystem	InstalledProduct	Product	ComputerSystem	Name, Version, Vendor

TABLE D.4 Network Objects in the ZENworks Inventory: Associations and Attributions

LOOKUPCLASS	TARGET CLASS	ASSOCIATION CLASS	ASSOCIATION ATTRIBUTE 1	ASSOCIATION ATTRIBUTE 2	CLASS ATTRIBUTES
CIM.Ethernet Adapter	CIM.Unitary ComputerSystem	SystemDevice	PartComponent	GroupComponent	Name, MaxSpeed, PermanentAddress
ZENworks. NetworkAdaptor Driver	CIM.Unitary ComputerSystem	Installed Software Element	Dependent	Antecedent	Name, Version, Description
CIM.IPProtocol EndPoint	CIM.Unitary ComputerSystem	HostedAccess Point	Dependent	Antecedent	Address, SubnetMask

(continued)

TABLE D.4   Network Objects in the ZENworks Inventory: Associations and Attributions (continued)

LOOKUPCLASS	TARGET CLASS	ASSOCIATION CLASS	ASSOCIATION ATTRIBUTE 1	ASSOCIATION ATTRIBUTE 2	CLASS ATTRIBUTES
CIM.IPXProtocol EndPoint	CIM.Unitary ComputerSystem	HostedAccess Point	Dependent	Antecedent	Address
CIM.LANEndPoint	CIM.Unitary ComputerSystem	HostedAccess Point	Dependent	Antecedent	MACAddress
ManageWise.MS DomainName	CIM.Unitary ComputerSystem	Designates	Designation	Host	Label
ManageWise. DNSName	CIM.Unitary ComputerSystem	Designates	Designation	Host	Label

TABLE D.5   Disk Objects in the ZENworks Inventory: Associations and Attributions

LOOKUPCLASS	TARGET CLASS	ASSOCIATION CLASS	ASSOCIATION ATTRIBUTE 1	ASSOCIATION ATTRIBUTE 2	CLASS ATTRIBUTES
CIM.DiskDrive	CIM.Unitary ComputerSystem	SystemDevice	PartComponent	GroupComponent	
ZENworks.Physical DiskDrive	CIM.DiskDrive	Realizes	Dependent	Antecedent	
ZENworks.Logical DiskDrive	CIM.Unitary ComputerSystem	SystemDevice	PartComponent	GroupComponent	DeviceID,TotalSize, VolumeSerial Number, Caption

LOOKUPCLASS	TARGET CLASS	ASSOCIATION CLASS	ASSOCIATION ATTRIBUTE 1	ASSOCIATION ATTRIBUTE 2	CLASS ATTRIBUTES
ZENworks.Storage PhysicalMedia	ZENworks.Physical DiskDrive, ZENworks. Physicaldiskette, ZENworks.Physical CDROM				Description, PhysicalCylinders, SectorsPerTrack, PhysicalHeads, Capacity, Manufacturer
CIM.DiskettDrive	CIM.Unitary ComputerSystem	SystemDevice	PartComponent	GroupComponent	
ZENworks. Physicaldiskette	CIM.DiskettDrive	Realizes	Dependent	Antecedent	
ZENworks LogicalDiskette	CIM.DiskettDrive	MediaPresent	Dependent	Antecedent	DeviceID
CIM.CDROM Drive	CIM.Unitary ComputerSystem	SystemDevice	PartComponent	GroupComponent	
ZENworks. PhysicalCDROM	CIM.CDROM Drive	Realizes	Dependent	Antecedent	Manufacturer, Description, Caption
ZENworks. LogicalCDROM	CIM.CDROM Drive	MediaPresent	Dependent	Antecedent	DeviceID

(continued)

TABLE D.5   *Disk Objects in the ZENworks Inventory: Associations and Attributions (continued)*

LOOKUPCLASS	TARGET CLASS	ASSOCIATION CLASS	ASSOCIATION ATTRIBUTE 1	ASSOCIATION ATTRIBUTE 2	CLASS ATTRIBUTES
ZENworks.SCSI Drive	CIM.Unitary ComputerSystem	SystemDevice	PartComponent	GroupComponent	Name, Description
ZENworks. LogicalSCSIDrive	ZENworks. SCSIDrive	MediaPresent	Dependent	Antecedent	DeviceID
ZENworks.Local FileSystem	CIM.Unitary ComputerSystem	HostedFile System	PartComponent	GroupComponent	Name, FileSystemSize, Description, FileSystemType

Sample Inventory Database Queries

The tables in the previous section give you a glimpse at the schema of the ZENworks inventory database. This sections lists some sample queries based on those tables to help you better understand how to use them to perform queries and create your own reports. The following are sample queries for retrieving the inventory information from the ZENworks for Desktops Inventory database.

Query I

Retrieve the name and ID of all workstations from the database and also to the tree to which these workstations are registered. The query is as follows:

```
SELECT u.id$,m.label,m.tree FROM managewise.NDSName
m,cim.UnitaryComputerSystem u,managewise.Designates s
where s.Designation=m.id$ and s.HOST=u.id$
```

Query 2

Retrieve the asset tag, manufacturer, and serial number of all the workstations in the database. The query is as follows:

```
SELECT m.Tag,m.Manufacturer,m.SerialNumber FROM
cim.UnitaryComputerSystem u,zenworks.SystemInfo
m,cim.ComputerSystemPackage s WHERE s.Antecedent=m.id$ and
s.Dependent=u.id$
```

Query 3

Retrieve all the software applications with their versions that are installed on the workstation 'SJOHN164_99_139_79.WS' registered under 'NOVELL_ AUS' tree. The query is as follows:

```
SELECT m.name,m.version FROM cim.Product
m,cim.UnitaryComputerSystem u,zenworks.InstalledProduct
s,managewise.NDSName m1,managewise.Designates s1 WHERE
(s.Product=m.id$ and s.ComputerSystem=u.id$) AND
(s1.Designation=m1.id$ and s1.Host=u.id$) AND
m1.label='SJOHN164_99_139_79.WS' and m1.tree='Novell_AUS'
```

Query 4
Retrieve the processor information for the workstation 'SJOHN164_99_139_79.WS'.

```
SELECT
m.DeviceID,m.Family,m.Stepping,m.OtherFamilyDescription,
m.MaxClockSpeed,m.Role,m.UpgradeMethod FROM cim.Processor
m,cim.UnitaryComputerSystem u,cim.ComputerSystemProcessor
s managewise.NDSName m1,managewise.Designates s1 WHERE
(s.PartComponent=m.id$ and s.GroupComponent=u.id$) AND
m1.label='SJOHN164_99_139_79.WS'
```

Query 5
Retrieve the ID of the UnitaryComputerSystem used for the workstation 'SJOHN164_99_139_79.WS'.

```
SELECT s.host FROM managewise.NDSName
m,managewise.Designates s WHERE
m.label='SJOHN164_99_139_79.WS' and m.id$=s.Designation
```

Query 6
Having known the ID of the UnitaryComputerSystem for a particular workstation from the query as shown in Query 5, Query 4 can be modified as

```
SELECT
m.DeviceID,m.Family,m.Stepping,m.OtherFamilyDescription,
m.MaxClockSpeed,m.Role,m.UpgradeMethod FROM cim.Processor
m,cim.UnitaryComputerSystem u, cim.ComputerSystemProcessor
s u.id$=? And s.PartComponent=m.id$ and
s.GroupComponent=u.id$
```

Substitute the ID of the specified workstation in place of the ? value for u.id in the query.

Query 7
List the IP Address, IPX Address, and MACAddress of all workstations in the database.

```
SELECT ip.Address, ipx.Address, mac.MACAddress FROM
cim.IPProtocolEndpoint ip, cim.IPXProtocolEndpoint ipx,
cim.LANEndpoint mac, cim.UnitaryComputerSystem u,
cim.HostedAccessPoint s WHERE (s.Dependent=ip.id$ and
```

```
s.Antecedent=u.id$) AND (s.Dependent=ipx.id$ and
s.Antecedent=u.id$) AND (s.Dependent=mac.id$ and
s.Antecedent=u.id$)
```

Modify the same query to get the information for a specified workstation as follows:

```
SELECT ip.Address, ipx.Address, mac.MACAddress FROM
cim.IPProtocolEndpoint ip, cim.IPXProtocolEndpoint ipx,
cim.LANEndpoint mac, cim.UnitaryComputerSystem u,
cim.HostedAccessPoint s WHERE (s.Dependent=ip.id$ and
s.Antecedent=u.id$) AND (s.Dependent=ipx.id$ and
s.Antecedent=u.id$) AND (s.Dependent=mac.id$ and
s.Antecedent=u.id$)AND u.id$=?
```

Use the query as shown in Query 5 to retrieve the ID of the specified workstation and substitute the ID in place of the ? value for u.id in the query.

Query 8

Retrieve the name and other properties of the drives on the hard disk of the specified workstation.

```
SELECT m.DEVICEID, m.TotalSize, m.VolumeSerialNumber,
m.Caption FROM zenworks.LogicalDiskDrive m,
cim.UnitaryComputerSystem u, cim.SystemDevice s WHERE
s.PartComponent=m.id$ AND s.GroupComponent=u.id$ and
u.id$=?
```

Use the query shown in Query 5 to retrieve the ID of the specified workstation and substitute the ID in place of the ? for u.id$ in the query.

Index

Continued

assigning licenses to users, 400
creating metered certificates, 398–399
creating reports within, 402
installing license certificates in, 396–397
viewing reports, 403–404

O

operating systems, filtering workstations by, 127–128
operators
    Boolean, 257
    meanings for, 256–257
    relational, 345
    types of, 256
Option property panel (Distribution tab), 113
Other Property page (Container policy), 268–269
Other Property page (Server policy), 295
Other Property page (Service Location policy), 281–282
Other Property page (Workstation policy), 229–230

P

partial installation detection, 66
personal folders, 155
Platforms page (Workstation Import policy), 306–308
Policy Package Wizard, 38–39
policy packages
    association of, 48
    enhancements to, 38
    troubleshooting, 436–438
Policy Property page (Server policy)
    general policies, 289–290
    netware policies, 290
    WinNT-2000 policies, 291
Policy Property page (Service Location policy), 277
Policy Property page (Workstation policy)
    general policies, 224–225
    Win95-98 policies, 226–227
    Windows NT-2000 policies, 225–226
Policy Schedule page (Computer Extensible policy)
    advanced settings, 240–242
    daily, 239
    events, 238
    monthly, 239
    weekly, 239
    yearly, 240
Policy Schedule page (User Extensible policy)
    advanced settings, 216
    daily, 215
    event, 214
    monthly, 215–216
    weekly, 215
    yearly, 216
ports, adding for capturing of application launch, 139
post-termination scripts, 178
printers
    adding to printer policy, 206
    removing from printer policy, 207
processors, filtering workstations by, 128–129
product installation, 23
Prompt Before Distribution option (Distribution tab), 114
prompted drive macros, 143
prompted macros, setting up, 173
prompted string macros, 144

Q

Quick Launch menu, adding applications to, 169

R

rebooting, prompting user before, 114
Refresh Interval page (Search policy), 273
Registry, uninstalling entries, 148–149
registry settings, filtering workstations by, 130
Registry Settings property panel (Distribution tab), 107
relational operators, 345
Remote Control policy
    activating, 207
    Remote Management page, 208–211
remote controlling workstations, 388–390
Remote Management
    enhancements of, 13
    overview, 5–6
Remote Management page (Remote Control policy)
    execute functions, 211
    file transfer functions, 211
    general system functions, 208–209
    remote control functions, 209–210
    view functions, 201, 211
removing printers from printer policy, 207
reporting capabilities, 52
Reporting option (Common tab), 140–142
    accessing, 140
    events, 141
reports
    creating within NLS Manager, 401–402
    creating within NWAdmin, 402
    viewing, 403–404
restoring image commands, 377–379
Rights to Files and Folders property page (Container policy),
    269–270
Rights to Files and Folders property page (Server policy), 296
Rights to Files and Folders property page (Service Location
    policy), 282
Rights to Files and Folders property page (Workstation policy),
    230–231
Roaming Profile feature, 192–194
roll-up log, 350
roll-up status, 351
root servers, 322
Rules page (Imaging Server policy), 297–300
Rules page (Workstation Imaging policy), 254–257
Run Application Install button, 74
Run Options tab
    environment variable option, 120
    Install Only option, 116
    licensing/metering variable option, 120

S

scanning, customizing software, 342–343
scripting commands, 180, 381
scripts
    post-termination, 178
    Startup, 178
Scripts property page, automating Application objects with,
    178–180

V

W

Z

my2cents.idgbooks.com

Register This Book — And Win!

Visit **http://my2cents.idgbooks.com** to register this book and we'll automatically enter you in our fantastic monthly prize giveaway. It's also your opportunity to give us feedback: let us know what you thought of this book and how you would like to see other topics covered.

Discover IDG Books Online!

The IDG Books Online Web site is your online resource for tackling technology — at home and at the office. Frequently updated, the IDG Books Online Web site features exclusive software, insider information, online books, and live events!

10 Productive & Career-Enhancing Things You Can Do at www.idgbooks.com

- Nab source code for your own programming projects.
- Download software.
- Read Web exclusives: special articles and book excerpts by IDG Books Worldwide authors.
- Take advantage of resources to help you advance your career as a Novell or Microsoft professional.
- Buy IDG Books Worldwide titles or find a convenient bookstore that carries them.
- Register your book and win a prize.
- Chat live online with authors.
- Sign up for regular e-mail updates about our latest books.
- Suggest a book you'd like to read or write.
- Give us your 2¢ about our books and about our Web site.

You say you're not on the Web yet? It's easy to get started with IDG Books' *Discover the Internet*, available at local retailers everywhere.